HOLMAN
New
Testament
Commentary

HOLMAN *New Testament* Commentary

Luke

GENERAL EDITOR

Max Anders

AUTHOR

Trent C. Butler

HOLMAN
REFERENCE

Nashville, Tennessee

Holman New Testament Commentary
© 2000 Broadman & Holman Publishers
Nashville, Tennessee
All rights reserved

ISBN 0-8054-0203-9

Dewey Decimal Classification: 226.6
Subject Heading: BIBLE. NT. Luke
Library of Congress Card Catalog Number: 98–39365

Butler, Trent C.
        Luke / Trent C. Butler
            p.   cm. — (Holman New Testament commentary)
        Includes bibliographical references.
        ISBN 0-8054-0203-9 (alk. paper)
            1. Bible. N.T. Luke—Commentaries.   2. Bible. N.T. Luke—
        Commentaries. I. Title.   II. Title: Luke.   III. Series
        BS2775.3.L43   1999   98–39365
        226.6'07—dc21   CIP

1 2 3 4 5 6   02 01 00
D

To

Mary Martin

and

Mary Webb

Used by God in the

midst of darkness

To let His light shine

again in my life

Contents

Contents

Editorial Preface

Today's church hungers for Bible teaching, and Bible teachers hunger for resources to guide them in teaching God's Word. The Holman New Testament Commentary provides the church with the food to feed the spiritually hungry in an easily digestible format. The result: new spiritual vitality that the church can readily use.

Bible teaching should result in new interest in the Scriptures, expanded Bible knowledge, discovery of specific scriptural principles, relevant applications, and exciting living. The unique format of the Holman New Testament Commentary includes sections to achieve these results for every New Testament book.

Opening quotations from some of the church's best writers lead to an introductory illustration and discussion that draw individuals and study groups into the Word of God. "In a Nutshell" summarizes the content and teaching of the chapter. Verse-by-verse commentary answers the church's questions rather than raising issues scholars usually admit they cannot adequately solve. Bible principles and specific contemporary applications encourage students to move from Bible to contemporary times. A specific modern illustration then ties application vividly to present life. A brief prayer aids the student to commit his or her daily life to the principles and applications found in the Bible chapter being studied. For those still hungry for more, "Deeper Discoveries" take the student into a more personal, deeper study of the words, phrases, and themes of God's Word. Finally, a teaching outline provides transitional statements and conclusions along with an outline to assist the teacher in group Bible studies.

It is the editors' prayer that this new resource for local church Bible teaching will enrich the ministry of group, as well as individual, Bible study, and that it will lead God's people to truly be people of the Book, living out what God calls us to be.

Contributors

Vol. 1 Matthew
Stuart Weber
Pastor
Good Shepherd Community Church
Boring, Oregon

Vol. 2 Mark
Rod Cooper
Professor
Denver Theological Seminary
Denver, Colorado

Vol. 3 Luke
Trent C. Butler
Editor, Bibles
Broadman & Holman Publishers
Nashville, Tennessee

Vol. 4 John
Kenneth Gangel
Professor of Practical Theology and Ministry
Toccoa Falls College
Toccoa Falls, Georgia

Vol. 5 Acts
Kenneth Gangel
Professor of Practical Theology and Ministry
Toccoa Falls College
Toccoa Falls, Georgia

Vol. 6 Romans
Kenneth Boa
President
Reflections Ministry
Atlanta, Georgia

Vol. 7 1 & 2 Corinthians
Richard Pratt
Professor of New Testament
Reformed Theological Seminary
Maitland, Florida

Vol. 8 Galatians, Ephesians, Philippians, Colossians
Max Anders
Senior Pastor
Castleview Baptist Church
Indianapolis, Indiana

Vol. 9 1 & 2 Thessalonians, 1 & 2 Timothy, Titus, Philemon
Knute Larson
Senior Pastor
The Chapel
Akron, Ohio

Vol. 10 Hebrews, James
Thomas Lea
Dean, School of Theology
Southwestern Baptist Theological Seminary
Fort Worth, Texas

Vol. 11 1 & 2 Peter, 1, 2, 3 John, Jude
David Walls & Max Anders
Senior Pastor
Church of the Open Door
Elyria, Ohio

Vol. 12 Revelation
Kendell Easley
Professor of New Testament
Mid-America Baptist Theological Seminary
Memphis, Tennessee

Holman New Testament Commentary

Twelve volumes designed for Bible study and teaching to enrich the local church and God's people.

Series Editor	Max Anders
Managing Editors	Trent C. Butler & Steve Bond
Project Editor	Lloyd W. Mullens
Marketing Manager	Greg Webster
Product Manager	David Shepherd

Introduction to

Luke

Luke, the physician, wrote his friend Theophilus to assure him that what he had heard was true: God had indeed fulfilled his purposes in the life and ministry of Jesus. Luke wrote from an unknown location about A.D. 70 to 75.

AUTHORSHIP

- Luke, the doctor (Col. 4:14), traveled with Paul on parts of his missionary journeys as indicated by the "we" passages in Acts (16:10–17; 20:5–21:18; 27:1–28:16). He:
- Received the Christian tradition from eyewitnesses.
- Was not an apostle or earthly follower of Jesus.
- Was highly educated and widely read.
- Was a research historian in his day.
- Was a Gentile who avoided controversial Jewish topics.
- Had a special interest in healings.
- Wrote Luke and Acts, over one-fourth of the New Testament.

GOSPEL PROFILE

- Sent by Luke to his friend Theophilus, whose Greek name means "friend of God."
- Addressed to a Gentile audience.
- Showed continuity between God's promises in the history of Israel with Jesus' ministry.
- Emphasized Jesus' compassion for the needy and unfortunate.
- Showed work of the Holy Spirit.
- Used Mark and other early traditions as sources.
- More succinct, less emotional than Mark, describing a more gentle, sensitive Jesus.
- Centered in Jerusalem as the starting point of the universal mission of the church.

Luke 1

A Heavenly Savior in an Earthly Womb

I. **INTRODUCTION**
Fear, Awe, and Joy

II. **COMMENTARY**
A verse-by-verse explanation of the chapter.

III. **CONCLUSION**
Two Special Babies

An overview of the principles and applications from the chapter.

IV. **LIFE APPLICATION**
A Promise Fulfilled

Melding the chapter to life.

V. **PRAYER**
Tying the chapter to life with God.

VI. **DEEPER DISCOVERIES**
Historical, geographical, and grammatical enrichment of the commentary.

VII. **TEACHING OUTLINE**
Suggested step-by-step group study of the chapter.

VIII. **ISSUES FOR DISCUSSION**
Zeroing the chapter in on daily life.

Quote

"The New Testament does not present the virgin birth of Jesus as some outlandish event but as simply the fulfill-ment of a promise by Almighty God made to a poor but devout Hebrew woman."

Aida Besancon

Luke 1

 I N A N U T S H E L L

In the clear, direct style of a historian, Luke tells the joyous story of the angels announcing the births of John the Baptist and Jesus, the remarkable reaction of John's father and mother, the glorious song of praise Mary sang, the awesome birth of John, and the powerful proph-ecy of Zechariah.

A Heavenly Savior in an Earthly Womb

I. INTRODUCTION

Fear, Awe, and Joy

*L*ight and joy flashed from my son's eyes as he announced, "Dad, you're going to be a grandpa." This led to months of waiting and planning. (Things became even more complicated in August when Mary Martin became my new bride and an immediate grandmother-in-waiting.) Everyone was excited about what was about to happen, but none of us had traveled this route before. A bit of fear and awe and wonder tinge the expectancy and excitement. When he was within a week of the big event, my son took me to lunch. Finally, he looked up and said: "Dad, I'm scared. I don't know that I can handle all of this."

A similar bag of mixed feelings tied up the heroes of Luke 1. Two couples looked forward to the birth of their first child. Each couple had the normal feelings of fear, awe, inadequacy, and overwhelming joy that my son, daughter-in-law, wife, and I felt. These two Bible couples had even more reason for the great mixture of contradictory feelings. The sons they expected were the two most important children ever born on this planet. Their intertwined ministries would change the world forever. Through the life and death of these two babies, God would act to redeem a lost world. What a responsibility for the expectant parents! The way they responded gives good news to us, not only as expectant (grand) parents but as people who need redemption. Because these two couples proved true to God's commission and performed their role as parents in exemplary fashion, every person in the world can find salvation from sin, eternal life, and unequalled joy.

II. COMMENTARY

A Heavenly Savior in an Earthly Womb

MAIN IDEA: *Luke's trustworthy account of the gospel story begins by showing that in his mercy, God—who does the impossible—prepared the way for the miraculous birth of the Savior's forerunner and for the virgin birth of the world's redeemer . . .*

🅰 Preface: The Tradition Is Certain and True (1:1–4)

SUPPORTING IDEA: *You can know all you need to know about Jesus because the gospel accounts about him are accurate—based on personal research and knowledge by trustworthy writers.*

1:1. Luke did not innovate. He compiled and clarified. He readily saluted the work of his predecessors but saw the need to tell Jesus' story one more time to help his Gentile friend(s) understand and accept it. He gladly used the work of Mark and other writers to show Theophilus how Jesus' life, death, resurrection, and ascension fulfilled and completed what the Holy Scriptures of Israel expected. The word **fulfilled** also means "convince fully," something Luke also wanted to accomplish. Luke used a classic literary form that his Greek-speaking audience would recognize to introduce these educated people to Jesus.

1:2. Luke claimed to be a good historian. He knew the value of accurate sources. They came from the right time: **the first**, that is the very beginning of Jesus' ministry. They came from the right people: **eyewitnesses**, those who knew Jesus. They came through the right channels: those set up to hand down tradition, **handed down** being a technical term for passing on oral tradition. They came for the right reasons: service of the word. Luke's sources of information were not propagandists seeking to twist the facts for their purposes. They were **servants of the word**. The message was of prime importance. The messengers and their causes remained anonymous. The word was the tradition about Jesus. Luke used the same word that John used to speak of Jesus as "the Word" who "became flesh and made his dwelling among us" (John 1:14).

1:3. Luke's claim as a historian rested on more than just choosing the right sources. He did firsthand research. He researched **carefully**, that is, he paid close attention and made sure everything was accurate. He researched **everything** so his readers could trust each part, not just the sum of the whole. He researched **from the beginning**: he had the total story and not just the interesting parts or the climax. Where his sources such as Mark did not include Jesus' childhood years, Luke included everything, even tracing the family tree back to make Jesus not just "the son of David" or "son of Abraham" but "the son of Adam, the son of God" (3:38).

Thus prepared, Luke carried out his writing task to produce **an orderly account**, that is, in a logical order a person could easily understand and in a chronological order a reader could easily follow. Luke's writing was directed to an honored friend who may or may not have held a high social or political position. The friend was Theophilus. His name means "friend of God." He may have been Luke's financial backer for publication of the work. He may have been Luke's channel for getting into higher political and social circles with the gospel of Christ. He may have been no more than a respected friend whom Luke honored by dedicating his Gospel to him. As with so many important persons in Scripture, we have a name without a resumé.

1:4. Theophilus knew the Christian story. Others, probably including Luke, had taught him. Still, doubts remained. He needed reinforcement to believe. Luke wrote his Gospel and then the Book of Acts to supply such reinforcement. Luke wanted **certainty** about Jesus so firm and secure that we can trust its truth absolutely. Reading Luke, Theophilus should have had no more reason to doubt who Jesus was and what Jesus had accomplished.

B Preparing for the Forerunner (1:5–25)

SUPPORTING IDEA: *God used unlikely people to prepare the way for the forerunner of the Savior.*

1:5. God works in the middle of human history. Thus, the Old Testament is full of specific people doing specific things in specific places. Luke began his Gospel in similar fashion. He pointed to a specific person: **Herod**, the great temple builder who ruled Judea from 39 B.C. to 4 B.C. This means that a few miscalculations in establishing the zero hour of chronology cause us to set Jesus Christ's birth to at least 4 and probably 6 years B.C.

Luke did not focus on the power-hungry King Herod the Great. He focused on the temple Herod was building, to one order of priests in the temple—the order named for its founder, Abijah (see 1 Chr. 24:10), and then to one man among those priests. This humble priest was the aged Zechariah, whose wife Elizabeth also belonged to an honored priestly family.

1:6. Impeccable priestly and religious credentials marked Zechariah's family. They followed every part of God's law. God judged them **upright.** They, rather than Herod, qualified to be God's instruments as he prepared the Savior's way. God continually looks among his people not for the rich and famous but for the righteous and holy to join him in his work of salvation. He saves you with imputed righteousness and uses you through realized righteousness.

1:7. Impeccable priestly credentials and impeccable religious, spiritual credentials did not guarantee life's blessings. Zechariah and Elizabeth suffered personal and social disgrace because Elizabeth could not have children. Leviticus 20:20–21 shows that the Hebrews thought childlessness was a sign of divine punishment. Couples were expected to have children, thus fulfilling God's command at creation to multiply and fill the earth (Gen. 1:28). Since they were **well along in years,** they had no hope of removing the disgraceful situation. They had to resign themselves to enduring disgrace the rest of their lives.

1:8. Five times a year Zechariah left home for the temple. During the three major Jewish festivals (Passover, Weeks, and Tabernacles) all priestly divisions served at the temple as pilgrims swelled Jerusalem's population. Each priestly order or division had two other weeks a year when they carried out the daily temple sacrifices and rituals.

1:9. With approximately eighteen-thousand priests in Judea, special duties were assigned by **lot**. Lots were sacred objects of unknown shape and material that would give a yes or no answer to questions or select one person over another. They may have resembled dice (see Num. 26:52–56; 1 Sam. 10:20–24; 14:41–42; 1 Chr. 24:5–19; Prov. 16:33; Acts 1:26). Once in a lifetime a priest had opportunity to enter the temple and offer the incense offerings. After all these years, Zechariah's lot came up. He had the awesome responsibility of entering the holy place, just in front of the Holy of Holies where God was present with his people. There on the incense altar he burned the special spices. Their aroma symbolized the prayers of the people ascending to God. As the incense burned, Zechariah would fall to the floor in humble prayer.

1:10. The time was either the morning or evening offering, probably in this case the evening (cf. Dan. 9:21). Only Zechariah could enter the holy place. Outside, the pious Jewish worshipers and priests joined in prayer, the rising incense giving assurance that God was listening to them. Luke repeatedly emphasized the power of prayer and the need to learn to pray, and to pray together. A praying church finds God's power coming to work among them and accomplish the church's mission.

1:11. Zechariah was visited by **an angel of the Lord**. This represents the heavenly council bringing God's news to God's people, revealing what God is about to do (see Gen. 16:7–11; Exod. 3:2; Num. 22:21–35; Judg. 6:21; 13:20; 1 Sam. 3; Isa. 6). Zechariah expected to see God's messenger about as much as we do. The angel stood in the holy place beside the altar where Zechariah served and prayed.

1:12. Zechariah responded to the angel just as we would and as biblical characters usually did—with pulse-stopping fear and hair-raising terror. The thought must have entered his mind, *What have I done to deserve this?*

1:13. God's angel responded in words God always used to announce salvation to the prophets: **Do not be afraid.** Now Zechariah could listen. The angel could deliver God's message: **your prayer has been heard.** Which prayer? The one I am now praying for the people and the nation? Yes, in a way, but really, No! God is answering your personal prayer. The one you and Elizabeth have uttered for years, the one you think has passed you by. You will be a father. You will name your son John.

1:14. The angel gave Zechariah no time to reply. He must hear the heart of the message. This will be no ordinary son. He will be a son who delights you and brings joy to your life. Here Luke raised a theme he would repeat often as he wrote Luke and Acts. Joy, not fear, is God's desire for his people. God's work brings joy to us and lets us delight in the life he gives. A firstborn son is reason for joy for any parent. This firstborn son was special: **Many will rejoice because of his birth.** John's birth would inject a note of joy into world history. Reading about it should bring joy to us as we contemplate God's work in our lives.

1:15. The picture is not yet fully clear. What is so special about this promised son to parents beyond childbearing age? He will meet God's standards for greatness. One thing will set his life apart from his peers. Priests like Zechariah could not drink alcoholic drinks while serving in the temple (Lev. 10:9). John would never follow his father's footsteps into the temple, but he would take this part of their priestly life as his permanent lifestyle. In this he would be like the devoted Nazirites (Num. 6:1–21), but in other ways he would not.

God laid out specific instructions to set the Savior's forerunner off from all other people. One thing above all would set him apart: **he will be filled with the Holy Spirit.** As we read Luke's writings we will notice how the Holy Spirit works with John, with Jesus, and with the early church. Luke is the Gospel of the Spirit. John was the servant of the Spirit. John would never know a minute without the Spirit, for the Spirit filled him in his mother's womb. Just as God called Jeremiah to be a prophet before he saw the light of day (Jer. 1:5), so John was set apart for God's special service before the first day of his life.

1:16. The Spirit came not for honor but for mission. John would call many people of Israel back to God. God has to begin his work of revival and renewal among people who think they already belong to him. The remainder of Luke's Gospel will feature people opposing John and Jesus—people who claim to be examples for God's people. The priest's task was to turn many people from sin (Mal. 2:6), so naturally the promised new Elijah, the Savior's forerunner, would have the same mission (Mal. 4:5–6). John could not be a missionary to the nations. Israel first had to hear God's message of repentance and conversion.

1:17. John had one major mission: **to make ready a people prepared for the Lord.** To do this he had to live in God's presence, assume the role of the new Elijah (Mal. 4:5–6), and unite families in God's way of righteous living. The Savior cannot come to a people fighting and feuding and disobeying all that God has taught.

1:18. Zechariah was overwhelmed. He could not take in this angelic announcement. Too old for this to happen, he needed a sign that he was not hallucinating. He acted like Gideon of old (Judg. 6).

1:19. The angel had a quick answer. My presence should be enough for you. I am the angel Gabriel sent directly from God's presence to share this good news with you. Just as I represented God to Daniel (8:15–27; 9:20–27), so I represent him to you. Now, listen.

1:20. Zechariah could not believe his eyes. This was too much for him to take in. Even in such an awesome situation, unbelief faces divine discipline. Gabriel announced it: You will not be able to tell anyone about this unparalleled experience. Until the baby cries, you will say nothing. Be assured, your unbelief cannot stop God's plans. My words will come true.

1:21. Zechariah's incense offering took too long. People outside quit praying and began worrying. Where is he? Do we need to do something to rescue him? What could have happened?

1:22. Finally, Zechariah appeared, but something strange was afoot. He was supposed to pronounce the blessing of Aaron (Num. 6:24–26) on the people. He could not talk, and apparently he could not hear (see v. 62). **He kept making signs**, nodding his head, trying to make them understand. What did he mean? He had experienced something unusual—a vision or something.

1:23. The week of priestly duty was over. This time Zechariah could not wait to return home. He had news to share with his family, even if he must write it all out.

1:24. Gabriel's word came true. Elizabeth became pregnant. What a surprise for her friends and all the townspeople! Elizabeth did not let anyone know. **For five months** she **remained in seclusion**. She was part of God's great plan of salvation history. She waited until God was ready to make his plan known. Apparently, she gave up an expectant mother's great joy—the joy of sharing her news—to wait for God's timing.

1:25. Elizabeth declared, **The Lord has done this for me.** She suffered because of her husband's silence and deafness. Still, she knew God was at work in her life. She joined Sarah, the wife of Abraham, and Hannah, the mother of Samuel, in bringing God's child of promise to birth long after all hope and expectation for childbearing had vanished. Failure to bear children resulted in earthly **disgrace**. Failure to believe God resulted in inability to hear or speak. Acknowledging and obeying God swept away disgrace and resulted in praise. No human could have written a script like this, centering the first subplot on an unknown priest's wife secluded in her small town in the hills for five months. No human could make such a script come true in life. God was at work miraculously carrying out his plan of salvation. No other explanation can explain what happened to Zechariah and Elizabeth. Theirs is only one piece of the evidence that God is mysteriously at work.

Ⓒ Earth Prepares for the Savior (1:26–38)

> **SUPPORTING IDEA:** *God did the impossible, bringing the Son of God to earth in a virgin womb to become the Son of David who rules an eternal kingdom.*

1:26. Six months into Elizabeth's pregnancy, God took the second step in his climatic act in salvation history. The scene of action was far from the nation's religious center where Zechariah sacrificed and met Gabriel, far even from the Judean hill country of Elizabeth. The angel Gabriel was again in action, but this time in Nazareth—an insignificant village known only as the home base for the eighteenth of the twenty-four courses of priests.

1:27. The virgin birth is Luke's central emphasis in this section. Having set the scene in verse 26, he begins the narrative with the words **to a virgin.** He will conclude this narrative section by telling how the virgin birth is God's possible impossibility (vv. 34–37). The epilogue to the narrative (v. 38) shows Mary's willingness to be a part of God's impossible acts.

Mary the virgin was **pledged to be married to a man named Joseph.** The language comes from Deuteronomy 22:23. It describes an engagement, the result of a public ceremony before witnesses by which a man and woman were legally considered married but did not live or sleep together. At this stage the bride price had already been paid to the woman's family, and the man had legal responsibility for the woman. This engagement could be broken only through divorce. Engagement usually lasted about a year, with the girl living with her parents. Often the girl was only twelve to fourteen years old. In the forerunner's birth, the expectant father occupied center stage. Here it is the expectant mother. The father is mentioned at this point only to introduce his Davidic ancestry.

1:28. Mary is the **highly favored** one—the recipient of a special blessing from God. She has experienced God's undeserved, unmerited grace in a special way. This does not change who Mary is or give her a status beyond other people. It singles her out as a special instrument whom God chose to use in his gracious plan of salvation. The grace Mary received was God's presence with her.

1:29. The **highly favored** becomes the **greatly troubled.** Luke uses *Siatapaxthe,* the only appearance of the word in the New Testament. It describes something thoroughly stirred up, confused, and perplexed. A divine messenger should be enough to stir up confusion in a young teenager. An angel who promises a special audience with God is even more confusing. So Mary stirred these thoughts around in her mind, trying to find a meaning to them and the steps to take in light of them. She had never received such a greeting! What was she to make of it?

1:30. The heavenly messenger understood her troubled mind, so the angel repeated the comforting words Zechariah had heard (v. 13): **Do not be afraid.** Why should she not be afraid? Mary found **favor.** The Greek word is *xaris*—unmerited, undeserved grace from God. God's grace removes all fear.

1:31–33. The angel's message did not ease Mary's confused mind immediately—not with a divine birth announcement for a baby named "Yahweh is salvation." Not with an explanation that this baby would be the new David, king over all Israel, bearing the awesome title, "Son of God" (see Ps. 2:7). But what a kingdom—an eternal rule without end. No other king had such a kingdom! Who could this baby be?

1:34. Confusion reigned. Mary's questions poured forth. One major obstacle to such a "blessed event" was that she was a virgin. A birth announcement to her was premature, if not nonsense.

1:35. God's messenger had the answer. The Holy Spirit would work a miracle. This child would be born through a special miracle of God—the creation of God's Son in a human womb. This Son of God would be different from kings in Jerusalem. He would be the **holy one.**

1:36–37. Mary's was not the only divine miracle. Elizabeth the barren one would be Elizabeth the rejoicing mother. Her six-month pregnancy verified that God was at work again in mysteriously wonderful ways. He does the impossible. Then and now!

1:38. In humble submission, Mary was now ready to serve God and follow his will. As pregnancy had lifted Elizabeth's disgrace it would soon bring the virgin Mary disgrace. Both agreed to do what God required (see v. 25). With his mission accomplished, the angel left.

ⅅEarth Affirmed Heaven's Way (1:39–56)

SUPPORTING IDEA: *God provides confirmation for the promises he gives.*

1:39–41. Ready to serve but also anxious to see evidence of God's other miracle, Mary headed for **the hill country** to visit relatives. First words of greeting brought encouraging confirmation in two ways: the baby jumped in the womb and the Spirit spoke.

1:42–45. Spirit-inspired words from Elizabeth rained blessing on Mary. They distinguished Mary from all other women. She had God's grace and presence (v. 28) in unique measure, but not in measure that lifted her up for eternal praise and worship. Mary's blessing came not from who she was or would become. Mary's blessing came from the holy baby whom she carried in her womb. This blessed child placed Mary in the position of blessing. God had turned his eyes to Elizabeth (v. 25) but had set his Savior in Mary. Just to stand in such presence awed Elizabeth. How did she deserve the opportunity to stand in the presence of the mother of her Lord? Even before his birth, Jesus was recognized as Lord, the Messiah of God. Such recognition came from humble priestly folks in the Judean hill country, not royal people in the nation's capital. The same humility characterized Mary. Now we see why she was blessed. She believed God's promise. She expected God to accomplish what he said he would do. Faith brings blessing.

1:46–49. Mary's faith displayed itself in praise. In a song resembling Hannah's in 1 Samuel 2, Mary praised God for his great acts for her. Her praise included two actions: giving glory to God and rejoicing in the presence and actions of God. The Lord had looked down on Mary with loving care. He saw the low economic and social state in which she lived. Such a state would be short-lived. God had placed her in a state of blessing. Because of her son, humiliation would disappear. From now on throughout all history people would recognize who she was and the state of blessing she occupied. She did nothing to earn or deserve this. The almighty God had caused it with his mighty acts. So praise him. Call him holy. See him as the transcendent God so uniquely pure and separated from sinful humans.

1:50–53. This holy one is not totally separated. He reaches down in mercy, finding in each generation people who worship him. He attacks the proud, removing them from political power and position. He pays careful, loving attention to the humble, raising them up to new positions of importance. The poor find food from him, while the rich are given nothing. No wonder the young virgin praised God.

1:54–55. Such praise reflected historical reality. The history of Israel tells the story of God's mercy. Start with Genesis 12 and read onwards. Each page recalls tender, loving salvation for an undeserving people. Yes, God does what he promises (cf. v. 45).

1:56. Mary stayed until Elizabeth was ready to give birth to John (see v. 36), then she returned to her people. What a surprise for Nazareth! An unmarried local girl comes down from the hills at least three months pregnant. It made no difference to Mary. God had confirmed his word for her. A baby leaped. The Spirit moved. Elizabeth blessed. God gave her a song of praise. Let the people say what they would. Mary was willing to bear the disgrace in order to become God's instrument of grace.

▣ The Forerunner's Earthly Birth and Heavenly Mission (1:57–80)

SUPPORTING IDEA: *God prepares the way to complete his eternal mission of forgiveness and salvation for his people.*

1:57–58. At the proper time, God fulfilled his promise to Zechariah and Elizabeth. Can you imagine the neighbors' reaction to this grace-child of their old age. They knew this was no ordinary child. This was the Lord's mercy. Elizabeth's attitude was infectious. Joy broke out all around.

1:59–63. God followed proper timing. So did the parents. They followed the law and on the eighth day presented the child for circumcision (Lev. 12:3). The ceremony included officially naming the child. Neighbors assumed the obvious. First child, child of old age—naturally he would have no other name but his father's. So they agreed the boy was a new Zechariah. Elizabeth interfered. Not so! John is his name. Confusion erupted. That name appears nowhere on the family tree. Why would you do a thing like that? Let Dad decide. Still silent (vv. 20–22), Zechariah wrote the name *John.*

Astonishment filled the room. Zechariah had learned his lesson. Do not ask why or how. Just obey God.

1:64–66. Obedience brought renewed fulfillment of God's words (v. 20). Zechariah had words—no longer words of questioning and doubts but words of praise and joy. Silence now moved to the neighbors. Awestruck, they tried to figure out what had happened. The news traveled fast. The entire hill country spread the word. As they talked, they also questioned. Evidence was clear: In this child of the barren and the silent, God was at work. If God could show his hand so strongly in this birth, what would he do when the child matured? What was God getting ready to do among them?

1:67. God had one more word for the pondering people. The Spirit promised for the son (v. 15) and pledged to come to Mary (v. 35) now spoke through Zechariah as he had through Elizabeth (v. 41). Thus, Zechariah's song of praise, reflective of so much of Mary's song (vv. 46–55), was more than human singing. It was divine prophecy, declaring God's word for God's people.

1:68–75. Praise and adoration belong to God alone. As he redeemed Israel from Egyptian slavery (Exod. 15:13; Deut. 13:5; Ps. 77:15; 111:9), so through the forerunner and the Savior he would again pay the price for his people's salvation. He will accomplish this through the Messiah whom everyone expected—the king anointed from a horn of oil and given divine strength like the strength of the great horned deer and oxen (1 Sam. 2:1,10; 2 Sam. 22:3; Ps. 89:17). The prophets said he would do this. Just think of Isaiah 9 and 11 and Jeremiah 23. The promise to David in 2 Samuel 7 is coming to pass.

Just look what will happen: Victory over our enemies. Everyone who hates us is doomed. The oppression and persecution we have suffered so long from the nations is past history. A new day has dawned. Why? Because God is faithful. He did not forget the covenant of mercy he made with our fathers. He promised Abraham a great nation. We will see that happen. Free from enemies, we can devote our lives to serve God without fear or hindrance. That means we will be a different people. We will be holy, set apart to serve and obey him, different from all other peoples on earth. We will be righteous, fulfilling the covenant promises we made to God just as he fulfilled his promises to us.

1:76–79. These wonderful hopes can come true through the little baby Zechariah held in his hands. This helpless, miraculous baby will be God's first prophet since Malachi over four hundred years before. He will not be the Messiah. He will be the one who prepares the way. He is the forerunner whom Malachi promised (see Mal. 3:1). He will let people know what God is up to. He will show them they can have salvation by letting God forgive their sins. Then they can be righteous keepers of the covenant.

Zechariah continued his song of praise: This is not to say how great this son of mine will be. This is to say how wonderful God is. This is all due to his mercy. God wants to send the rising sun of righteousness Malachi said would come (Mal. 4:2). For too long God's people have lived in the darkness of foreign governments, the darkness of economic oppression, the darkness of our own sins. We have experienced living death all these years. Now God is changing all that. God will let his sun shine on us. His pathway for us will become clear. No longer will we have to plot war and subversion against the enemy nations. We will know his perfect peace.

1:80. God has promised salvation and forgiveness. Zechariah and his family and Mary and her family can see it coming. But first, they must wait. Babies cannot accomplish God's plans. They must grow up. John did just that, growing physically and spiritually. When he retreated to the Judean wilderness, we do not know. But Luke prepares us in John's birth story for the strange lifestyle this prophetic forerunner would live. He did not appear in the city streets compelling people to listen. He appeared in the wilderness, expecting city people to come out to him. Just as God prepared Israel in the wilderness before giving them the salvation of the promised land, so he prepared his forerunner in the wilderness before the Messiah's salvation.

> **MAIN IDEA REVIEW:** *Luke's trustworthy account of the gospel story begins by showing that in his mercy, God—who does the impossible—prepared the way for the miraculous birth of the Savior's forerunner and for the virgin birth of the world's redeemer.*

III. CONCLUSION

Two Special Babies

Luke's trustworthy report sings forth the good news. After centuries of silence, God chose one special moment in history to act for his people in forgiveness and salvation. He did this by bringing two special babies into the world—one from the womb of an aged barren woman, the other from a young virgin teenager celebrating her betrothal and approaching marriage. This is the God we serve—a God who chooses his time to bless his people in ways we could never expect. Here is the center of God's work—a work of forgiveness and salvation, a work completing covenant promises made over a thousand years before. Here is the center of human hope—a hope based not on human power and ability but on divine promise and miracle.

God came in the person of John in the wilderness to call his people to repentance and forgiveness. He came in the person of his own Son Jesus to deliver the salvation he had promised. He came through channels people called impossible. He came through people seen as ordinary. He came in places snubbed as unworthy. As he came, he called people to join him in giving salvation to his people and then gave them miraculous signs confirming his presence and his call to them. No wonder the people responded in praise and wonder, singing forth their Spirit-inspired understanding of what God was doing in their lives.

PRINCIPLES

- God often accomplishes his will in unusual and unexpected ways.
- Born as a baby, Jesus was human in every respect.
- Jesus lived his life in dependence on the Holy Spirit.
- God fulfills his promises.
- God works out his will according to his perfect timing.
- Faith brings blessing.
- Praise and adoration belong to God alone.

APPLICATIONS

- Do not limit God by your thinking or with your actions. He is the most creative being in the universe and often accomplishes his will in ways we might not expect. Let him surprise you!
- Take God at his word. Trust God to be true to his promises. God responds to our faith and rewards our obedience.
- Be patient in the life of faith. Although circumstances may often give us a "false reading," God's timing is always right. In spite of circumstances and the consequences, let God work out his will in your life according to his timing.
- Be receptive to the leading of the Holy Spirit in your Christian walk. As Jesus lived in dependence on the ministries of the Holy Spirit, so should we. The indwelling Spirit empowers us to live the life of victorious faith.
- Give praise and thanks to God continually for his gracious gift of salvation.

IV. LIFE APPLICATION

A Promise Fulfilled

Look what God has done. He has surprised the world. Yes, he has surprised his own people. He has gone to out-of-the-way places. He has spoken to unsuspecting, ordinary people, who appeared not to be in a situation to do what God announced would happen. God had two tasks to accomplish. He planned to prepare an unrighteous people to receive a holy Savior. He planned to provide forgiveness and salvation for these people. And he did it. We know he did it because he also prepared a well-educated writer to gather the details and put them in a stimulating and trustworthy literary form so we can enjoy reading what God has done. We know Luke's story of two miraculous births. We know God's surprises for his people. So what? How do we react?

We cannot expect angelic visitations to call us to such miraculous tasks. Mary's and Elizabeth's roles were one-time miracles, never to be matched in human history. They stood at the zenith of God's salvation history. We cannot imitate them. The important thing is what God did and why He did it.

God completed his salvation promises, promises that he first made to Abraham and to David. He brought forgiveness and salvation. He established his covenant once and forever. He invites us to be a part of that covenant. He invites us to believe that God has done the impossible. God has opened a path for us to be in constant relationship with his mercy. He invites us to admit our sins, let him forgive them, and thus know his salvation. He wants to make us holy, separated from the world to serve him in moral purity.

What must happen before we are willing to believe and become what God wants to make of us? Does he have to silence our lips for nine months as he did Zechariah's? Does he have to send us into five months of seclusion to ponder what he has done as he did for Elizabeth? Does he have to answer our questions about how God does the impossible as he did for Mary? What stands in the way of our forgiveness and salvation? God has prepared the way for us. He has sent his Son of righteousness for us. Will we follow Mary in believing what God has said, accepting the promises he has made, and becoming servants through whom God can do his will? If we respond in faith to God, we can know forgiveness for our sins. We can experience the salvation God promised. We can join Mary and Zechariah in singing praises to God for his mercy, forgiveness, and salvation.

V. PRAYER

God, you are the miracle worker, the covenant keeper, the mercy giver, the salvation bringer. We sing in amazement at what you have done for us. No enemy can defeat us. No hatred can stifle us. No rebuke can deter us. We are your covenant people—people called to salvation and forgiveness, people led to holiness and righteousness by your covenant power. Our gratitude knows no bounds as we praise you for sending John to prepare the way and Jesus to fulfill all your promises so we can be your people. Show us the path you have for us to walk, even if it is a path through the wilderness. Amen.

VI. DEEPER DISCOVERIES

A. Fulfilled (1:1)

Luke did not limit his horizons. He stretched his vision back to Scripture's beginning point, which is, of course, the world's beginnings. Every bit of God's historical plan and every scriptural promise found their focal point in the brief span of years Luke wrote about. The years since Malachi had darkened Israel's vision. God's works had been difficult to discover. Once again, God said, "Let there be Light!" The light of two baby boys changed the focus of history. God accomplished his plan to save his people.

The Greek word *peplérophoremenon* refers to something filled up, complete, accomplished but also to the assurance and satisfaction that come from such fulfillment. Luke said the story he was about to tell had been told by many others but was worth telling again. Why? Because this story and only this story ties together all God has ever done in history into one complete, assuring, satisfying whole that will persuade us to believe in Jesus of Nazareth, the Son of God, the Savior. This was not a one-time thing for Luke. He repeatedly used this basic Greek word to show God had a reason for doing what he did and for leading his people to write and preserve Scripture (see 1:20; 4:21; 21:22; 22:16; 24:44; cf. 21:24).

B. Eyewitnesses (1:2)

Luke had a credibility problem. He and the church knew he had never seen Jesus. He was not an apostle. What right did he have to write a Gospel? We would expect him to pile up letters of recommendation and start throwing out names on his network of friends. Surely he would hold up Paul as exhibit number one for his credibility and authority to write. Instead, Luke proceeded like a trained historian. He described his historical method. He admitted his was not an original idea. Many before him had written about Jesus. These included Mark and someone who collected sayings of Jesus, a collection both Matthew and Luke appeared to have used. Scholars refer to this common material shared by Matthew and Luke but not appearing in Mark as Q. Why such an odd designation? Because Germans first talked about it and called it the Source, or in German, *Quelle*. To make this source easy to talk about, scholars simply refer to it as Q.

Luke had access to some of these accounts, at least Mark and Q. He had something more. He had tradition that the church had used in its teaching and preaching during the forty years since Jesus' resurrection and ascension. These were stories the church cherished, stories they carefully taught, stories they memorized to be sure they told them correctly. These stories reached all the way back to the apostles, those who were eyewitnesses of Jesus.

So Luke could not acclaim apostolic authority for himself. But he had the next best thing. He had access to what the apostles said. He had access to what the church taught. He told what servants of God's word taught. What more could you ask for? You want Luke's credentials, too. He had one qualification. He had "investigated everything from the beginning." Luke had not just relied on hearsay evidence. He had not just picked up what information about Jesus was easily at hand. He had become a true student of history. He had traced each piece of information as accurately as possible to its source. He could vouch for the accuracy and reliability of everything he wrote.

Theophilus must have had a serious interest in understanding what this Christian story was all about. Luke assumed he would be willing to read this voluminous Gospel and then keep on and read Acts, too. Luke wanted to make sure Theophilus understood the facts about Jesus.

C. Orderly Account (1:3)

Luke's preface sounds like a secular historian's. He did not use church talk. He did not set out a high-sounding theological purpose. He described a literary purpose. He had taken the reliable information from reliable sources, carefully examined it for himself, and then set it out in a way no writer before him had done. This was not to criticize the presentation of previous accounts. It was to assure Theophilus that Luke's report could be easily followed and its purpose would be clearly evident. Luke had reasons for including the materials he included, for placing them in the order in which he placed them, and for emphasizing certain elements about the life and ministry of Jesus. Finding the order and purpose to Luke's account would be Theophilus's task. Once found, the order and purpose might surprise, for it would be good news, news of salvation available to Theophilus.

Today, we are the Theophilus for whom the Gospel is written. Will we search as diligently as Luke wanted Theophilus to so we can determine the order and purpose of the Gospel and apply its message to our lives? If so, we may have "certainty" (v. 4). Such certainty means we believe Luke reported the facts accurately. Luke wants it to mean more for us. He wants us to have certainty as to who Jesus is and thus find certainty about the salvation Jesus offers. Theophilus had already been taught. He needed more. He needed assurance that what he heard was true, and he needed certainty about how that truth related to his life.

D. Certainty (1:4)

Luke had a goal in writing the honorable Theophilus. He sought to convince him that his account locked up the truth, made it certain and secure so no one had any reason to doubt it. Luke did not intend to introduce Theophilus to new information. He wanted to place common teaching into a framework and order that would bring this "friend of God" to trust the God who came in Jesus.

E. Blamelessly (1:6)

God uses obedient people. Zechariah and Elizabeth met all obedience qualifications. They desired with all their hearts to do what God had commanded in the Old Testament. They apparently passed all the qualifications for God's blessings (see Deut. 28–29). Their reward was the loneliness of childlessness. Aging Elizabeth could not bear children. So many people suffer so many things they seem not to deserve. They ask *Why me?* God's answer: So you can be ready to participate in my future plans. Despite their sorrow, emptiness, and shame over not having children, Zechariah and Elizabeth looked ahead to God and not to the side to sin.

F. Your Prayer Has Been Heard (1:13)

This was the greatest day in Zechariah's life as a priest—the one time when he got to enter the holy place to offer the incense. Certainly he joined the host of priests and people praying on the outside (v. 10) as he entered to pray on the inside. What did he expect to happen? Not at all what did. An angel told him that his prayer had been answered. How many times had he prayed the same prayer over the years? Never had an angel jumped in front of him with immediate response. No wonder the hill-country priest was terrified. Prayer is not just a religious rite carried out to be pious and blameless. Prayer is direct access to God's ear which allows God direct access to you. A people united in prayer had better be ready. There is no telling what you can expect from God. He answers prayer.

G. Filled with the Holy Spirit (1:15)

Luke is the Gospel of the Holy Spirit, preparing the way for the great outpouring of the Spirit at Pentecost (Acts 2). The work of the Spirit indicates the rebirth of prophecy, silent for four hundred years since the days of the prophet Malachi. The work of the Spirit ties John closely to Elijah (v. 17). The work of the Spirit explains why crowds came to hear John in his unlikely pulpit in the isolation of the Jordan River. The working of the Spirit explains why strongly religious people would repent and seek renewal from God. The working of the Spirit assures that what John said and did was precisely what God wanted said and done. John was not some power-mad preacher putting on a show for the crowds. John was God's instrument at history's most important moment. We know this because God promised it, even before John's birth.

The Holy Spirit is the star of Luke's infancy narratives. The Spirit would make John's ministry possible. The Spirit made Jesus' birth possible (v. 35).

The Spirit led Elizabeth to recognize that God was working miraculously in Mary's womb in an even greater way than in her own (vv. 41–45). The Spirit spoke through Zechariah after his months of silence, as he praised and explained what God was doing through his son (v. 67).

H. To Make Ready a People Prepared for the Lord (1:17)

Isaiah (ch. 40) surprised Israel by announcing a return from exile on a highway God would construct. Luke picked up Isaiah's language (Isa. 40:3) as a summary of John's job description. Israel under Roman rule resembled Israel under Babylonian rule. Isaiah's words led a nation across the desert wilderness from Babylon to Palestine. Now his words would awaken a nation in a spiritual desert and lead them to the Jordan wilderness to hear a strange preacher point them to God's way so they would be ready when the Lord appeared. To be ready meant to restore family relationships and righteousness (cf. Mal. 4:5–6) in a nation so dedicated to scoring itself on obedience to the law that it had forgotten God's scorecard emphasizes relationships and righteousness.

I. The Lord Has Done This for Me (1:25)

Prayers uttered became prayers answered. Elizabeth recognized this and gave God credit. A barren woman beyond childbearing years was pregnant. That was God's kind of work—work preparing for an even greater work of God. God's work removes disgrace, restores favor, and prepares for revival. The human who recognizes God's grace at work praises God for it. Soon Mary and Zechariah would expand this brief note of praise, but Elizabeth's expression of praise is the basic hymn for all people—a first-person confession recognizing God at work in human affairs.

J. Jesus . . . Son of the Most High . . . Son of God (1:31–35)

Luke used titles for Jesus in special ways. His basic name reaches back to that of Joshua who first gave Israel the land as a permanent home. The name Jesus means "Yahweh (personal name of the God of Israel) saves." It was a common name that represented a parent's praise for what God continued to do in the life of the family and the nation. Only with Jesus did the name take on a special meaning. Now the world would learn for the first time the true meaning of salvation. For the first time God's eternal way of salvation would become clear. Yahweh's salvation would become incarnate in this baby named "Yahweh saves." "Jesus" as a name or title did not sufficiently express all that God was doing.

Who Jesus was is as important as what Jesus would provide for us. Jesus is the "Son of the Most High." He is directly tied to the ancient name the patriarchs used for God—El Elyon (Gen. 14:18). He is tied to God's allotment of land to the nations (Deut. 32:8). He is tied to the God who comes and delivers in time of urgent need (2 Sam. 22:14; cf. Ps. 7:17). He is tied to the king of all the earth who is "exalted far above all gods" (Ps. 97:9). This baby announced in the insignificant village of Nazareth to an unmarried teenager can claim the most awesome title imaginable. He is Son of God, tied to the language of kingship (2 Sam. 7) and to the rituals used to install David and his successors in office (Ps. 2:6–7). He is Son of God, not just in a sense of one adopted by God for special service as was the king. He is Son of God in the most intimate sense possible—Son of God by his very nature. What better time to express this than at his birth.

Interestingly, Luke holds tightly to this title for Jesus. It belongs to demonic profession (4:3,9,41; 8:28) and to the priests' accusations (22:70), never to the disciples' confession as in Matthew 16:16; Mark 15:39. Instead, it occurs in private conversations as God speaks to Jesus (3:22; 9:35) or in Jesus' coded messages to his disciples (10:22; 20:13). Luke wanted the readers of his Gospel to know that Jesus is the Son of God, but he used the Son of God role to characterize how Jesus ministers on earth. Jesus is the intimate Son loved by the Father and held in awe by the demons. He is not the miracle-working Son sent to display overpowering divine works that force all observers to recognize him as unearthly.

K. All Generations Will Call Me Blessed (1:48)

God used Mary in a unique way. In what way did this make her a unique person? The church has debated this issue for centuries. Mary described herself as humble (v. 48), "the Lord's servant" (v. 38). She also recognized that God was doing something extraordinary in her life, something which would make the rest of history take notice of her. Future generations would unite in calling her "blessed." Does this mean that Mary entered a new state of existence, a state different from other people, a state that provided power for future prayers and hope for future miracles in her name? Is it not much more a recognition of changed circumstances rather than a changed state?

Mary was a humble, unmarried teenager from Nazareth with little of the world's goods. She received a gift from God, a gift of service. She served as God's means of bringing his Son into the world. That gift of service means she received God's blessing. It is as a recipient that she is blessed, not as a giver of blessing to others. The church in gratitude for her attitude of obedience and service recognizes what God has done for her and calls her blessed of God.

VII. TEACHING OUTLINE

A. INTRODUCTION

1. Lead Story: Fear, Awe, and Joy
2. Context: We study the gospel, God's good news to his people, good news centered in the life of Jesus, son of Mary and son of God. Such good news is overwhelming, even fearful. How can we believe such extraordinary reports? Luke tells us clearly in his first chapter. The tradition is certain and true based on personal research and knowledge by trustworthy writers. Heaven, not earth, prepared the way by using unlikely people to bring the forerunner to birth. God did the impossible, bringing the Son of God to earth in a virgin womb to become the Son of David, ruling an eternal kingdom. God provides confirmation for the promises he has given. God prepares the way to complete his eternal mission of forgiveness and salvation for his people.
3. Transition: Today we look at the impossible. We talk about a heavenly Savior in an earthly womb. What in the world can bring us to believe the impossible? Nothing! Nothing in this world can bring us to believe the impossible. We must suspend dependence on earthly ways of thinking. We must go beyond human means of logic and persuasion. Can our minds stretch far enough to look at things from heaven's perspective instead of earth's? If so, we will join good company—a humble priest, a secluded hill-country woman who could not have children, and a young, vibrant teenager looking forward to her wedding day. They will help bring us to believe in God's impossibility.

B. COMMENTARY

1. Preface: Certainty about the Tradition (1:1–4)
2. Preparing for the Forerunner (1:5–25)
   a. The earthly setting: righteous priestly parents (1:5–7)
   b. The divine setting: temple worship (1:8–10)
   c. The heavenly visit: angelic birth announcement (1:11–13)
   d. The heavenly job description: prepare for the Lord (1:14–17)
   e. The earthly uncertainty: how can I be sure? (1:18)
   f. The heavenly certainty: sign of silence (1:19–20)
   g. The earthly fulfillment: pregnancy as heavenly favor (1:21–25)
3. Preparing for the Savior (1:26–38)
   a. The earthly setting: royalty in Galilee (1:26–27)
   b. The heavenly setting: God with you (1:28)
   c. The heavenly visit: angelic birth announcement (1:29–31)

      d. The heavenly job description: eternal king (1:32–33)

      e. The earthly uncertainty: how will this be? (1:34)

      f. The heavenly certainty: the Spirit's work (1:35)

      g. The earthly fulfillment: pregnant together (1:36–38)

4. Earth Confirmed Heaven's Way (1:39–56)

5. Confirmation from Baby and Spirit (1:39–45)

6. Confirmation in Human Praise (1:46–55)

7. Confirmation in Togetherness (1:56)

8. The Forerunner's Earthly Birth and Heavenly Mission (1:57–80)

      a. The forerunner's earthly birth (1:57–66)

      b. The forerunner's heavenly mission (1:67–79)

      c. Earthly growth for heavenly mission (1:80)

C. CONCLUSION: A PROMISE FULFILLED

VIII. ISSUES FOR DISCUSSION

1. In what ways are the two birth announcements similar? Different? How do they resemble and differ from the birth announcement to Hannah in 1 Samuel 1–2?

2. What role does the Holy Spirit have in the birth announcements?

3. What character traits do Zechariah and Elizabeth share with Mary? Why would God choose such people to prepare the way for the Lord?

4. How many references to prayer can you find in Luke 1? What different types of prayer are represented? What do you learn about God's response to prayer and praise?

Luke 2

The Savior's Earthly Birth and Heavenly Mission

I. **INTRODUCTION**
Why Can't Booker Come to Church?

II. **COMMENTARY**
A verse-by-verse explanation of the chapter.

III. **CONCLUSION**
Son of Earth, Son of Heaven
An overview of the principles and applications from the chapter.

IV. **LIFE APPLICATION**
Believing Is Not Easy
Melding the chapter to life.

V. **PRAYER**
Tying the chapter to life with God.

VI. **DEEPER DISCOVERIES**
Historical, geographical, and grammatical enrichment of the commentary.

VII. **TEACHING OUTLINE**
Suggested step-by-step group study of the chapter.

VIII. **ISSUES FOR DISCUSSION**
Zeroing the chapter in on daily life.

> ## Quote
>
> "*The* virginal conception . . . is the divinely ordered method of the incarnation of God in Jesus Christ. . . . It is possible, of course, that God could have chosen and effectuated another method, but it is difficult to conjecture a more appropriate method for the incarnation. To be the Redeemer of humankind, Jesus must identify himself with human beings and at the same time transcend the human race. Thus he was fittingly begotten of the Holy Spirit and born of a woman."
>
> J .   L e o   G a r r e t t

Luke 2

IN A NUTSHELL

Luke in chapter 2 ties the earthly and the heavenly natures and missions of Jesus closely together while continuing his theme of God using earth's lowest to do God's highest. Heaven's angels join earth's shepherds to announce the birth of the One who would change history for Jew and Gentile alike. The young lad knew his place in his Father's house and in his father's home. He grew in earthly wisdom and heavenly grace.

The Savior's Earthly Birth and Heavenly Mission

I. INTRODUCTION

Why Can't Booker Come to Church?

I will never forget Booker, though I cannot remember his exact name. I was in the fifth grade. I drove with my parents by a school on the other side of town. There everything seemed different. Only black people populated that school. All the teachers, all the parents, all the students were black. And there among them stood my friend Booker. He had been the savior for our Little League baseball team. We counted on him to win every game he pitched, and he almost did. No one could hit his fastball, and the pitch they did not want to see was his curve ball. When not pitching, he starred at shortstop and at the plate. He was the center of our team.

That afternoon, it dawned on me that something was wrong. I could play ball all summer with Booker and other black friends, but come fall, we had to say good-bye, go our separate ways, and get our separate educations. This practice eventually led Booker to leave west Texas and live with relatives in New Mexico, where he could go to school wherever he desired. Even later it dawned on me that Booker was not welcome where I worshiped either. We had a mission for his kind. As a teenager dedicated to the ministry, I could go preach in the mission, but I could not invite Booker and his friends to my church.

From his birth on, Jesus came with a resounding note that clashed with the culture of his day. He was the Savior not just of Jews but of all people. Whoever believes on him will be saved. Jews far beyond the fifth grade saw no problem at all in excluding everyone else from salvation. They could not hear Jesus' message about salvation for the entire world. A visit to our churches today makes one wonder how well we have heard the message. Have we excluded from salvation all who do not belong to our social class, our side of town, our race, our clothing standards?

Luke should threaten the church today; it still calls out "good news of great joy that will be for all people."

II. COMMENTARY

The Savior's Earthly Birth and Heavenly Mission

MAIN IDEA: *Jesus is the promised Messiah and Savior who brings salvation to people from all classes, races, and nations of the world.*

Ⓐ The Savior's Earthly Birth (2:1–21)

SUPPORTING IDEA: *God works through history-making governments and anonymous people like shepherds to accomplish his saving purposes.*

2:1–3. Luke changes the scene quickly and radically. We go from the isolated Jordan wilderness to the senate in Rome, from a young man waiting for his chance to perform to the Roman Emperor seeking taxes.

Luke shows his historical concerns by setting Jesus' birth in a world history framework. The problem lies in the ability of modern historians to recreate his historical framework. We can list governors of Syria around the time of Jesus' birth:

M. Titius	10 B.C.
C. Sentius Saturnius	9–6 B.C.
P. Quintilius Varus	6–4 B.C.
* * * * * *	
P. Sulpicius Quirinius	A.D. 6–7

Jesus was born at least by 4 B.C. How could Quirinius have been responsible for the census? Also, Luke claims the entire world participated. No other records show such an extensive Roman census. Records do show Augustus sought to reorganize the financial policies and procedures of the empire. The census was one means he used to gain financial resources. Records also show Quirinius carried out an important census (referred to obliquely in Acts 5:37) but a decade after Jesus' birth. Without further records, we cannot solve this historical problem. Such solving is not necessary, however, to maintain confidence in God's Word. It would answer human questions but would not provide new theological insights or new directions from God for life.

2:4–7. Joseph, barely introduced in 1:27, enters center stage. Taxation followed his lineage, so he obediently traveled the ninety miles to Bethlehem, David's home, where the Scriptures said Messiah would be born (Mic. 5:2). Finally, we see Joseph, too, can trace his family tree to David. Joseph did not make the trip alone. Mary, still only engaged, not married but pregnant, joined him. Perhaps, she, too, like Syrian women over age 12, had to register for the census and pay taxes. Luke surprises us with his next statement, just as the event must have surprised Mary and Joseph. Jesus' appearance time had come. Simply, Luke reports, **she gave birth to her firstborn, a son.**

Following the practice of her day, Mary wrapped the baby in strips of cloth to keep his arms and legs straight. Jesus' first crib had usually served as a dining table for animals. Where they had eaten, he now slept. Why? Because all normal lodging places were full. Or perhaps because Joseph found a small one-room house with just enough room for him and his wife. The only available space for the child was in the animal trough attached to the wall that their room shared with the animals' quarters. The promised king came to his people but did not have enough power to secure a resting place for his birth. The descendants of David descended to a stable to find a place to lay the head of the King of kings. This is how God used earth's lowest to bring salvation from heaven's highest.

2:8–12. Luke quickly shifts scenes from the king lying where animals eat to burly men protecting animals in their natural homes. Shepherding had changed from a family business as in David's time (1 Sam. 16:11) to a despised occupation. Many shepherds were accused of robbery and using land they had no rights to. Shepherding was also a lonely occupation, particularly at night, as a shepherd stood his watch, making sure sleeping sheep did not wake up and wander and that prowling predators did not attack and devour the sheep. Only God would visit those in such a low occupation and raise them to witness to his salvation. Yet, shepherds had a tender side, counting the sheep constantly (Jer. 33:12–13), lifting the weak on their shoulders (see Isa. 40:11), and creating crude pens where the sheep could sleep (John 10:1).

Shift the spotlight once more from earth's lowly shepherds enduring a dark night to heaven's most glorious messenger. With the angel came God's glory, his shining majesty, the side of God humans can see and to which they can respond in confession, worship, and praise (see Isa. 60:1–3). As with Zechariah (1:12–13) and Mary (1:29–30), gazing at God's glorious angel terrified the shepherds and brought quick reassurance: **Do not be afraid.** Gospel is coming, **good news.** Gospel elicits joy, not fear. Joy is the inward feeling of happiness and contentment that bursts forth in rejoicing and praise. Joy comes not just to lowly shepherds or isolated parents far from home. Joy comes to all people. In the most unlikely place amid the most unlikely spectators, God brushed aside the world's fears and provided the world reason for joy (cf. Isa. 9:3).

Joy centers not in something you earn or possess. Joy comes from God's gift, a tiny baby in a feed trough. But what a baby! Born in David's town, the child clasps heaven's greatest titles in his small fist. **Savior,** God's title (1:47), becomes the baby's (cf. 1:69). He will follow in the biblical tradition of deliverers (Judg. 3:9,15; Neh. 9:27; Isa. 19:20; cf. Acts 5:31; 13:23). A troubled, powerless people will find a hero able to overcome the enemy. **Christ** or Messiah, the promised Anointed One, the king who would sit on David's throne and deliver oppressed Israel. The birthplace of the king who first united the nation now births the king who offers unity to the world. **The Lord** is the title Luke uses most often for Jesus. This title refers to the holy, unspeakable personal name of God himself. This baby in the manger was God himself (cf. 1:32,35), with all power and all authority under heaven. Bow in obedience to the baby of Bethlehem. You will easily find him, the only baby wrapped up like an infant but lying in the trough where animals eat.

2:13–14. An angelic chorus burst on the scene, confirming the original angel's message and singing heavenly praise to God. God revealed his glory in brilliance that shepherds could recognize. Angels recognize the worth and weight of God's presence and praise him for it. God gains glory. People get peace. God is in heaven; people, on earth. All this happens because God's favor, his good will, his choice rests on people.

2:15–16. Angelic presence does not last forever. Angels leave. People must respond. How would shepherds respond—these tough men whose theological education came from the heavens and meadows rather than the synagogue and its rabbis? No quibbling or quarreling! Rather, they made an immediate decision—to go to Bethlehem to see what God had reported to them. They wanted to be part of the work God was doing in his world. They saw God's work in the face of a baby lying in a manger. What audacity that God would use society's lowest occupations and its most meager resources to begin his awesome work of salvation.

2:17–20. Seeing the baby Jesus was not enough for the shepherds. They had to share the story. Everyone they met heard from them about angelic visits, angelic songs of praise, and a trip to a manger to find the baby of God's glory. Most important, they shared **what had been told them about this child.** The fact of the child was news. The function of the child was gospel. Shepherds found in a manger the Savior, the Messiah, the Lord himself. They let everyone in hearing distance know.

One word characterized their audience: **amazed.** Shepherds became Jesus' first evangelists. Surprise, astonishment greeted the first testimonies about Jesus. Surprise soon gave way to wonder and marvel at what God had done. Everyone in Bethlehem began talking about God's mysterious surprise—a surprise made known firsthand only to a couple from Nazareth and unappreciated shepherds carrying out their lonely nighttime tasks. The mother responded differently. She had incubated amazement for nine months. Now she incubated experiences in her mind, experiences that gradually became treasured memories, each showing something new and different about her son, each confirming Gabriel's promise of greatness for this Son of David and Son of the Most High. Surely nothing was impossible with God (1:30–37).

Shepherds came. They saw what God told them to expect. They proclaimed their findings to all who would listen. They turned back toward their jobs, a new song of praise in their hearts. What God had said, God had done. They returned to the sheep, never to be heard of again, but never to be forgotten.

The Son of God had to endure the rituals of a Jewish son. Obediently, Mary and Joseph performed the operation that dedicated the baby to the covenant faith of the Jews—a covenant faith initiated long ago as Abraham performed the first circumcision rites on his people (Gen. 17). Then the high moment came; they could officially announce his name. He would be called Jesus, just as the angel instructed (1:31). God's Savior was here.

B The Savior's Heavenly Mission (2:22–38)

SUPPORTING IDEA: *God uses devoted people to reveal his heavenly purposes to provide salvation and redemption for his people and for all the world.*

2:22–24. Obediently, Mary and Joseph followed all the Jewish customs based on God's Old Testament revelation. Thirty-three days after circumcision, the new mother entered the temple to purify herself and her family **(their purification)** from the impure postnatal bleeding and the contact the family must have had with her (see Lev. 12).

Fulfilling the demands of Exodus 13:2,12 (cf. 13:11–16; 22:29–30; Lev. 27:26–27; Num. 3:13; 8:17–18), Mary and Joseph took Jesus to Jerusalem for the purification rites to dedicate him officially to God as their firstborn. They carefully followed the regulations of Exodus and particularly of Leviticus 12. Unable to offer a lamb, they presented birds as a poor person's substitute (Lev. 12:6,8). The sinless Son of God could not in his humanity as a son of Mary exempt her from enduring the normal shame of being unclean, impure. The Son with his parents fulfilled all righteousness in fulfilling all the Law, as Luke repeatedly emphasizes. The Son, like Samuel, was dedicated to God and his service as a helpless infant (see 1 Sam. 2).

2:25–26. Two persons—pious, devoted servants of God—met Jesus in the temple and explained his calling and ministry. Both explanations came through the Holy Spirit. Simeon appeared first. Like Zechariah and Elizabeth (1:6), he was **righteous.** He conformed to God's expectations and lived in a right relationship with God. He was **devout.** He feared God and showed reverence for God. He took God's promises seriously.

God had promised **consolation** for Israel, a time of comfort and renewed hope (see Isa. 40:1; 49:13; 51:3; 52:9; 57:18; 66:10–11). Simeon expected that to happen any day. In his daily walk with God, Simeon had heard God's Spirit speak. God's personal word to Simeon guaranteed him the Christ, God's comfort in person, would come before Simeon died. God kept his promise to a man known in history only because he waited obediently for God to keep his promise.

2:27–33. The Spirit controlled everything Simeon did. He spied Mary and Joseph, Jesus' **parents,** as they entered the temple. They were simply obeying God's law. Simeon intercepted them and took the child in his arms. He gave them a blessing they did not expect. Praising God (cf. 1:68), Simeon first claimed his dismissal from God's army. His tour of duty was done. God had fulfilled his promise. Simeon could now die and claim his eternal peace. He had seen God's **salvation.** Named Jesus, "Yahweh is salvation" (v. 21) and proclaimed by the angel as Savior (v. 11), Jesus was what Simeon had longed for and looked for all these years—the salvation, the deliverance of his people.

Such salvation is not a human act or human possession. It is God's salvation. He prepared for it clearly on the stage of world history where all people could see. He made it a **light for revelation** to the Gentiles. Yes, salvation was more than fulfillment of Israel's nationalistic hopes. Salvation was a light revealing God and his purposes and ways to all people, Jew and Gentile alike (see Isa. 40:5; 42:6; 46:13; 49:6; 52:9–10). Israel did have a special place. They were **your people.** In Jesus they received **glory,** for the Gentiles saw them as the important instrument God used to bring salvation to the whole world.

Shepherds amazed Bethlehem with their message (v. 18). Simeon amazed Joseph and Mary with his. News about Jesus is never ordinary, daily newspaper stuff. News about Jesus leaves the audience wondering: How can this be? Who is this?

2:34–35. Simeon continued his blessing, not directing it to the parents but to God. The words hardly sounded like blessing. They described pain and separation. Israel must fall and fail in the face of Jesus before they would rise as he arose (see Ps. 118:22; Isa. 8:14; 28:16; cf. Luke 20:17–18; Rom. 9:32–33; 1 Pet. 2:6–8). Some would never rise, for Jesus' own people would reject him. This is clear at the start of the gospel story, not part of a surprise ending. God's incarnate symbol and instrument of salvation would be sneered at, spoken against, rejected. True Israel will be revealed, for hearts and minds will become clearly visible. Those of faith and those without faith will be clearly distinguished.

Such response to a Son is difficult for a mother. Her heart would be pierced as if by a sword, broken apart because of the treatment her Son must suffer. God has provided a Savior, but salvation is not automatic. People must believe, trust, and embrace God's Savior and his salvation. Gentiles will; many in Israel will not.

2:36–38. Simeon acted like a priest, much like Eli in 1 Samuel 1–2, but he received no official title from Luke. He was simply a dedicated servant of God led by the Spirit of God. Anna immediately received a legitimating title. She was a **prophetess**, one with great age and experience, apparently having been married seven years and widowed eighty-four (NIV textual note), perhaps being 105 or so as she stood in the temple. She made the temple her permanent home; worship, prayer, and fasting, her occupation. Without invitation, she approached the baby Jesus just as Simeon returned him to his parents. She recognized what God was doing in the person of this baby and **gave thanks.** This term appears only here in the New Testament.

Anna then turned to other worshipers and spoke her prophetic words about the child to all who **were looking forward to the redemption of Jerusalem** (see Isa. 52:9). Not all Jews rejected Jesus. Simeon waited for God to comfort Israel (v. 25). Anna and the other worshipers looked to God for Jerusalem's redemption (cf. 1:68). Israel raised praises at Jesus' birth, looking forward to what he would do in his death. There he died, giving his life in payment for the death penalty all people deserved because of their sins.

Ⓒ Earthly Growth for Heavenly Mission (2:39–52)

SUPPORTING IDEA: *The human Jesus grew in the ways that all children do, each step of growth preparing him to fulfill his Father's eternal mission.*

2:39–40. Mission accomplished, census enrollment completed, miraculous baby birthed, circumcision performed, name given, purification carried out, firstborn presented and dedicated, blessings and prophecies heard and stored away in amazement—the new family returned home to the obscurity of Nazareth, having **done everything required by the Law.** There where no one expected anything of significance to happen, the son of Mary and Joseph who was also the Son of God grew up in the ways all children do, the way John had grown in the desert (1:80). He gained physical strength. He was filled with wisdom, including intellectual abilities and knowledge but guided by the "fear of the LORD" (Prov. 1:7). He would soon demonstrate his growth in this capacity (vv. 46–49). And most important of all, God's grace covered him (cf. 1:30). From childhood God's loving presence filled Jesus' life.

2:41–50. Pious parents attended the Passover each year in Jerusalem, again fulfilling God's expectations (Exod. 23:14–17; 34:23–24; Deut. 16:16). Each year the growing Jesus learned more about the history and worship of God and God's people (Exod. 12–13). The twelfth appearance proved special. Next year he would officially enter the community of Jewish men. At the temple he showed he was more than ready. His earthly growth was preparing him for heavenly mission. Absorbed in such preparation, Jesus did not realize his parents had left. Absorbed in preparations for the journey, apparently with a crowd of friends and fellow pilgrims, his parents did not notice the missing child.

When the time to camp out for the night arrived, the parents could not locate Jesus. Immediately they turned back to Jerusalem. They found him in the temple. Had he like Anna spent day and night there, ignoring everything in the service of the Father? Finding him in the temple was not surprising. Seeing him a full participant in rabbinical Bible studies was. The reaction (v. 47) was a different kind of astonishment than that of 1:21,63; 2:18,33. There some understanding is implied of God's part in the wonderful, miraculous nature of the event causing amazement. Here confusion and inability to understand plays a greater role. The people had never seen anything like Jesus, nor would they ever again. His parents showed still another type of amazement. They were both frightened and overwhelmed at what they saw and heard but more overwhelmed that a son with such promise and brilliance would have treated them the way they perceived he had done.

Jesus endured the normal parental scolding, **Son, why have you treated us like this?** He was amazed at their lack of growth in understanding about who he was and about his priorities. The miracles surrounding his birth and the years watching his growth should have prepared them for the identity he had assumed. Yes, he was their child and would go home to live with them. Still, they did not give him his primary identity. That came from his Father. He must—a necessity laid on him by the Father and by his identity as the Son—do the things of the Father, not of the parents. That was the goal of his growth.

2:51–52. Jesus' growth was not yet complete. He returned obediently with his parents to the normal childhood life. Mother would never be the same. More treasures entered her mind (see v. 19), some now that she could not understand (v. 50). Jesus resumed his growth pattern (see v. 40). The relationship to God's grace now became evident in a similar relationship with people. Jesus had all his relationships in order, those with people and with God. He was going through all types of earthly growth so he could embark on his heavenly mission.

MAIN IDEA REVIEW: *Jesus is the promised Messiah and Savior who brings salvation to people from all classes, races, and nations of the world.*

III. CONCLUSION

Son of Earth, Son of Heaven

Two chapters into Luke, we know what to expect from Jesus. He is son of his parents and Son of his Father. He is good news, gospel, joy, Savior, Messiah, Lord God, cause of amazement and wonder, one who fulfills every clause of the Law, full-fledged member of the covenant people Israel. He is the source of comfort and consolation for which Israel waited, the promised bringer of salvation, the light giving revelation to the Gentiles and glory to Israel, the fulfillment of God's promised redemption.

More ominously, he is the source of falling and rising, the target of sneers and rejection, the revelation of the true thoughts and belief of Israel, the cause of a heart-piercing pain for his mother. Still, he is only a child, gradually growing up like every other child, but precocious, full of wisdom and intent on fulfilling the things his Father expects of him, even when this brings consternation and anguish to parents who cannot understand all that is going on with this human, yet divine Son whom God has given them to raise. Thus, we are set for the gospel story—the story of how the world received this God/man as he left his parental home to enter his Father's ministry.

How can a baby isolated in Nazareth bring salvation to a world so unaware of his presence? Will this son of David find political answers for Israel and redeem the nation by the sword as David had? Or will the focus remain on the "little people," the people whose only claim to historical fame is that they came in contact with Jesus, and God used them to tell his story? Are we entering a story of kings and princes and counselors? Or are we entering a story of country priests and pious servants of God waiting for God to act to fulfill his promises? We know who Jesus is, yet we cannot fathom how the world will learn who he is and how he will accomplish the role of Savior, Messiah, Lord God given to him at birth. We remain like his parents, treasuring what we know in our hearts but not yet understanding how all the parts fit together.

PRINCIPLES

- Jesus' role as Savior was proclaimed before his birth.
- Jesus' salvation is intended for all people.
- Jesus' salvation comes to us through the dedicated lives of the "insignificant people" of the world who choose to serve God in obedience and trust rather than carve out a niche in history for themselves.

- Jesus' salvation comes to us in the midst of world history and even through the unsuspecting actions of unbelieving historical rulers.
- Jesus' salvation does not come automatically. People retain the freedom to reject him.
- Jesus' salvation often brings pain to those closest to him.
- Jesus' salvation was accomplished only because a human baby faithfully accomplished the growth tasks of a child in order to enter a heavenly mission.

APPLICATIONS

- Extend the ministry of your church to all people whom Jesus came to save.
- Expect pain and opposition as you learn from and serve Jesus.
- Model yourself on the "insignificant people" of life, like a priestly couple from the hills, unappreciated shepherds toiling alone through the night hours, a righteous man doggedly following the Holy Spirit and waiting for God to fulfill his promises, and an aged woman living in God's house occupied with worship and prayer until God blesses her.
- Expect to find God at work in places where people would never think to look, even in animal feeding troughs.
- Live each day in obedience so God can use you when his time comes.
- Tell everyone you meet the good news that God has shared with you.

IV. LIFE APPLICATION

Believing Is Not Easy

Believing Jesus is God's Savior and Messiah is not easy. God seems to do his best to make it difficult. God works with people we would never choose. He makes claims for Jesus that defy human reason. He expects us to endure loneliness, long waiting periods, pain, grief, rejection, and lack of under-standing when we do choose to follow Jesus. He looks to us to follow the Holy Spirit rather than rely on our own intelligence. Yet he commands us to mature physically, intellectually, and spiritually.

How can I possibly believe when God acts like this? You can believe the same way my friend believes in his son. The father knows his son's life story—a story of being uprooted from one home to another, even from one culture to another. A story of rejection by friends, denial by people he thought loved him, even the death of a parent. A story of delving into the ways of the world to see if it offered fun or at least escape from the unrealized hopes of family, friends, and church.

How can a father stand to watch a son act out this story? How can a father show patience waiting on God to bring change in the son rather than bursting into action himself and trying to force the son to act "normal"? Reason offers no answer, for the son's story is unreasonable and the son does not respond to reason. Emotional appeals offer no answer, for the son is rebelling against the emotional atmosphere of home, school, friends, and church. Rejection and denial offer no hope, for the son has grown to expect this as the way life treats him.

But the true story does become one of return to home, friends, a moral way of life, church, God, and hope. How? Because the father prays, hopes, and waits patiently for God to fulfill his promises in his time. The father trusts that what God has said, God will do. This is your response to Jesus. God has promised that Jesus will save, that Jesus is the Messiah bringing hope to the people of Israel and bringing new revelation and salvation to all those outside the people of Israel. God has pointed to Jesus as the only source of good news in life.

You may not be able to see just now in the circumstances of your life just how God can make this true. You may not see any hope for deliverance from the situation you face. God calls on you to trust him and wait to see how he brings your story to a close. Stay on the job faithfully like the shepherds. Watch and trust faithfully like Simeon. Worship and pray faithfully like Anna, even until you are 105. Store up all you know as God's treasures in your mind, waiting for the time when he will give you the key to understanding them. Endure the pains and rejections of life until he causes you to rise up rather than fall down.

The father does not find it easy to wait on God to bring his son back. Mary and Joseph did not find it easy to endure the criticism and judgment that friends put on the pregnant, unmarried couple. Simeon did not find it easy to wait for Israel's comfort and consolation. Anna did not find it easy to pray, fast, and worship when each day could easily be her last. Mary and Joseph did not find it easy to give their son up to the things of the Father. But God came through for them. God eventually showed them their faith in him was well placed. Yours will be, too. Christ is the Savior. He proved it in the virgin birth. He proved it on the cross. He proved it by the empty tomb. He proved it to the father of the wayward son. He will prove it to you. Give him a chance. Trust him. Believe him. Wait on him. He will be your Savior, too.

V. PRAYER

Waiting, patient Father of Jesus Christ, teach me the patience to believe. Your gospel begins with high claims for Jesus, yet claims that seem too wonderful to be true and claims that have yet to become totally true in our lives. Give us the gift of faith to believe you are who you say you are, even when our minds cannot understand and our experience does not seem to confirm it. Show us the work you are doing, and let us, even as insignificant as we are, become a part of the work of extending Jesus' salvation to all peoples of all classes, races, and nations. In Jesus' name. Amen.

VI. DEEPER DISCOVERIES

A. Census (2:1)

Taking a census was a custom of the Roman government. They used the census to establish official lists that were used for taxing the population. They conformed to the practice of the country where the census was held. Following the customs of the Jews, they sent everyone back to their ancestral homes. Although Joseph and Mary lived to the north in Nazareth, they still had to travel south to Bethlehem because they traced their lineage to King David, whose home was Bethlehem. Luke thus tied Jesus' birth to a normal historical happening, showing that God works through the decrees of government to bring about his perfect will.

The problem lies in relating biblical records to historical records. A study of the development of the modern calendar shows that its beginning with the birth of Jesus was a great idea, but the original calculation was a few years off. We know from the work of Josephus, matched with calculations of eclipses, that Herod the Great, the governor of Judah when Jesus was born, died in 4 B.C. Jesus was born between 6 B.C. and 4 B.C., rather than in year 1. Roman records show several facts about Sulpicius Quirinius. He became a Roman consul in 12 B.C. and fought wars in southern Galatia. He was legate over Syria in A.D. 6–9. This would be when Jesus was already 12 to 15 years old. Elsewhere Luke reports a census in A.D. 6 which caused trouble for the Romans (Acts 5:37).

The census Luke records in 2:1 stands outside our records of Roman censuses, but this does not mean that Luke wrote fiction or mistaken history. As Bock well documents (pp. 904 to 909), Augustus periodically called for a census in different parts of the Roman Empire and established a cycle for censuses to be held in some parts of the empire. Extensive chronological, literary, and lexical studies have sought to solve the problem. Quirinius may have served in an administrative position in Palestine in relationship to the census and may have assisted more than one Syrian legate or Judean governor in establishing and carrying out the census. It may even be possible to read the Greek text in such a way as to conclude that the census occurred before Quirinius became governor in A.D. 6.

We must conclude that no clear solution is possible to the chronological problem, but that it is not outside the realm of Roman custom to posit a census in Palestine about 6 B.C. led by Herod and the Roman government. The major problem is not whether such a census occurred but how Quirinius related to it. That question is at the moment beyond solution.

B. Pledged to Be Married (2:5)

A Jewish girl generally was pledged in marriage to a man when she was about thirteen years old. They were considered to belong to one another, although they did not live together, nor did they have sexual relationships during the betrothal period. About a year later the actual marriage occurred. Luke used this language in an unusual way to emphasize the virginal conception of Jesus. Joseph and Mary were "pledged" to each other. They were obviously traveling together as only a husband and wife would normally do. They were expecting a child, another situation normally experienced only by husband and wife. But they had not consummated the marriage with sexual relationships and so were not fully married.

C. Circumcision and Purification (2:21–22)

Circumcision was a sign that a person belonged to the Jewish covenant. This rite had been performed by all Jewish parents since the time of Abraham (Gen. 17:11–12; 21:4; Lev. 12:3). This marked a person off as a Jew (see Phil. 3:5). Circumcision rites were accompanied by celebration and rejoicing. Friends and neighbors joined in. Usually, the head of the house performed the operation on the child. Other nations also circumcised, but the Jews held it sacred as a part of their covenant identity. This ritual brought the child into God's family and obligated the child to fulfill the duties of the covenant, including keeping the Jewish laws and customs. As with John in 1:59, so Jesus is pictured as fulfilling the expectations Jews placed on a family for their male children. Jesus fulfilled the requirements of Jewish law. No one could accuse him of sin in that regard.

Purification rites were for the mother of a child (Lev. 12:6). The mother was ceremonially unclean for seven days after the birth and then she could circumcise the child on the eighth day. But she had to remain home for thirty-three more days. On the fortieth day she offered a sacrifice at the Nicanor Gate on the east side of the Court of Women in the temple. Jesus' mother, like the Son, completed all the requirements of the law. Even the birth of the Messiah brought ritual uncleanness on his mother and forced her withdrawal from social activities for forty days. Incarnation came amid life's daily rites and rituals. Joseph and Mary revealed their lowly financial status by offering a pair of birds (Lev. 12:8) rather than the normal lamb with a bird (Lev. 12:6).

D. The Presentation (2:22–24)

Jewish law required parents to redeem a firstborn child. This goes back to the redemption of the firstborn of animals (Exod. 13; 22:28–29; 34:19–20; Num. 3:11–13,40–51; 8:16–18; 18:15–18; Deut. 15:19–20). Numbers 3:46–47 shows the first instance of a ransom price paid for firstborn sons, but in Judaism this payment of five shekels became standard for all firstborn. A parent could pay the redemption price to any priest at any place.

The story of Jesus is complicated by placing it at the temple in some parallel to the dedication of young Samuel by parents (1 Sam. 1–2). The story shows that his parents fulfilled every point of the law, although no mention of the redemption price is made. They also presented Jesus to the Lord for his service similar to the way Hannah fulfilled her vow and gave Samuel to the Lord for temple service. The service to which Jesus was dedicated was much greater. He was to save his people from their sins. Thus, the parents did more than the law required. They dedicated him and also went through the purification and redemption rituals.

VII. TEACHING OUTLINE

A. INTRODUCTION

1. Lead Story: Why Can't Booker Come to Church?
2. Context: Luke 1 set up the comparison between John the Baptist and Jesus, showing us who Jesus was and what he would do for the world. Chapter 2 described the birth of the Savior and the acclamation given him by angels, shepherds, and a pious man and woman. It showed how Jesus and his parents fulfilled all the Jewish requirements for a firstborn son. And it showed how Jesus proved to be an extraordinary child, his brilliance and acumen acknowledged by the Jewish religious leaders. His parents began to have trouble understanding who this child was and what he was about. Meanwhile, Jesus underwent the growth pattern expected of a normal child. These were his first steps from cradle to Calvary as he prepared to become the Savior of all the world.
3. Transition: The first persons to hear the news of Jesus' birth were not those we would expect. God sent angels out to the fringes of society to announce his birth to shepherds and then revealed his identity to two

pious senior adults in the temple. Finally, at age twelve, Jesus appeared before the religious leaders in the temple. In appearing to such a wide diversity of people, Jesus began to prove the angels' message to the shepherds was true. His good news of great joy was for all people.

B. COMMENTARY

1. The Savior's Earthly Birth (2:1–21)
   a. The earthly occasion: Roman taxation (2:1–3)
   b. The heavenly destination (2:4–5)
   c. The secluded birth (2:6–7)
   d. The heavenly announcement of good news (2:8–12)
   e. Heavenly praise for earthly peace (2:13–14)
   f. Earthly visit to heaven's child (2:15–16)
   g. Earthly witness to heaven's child (2:17–20)
   h. Earthly rites bring heaven's names (2:21)
2. The Savior's Heavenly Mission (2:22–38)
   a. Heavenly setting: purification rites (2:22–24)
   b. Earthly setting: saint waiting for promise fulfillment (2:25–26)
   c. Certainty of salvation for all peoples (2:27–33)
   d. Certainty of opposition (2:34–35)
   e. Hope for Israel's redemption (2:36–38)
3. Earthly Growth for Heavenly Mission (2:39–52)
   a. Growing physically and spiritually (2:39–40)
   b. Growing in relation to the Father (2:41–50)
   c. Growing in obedience, size, and relationships (2:51–52)

C. CONCLUSION: BELIEVING IS NOT EASY

VIII. ISSUES FOR DISCUSSION

1. How important is the doctrine of the virgin birth in biblical theology? What does it mean to you and your faith in Jesus?
2. Does your church bring joy and good news to all people or just to a privileged class?
3. In what ways will you give glory and praise to God for the birth of Jesus?
4. Why did Mary and Joseph go through all the Jewish rituals if Jesus was coming with a way of salvation for all people that freed them from following Jewish ritual?
5. Having read the testimonies of Simeon and Anna, what personal testimony can you give about Jesus?
6. How can the Son of God, the Savior of the world, grow? What does this say about the biblical teaching of incarnation?

Luke 3

The Forerunner's Call to Repent and the Savior's Ministry of Good News

Quote

"*Nearly two thousand years ago He came to this world, and His spirit has made an impact deeper than that of any other personality that has ever touched this world. His spirit pervades all the realms of life. His spirit pervades literature and government and law and religion and art and music. All the spheres and realms of life have been influenced by Christ and Christianity. What if He had not come? Where would the world be, at this moment, if Christ had not come?"*

George W. Truett

Luke 3

IN A NUTSHELL

In Luke 3 John the Baptist prepares the way for the coming of the Messiah by calling on people to repent from their sins. He leveled scathing rebukes at the hypocritical religious leaders and at Herod, the king, for not turning from their sins. Then Luke describes Jesus' baptism and gives his family tree to show his credentials as son of David and son of Adam.

The Forerunner's Call to Repent and the Savior's Ministry of Good News

I. INTRODUCTION

Standing Alone

*I*n 1814 Louis XVIII banished Napoleon to the island of Elba, apparently ending the brilliant military and political career of the little general. But in March 1815, barely a year later, he returned to France. The emperor sent an army to recapture the returning exile. Seeing the army, Napoleon stepped down from his carriage and advanced toward the army all alone. One lone man faced a mighty French army. Approaching the army, Napoleon quietly opened his coat, giving the marksmen clear aim at his heart. Quietly he said, "Frenchmen, it is your emperor." They went wild. They kissed his hand, fell at his feet, picked him up, and carried him on their shoulders, shouting all the while, "Long live the emperor."

Long before Napoleon, a lone man stood in the Judean wilderness defying the religious authorities by demanding that they repent and change their way of life. Everything was set for John's arrest and execution for defying local authorities. Long before this occurred, crowds swarmed John as they later did Napoleon. They trekked long miles into the lonely wilderness to listen to this lone preacher of repentance and let him baptize them rather than heed the learned priests and scribes in Jerusalem. As we study the ministry of John the Baptist, we need to ask what kind of preaching would draw us out into the wilderness. We need to hear John's message calling us to repent. We need to ask God if he is calling us to a lonesome ministry and if we are faithful to hear and answer his call. Most of all, we need to see if our life is pointing away from ourselves toward Jesus as John's did.

II. COMMENTARY

The Forerunner's Call to Repent and the Savior's Ministry of Good News

MAIN IDEA: *Jesus is the beloved Son, descended from Adam through David and Abraham, who takes up the role John proclaimed for him and receives the Spirit as a sign of the Father's love and pleasure.*

Ⓐ The Earthly Setting: In the Desert under Rome (3:1–2)

SUPPORTING IDEA: *Jesus ministered in real time and space under difficult conditions.*

3:1–2. Historian Luke faithfully set out the historical conditions Jesus and John faced as they ministered. Luke introduced us to the historical odds stacked against Jesus from the beginning of his ministry. He introduced the enemies, the government leaders whose opposition Jesus faced throughout his ministry. Tiberius Caesar ruled Rome from A.D. 14 to 37. Luke thus placed John's ministry in A.D. 28–29. Tiberius excelled as a military commander and governmental administrator, although his problems with the Roman Senate led him to abandon Rome for the isle of Capri from A.D. 26 until his death in A.D. 37. Luke mentioned Tiberius to help his patron Theophilus set Jesus in universal history and to show his readers that the gospel was not just a Jewish matter but had universal importance. Eventually Jesus would have to face Roman authority, not Tiberius but Pontius Pilate.

Pilate haunted Jesus throughout his ministry, though as ruler of Galilee Herod had opportunity to question him (23:6–12). John's ministry had a different political locale: Perea. He dealt with Herod Antipas, son of Herod the Great. Antipas inherited Galilee and Perea from his father and ruled there from 4 B.C. to A.D. 39 when the emperor Gaius exiled him. Herod's mother Malthace was a Samaritan and raised her sons Antipas and Archelaus in Rome. Antipas at times placated the Jews and at other times antagonized them. He married the daughter of the king of Nabatea, then divorced her to marry Herodias, his own niece and wife of Antipas's half brother. Aretas of Nabatea defeated Antipas in battle. John and other Jews attacked him for a marriage they considered unlawful (Lev. 18:13,16; 20:21). Herod Antipas retaliated against John by imprisoning him (v. 20).

Herod Philip was another son of Herod the Great who inherited Batanaea, Trachonitis, Auranitis, Gaulonitis, and other territory, ruling from 4 B.C. to A.D. 33/34. Known for his desire for justice and as a builder, he created Caesarea Philippi. He married Antipas's daughter, Salome (see Mark 6:22).

Lysanias ruled Abilene, west of Damascus, but brief mention of him in Josephus and in an inscription from Abila give us scant information about Lysanias. Luke apparently mentioned him to give a feeling of completeness to his historical setting.

Jesus and John faced another power structure—the Jewish religious leaders. Here Annas and Caiaphas ruled supreme. Quirinius (see 2:2) appointed Annas high priest in Jerusalem about A.D. 6. He served until Valerius Gratus removed him from office in A.D. 15. His son-in-law Caiaphas (John 18:13), and five of his sons also became high priest. Annas remained the priestly power broker and leader of opposition to Jesus and the early church even after he no longer held office (see John 18:12–24; Acts 4:6).

Joseph Caiaphas was appointed high priest by Valerius Gratus about A.D. 18 and was removed about A.D. 36 by Vitellius, thus actually serving during the ministries of John and Jesus, though Annas retained great influence. Caiaphas prophesied that Jesus would die for the nation (John 11:47–53). He apparently cooperated closely with the Roman authorities throughout his term of office, seemingly not challenging Pilate. He also established the practice of allowing vendors to sell their wares in the temple.

In this political and religious setting, God renewed his activity in human history. He gave his word to John just as he had to the prophets of old. Such word came in the desert where John lived (see 1:80). Political and religious activity centered in urban Jerusalem. God's activity centered in the desolate wilderness of the Jordan River. The remainder of Luke's Gospel shows which activity proved most effective.

B The Heavenly Message: Baptism, Repentance, and Forgiveness (3:3–6)

SUPPORTING IDEA: *John prepared the way for Jesus to show God's salvation by calling people to repent, be baptized, and experience God's forgiveness.*

3:3. God often mystifies people when he acts. Four hundred years after Malachi, another prophet appears. What an appearance! People left the civilization of the city and came to him in the wilderness. They had to search him out, for he did not stay in one place. His message drew them to him. It was simple, but haunting: Be baptized. Why would a Jew be baptized? Perhaps Gentile baptism had entered Judaism by this time. Certainly the strange people at Qumran loved to purify people with water. John called for more than immersing one's body. He called for cleansing one's soul, admitting the wrongs done against God and against other people and turning away from such actions and attitudes. Yes, pious Jews must admit they, not just Gentiles, are sinners.

According to John, even religious leaders had to escape their pious pretense of pleasing God and seek God's forgiveness. Why? Not just to establish a right relationship with God, what Christians would term salvation. No, John's baptism qualified a person to meet the One to come. In God's special time of activity, John consistently played the role of preparing. His baptism prepared people to meet the holy Son of God and receive the good news of salvation that he would bring.

3:4–6. Strange activities renew God's prophetic actions and prepare the way for the Worthy One. At least, that is what John said. What authority did he have to make such claims? He rested completely on the authority of

Scripture. As seen in chapters 1–2, Luke sought at each step to show that God's good news is based on God's old news. Isaiah 40:3–5 promised Old Testament Israel God's deliverance from Babylonian exile along a path God would provide in the wilderness. John's audience was promised an even greater experience of deliverance—salvation from sin. Such salvation was not a secret that God hid in the wilderness. It was a salvation God was proclaiming for **all mankind** (literally, "all flesh").

God is consistent. He sticks to his purposes. He fulfills his word and then uses the word to bring new fulfillment and meaning to a new generation. For John's generation, salvation came in the same setting as for the exiles: the wilderness. It came in a new way. People did not have to cross the dry desert between Babylon and Palestine. They had to cross the hard line from self-centered religious pride and piety to humble acceptance of baptism based on confession of their sins. Then they would be ready to see the salvation God had prepared in Jesus.

🄲 The Earthly Ministry: Call to Repent and Reform (3:7–14)

> **SUPPORTING IDEA:** *Repentance is more than submitting to a ritual act; it is a change of lifestyle in relationship to people in need.*

3:7–9. The heavenly message needed earthly application. John supplied this vigorously. Seeing Jews proud of their religion standing in the baptismal line, he shocked them. No words of congratulations, gratitude, or praise to God. Instead, he issued a stinging attack. John practiced prophetic name calling. He saw straight through those wanting to be baptized. They wanted one more credential behind their name, one more religious act they could tell everyone about. They were not saints. They were snakes. They needed to take John seriously, along with the God who stood behind John. They needed to know divine wrath was coming.

Just as prophets of old tried to warn the nation and prevent God's discipline and judgment, so John played out the prophetic role. If you want to go through the ritual, be ready to live the life. Gaining God's forgiveness requires more than carrying out another religious ritual. Forgiveness means changing your way of living, producing new fruit in your life. Repentance is not a one-time performance. Repentance is a continuing way of life—a life totally different from the one that required repentance in the first place. Repentance is a change of life, not just an exchange of words. Repentance depends on much more than keeping up family traditions and relying on proud and proper family trees.

John declared that God does not have to work with the family of Abraham. He can start over again. He can pick up the rocks in the wilderness and start a new family of Abraham. He can fulfill his promises to bless Abraham (Gen. 12; 15; 17) with the new family of Abraham.

John told these religious leaders that they had no claim on God. They could never bring pressure to bear on him to fulfill his promises. He will do so in the ways he chooses with the people he chooses. God's threat is not an empty gesture. He is already at work. He has picked up his sharpened ax and is chopping away at the roots of Israel's family tree. One factor determines which trees get chopped and which may continue living. God is the fruit inspector. Trees with good fruit live. Others die and burn.

3:10–14. John, these leaders said, your language is too theological, too full of pictures. What do you really want us to do? His reply: Go look at your clothes. Do you have a change of clothes? Take one and give to a person who needs it. Do you have a food supply for today? Invite someone to share it with you. Yes, these words fit everyone. You do not have to be rich to show fruits of repentance. Just have a little extra for today and give it away.

The message is not just for religious folks. Those people everyone knows are traitors and sinners can come to repentance, too. Yes, tax collectors, Jews who work for the Roman government and make a good living because they charge more than the government demands—these hated national traitors can repent. What must they do? Stop unjust practices. Collect exactly the amount of tax you are supposed to. Live on what the Roman authorities allot you, not on what you can extort from the Jewish people.

Even members of the Roman army can ask for repentance. These were probably Jews who signed up for military service or were conscripted by the government. They may have been Jews assigned to protect the tax collectors. They received small wages. They could use their authority and the fear of Rome to force people to give them money. Repentance for them meant refusing the temptation to get extra money just because they had the power to do so. Repentance meant living on what they had agreed to work for, whether that proved to be a living wage or not.

According to John, repentance is not confined to religious acts or private life. Repentance enters the place where you work. You must carry out your job in ways that reflect the life God approves of. No matter how much power and authority you have, no matter how much money you can get by exercising such authority, you do not have God's authority to use your power to get that money. Like the prophets of old, John called for justice, righteousness, and mercy in every area of life (see Amos 5:24; Mic. 6:8).

D The Heavenly Promise: A Greater One Coming (3:15–17)

SUPPORTING IDEA: *One greater than John is coming with the baptism of the Spirit and fire to bring judgment to the world.*

3:15. Who was John? The crowds could not quite make up their minds. Could he possibly be the deliverer whom Judaism was waiting for? Was he the promised Messiah whom God would anoint to deliver them from Rome and restore the kingdom to Israel? Suspense built as the people talked among themselves who this John really was.

3:16. John quickly shattered the suspense and messianic hopes. He knew his role. He baptized **with water**, seeking repentance and cleansing from sin. He was weak and insignificant in face of the coming One, who was mightier and more powerful—so powerful that John did not consider himself qualified to touch him and serve him as the most humble slave. Only a slave would do the dirty job of untying sandals caked with dust from the roads of Galilee and Judea. No Hebrew could be required to do this for another Hebrew. Pride prevented Jews from even considering such action for a fellow Jew.

John looked at it from the other perspective. He did not have the qualifications to accomplish this filthy, humiliating task for Jesus. Jesus was too great for John to touch. Not only was Jesus' character and power far superior to John—so was his mission. He brought the Holy Spirit as he baptized. But not just the Holy Spirit. He also brought fire as he baptized. The Spirit set the recipient apart as belonging to God's people, empowered to do God's work. Fire purged and burned. Those who responded to Jesus received a purging baptism that implanted the Spirit in them (v. 21) and incorporated them into Christ's people of the kingdom. Those who rejected Jesus received the Spirit's judgment, a judgment expressed as a burning fire that destroyed them (cf. Isa. 4:2–6).

3:17. John used a twofold agricultural image to explain Jesus' baptism with Spirit and fire. A farmer took a large fork-shaped shovel and tossed grain into the air. The heavy grain fell to the threshing floor to be gathered and prepared for use. The lighter chaff flew off in the breeze and had to be swept up and burned because it was useless. So Jesus' coming divided people into two camps: the people of the Spirit and the people destroyed and made useless by the fire.

E The Forerunner's Passing: Imprisonment (3:18–20)

SUPPORTING IDEA: *John's role was temporary and could be contained by political powers.*

3:18. Luke summarized John's role. He was a comforter, an encourager. That is the meaning of *parakalon,* **exhorted.** He **preached the good news.** Jesus would also preach good news of the kingdom (4:43).

3:19–20. But the big difference is that no one could stop Jesus until his hour had come, no matter how much his preaching upset them. The first time John **rebuked** Herod, Herod got the best of him, putting him in prison and locking him up. Why would John risk so much? Because he knew repentance needed to begin in high places. The political representative of Rome masqueraded as a person who cared for and was obedient to the Jewish way of life. His marriage to his brother's wife unmasked the masquerade. Not only did he participate in divorce; he also married his own niece, violating the law (Lev. 18:13,16; 20:21). The sinful king showed he had more power than a saintly prophetic wilderness preacher. John's ministry was over. He had accomplished his task for God. A new ministry began—a new day in the history of God's kingdom.

☐ Earthly Dedication: Pleasing the Father (3:21–22)

> **SUPPORTING IDEA:** *Although Jesus needed no repentance, he identified with those who did.*

3:21. Jesus identified with the crowds, and implicitly against leaders like Herod, by joining the line for John's baptism. For him baptism became an hour of prayer. For God the baptism became opportunity to testify, as he opened heaven to speak to earth. Modern disciples seek answers to the Bible's unanswered questions. Why was Jesus baptized? How could a person who had no sin identify with those whom he knew were sinners? How did the sinless Son of God relate to a baptism for repentance and the forgiveness of sin?

3:22. God did not answer our question. He chose to testify to the greatness of Jesus. He sent his Holy Spirit to Jesus incarnate as a dove, where Jesus was incarnate as a person. Jesus is the Son of God, loved by God and pleasing to God. Other questions need no answers when you see who Jesus is and what he is up to. Of course, he did not need to repent. He did not need forgiveness. He did need the Spirit's power. Now he could fulfill his task and baptize with that Spirit and with fire.

☐ The Earthly Setting: Son of Man and Son of God (3:23–38)

> **SUPPORTING IDEA:** *Jesus' family tree qualifies him from a human and a divine standpoint to bring God's salvation.*

3:23–38. Luke takes the genealogy of Jesus back to Adam to show that in Jesus God offers salvation to all people, not just to the children of Abraham.

> **MAIN IDEA REVIEW:** *Jesus is the beloved Son, descended from Adam through David and Abraham, who takes up the role John proclaimed for him and receives the Spirit as a sign of the Father's love and pleasure.*

III. CONCLUSION

What Does the Future Hold for My Children?

Even when my sons were through school, married, and into their first jobs, I still sat and wondered, what would they become? Would they be able to complete in the day's difficutl job market? Would they maintain their ties to the church and let God lead their lives by his Spirit? Would they become successful parents? What did the future hold for my children?

Luke 3 completes the parallel description of the lives of two young men. John the Baptist follows God into the wilderness, brings people to baptism for repentance of sins, and points them to Jesus. Then John falls prey to a greedy, proud, paranoid political leader and goes to jail. His ministry is complete. His life is almost over. He leaves the scene so Jesus can occupy it. Jesus, at the age of thirty years, enters his ministry. Will the parallel continue? Will a brief ministry give way to prison and death? Can that be what the future holds for the Son of God, Son of Man, Messiah? Luke wants us to ask: What will Jesus become in light of John's powerful witness and quick departure?

PRINCIPLES

- Forgiveness of sins comes only through repentance.
- God's salvation is available for every person, not just a chosen few.
- Repentance involves a change of lifestyle, not just a momentary feeling or statement.
- A family tree of faith cannot guarantee salvation.
- Christ's ministry was to bring the Holy Spirit to people and to bring judgment on those who refused to repent and believe in him.
- Faithfulness in ministry does not protect us from earthly hurt, suffering, and injustice.
- Jesus is the beloved Son of God.

APPLICATIONS

- Confess your sins, repent, and ask God for forgiveness.
- Ask God to show you the changes repentance should bring in your daily life.
- Change your life in the ways God shows you.
- Let God teach you to be content.
- Find your place in ministry for God, and carry out this ministry by seeking what God has called you to be and do.
- Pray for an awareness of the Holy Spirit guiding your life.
- Confess that Jesus is the Son of God, and ask him to save you.

IV. LIFE APPLICATION

More Than Anything Else in the World I Want . . .

Fan mail poured in from all over the country. Everyone wanted to congratulate Pepper Martin. He had just led the St. Louis Cardinals to victory in the World Series, making them world champions of baseball. After the final game, reporters crowded around Martin wanting an interesting quote to headline the next day's newspaper. Finally, one enterprising reporter asked Pepper, "Having won the World Series single-handedly, now, what do you want more than anything else in the world?"

Martin stopped to think for a few moments, then startled the gathered newsmen with his answer: "Above everything else in the world I want to go to heaven." The reporters laughed vigorously. Martin stared them into silence, then asked calmly, "What's so funny about that? I do want above everything else to go to heaven. I want to live so right that when I come to the end of life there will not be any question about where I am going to spend eternity."

The picture of John the Baptist would be funny if his message were not so strong and pertinent. He called people to get ready for the final judgment. The only way to be ready was to repent, but repent meant to change one's way of living. Unexpectedly, hundreds of people mobbed him daily, wanting to know more, and wanting to be baptized to show they had truly repented.

Today's generation may have heard the story too often. Maybe we have been told we need to repent too many times. Perhaps the call seems always to be for the other fellow and not for us. Jesus and John kept telling self-secure, religious people that the call to repentance was for them, not someone else. Are you willing to hear God's call to your life today? Are you willing to repent, change your course, and become who God wants you to be? Will you follow Jesus Christ, the Son of God? This is the most important question of life. To put it off is to miss life itself. To apply it to someone else is to turn a deaf ear to God. To repent and follow Jesus is to find assurance that when you die you will go to heaven.

V. PRAYER

Father in heaven, you know my life better than I know it myself. You can show me exactly what changes I need to make in my life. I know I have sinned and disappointed you. I know I deserve nothing but your judgment. I do repent of my sins. I turn away from them. Give me strength and faith never to repeat that style of life again. I will follow Jesus, the Christ, the Son of God wherever he leads. Lead me, Lord, even to the cross. Amen.

VI. DEEPER DISCOVERIES

A. Baptism of Repentance for the Forgiveness of Sins (3:3)

John's message had only one theme: Repent of your sins and be baptized. Repentance can be defined as "turning." To repent is to turn from a life of sin to a life directed by God. John the Baptist put more into the term. To him, repentance meant caring for other people more than for yourself, being fair in your dealings with other people even at personal sacrifice. Repentance meant giving up any reason to feel secure and satisfied with your relationship with God. Repentance recognizes God's call on one's life and life's inability to sustain itself in the face of God's call and God's coming judgment. Thus, a repentant person chooses to prepare for judgment by changing his or her lifestyle. One who repents feels personal responsibility before God rather than personal success in view of life. John's call to repentance begins this theme in Luke's Gospel (see 5:32; 10:13; 11:32; 13:3,5; 15:7,10; 16:30; 17:3–4).

Repentance was more than a private transaction between a person and God. Repentance involved one's total relationship to the community of God's people. Thus, repentance led to an action testifying of this repentance to the community and symbolizing what this repentance meant. This action was baptism.

Jews knew of baptism from several sources. The community of the Dead Sea Scrolls at Qumran had many rituals involving water purification, so that a person frequently entered the waters. In contrast, John called for a one-time action symbolizing an entirely new approach to life. Jews also baptized Gentiles who wanted to become Jews. Such Gentiles were called proselytes. Baptism initiated them into Judaism. But John baptized Jews, not Gentiles. He was not initiating them into a new relationship with God. Rather, he was asking them to reaffirm their relationship by admitting they had not lived up to God's covenant demands and that they would commit themselves to do so.

John's baptism was unique to his own ministry before God. It was a call to confess one's sinful life, renew one's commitment to God, and seek forgiveness of sins and renewal with God. It was a baptism that looked to coming judgment and also to a coming Savior, who would bring a new baptism—the baptism of the Holy Spirit. Thus, John's baptism was a precursor of Christian baptism, but it was not Christian baptism. It was baptism preparing for Jesus' coming, preparing for Christian baptism, and preparing for the coming judgment.

B. Baptism with the Holy Spirit and with Fire (3:16)

John refused to take credit or praise. He wanted only to point to the One who came after him and was far superior to him. Whereas John baptized with water for repentance, this One would baptize with Spirit and fire. Many questions can be raised about the meaning of such baptism, especially in light of the fact that Jesus apparently did very little baptizing.

Baptism with the Holy Spirit means that Jesus gave his followers the power and presence of God in their lives in the person of the Holy Spirit. Every believer could call on the Spirit for direction and understanding. John's baptism purified from past sins and prepared for future service. Jesus' baptism empowered for current living.

But what is baptism with fire? Many link it to the coming of the Spirit at Pentecost in tongues of fire in Acts 2. Some see it as continuation of John's message of judgment so that the coming of the Spirit was not a coming to lead but a coming to destroy. Others have tried to separate two different baptisms here—one on those who are saved and receive the Spirit and the other on those who reject salvation and are condemned to the judgment of fire. Perhaps the best approach to the statement is that baptism has consequences. It separates those baptized by the Spirit into obedient people of God. It separates those who are not baptized into a disobedient people facing God's judgment by fire (cf. Isa. 4:4–5).

VII. TEACHING OUTLINE

A. INTRODUCTION

1. Lead Story: Standing Alone
2. Context: Luke 2 concluded the childhood of Jesus and prepared us for his adult ministry. Luke 3 pushed that ministry aside for a moment to introduce the last parallel between John and Jesus, their purpose and ministry. John ministered briefly, calling a nation to repent, to turn back to covenant faithfulness, to show care for those in need rather than for themselves, and to be ready for God's coming judgment. John never pointed to himself, but always pointed ahead to a coming One who was more worthy than he. Jesus would baptize with Spirit and fire, separating the population into people of the Spirit and people waiting for the judgment of fire.

   Then Luke gave one more qualification of Jesus as Messiah. He is the Son of God whose lineage may be traced back through David to Adam and then to God. This qualified One was the Messiah to whom John pointed. He would bring salvation in the Spirit and judgment in fire.

3. Transition: Are you ready to face this Jesus? Do you need first to repent, find forgiveness, and change your way of living? Luke 3 showed the deeper meaning of repentance and served as a call for you to prepare to meet Jesus. As you meet him, how will you respond? Does Jesus' baptism bring the Spirit to guide your life and prepare you for the time of judgment? Or will you refuse to accept Christ's baptism and thus be separated out for the judgment of fire? You ignore the call to repentance, baptism, and forgiveness at great peril to your life both now and in the judgment to come.

B. COMMENTARY

1. The Forerunner's Ministry of Repentance (3:1–20)

    a. The earthly setting: in the desert under Rome (3:1–2)

    b. The heavenly message: baptism, repentance, and forgiveness (3:3–6)

    c. The earthly ministry: call to repent and reform (3:7–14)

    d. The heavenly promise: a greater One coming (3:15–17)

    e. The forerunner's passing: imprisonment (3:18–20)

2. The Savior's Ministry of Kingdom Good News (3:21–38)

    a. Earthly dedication: pleasing the Father (3:21–22)

    b. The earthly setting: Son of Man and Son of God (3:23–38)

C. CONCLUSION: MORE THAN ANYTHING ELSE IN THE WORLD I WANT . . .

VIII. ISSUES FOR DISCUSSION

1. What place is there in your church for a preaching ministry like John's that issues a call to baptism of repentance for forgiveness of sins?

2. What sins plague members of today's church? Why? How should the church react?

3. Do you see in your life and in your church fruit in keeping with repentance?

4. What is baptism with the Holy Spirit and with fire? Have you received this baptism?

5. Can God's faithful servants expect to survive the world's persecution and receive God's justice and blessings? Why? Why not?

6. What does it mean to confess Jesus as Son of God?

Luke 4

The Savior's Ministry of Kingdom Good News: Testing, Rejection, and Authority

I. **INTRODUCTION**
Prom Rejection

II. **COMMENTARY**
A verse-by-verse explanation of the chapter.

III. **CONCLUSION**
Authentic Ministry
An overview of the principles and applications from the chapter.

IV. **LIFE APPLICATION**
Jesus Our Model
Melding the chapter to life.

V. **PRAYER**
Tying the chapter to life with God.

VI. **DEEPER DISCOVERIES**
Historical, geographical, and grammatical enrichment of the commentary.

VII. **TEACHING OUTLINE**
Suggested step-by-step group study of the chapter.

VIII. **ISSUES FOR DISCUSSION**
Zeroing the chapter in on daily life.

Quote

"*It little matters where we are if we can pray; but prayer is never more real and acceptable than when it rises out of the worst places. Deep places beget deep devotion. Depths of earnestness are stirred by depths of tribulation. Diamonds sparkle most amid the darkness. He that prays in the depth will not sink out of his depth. The one that cries out of the depths shall soon sing in the heights.*"

Charles Haddon Spurgeon

Luke 4

IN A NUTSHELL

After Jesus was baptized, the Holy Spirit led him into the wilderness. There Satan tempted him to reject the Father's plan for his ministry. Triumphing over Satan's temptations, Jesus returned to Galilee, where his own friends rejected him. Moving on to Capernaum, Jesus began to give evidence of his unique authority through signs and wonders.

The Savior's Ministry of Kingdom Good News: Testing, Rejection, and Authority

I. INTRODUCTION

Prom Rejection

*H*igh school prom! Highlight of a senior's high school career. Everyone will see him and the beautiful young lady on his arm. With joy and anticipation, he picks up the phone and calls the young lady he has dated for two years. "I do want to take you to the prom. You will go with me, won't you?" he asks confidently.

"I am so sorry," the reply comes. "Mark asked me last week. I am going to go with him."

"What? You are going with my best friend? What happened? I thought we were going steady. I was serious about our relationship."

"I was, too, but you know how important Mark is on campus. I want to be seen with him at the prom."

Dejectedly, the young man hung up the phone. Life started downhill at record speed. It would take almost ten years to put it back together. Rejection by the one he thought would be part of his family and rejection by his best friend were too much. He opted out of life for a decade.

Jesus had the same opportunity. Rejection met him in double-barreled fashion just as he began his public ministry. He set forth to bring good news to the world. He had a message of hope for the hopeless, deliverance for the captive, healing for the sick, release for those whom demons had captured. Before ministry came testing. First he had to face the devil whose kingdom was threatened by Jesus. Scripture got him by that one. Then his family and friends rejected him. Jesus survived rejection through the power of God's Word, God's Spirit, and God's personal presence in prayer.

II. COMMENTARY

The Savior's Ministry of Kingdom Good News: Testing, Rejection, and Authority

> **MAIN IDEA:** *Jesus passed earthly testing by the devil, and ministry rejection by hometown people, before he entered the ministry of kingdom good news.*

A The Earthly Testing: Following the Spirit to the Devil (4:1–13)

> **SUPPORTING IDEA:** *Testing people who minister for him is God's way of preparing them to minister. He wants to give them experience in relying on Scripture and experiencing him rather than on human qualifications, methods, and abilities.*

4:1–2. John the Baptist disappears and Jesus takes center stage. The One coming to baptize with the Spirit and with fire (3:16), and acknowledged by the dove-appearing Spirit (3:22), now followed the Spirit into ministry. His first stop was the **desert**, a place of isolation and desolation, outside the urban life of the city, outside the cultivated life of the farm country. It was on the stony, barren slopes of the Judean mountains toward the Dead Sea and lower Jordan River valley. Here robbers and revolutionaries gathered. Civilized people avoided the wilderness. But here Jesus followed the Spirit in faith. The stay proved long and arduous—forty days without family, friends, fellowship, or food. Only one other person ventured into the desert with Jesus: the devil, Mr. Temptation himself. Jesus faced the slandering, tempting adversary for over a month with no physical resources. He had to depend on spiritual strength.

Jesus did not fast because this was a religious requirement. Only the Day of Atonement called for national fasting in Israel (Lev. 16:29,31; 23:27,32; Num. 29:7), although Israel apparently developed other fast days (Jer. 36:6; Zech. 7:5). Other fasts were special occasions of national need (1 Sam. 14:24). People in grief, repentance, and intercession might also fast (Num. 30:13; 1 Kgs. 21:27; Ps. 35:13). Jesus fasted to devote full time to God's business and God's presence rather than devote time to satisfying his personal needs. Ministry and devotion took top priority over physical hunger and self-satisfaction.

Later, Jesus would teach people to make fasting an intensely personal relationship with God, hiding all signs of it from the outside world (Matt. 6:17). Facing the devil is certainly the time to fast, to face God as intensely as possible at the same time the devil faces you. So as Israel wandered forty years in the wilderness for disobeying God, so Jesus stayed forty days in the wilderness in complete obedience to God.

4:3. Satan's first test: "Prove **you are the Son of God.** Serve yourself, show divine power. You are hungry and you have the right to eat. Pick up one of the many rocks lying around here in the desert and let God turn it to **bread** so you can eat. Surely he will supply your every need."

4:4. Jesus' answer: "The Bible has a better answer. Look at Deuteronomy 8:3. A person needs something much more substantial than bread. God supplies my needs. He knows that my need now is something much better than bread. I need power from him to enter the ministry of kingdom good news. He is giving me what he knows I need, not what you try to trick me into thinking I need. I will listen to God's Word, not your word. I will serve God, not self."

4:5–7. Satan's second test: "Build the kingdom the quick way—serve me. God wants you to establish the kingdom of God. Easily enough done. Come up here a minute. What do you see spreading out below you? You can see forever, can't you? Looks like every kingdom and nation in the world spreading out before your eyes." Note that Matthew places this temptation as the last one and situates it on a high mountain. Luke skips this detail. Location makes no difference. Purpose makes all the difference.

Satan makes a startling claim: he has all earthly glory and authority to give away to whomever he wants. The Bible makes great claims for him, too. He is "the prince ("ruler," NRSV) of this world" (John 12:31; 14:30; 16:11). "The whole world is under the control of the evil one" (1 John 5:19). He can give it away (Rev. 13:2). Such power is only temporary and delegated power. Satan faces ultimate defeat. God's kingdom will rule the world.

Jesus must choose between a temporary, worldly kind of power with earthly glory or an eternal kind of power with God's glory. The decision is difficult because the methods are so different. God's method leads to preparation in the desert, a preparation to a cross-carrying ministry. Satan's method leads to a high place with a vision of the whole world. God's method demands death. Satan's method calls for high living—with one catch.

So if you worship me, it will all be yours. What a tempting trade! Could the god of this age blind the Son of God (see 2 Cor. 4:4)? What is wrong with one moment of worship for full-time authority over the world? One-time worship reveals something much deeper. It shows devotion to selfish interests, hunger for personal power, willingness to doubt God's way and go Satan's way, a starting point on a path that has no way back to worship God.

4:8. Jesus' answer: "The Bible again has a better answer. Deuteronomy 6:13 says to worship God and no one else. That means every minute of my time is devoted to the worship and service of God. No time left for you, Satan. I will do it God's way, even if it is the way of the cross. Nothing you have to give is worth giving up my experience and relationship with the Father. He has ultimate power. He alone loves me and cares for me. He alone deserves my worship. I will listen to Scripture, not to you. I will serve God, not Satan."

4:9–11. Satan's third test: "Show the world who you are. Prove to them in one instant how much power you have, what you can do for them. Let God serve you one time. You serve him all the time. I will show you how. Come with me to holy Jerusalem, certainly the city of God's kingdom. Stand up here on the highest point of the temple. Look down on the beautiful holy city at your feet. They will really be at your feet in a minute if you just listen to me. Scripture tells you how to do it. Read Psalm 91:11–12. Surely this passage was talking about Messiah. God will take care of his Messiah. He does not want you even to stub your toe. Jump right down. God is faithful. He will rescue you in midair. Everyone will see. All will fall at your feet. Your ministry mission will be accomplished. I will help a little. Just quickly jump off and wait for God to help."

4:12. Jesus' answer: "You must read the Bible in its context and find its governing principles. Deuteronomy 6:16 gives one: 'Do not put God to the test.' You are the tempter, the one who puts people to the test. God is not a tempter, nor is he to be tempted. I will trust God to do things his way. We will work on the ministry of kingdom good news like he wants to. Your way is slick and sassy. It makes great marketing sense. One problem: It is not God's way. I will serve God and never ask him to serve me. Worshiping God is not a trade-off, give me this and I will give you that. Worshiping God is total devotion to him no matter the cost. I will serve him even to the cross. I will never serve you. I will never ask God to serve me. I will never do things your way. I will follow God's way."

4:13. Satan is not constantly on the job with us. He comes and goes. He strikes when we are most vulnerable. Then he goes on to other pursuits. He knew Jesus had gotten the best of him this time. "Okay, so I will try again," Satan said. Continued temptation is fruitless against a person who has been strengthened by previous rejections of temptation. Let him get into another crisis point. See how strong he is then. Perhaps that will be the **opportune time.**

B The Ministry Rejected: Familiarity Breeds Contempt (4:14–30)

> **SUPPORTING IDEA:** *Ministry for God does not always meet the world's success standards. It must be done even in the face of rejection by important people.*

4:14–15. The Spirit was Christ's guide, from desert temptation to synagogue service and ministry. Satan tried to lead Jesus to Jerusalem to do miracles before the multitudes. The Spirit led him to rural Galilee to teach in the small worship places. Interestingly, Matthew has Jesus take refuge in Galilee because John the Baptist had been arrested. Luke did not connect Jesus' ministry to John's. John served to prepare the way. Jesus is the sole focus. In Galilee Jesus escaped the major political centers and ministered to the farmers, fishers, and traders who were the center of Jewish civilization. In Galilee Jesus found wide acceptance. People thronged to hear him. No one had ever taught like him before. He was the popular hero of the hour. Then the time arrived for Jesus to go home.

4:16–22. In a setting of universal praise, Jesus went home to Nazareth to preach. He followed his family's normal habit and went to synagogue worship. There they repeated Deuteronomy 6:4–9; 11:13–21; Num. 15:37–41 (called the *Shema*), the central verse of Judaism, pledging allegiance to the one God. Next, they prayed, heard a passage read from the Pentateuch or Torah, then a passage from the prophets, a sermon, and a final priestly blessing. Jesus was given the honor of reading the scroll and then preaching. He read Isaiah 61:1–2. Then he claimed that the passage was **fulfilled** as they heard him read it.

This claim was too big for neighbors and friends to stomach! What delusions of grandeur. He says God's Spirit has brought him to us. He has news that the poor, impoverished people have been waiting for. He is God's anointed. Does that mean he thinks he is the Anointed One, the Messiah? People in prison, he will free. The blind he will make see. Our oppressed nation he will release from captivity and renew its strength. Today is the day. This is the year God will show favor and grace on his people. A young man from Nazareth can do all this? He can bring in the true Jubilee year when we release not only our slaves but also our nation from oppression and captivity (see Lev. 25:8–55)?

It sure sounds good. Nazareth can be proud of a young man who can make such a fine speech. Can you believe it? Joseph's son doing so well? Wish he could really do all this, but you know him as well as I do!

4:23–27. Jesus knew the people's hearts and thoughts. He also knew their traditions and could quote their proverbs—sayings preserved orally among the rural people without ever being reduced to writing. They told him *to put up or shut up*: "If you have such a calling from God, let us see you prove it." Here they echoed Satan's temptation to Jesus: "We will believe you and follow you if you do things our way." Jesus sought faith in his word and in his person, not faith in miracles. The people felt slighted. They had heard of a ministry he performed in Capernaum—the significant military, trading, and commercial city of the area. Why not do the same at home for his friends and neighbors?

Jesus would not be reduced to a local side show attraction. He did things only when they were God's will leading to God's purposes for God's kingdom. So Jesus had another proverb for them. He knew the fate of prophets as well as they did. Prophets receive honor only years after their death, and certainly not among the people who know them best. The Bible itself proves that. First Kings 17 shows how Elijah had to go up to Phoenicia to do his miracles and find faith. Naaman (2 Kgs. 5) was the only person with the horrible skin disease that Elisha chose to cure. Naaman was from Syria.

Yes, prophets often have to go far afield, even outside Israel—certainly outside their hometown—to do God's work. Nazareth is not going to force Jesus to do God's work when they have no faith in him. Yes, God can send the Messiah and see Israel reject him. God can take his message of hope and grace clear outside the chosen people Israel to Gentiles like the widow and Naaman.

4:28–29. Amazement turned to fury. Mob mentality took over. By brute force, the crowd forced Jesus to the brink of the cliff outside the city. They had every intention of throwing him down.

4:30. There was no miracle, no angels called down from heaven. Jesus just walked right through the crowd. His person was enough to quiet them. They had no response to his quiet self-assurance as he walked away, leaving them looking foolish, a collected mob without a victim. Rejection at home did not call forth desperate measures from him to win back the crowd. Rejection at home simply sent him elsewhere to do his mission. How far would that mission reach? Luke will eventually follow it to Rome, where Paul can preach about Jesus unhindered (Acts 28:31) even though Jesus could not so preach among his friends. Rejection is not the end of ministry.

◼C The Ministry Witnessed: Exorcism Creates Excitement (4:31–37)

SUPPORTING IDEA: *Ministry done God's way in God's time at God's place brings amazing results from those who witness this ministry.*

4:31–32. Jesus remained consistent. Sabbath came and he went to worship. His presence led to his selection as Scripture reader and preacher. His teaching style and skill left the audience gasping for parallels. They had never seen anything like him. They had heard teachers every Sabbath all their lives, not to mention all the ones in Sabbath school during the days of childhood. Those teachers were all alike. They set out a problem and then told you what every rabbi who ever taught had said about that problem. Then they went on to the next one without solving the problem. Jesus was different. He did not mention what other teachers had to say. He simply said, This is the truth. Take it or leave it. Crowds came to hear such a message.

4:33–34. Worshipers are not perfect people. The crowd who listened to Jesus in Capernaum included **a man possessed by an evil spirit**.

The demon-possessed man soon took possession of the worship and Scripture study. He screamed at Jesus. What are you doing here? What do you want with us? Are you trying to destroy us? Do not think you can get away with anything. I know your name. You are the Holy One of God. Knowing your name, I can control you. Yes, you will have to worship the devil because I have control of you. I know your name!

Did the demon say more than he meant? Jesus did come to destroy the demonic. His kingdom will win over all demonic forces and powers. Jesus also came in judgment on those who will not believe. Would this synagogue, like Nazareth, become a crowd of unbelievers facing Jesus' judgment?

4:35. Demons did not control Jesus. He always remained in control. He had kingdom news but not good news for the demon. This kingdom news was short but not sweet: "Be quiet. Get out of him! You have no control over anyone. Yes, you know who I am. All demons do. They have that kind of knowledge, but they use it wrong! You do not believe me even though you know me. I do not need your kind of witness. Get out!" There was one last struggle. The demon threw the poor man to the floor. Then it did what Jesus said: "Get out and stay out. Do not hurt the man. Leave him alone." Jesus had power over demons. They had no power over him!

4:36–37. The chorus of amazement continued. Not only his teaching (4:14–15,22,32) but also his actions astounded the crowd. They had never heard or seen anyone like this who had such authority in teaching as well as authority over demons. Let the gossip lines open up! Everyone is talking about Jesus. But do they believe? Is this the kind of witness Jesus wants? What must be added to their stories of authority before it becomes faith?

Ⅾ The Ministry Continues: Heal, Exorcise, Pray, Preach (4:38–44)

SUPPORTING IDEA: *The ministry of kingdom good news is not a one-stop performance but it continues through Jesus' teaching and healing.*

4:38–39. The synagogue, the worship and teaching center, was not the only place for ministry. A private home offered just as good a setting. Jesus went where there were people in need. First, he went to those who were close to him, the mother of Simon Peter. Those close to the sick woman asked Jesus for help. His word dismissed the fever. No slow recuperation here, no leftover signs of weakness. She got up and went about her business, serving the guests. Home is a good place for ministry. Those in charge of the house are good subjects to receive ministry. Christ's authoritative power is sufficient for all kinds of ministry.

4:40–41. The crowds brought sick people to Jesus. He had time to minister personally to each one, to touch them. Each received healing. Bringing needy people to Jesus to have their needs met was ministry that he blessed. Demons could confess who he was, just as Satan could at his temptations in the wilderness. They had good theology. They knew he was Messiah. But knowing the title was not enough. They did not respect the title, obey the titleholder, and believe in what God was doing through him. Thus, **he rebuked them and would not allow them to speak.** He did not need their witness.

4:42–44. Jesus showed what ministry is. It starts with a relationship with God in the lonely place of prayer. No ministry is sufficient if it does not have the daily prayer base. Prayer guides the minister to the right relationship, the right beliefs, and the right places and opportunities for ministry. Prayer is the ministry enabler. Crowds in need seem to have no time for prayer or pray-ers. They have an agenda for Jesus and expect him to carry it out. Just as Satan tried to give Jesus an agenda for ministry, just as the friends and family in Nazareth had directives for doing good, so Capernaum wanted to tell Jesus how to minister. The first requirement was, "Stay here among us."

Jesus had a different agenda. He did not respond to popular demand. He did not look to find where the biggest crowds, the loudest acclamation, and the greatest number of results could be recorded. Jesus had been in prayer. He knew where the Father was at work. Jesus went where the Father was working, not where the people were clamoring for miracles. He must let all people hear, not just a privileged few. Ministry of kingdom good news is ministry to the world, not the local population center. Ministry sends you out rather than keeping you at home. Ministry tells everyone the good news of the kingdom, so they all may have a chance for salvation, not just for healing.

So Jesus kept on preaching! Never in Nazareth, where he was rejected. Not just in Capernaum, where he was received with amazement. Not just in Galilee, where he was for the moment. But throughout Judea, every place where the Jews lived. Ministry must preach good news, not just act out good news. The gospel has content as well as action. Jesus was doing what the Spirit said. He was finding people in need and saying and doing what was good news for them (see vv. 18–19).

MAIN IDEA REVIEW: *To please the heavenly Father in ministry, we—like the Son of God—have to pass testing by the devil and ministry rejection by hometown people before we can enter the ministry of kingdom good news.*

III. CONCLUSION

Authentic Ministry

Ministry for Jesus is the same as ministry by Jesus. It is ministry of kingdom good news. It is telling people who Jesus is: the anointed Messiah, Son of God, the Holy One of God come to help the poor, the imprisoned, the blind, the oppressed. It is acting on behalf of people in need: healing all kinds of diseases and overcoming anything that would oppress people and rob them of God's freedom. It is sending people back to their own ministry of serving others. It is opposing Satan in all his guises: tempter, kingdom giver, adversary, ministry planner, theology teacher, and evil spirit inhabiting and inhibiting people.

Such ministry brings many responses. Sadly, too often the responses hurt. Friends and family do not understand. Those we help demand more help rather than joining us in faith and ministry. All have alternatives to ministry that lead to success in the world's style but do not come from the Father. Ministry not guided by relationship with the Father is not ministry at all. Ministry is being anointed by the Spirit to carry on the work of the Son in obedience to the Father who sends us.

PRINCIPLES

- The devil tempts all of God's people.
- Scripture is the best weapon against temptation.
- We do not have to give in to temptation.
- Worship belongs to God.
- The Spirit gives direction in all ministries for God.
- God's ministry focuses on those whom the world ignores.
- Jesus is the fulfillment of the Old Testament.
- Jesus has unequaled authority in his ministry and teaching.
- Ministry for Jesus must not be confined to one responsive place.

APPLICATIONS

- Pray for God's wisdom in recognizing and facing Satan's temptations.
- Memorize Scripture so that you will have it as a resource to use against temptation and trial.
- Review your daily ways of living to be sure you are worshiping God and him alone.
- Ask God to show you how to carry out his ministry to the poor and needy that Jesus began.

- Be ready for rejection, and do not let it lead you away from Jesus.
- Find out where God is at work preaching the good news of the kingdom, and ask him to show you how to join in his work there.

IV. LIFE APPLICATION

Jesus Our Model

In 1997 nine brave souls from my workplace ventured on a pioneering effort in volunteer mission work. Several of the nine were bookish types like me unused to long walks, long talks, or one-on-one evangelistic efforts. Still, each of us was convinced of a call from God to participate in a fourteen-day mission tour in western Kenya. We actually spent about eight days in the Busia, Kenya, area going from door to door witnessing to people about Jesus.

People back home wondered what we were expecting to accomplish. Missionaries on the field in Kenya had low expectations for our work in an area they did not even bother to enter. One man dared urge us on into the field—Samson Kasia, a major church leader in Kenya. He planned every detail of the trip and went with us. As a result, five-thousand people came to know Jesus as Savior, and two more groups came to western Kenya in succeeding years. Twenty-nine volunteers went the second year, and nearly one hundred of us went this year. Six churches became more than one hundred churches. Over twenty-thousand Kenyans gave us their names and repeated the sinners' prayer to accept Jesus as Savior.

How do we explain such missionary "success"? Simple. We followed Jesus' model. Do not let human or satanic opposition stop you. Find people who need God. Share in love the Word of God with those people. Depend on God to bring people to himself. Yes, Jesus was the model for the ministry in Kenya. He is the model for ministry. If you belong to his people and know his salvation, you are called to minister as he did. Such ministry sets you apart from the world. It leads you into isolated, lonely places where only the devil visits you and tempts you with massive programs that promise immediate gratification and reward—immediate ministry success. It leads you to people you know, love, and respect, only to have them laugh at you, confident you will never be anyone capable of the kind of ministry you know God has given you. They never expect God-sized work from your feeble hands. Yet God does. Acceptance from God means rejection by those whose respect, honor, and love you desire. Ministry eventually brings great results. People applaud. People crowd around for more. People say wonderful things about you. How do you react? Jesus retreated to the lonely place of prayer to find God's next step. He left fruitful ground for unplowed soil to do God's will in God's way. Do you have the faith to go where he sends rather than where worldly success beckons? Ministry of kingdom good news has a larger crowd in view than you ever see. Such ministry, modeled on Jesus the Minister, sees a world that needs to hear good news. Such ministry is always willing to plant seeds here and then move on to where God is working next. Are you too rooted down where you are to find where God is at work?

V. PRAYER

Amazing Lord, you ministered in awesome ways. You cared not for the world's success paths. You cared not for immediate victory for the kingdom. You responded not when loved ones rejected you. You continued seeking the Father's will and doing it. Teach me to minister like you. Teach me to love the poor and oppressed whom no one else loves. Show me how to bring good news to lives that face only bad times. Give me the power to overcome Satan and his ways. Let me empower people through the Holy Spirit rather than inhibiting them through the devil. Thank you for the opportunity to minister kingdom good news. Amen.

VI. DEEPER DISCOVERIES

A. The Devil (4:2)

Scripture teaches that we are embroiled in a battle between two personal powers—the all-powerful God and a personal representative of evil who has great powers in this world. This evil one is called the devil, Satan, the Tempter, the Adversary (a translation of Heb., *satan*), and Beelzebub. He appears in Job 1–2 as a member of the heavenly court seeking out persons to bring charges against before the heavenly council (cf. Zech. 3:1). In 1 Chronicles 21:1 he encouraged David to do evil (cf. 2 Sam. 24:1).

In the New Testament the devil is the one who opposes Jesus in his ministry in the form of a tempter and in the form of evil spirits and demons that possess people, leading Jesus to expel them. Jesus stands opposed to everything the devil stands for (Matt. 12:26; Mark 3:23,26; Luke 11:18) and he frees people from Satan's control (Luke 13:16). Satan seeks to mislead Christ's followers (Matt. 16:23) and wants to test and tempt all of them (Luke 22:31). He captured the heart of Judas (Luke 22:3; cf. his work with Ananias in Acts 5:3). Satan has many ways of fooling people into thinking he possesses more power than he actually has (2 Thess. 2:9) or thinking he is good rather than bad (2 Cor. 11:14). He opposes the gospel (Mark 4:15; Luke 8:12) and inflicts suffering on God's people (2 Cor. 12:7). Human anger provides opportunity for the devil to work in our lives (Eph. 4:26). He can lead some people away from God to follow him (1 Tim. 5:15). At times God has to hand his people over to Satan for discipline (1 Cor. 5:1–5; 1 Tim. 1:19–20). But wearing God's armor lets God's people defeat the devil (Eph. 6:11–16).

God's power displayed in the mission of the church brings Satan's downfall (Luke 10:18; cf. Rev. 12:9). The power of the cross defeats Satan (John 12:31; cf. Rev. 12:11), who cannot control the sinless Christ in any way (John 14:30). Thus, Satan stands condemned (John 16:11). Jesus came to destroy his wicked works (1 John 3:8). Those opposed to Jesus belong to the devil's family (John 8:44).

B. Tempted by the Devil (4:1–13)

Luke tells us that Jesus was "led by the Spirit in the desert, where for forty days he was tempted by the devil" (vv. 1–2). The good news for every believer is that the temptations he faced were like ours in the sense that they were real. Jesus' experience, however, was unique in that (1) he resisted the temptations and did not sin; and (2) he met temptation on the field of battle and emerged victorious. Hebrews 4:15 tells us that Jesus was tempted in every way, just as we are—yet without sin. This underscores the reality of Jesus' temptations.

C. Proverb (4:23)

This word *proverb* comes from the Greek term *parabole,* which has several meanings, ranging from story and example parables, allegories, similitudes, and metaphors to proverbs. This particular proverb has numerous parallels in both form and context. For context, see Luke 23:35. For form, we find in Greek literature, "Physician, physician heal thine own limp." Here as elsewhere (Luke 5:22; 6:8; 7:40; 9:47; 11:17), Jesus had a unique awareness of others' thoughts.

VII. TEACHING OUTLINE

A. INTRODUCTION

1. Lead Story: Prom Rejection
2. Context: We follow Jesus' first steps as he ministers. We find true surprise. Ministry begins under the Spirit in the loneliest, most desolate place you can imagine, with only the devil as company and no food for sustenance. We watch Jesus face the devil, face hometown loved ones and friends as they laugh in his face, and then face success that drives him to the Father. Jesus models ministry of kingdom good news for his followers. Are you ready to take his model as the pattern for your ministry?

3. Transition: As we study Luke 4, we examine the very nature of Jesus Christ and the way he represents the presence of the kingdom of God. We see that he engages in ongoing battle with the devil, who tempts him to accomplish his purposes in ways opposed to God's ways. Thus, the chapter calls into question our methods of doing God's work. It demands that we ask if we are using human ways to try to attain divine goals. It reminds us that God's way consists of ministry to the poor, needy, and unappreciated. Jesus' example calls us to a solitary place to be alone with God, learn his will, and find his place of ministry so all people can hear the gospel message of the kingdom.

B. COMMENTARY

1. The Earthly Testing: Following the Spirit to the Devil (4:1–13)
   a. The setting: led by the Spirit but hungry for food (4:1–2)
   b. The first test: serve self (4:3–4)
   c. The second test: serve Satan (4:5–8)
   d. The third test: let God serve you (4:9–12)
   e. The epilog: Satan's timing (4:13)
2. The Ministry Rejected: Familiarity Breeds Contempt (4:14–20)
   a. Setting of rejection: universal praise (4:14–15)
   b. Message rejected: Scripture fulfilled (4:16–21)
   c. Rejecting reception: don't we know him (4:22)
   d. Rejection recognized: hometown boy (4:23–27)
   e. Rejection realized: throw him down (4:28–29)
   f. Rejection rejected: on the way (4:30)
3. The Ministry Witnessed: Exorcism Creates Excitement (4:31–37)
   a. The setting: authoritative teaching on the Sabbath (4:31–32)
   b. The scene: informed demon (4:33–34)
   c. The healing: exorcism without harm (4:35)
   d. The response: amazement and witness (4:36–37)
4. The Ministry Continues: Heal, Exorcise, Pray, Preach (4:38–44)
   a. The setting: sick at home (4:38)
   b. The scene: immediate healing (4:39)
   c. The reaction: multitudes to heal and exorcise (4:40–41)
   d. The Master's response: pray, preach to all (4:42–44)

C. CONCLUSION: AUTHENTIC MINISTRY

VIII. ISSUES FOR DISCUSSION

1. Discuss the devil's role in temptation as well as our part in temptation.
2. Describe how you have experienced and withstood temptation.
3. In what ways do we put God to the test?
4. In what ways are you continuing Christ's ministry to the poor, needy, and unappreciated people of this world?
5. In what ways do you reject Jesus?
6. How do you know where God wants you to share the good news of the kingdom?

Luke 5

The Savior's Call for Faith (Part I)

"*G*od knew that I had hands and feet and arms and legs that did not work. He knew what I looked like. And none of these things really mattered. What counted was that I was His workmanship created in His image. And He wasn't finished with me **(Eph. 2:10)**."

Joni Eareckson Tada

Luke 5

IN A NUTSHELL

*C*hapter 5 begins a long section (5:1–7:50) about the Savior's call for faith. Combining miracle stories, call narratives, dialogues with his opponents, and a parable, Jesus showed the reason to follow in faith, the will to follow, the power to follow, the position to follow, and the lifestyle to follow. In each case he stood in direct opposition to the Jewish religious leaders. Jesus showed himself to be equal with God in power, authority, and preaching, an equality the leaders could not accept and an equality that would lead to the cross.

The Savior's Call for Faith

I. INTRODUCTION

Strangely Effective

*W*ally was strange. Everyone in the university thought so. He joined us on Saturday night at the student mission service for the black kids. Somehow, we could not communicate well with the kids. They came to us for the refreshments and fun times. We certainly could not communicate with Wally. He lived on a different planet. Strangely, the black kids swarmed around Wally. The swarming continued Sunday morning when Wally attended the black church. And again Sunday evening when he met with the black church where he was a full member in good standing. Strange how no one on campus wanted to be associated with Wally, but no one on campus had an effective ministry like Wally's either. Why were both Wally and Jesus snubbed, sneered at, and abused by the religious establishment? Why were they both loved and followed by those to whom they ministered?

II. COMMENTARY

> **MAIN IDEA:** *Jesus' divine power and authority give us reason to follow him in the new ways which the old religion rejects.*

The Savior's Call for Faith (Part I)

A Reason to Follow: Revelation of Divine Power (5:1–11)

> **SUPPORTING IDEA:** *Jesus' divine power reveals human sinfulness and calls people to follow him in a new profession.*

5:1–3. Having inserted his section on Jesus' ministry (ch. 4) in place of Mark's quick summary of Jesus' preaching (Mark 1:14–15), Luke picked up Mark's calling of the disciples (1:16–20) but did so with an extended miracle story (Luke 5:1–11) without parallel, except for the story John used to end his Gospel (John 21:1–11). Luke turned the miracle story into a call narrative, setting forth the mission of the disciples who joined in Jesus' ministry. The call to mission did not come in a quiet time of relaxation and rest with a few friends. It came in the midst of crowded, busy ministry as people listened to this uniquely authoritative preacher. The crowds pushed him to the brink of the sea. A fishing boat belonging to Simon Peter became Jesus' platform for teaching.

5:4–5. Teaching was over; it was time for fishing. No recreational fishing for these professionals. Back to daily work, but not ordinary daily work. That was completed for the night, because night was the best time to fish. Jesus called for overtime labor in the least productive time of day. Exercising his normal gift for immediate response, Simon Peter protested: "No more fruitless labor for us. We have already done a night's work without anything to show for our efforts."

Then Simon caught himself: "You are talking, Jesus. You are the Master. What you say, we will do." Note that **Master** (Gr. *epistata*) was Luke's word of address from the disciples to Jesus where other Gospels used "Rabbi." Luke thus shows his aim toward a Gentile rather than a Jewish audience. The Master's word takes precedence over human experience and human knowledge. Tough, experienced fishermen let Jesus show them when and where to fish. They had seen the power and authority of his ministry.

5:6–7. The Master proved that he was the master fisherman. Following his instructions brought a record catch. Not just a net full, but two boats full—so full the boats **began to sink**. What kind of revelation is this?

5:8–10a. Instantaneously, spontaneous Peter knew immediately. This revealed divine power placed him in the presence of God. Only God could bring such amazing fishing results. But this meant Peter stood facing God. His was the normal reaction to revelation: confession of sin. The holy purity of deity brings consciousness of the unholy sinfulness of humanity. Peter knew that the unholy cannot stand in the presence of the holy. What fate awaited him? He was not alone in his reaction. His partners shared his amazement at such revelation. Now we learn who the partners were: brothers James and John, the sons of Zebedee.

5:10b–11. Salvation oracle language reappears (see 1:13). Sinful Peter did not have to fear when facing a holy God. God accepted him as he was and made him something new. Interestingly, the call to mission came in singular to Peter, not in plural to the partners. A person who recognizes his limits and stands awefully and fearfully before God finds God coming not with a hand of judgment and discipline but with a call to join in dedicated labor, seeking others for the kingdom. The Savior's call for faith found fruitful ears. The partners joined Peter in steering the boat immediately to shore, leaving the job of cleaning and refitting it to someone else as they followed Jesus in faith. Divine power had unleashed faith to follow the Master.

⬚ The Will to Follow: Asking for Cleansing (5:12–16)

SUPPORTING IDEA: *People with a reason to follow Jesus must also have a will to let him clean them and prepare them for service in the kingdom.*

5:12. Chronology and geographical exactness were not major interests of the inspired Gospel writers. Matthew inserted the Sermon on the Mount at this point in Mark's outline. Luke followed Mark (1:40–45) in telling about the cleansing of the leper. Mark gave no location for the story. Luke gave the location as **one of the towns.** The focus is not on place but on person. The leper was an exile, excluded from society because his skin did not look right.

Somehow, the excluded leper entered society long enough to talk to Jesus. He prostrated himself as one would before kings or slave owners or God. He recognized Jesus' higher position of authority over him and made no demands. He just begged for mercy. His term of address matched his prostrate position. **Lord** is a term of respect that recognizes the higher status of the person addressed. Of course, it was also the Jewish way of referring to God without using the sacred divine name. "If you want to, Lord Jesus," the leper pleaded, "you can heal me and let me back into society with my friends and family. I know you can. Will you, please, Lord?" This was a call of faith, leaving the initiative and choice to God.

5:13. The unthinkable happened. Jesus touched an unclean leper, making himself just as unclean in the eyes of the religious authorities, and thus identifying himself with the leper rather than with the religious establishment. Jesus uttered the cleansing words, **I am willing . . . Be clean.** No sooner said than done the leprosy disappeared, and with it the status of unclean and the social position of ostracized. The Master's power rested not only in the natural world of lakes and fish. It lay in the human world of isolation, uncleanness, and health.

5:14. Cleansing came with commands: "Don't tell anyone. Show your skin to the priest. Obey God's word with the sacrifices demanded" (Lev. 14). The sacrifice did not cause cleansing. It testified to cleansing and expressed gratitude to God for cleansing. Jesus made it something more. It was an opportunity for witness. The priests who were busy with temple affairs could not know what was happening up north in Galilee. Through the leper's sacrifices, they came to know divine powers were at work in the Galilean teacher. Silence before the mobs, but witness to the priests. Why? So mobs would not riot wanting more than Jesus was ready to give and so priests had no excuse when they led the charge to Calvary.

5:15. Jesus told the leper not to let the news leak. Such news was too good to keep quiet. Crowds who saw what happened started the good news mill. Everyone came running. They had two purposes as they came: to hear the authoritative teacher and to be healed of disease. Revelation of power brought people to hear Jesus.

5:16. Popularity drove Jesus to prayer—not just once, but **often**. The Son of God had to hear the Father's voice and determine where the Father was at work. Jesus did not follow the rule of demand and supply. Had he done so, he would have stayed in one place his entire ministry. Always people came to him. Jesus went where prayer led, not where people led. God knew where power needed to be revealed. The revealing Son went where his Power Source directed. Mobs of people were willing to be healed. Jesus had to find where healing led to kingdom growth.

C The Power to Follow: Finding Forgiveness (5:17–26)

SUPPORTING IDEA: *The power people need to follow is more than power to provide physical needs and health; it is the power to provide spiritual forgiveness and health.*

5:17. Jesus faced a crisis decision. Would he keep the healing powers to himself in the face of unbelieving leaders with political power? Or would he heal and let these leaders react as they would? His opponents certainly made a power play. They brought in the troops from every corner of the country to wait, watch, and react.

5:18–19. The people ignored these power confrontations. They saw a power source and did everything necessary to connect with it. At times crowds held the upper hand. Their physical presence prevented anyone from reaching Jesus. Not these resourceful men. If they could not carry the paralyzed man on his pallet through the crowds to Jesus, they would make their own doorway to the Master Physician. They cut away the roofing tiles and lowered the man's pallet attached to ropes. Now the sick man became the object of power-play politics.

5:20–21. Jesus made his power play on behalf of the sick man. He pronounced him cured from illness, sin, and death. Religious leaders made a power play against Jesus. Anyone who claimed to forgive sins put himself on an equal level with God. No one dared make such claims. Jesus must be arrested. He must not influence the crowds.

5:22–25. Jesus' power extended even beyond forgiving sins. He could read minds. He knew they saw him as a blasphemer, one who claimed for himself powers limited only to God. He proved his point. He told the man to walk. Immediately he walked, carrying away his pallet. Jesus' healing powers won this round of argument.

5:26. The people knew who had won. They knew who had divine power. They came to Jesus. Again amazement and praise filled their lives. What they saw made them awestruck. They stared in wonder at what God had done.

Revealing power is more than healing power. It is the power to put all life forces back together. As such, it is a gift from God. It reveals who has God's power. It also reveals who opposes God's power.

D The Position to Follow: Social Outcast (5:27–32)

SUPPORTING IDEA: *The position a person must occupy to follow Jesus is opposed to the position people occupy to attain worldly position and power.*

5:27–28. One day Jesus encountered Levi. The rebel with a cause against religious power structures met the man who represented foreign power structure at its worse—a man whose profession was to collect money for the Romans. Luke took up the Markan call narrative refrain: **Follow me** (Mark 1:17). Levi showed how to join the proper power structure. He left everything he had—his profession, his profits, and his personal identity. He followed Jesus.

5:29–30. Following meant more than just wandering the countryside listening to Jesus teach and preach. Following meant using your influence and skills for Jesus. Levi left the tax table to invite people to the supper table. Following Jesus meant telling others what Jesus had done for him. The others were friends Levi had known for a long time—not new acquaintances formed for convenience and prosperity.

5:31–32. In typical Jewish teacher fashion, Jesus cited a proverb to emphasize his message. Wellness did not drive people to the doctor. Illness did. Jesus was the spiritual doctor. He came with a message of repentance. That message seemed misdirected. It did not save Israel and the Middle East, where political confusion reigned. It saved those religious leaders considered unworthy of God's attention. Power began to reveal true positions in life. Who was sick? The tax collector's friends, people willing to work for the Roman government and thus against Israel? Or religious leaders who knew more about God than God did? The title Righteous One given them by humans was the only title they would ever receive. Jesus picked out the lowest social positions as the positions through which he would work.

E The Lifestyle to Follow (5:33–39)

SUPPORTING IDEA: *Jesus' revealing power forced a decision: old or new way of doing things, fasting for show or fasting for refreshing.*

5:33–35. The Pharisees noticed that Jesus' disciples failed to fast. Jesus explained that fasting meant mourning, grief, and loss. Israel had lost nothing. Israel had gained a groom. The groom will work until his time comes. Then they could fast.

5:36–39. Put it all together in parable form. You folks have all been on the grape farm. You know how new wine expands as it settles into the bottle. It needs new wineskins that has the resiliency to stretch and expand with the new wine. Old skins will not work. They are too set in their ways. They will cause you to lose all the wine. Old power structures built on human wisdom and human control will not work. God's system will work. So choose the power you want to follow: the lifestyle of the set-in-their-ways Pharisees and religious leaders with its wine, bread, and comfort—or do you prefer God's call to be persecuted, even killed on a cross for Jesus' sake. A Savior's call for faith became clear. We must not take things for granted. We are not yet included in the faithful. First we must forgive others and accept God's call for us, wherever that might lead.

> **MAIN IDEA REVIEW:** *Jesus' divine power and authority give us reason to follow him in the new ways which the old religion rejects.*

III. CONCLUSION

Unique Power

Jesus revealed unique power—power only God has—through his authoritative teaching, his miracle working, his mind reading, and his calling of disciples from the wrong social classes. Religious leaders rejected such power as false and blasphemous, claiming for man what only God possessed. They missed the meaning of their own Scriptures that pointed to Jesus. He had power to heal broken minds and bodies. He had another power: the power to forgive sins, to make people whole, and to empower them to do his work. Such power came to those of the wrong social status, the wrong religious affiliations. They were given the power to catch people for Jesus, to spread his church, to bring masses to hear the gospel.

PRINCIPLES

- Jesus is the source of all power.
- Jesus has revealed his power through his teaching, his miracles, and his calling of disciples to follow him in his mission.
- Human religion devises ways for people to earn power by obeying laws and traditions.
- Christ's mission invites people whom human religion rejects and excludes.
- Prayer is the source of power and direction for life.

- The power lifestyle does not come from religious ritual but from enjoying the presence of Jesus.

APPLICATIONS

- Let God be the power source in every area of life, even your business.
- See your mission as finding other people for Jesus.
- Find people whom your church excludes and include them in your circle of friends.
- Act in faith to help those who need help but cannot help themselves.
- Expect to find God at work revealing himself in the midst of human need.
- Know your greatest need is forgiveness of sin, not power in the world.
- When you think you are in the best religious health, you may be spiritually dead.

IV. LIFE APPLICATION

What Are We Fishing For?

If Luke's account of the miraculous catch ended with the nets bursting with fish, it would be an interesting but inconsequential miracle. It might feed our desire for a gospel of success in business and good grades in school, but it would hardly be worthy of our Lord Jesus Christ.

Fortunately, Simon Peter saw more than just the miracle. He was captured by the Lord behind the miracle. Thus, instead of responding with the bravado of a winner, he pleaded for forgiveness. Falling at Jesus' knees, he begged, "Go away from me, Lord; I am a sinful man," (Luke 5:8).

At first glance, this may seem an unlikely reaction to a moment of success. Sometimes, however, it is the experience of achievement that forces us to see how superficial our victories are. Andre Thornton, star home-run hitter with the Cleveland Indians and an exemplary Christian, has predicted that there may be a very real religious awakening among athletes as a result of the exorbitant salaries so many are now receiving. He feels that when they find themselves suddenly so financially secure, they will realize how little their wealth really means, and will be driven to look for deeper values.

The truth is that a person can have full nets but still have an empty life. After you have sold the fish in the market and have put the money in the bank, you may still feel an emptiness deeper than empty nets and a yearning more poignant than the desire for economic security (J. Ellsworth Kalas, *Reading the Signs*, 77).

V. PRAYER

Father, we hear and read of Jesus so much that we often lose sight of his awesomeness. Help us to see what Peter saw in him that morning on the shore of Lake Galilee. Give us the grace to give ourselves wholly to him, unworthy though we are. Amen.

VI. DEEPER DISCOVERIES

A. Pharisees (5:17)

The teachers of the Law who opposed Jesus were comprised primarily of the Pharisees. They were the most influential of the three major Jewish sects (the other two being the Sadducees and Essenes). We first read of them in the second century B.C. They believed in a strict keeping of the Law, as interpreted by their own traditions. They were separatists who sought to avoid contact with unclean things and unclean people. The teachers of the law, or scribes, were professional students of the law, and most of them were Pharisees.

B. Tax Collectors (5:27)

When Jesus attended a banquet given by a tax collector, he created a stir among the Pharisees. Tax collectors were outcasts from respectable society. They were collaborators with the Roman government. Tax collectors had daily contact with all kinds of "unclean" people. The word *sinners* means the common people who paid little attention to the religious scruples of the Pharisees.

C. Fasting (5:33–35)

Jesus fasted on occasion, and he often spent time in prayer. However, he did not fashion fasting into prescribed ritual. The kind of fasting he practiced was a natural fasting that resulted from preoccupation with more important matters (see John 4:31–34).

D. Wineskins (5:36–39)

Winemaking has always been a major industry in Syria-Palestine. In Old Testament times, the presses for making wine were usually pits hewed out of solid rock. These were connected to channels to lower vats, where the juice was allowed to collect. The juice was then poured into wineskins—skins of small animals such as goats, which were sewn together to hold the wine. The point of Jesus' parable was the incompatibility of the old wineskin with the new wine. New wine, if placed in old and hardened wineskins, will destroy both skins and wine. As the new wine ferments, the old wineskin will burst, spilling the wine.

VII. TEACHING OUTLINE

A. INTRODUCTION

1. Lead Story: Strangely Effective
2. Context: In chapter 4 Jesus withstood temptation and rejection. He demonstrated his authority in teaching and ministry. He aroused the curiosity of the crowds. He refused to let demons inform the people of his nature as Son of God. He set his course to discover the Father's will in the lonely place and then to preach where God directed, not where the crowds demanded. In chapter 5 he took the next step in his ministry. He called disciples to join him in full-time ministry and to be the nucleus who would continue the ministry after his departure. Their calling was to be fishers of men.

   Through his healing ministry, Jesus continued drawing the curious, miracle-seeking crowds despite all his efforts to get people not to talk about his miracles. Miracle working was not his main business. Preaching the kingdom and forgiving sins was. But the latter raised hostility as well as awe and praise. The company Jesus kept also raised hostility, but this only gave him opportunity to define his ministry as calling sinners to repentance. Still he pointed ahead to a time when his disciples would have to fast.
3. Transition: Jesus called people to follow him. Many followed because of his miracles. Some followed to check out his unorthodox teachings and reprimand him. A few followers were seeking to learn from him and to obey his teachings. As we study the life and ministry of Jesus, we must keep asking ourselves, why do I follow him? What are my true motives? Do I expect miraculous blessing? Am I trying to gain personal prominence? Or am I a dedicated learner, wanting to obey Christ's new teachings?

B. COMMENTARY

1. Reason to Follow: Revelation of Divine Power (5:1–11)
   a. The setting: teaching from a boat (5:1–3)
   b. The command: do your best at what you do best (5:4)
   c. The reaction: if you say so (5:5)
   d. The result: straining the nets (5:6–7)

    e.   The response: astonished confession (5:8–10a)

    f.   The commission: catch men (5:10b)

    g.   The conclusion: fishers without nets (5:11)

2.   The Will to Follow: Asking for Cleansing (5:12–16)

    a.   The setting: in town but out of touch (5:12a)

    b.   The request: cleansing (5:12b)

    c.   The scene: willing and able to cleanse (5:13)

    d.   The command: silent sacrifices (5:14)

    e.   The conclusion: crowds for cleansing (5:15)

    f.   The Master's response: lonely prayer (5:16)

3.   The Power to Follow: Finding Forgiveness (5:17–26)

    a.   The setting: teaching among opponents and power (5:17)

    b.   The scene: power to get to Jesus (5:18–19)

    c.   The Master's response: sins forgiven (5:20)

    d.   The opponents' reaction: blasphemy (5:21)

    e.   The Master's proof: foreknowledge and healing (5:22–25)

    f.   The conclusion: amazed at remarkable man (5:26)

4.   The Position to Follow: Social Outcast (5:27–32)

    a.   The setting: tax collector's office (5:27a)

    b.   The command: follow me (5:27b)

    c.   The reaction: leave all to follow (5:28)

    d.   The results: banquet for friends and foes (5:29)

    e.   The complaint: wrong company (5:30)

    f.   The Master's teaching: sinners need help (5:31–32)

5.   The Lifestyle to Follow (5:33–39)

    a.   The setting: questioning crowd (5:33a)

    b.   The question: why are you different (5:33b)

    c.   The Master's response: when the time is right (5:34–35)

    d.   The Master's conclusion: the nature of things (5:36–39)

C. CONCLUSION: WHAT ARE WE FISHING FOR ?

VIII. ISSUES FOR DISCUSSION

1.   Has God ever asked you to do something impossible or unreasonable? What happened?

2.   What does it mean to be in the business of catching men? Are you in that business?

3.   Why did Jesus feel it necessary to withdraw to lonely places in the face of needy crowds?

4.   What does it mean to say Jesus can forgive sins?

5. What events in your life in the last month give you reason to praise God?
6. Does Jesus have no place in his ministry for "righteous" people? Why?
7. Why would Jesus' disciples eventually have to fast?

Luke 6

❧❧

The Savior's Call for Faith (Part II)

Quote

"*It* is always so. Our choicest blessings invariably come to us by descending; our richest benefits come by going downward. We stoop to conquer. The farmer bows his face toward the earth both to sow the seed and to reap the harvest; the miner goes below for the precious things of the earth; the loveliest streams flow along the lowliest valleys; the sweetest flowers flourish in the shadiest dells."

F. W. Boreham

Luke 6

IN A NUTSHELL

The Savior's call for faith continues as Jesus shows himself to be Lord of the Sabbath and thus the authority to follow in faith. His Sabbath miracles continued to challenge the religious leaders' religious system—until they finally decided his call to faith was a call to death. In face of such threats, Jesus chose twelve men to follow him closely as apostles. Healing the sick provided the setting for Jesus' teaching in which he identified those blessed of the Father—a blessed crowd far different from the crowd the religious leaders picked out as chosen. His call to faith reached people whom the call to law had ignored.

The Savior's Call to Faith (Part II)

I. INTRODUCTION

WRONG EXPECTATIONS

"*H*ere, Mom! It is for you. He has finally called you."

The single mom picked up the phone with excitement. The weeks and weeks of paying attention to the new man at church was finally going to pay off. She was going to get a date at last.

"I need to tell you something," she heard him say. "You have been so kind and helpful to me these last weeks. You have lived up to what everyone said about you. You are kind and generous and thoughtful. I have really enjoyed getting to know your kids. They are great. You have done a wonderful job with them. But I think you ought to know that God has led to me a young woman in another town, and we have begun dating. I am sorry things did not work out for us as we once thought they might!"

Tears stung her eyes as she hung up the phone. How could she have been so wrong in her expectations? Just as everything seemed to be going right, it all turned wrong. If she could only get her hands on that man . . .

The religious leaders reacted in similar manner to Jesus. They had things all figured out. They knew what Messiah would be like. They knew what obedience to God meant. When they heard about a young preacher in Galilee whom many thought was Messiah, they went to check him out. He certainly did not meet their expectations. Their mood shifted immediately from expectation, thrill, and hope to disappointment, disbelief, and intense anger. No one who acted like Jesus could possibly be Messiah. Such an imposter threatened their religious power and their truce with Rome. He had to be stopped.

Jesus responded to the challenge in the simple way he always did. He prayed. He obeyed his Father. He healed. He taught. As the religious hierarchy issued the call for his death, Jesus continued to issue his call to faith.

II. COMMENTARY

The Savior's Call to Faith (Part II)

MAIN IDEA: *Faith follows evidences of divine power and authority, not human traditions and institutions.*

A The Authority to Follow: Lord of the Sabbath (6:1–5)

SUPPORTING IDEA: *Jesus has God's power and authority over all human institutions and traditions.*

6:1. Ever on the move, Jesus and his followers trudged through a grainfield one day. Almost subconsciously, the disciples began picking off a few grains, rubbing them in their hands to remove the husks, and snacking on the kernels.

6:2. The Pharisees made no allowance for subconscious acts. They held you responsible for anything you did that related to their law in any way. And what would not relate to the voluminous oral interpretations they collected and enforced? The shameful disciples were reaping, threshing, and preparing food, all on the holy day of rest.

6:3–4. The disciples acted; Jesus took responsibility. Following his pattern of response, he found scriptural proof for his defense in 1 Samuel 21:6. David satisfied the needs of his hungry army with bread that only priests were supposed to eat (note Lev. 24:5–9). Perhaps one could see David as the Lord's anointed qualified to be the nation's religious leader, but **he also gave some to his companions.** The Book of Samuel defends this action on grounds that they were entering holy-war battle and had sanctified themselves, but still they were not priests in the line of Aaron. David simply put human need above ritual law. God's priest cooperated with him.

6:5. Jesus' pronouncement gave the reason for telling this story. Scriptural precedent shows that human need ranks above ritual law in God's sight. If this is true for common soldiers, how much more for the Son of Man? Jesus is Lord or Master of the Sabbath. What implications were behind such a statement? The Pharisees surely did not miss this point. Only God could make such a claim. Jesus, the Son of Man, identified himself also as Son of God with divine authority. Such an authority makes the law and cannot be accused of breaking it. Such an authority forces people to choose: follow pharisaic interpretations of the law or follow the **Lord of the Sabbath.**

Ⓑ The Danger to Follow: Intent to Kill (6:6–11)

> **SUPPORTING IDEA:** *Faith faces decisions that may be risky and even life-threatening.*

6:6. Luke makes the point another way. Jesus followed pharisaic custom. He used the Sabbath to go to synagogue worship. As usual, he was chosen as visiting teacher for the day. Someone else shared the spotlight with him, a man with a shriveled right hand. Two mission statements stood diametrically opposed: the Pharisees' mission to ensure the observance of the law according to their interpretations and Jesus' mission to "release the oppressed" (4:18). Would Jesus be true to his mission, or would he seek to appease the religious power brokers?

6:7. The Pharisees were also on a mission. They wanted evidence against Jesus. They **watched him closely to see if he would heal on the Sabbath.**

6:8–10. Jesus knew their thoughts. He called the man to center stage so everyone could see. He called on the Pharisees for a decision: **which is lawful on the Sabbath: to do good or to do evil, to save life or to destroy it?** Silence greeted the question. Their law allowed exceptions to the Sabbath rules forbidding work, including healing, on the Sabbath. Healing was permissible for life-threatening situations. No question this was life-threatening. It was lifelong. **Stretch out your hand,** Jesus told the man. He accomplished one more part of his mission. Would the Pharisees dare attack him for helping a person in such need?

6:11. There was no time for action by the Pharisees—just planning and plotting. In great anger they plotted to get rid of this Sabbath-breaking nuisance who claimed to be Master of their Sabbath. How often do good intentions lead God's people to take over God's position and defend him?

Ⓒ The People to Follow: The Twelve (6:12–16)

> **SUPPORTING IDEA:** *Faith begins with a small group of dedicated followers chosen by God.*

6:12–16. It was decision time for Jesus. How would he set up an ongoing mission that would continue after his ministry on earth? Decision time for Jesus always meant prayer time (see 3:21; 5:16; 9:18,28; 11:1). Prayer time meant withdrawal time, escape from the crowds to the desolate, lonely place where nothing interrupted communication with God. Prayer time led to appointment time. From the band of disciples who followed him, he chose twelve for the special work of apostles.

Ⓓ The Teaching to Follow: Identifying the Blessed (6:17–49)

> **SUPPORTING IDEA:** *Faith must be informed by teaching that identifies the characteristics of kingdom members who receive God's blessing.*

6:17–19. Luke's sermon on the plain served the same purpose for him as Matthew's Sermon on the Mount (Matt. 5–7). The crowd was multifaceted: disciples, southerners from Judea came south, representatives from Jerusalem the capital, evidently including religious leaders who had been hounding Jesus, and persons from the Phoenician cities of Tyre and Sidon, perhaps Gentiles (cf. 10:13–14). Two purposes drove people to travel long, difficult distances to see Jesus. They wanted to hear his authoritative teaching and be healed of their diseases. The healing began immediately, evil spirits coming out of people and a simple touch bringing healing. The unique power of Jesus must not be overlooked. He had a power available to all.

6:20–23. Jesus' teaching was directed to his disciples. Others listened in. Three blessings underline the mission Jesus set out in 4:18–19.

The unhappy poor possess the kingdom of God. The hungry will find satisfaction. The NIV's "satisfaction" translates the Greek *chortasthesate,* literally "will be fed, will eat one's full." Jesus turned human need into human contentment. Those crying over their pitiful condition on earth will laugh at the new conditions Jesus creates for them.

Pitiful hunger and poverty are not the only conditions that the blessed face. They also face persecution. People turn against them, hating them, excluding them from society, insulting them, rejecting their very name, the only reputation they have now and after they die. If loyalty to Jesus brought such drastic consequences, fear not; Jesus promised his blessing. The question pops up at us: do we trust Jesus enough to wait on his blessing, or must we find instant gratification in fellowship and fame with the world? Look at the reaction Jesus expected. Given the dirtiest treatment earth can deal out, we should leap and shout for joy. We have joined the ranks of the prophets in receiving the world's harshest blows. Life here may be dastardly. Life with Jesus in heaven will be heavenly. Is that reward enough, or must we have something here and now? If so, depart from the company of the blessed.

6:24–26. The blessed life has a counterpart—the woeful life. The Greek *ouai* reflects a situation of horror, disaster, and calamity. Such awaits the rich, the one who has never known hunger, the person who has all the reason in the world to laugh, the individual who sits atop the social ladder hearing nothing but praises and adoration. These are short-lived in the face of eternity. False prophets gained the same adulation and wealth. Comfortable now, such people face eventual starvation and grief. Is power and praise at the moment prize enough for us? Or do we look to eternal rewards? That is Jesus' question for disciples of all ages.

6:27–36. Want to be among the blessed? Jesus has a recipe for life. This recipe calls for much more than silent endurance waiting for eternal reward. Turn the cards on the enemy. Repay hate with love, cursing with blessing, persecution and exclusion with intercessory prayer. If you lose a judgment so someone can give you blows on the cheek, give him opportunity for twice as many by turning the other cheek. If someone spitefully takes your cloak just because of having the power to do so, get in on the fun. Take off your inner garment and give it away, too. If other people want what you have, let them have it, whether you have to give it away yourself or simply let them keep what they stole. Put yourself in their place. Let them have what they want, what you would want if you were where they are.

Wait a minute, you complain. Is that not going a bit too far? After all, look at all the people I already love. Is it not enough to love good church people and share what I have with them? You are just doing what comes naturally. Anyone can return love for love. Even those who persecute others love people who love them. They do not act mean all the time. They have some people in their own family and inner circle of friends. The worst of people help somebody. You cannot pick and choose whom to love. Love everyone.

This goes so far as to share your material goods. If someone wants to borrow something from you, let them. Do not hold back in selfishness. Give in selfless love. Do not sit down and figure how much interest you will get or whether you have a good chance of getting the loaned item back. Just give away what you have to those who need it. Love everyone. Do good to everyone, even the worst enemy who has put you in the persecuted, impoverished condition you are in.

What will you get out of all this? You will be acting like your heavenly Father. You will be showing mercy to others who do not deserve your mercy. This is how God shows you mercy when you do not deserve it from him. Act like that in love. He will call you his sons. Can you ask for anything more?

6:37–38. Perhaps you had a different job description in mind when you decided to follow Jesus. You would join him in judging the world. You would point out all the evil people to God so he could give them what they deserve. God's ways are different. You experienced them from him. No judgment. No condemnation. No heaping punishment on others. Forgive! Give! Use fair, generous measuring cups to sell something to someone else.

Yes, be generous in what you give to others. God will give you the same kind of measure you give others.

6:39–40. You need a story to help you understand? Look at it this way. If you cannot see where you are going, do you want a blind person leading you?

Of course not! You would both fall into the trap by the road, and neither of you could get the other out. You need someone who is better equipped than you are to guide you. This is certainly true in discipleship. The new disciple must know that the teacher knows more and is to be honored and respected. The new disciple must not, however, remain a new disciple. The goal is for the disciple to become like his teacher. Ultimately the goal is for every disciple to become like the Master Teacher, Jesus himself. No disciple should have any lower goal than to be like Jesus.

6:41–42. The disciple never becomes the judge. As humans, our tendency is to be too easy on ourselves and too harsh on others. We see a tiny speck of dust in the other person's eye, and want to remove it. The other person must be perfect. All the while, other people wonder why we are so blind. Can we not see what is sticking out of our eye? No, that two-by-four in our eye goes unnoticed, no matter how many times we look in the mirror. We moan and complain about the hypocrisy in this world, even the hypocrisy in the church. Jesus looks lovingly at us and says, **you hypocrite, first take the plank out of your eye.** Until Jesus has helped us to see ourselves realistically and to deal with our spiritual problems, we cannot become mature disciples—the teachers of others whom he calls us to be.

6:43–45. Use another image to get the picture. Go to the orchards. Look at the fruit trees—old trees, limbs just barely hanging on, leaves dried and withered, infested with bugs. What kind of fruit do you expect from trees like these? Then look at the strong tree—limbs rising to the sky, loaded with beautiful green leaves, no bugs in sight. What kind of fruit will you look for on these trees? Now look in the mirror again. What kind of fruit do you expect from what you see there? Do you have a spiritual mirror to look at yourself? Does God's Word reflect back at you the kind of person you are and the kind of fruit you are bearing? You must fit some category. Fig tree or thornbush, grapevine or brier?

Listen carefully to fellow believers. Study God's Word diligently. Find out what category you are in. Get the real picture of the real you. Want to know what kind of person you are? Listen to yourself. God has a spiritual rule. You are what your heart is. An evil heart produces evil results. A good heart produces good results. How do you know what the heart is producing? Listen to the mouth. Your daily conversation issues from your heart.

6:46–49. Put all this teaching together, and what do you get? You get the definition of a hypocrite—a person who says with the mouth that Jesus is Lord and Master of life, then never listens to Jesus, never obeys Jesus. You also get the definition of a disciple—a person who listens to every word Jesus says and then puts those words into practice in daily living. Here is one final picture to bring the point home! A contractor agrees to build a house. He digs a deep hole, clear down to bedrock. He fills the hole with a strong foundation laid on top of bedrock. Then he builds the house on that foundation. What does he have to fear? Even the worst flood could not harm the house built on a deep foundation on bedrock.

Of course, there is the other kind. The contractor wants to get by as cheaply as possible. He does not even bother to dig a hole or lay a foundation. He just starts building a house on the surface of the ground. The flood comes. Instantly, the house falls. Why? It has no connection to bedrock, no foundation. The choice is yours: hypocrisy or faithful obedience; built on the bedrock of Christ or on sinking sand; eternal life or destruction? Which of these is truly you?

MAIN IDEA REVIEW: *Faith follows evidences of divine power and authority, not human traditions and institutions.*

III. CONCLUSION

What It Means to Follow Jesus

The Savior's call for faith means we have to decide if we will follow him. To follow him means to recognize his authority as Lord of all religion and all religious traditions. To follow him means to realize the end of the road—death at the hand of religious leaders who are not willing to let him be Lord of religious traditions. To follow Jesus means to join the apostolic faith, to know the people Jesus first entrusted his mission to, to know the source of authority—the Bible—they left behind, and to live out and pass on that apostolic faith to the next generation. To follow him means to follow his teaching—truths that stand in stark contrast to normal religious teaching.

Check your "hater" at the door. You have no more need of it. Love is the only theme—love for every person on earth no matter how they treat us. Retire from the judge's bench. That task should be left in God's hands. He is the judge. We are called to test ourselves and to make sure hypocrisy and evil have not gained control of our lives. We are called to be master teachers, setting our goal to become like the Master. We have no excuse for being blind to the truth or following those who are blind. We must build our lives on the solid rock of faith in Jesus Christ. Then we will bring forth good fruit for him.

PRINCIPLES

- Jesus and God's Holy Word are the only absolute authorities we have to follow.
- Church traditions too often become church laws, keeping people away from God rather than leading them to him.

- Doing good is more important than obeying traditions.
- Prayer should precede all of life's decisions.
- Kingdom blessings rest on the poor, the hungry, those who mourn, those who are persecuted.
- One's position in human society does not determine one's position in heaven.
- Earthly prosperity may be the only reward we will ever get.
- Love for others, especially those who oppose us—not protection of self—is life's guiding principle.
- We are called to judge ourselves, not others.
- God expects from us good fruit that is shown in obedience to him and love for others.

APPLICATIONS

- Beware the limits the church places on who, where, and when we can minister in Jesus' name.
- Look for opportunities to do good to other people no matter what people will say about the kind of people we are associating with or the way things have always been done in the church.
- We can expect to be attacked by religious people when we follow Christ completely.
- Pray every day and especially before every decision you face.
- See if wealth, position, or power in this world is preventing you from joining those God is blessing with eternal rewards.
- Take your enemy list down to zero by praying for and loving every person on the list. The question is not how they are behaving but how much we are loving.
- Every time you find reason to judge someone else for an action or an attitude, look inward and see how much of that action or attitude controls your life.
- Ask God to show you the foundation on which you have built your life.

IV. LIFE APPLICATION

No Need to Worry

Josiah Elliott was a North Carolina country preacher for over fifty years. He was a preacher's preacher. He labored hard to see God call young men to the gospel ministry, and then he labored hard to see that those young men got the education they needed to be faithful pastors. Five times Josiah Elliott mortgaged his house to pay for the education of one of his "preacher boys."

Five times the young preacher came back with the money to pay off the mortgage again.

Finally, the time came when Josiah Elliott could no longer preach. In fact, he could do nothing but lie in bed. People wondered if the old preacher could live on without a ministry? How would he have enough to eat if he could not preach? No need to worry. People knew the power of Josh Elliott's prayer life. They ran to him to kneel before his bed, let him place his hands on their heads, and pray for their needs and for their spiritual growth. These same people and many others who had found blessing from Elliott's ministry through the years came to his door with every kind of food imaginable. The man never went without ministry or food. He had lived out the teachings of Jesus among his people. Now they lived out those same teachings in relation to him.

The world continues to look for people like Josh Elliott. Luke 6 sets out the basic teachings about life in Christ's kingdom. If you want to be a citizen of this kingdom, you must follow Christ in all these teachings. To build on the rock you must hear the teachings and put them into practice. Then you will hear Christ's blessings, not his woes, pronounced on your head. The house you build on Christ's teachings will never be shaken, no matter how horrible the storms of life.

V. PRAYER

Jesus, my teacher, call me to follow you in faith. Point out the hypocrisy in my life. Show me my blind spots. Help me see the true fruit my life is producing. I want you to be Lord of my life and Lord of all the traditions that feed and guide my life. Put love in my heart and forgiveness in my soul. Let me become like you. You are the only role model I want to follow. Speak, Lord, and I will follow in obedience. Amen.

VI. DEEPER DISCOVERIES

A. Sabbath (6:2)

The Sabbath is the day of rest, considered holy to God. It is derived from God's rest on the seventh day following his creation of the universe. It was viewed as a sign of the covenant relation between God and his people and of the eternal rest, which he promised them. The habit of Jesus was to observe the Sabbath as a day of worship in the synagogues. But his failure to comply with the minute restrictions of the observance of the law by the Pharisees brought conflict and confrontation with the religious leaders of his day.

Christians view the Sabbath as a shadow of the reality that has been revealed (Col. 2:16–23). The Sabbath is a symbol of the heavenly rest to come (Heb. 4:1–11).

B. Disciples (6:1,13)

The term *disciple* implies several important ideas in the Scriptures. It speaks of repentance and faith for salvation, dedicated Christian living, identification with and service to Christ, and telling the good news to others.

The primary emphasis of the word points to various aspects of a person's Christian experience. The actual English term is derived from the Latin word *discipulus*. In the first century this meant a *pupil* or a *learner*. The word was often used in the philosophical world to speak of a philosopher's understudy. The equivalent of the term in New Testament Greek carries the same idea of *learner* or *pupil*.

We see the word used extensively in the four Gospels. Moses' disciples (John 9:28) and the followers of John the Baptist (Mark 2:18) are classic examples. It is also used to denote the disciples of the Pharisees (Matt. 22:16). Of course, the New Testament usage is primarily concerned with the disciples of the Lord Jesus Christ. Here, it is used once again as a *learner* or *pupil*. Those who encountered Jesus and became his committed followers and learners were known as disciples.

It is clear that the many people who came to Jesus had varying degrees of conviction and loyalty. Thus, there is a broad as well as a narrow connotation to the term as used in the four Gospels. The highest concept of *disciple* in the Gospels relates to the Twelve (Luke 6:12–18). In the Acts of the Apostles, the word takes on a definite absolutist connotation. It was the accepted description of those who had come into full faith and commitment to Jesus Christ.

This entire theme can be summarized by saying that a disciple was:
- a person who became a believer (Acts 11:26),
- one who became a learner of Christ and thus his follower or pupil,
- a believer who is committed to suffering and living a sacrificial lifestyle for the sake of Jesus Christ (Luke 14:26–27,33), and
- one who fulfills the ultimate obligation of discipleship—to make disciples of others (Matt 28:19–20).

C. The Golden Rule (6:31)

This is the name usually given to Jesus' command in Matthew 7:12 and restated in Luke 6:31. The designation, "Golden Rule," does not appear in the Bible, and its origin in English is difficult to trace. The principle of the Golden Rule is found in many religions; but Jesus' wording of it was original and unique.

VII. TEACHING OUTLINE

A. INTRODUCTION

1. Lead Story: Wrong Expectations
2. Context: Luke 5 began a brief section of Luke's Gospel in which the Savior called people to faith as he preached the good news of the kingdom of God. He sought people who would catch others for him—people who would celebrate while the bridegroom is here and fast when he leaves. He called people to a new adventure that would bring destruction to old ways of living and doing religion. Chapter 6 presents the Lord of the Sabbath, the one with new ideas splitting out of the old wineskins.

   The keepers of the old cannot endure the new. The religious leaders began to plan Jesus' destruction as he began to call out his disciples and teach them kingdom principles that stood in direct opposition to the world's principles. These made poverty, hunger, crying, and being hated the opportunities for God's blessing. Material wealth plays no role in this kingdom, for rewards come not here but in the future. Eyes on heaven cannot focus on earthly things. Lives filled with heaven's love cannot hate or judge earthly acquaintances. Kingdom people care for their hearts, not their pocketbooks. They come to Jesus, hear his words, and practice them in daily life. Thus, they have a foundation that will last into eternity.

3. Transition: Our world more than ever judges people and sorts them out into friends and enemies. Our world counts the value of one's bank account, the size of one's car, and the luxury of a person's home. Turning our back on such values becomes difficult in face of the public pressure to surpass the Joneses. As we study Luke 6, we must make hard decisions. These are not decisions for today or tomorrow and then to be forgotten. They are decisions that determine the direction we will take for the rest of our lives. Do you trust Jesus enough to take up the radical lifestyle he calls you to? Do you truly confess him as Lord, or do you give lip service to him while practicing someone else's words? This chapter calls for us to leap into action. On your mark. Get set.

B. COMMENTARY

1. The Authority to Follow: Lord of the Sabbath (6:1–5)
   a. The setting: hungry men on the Sabbath (6:1)
   b. The opponents' reaction: it is against the law (6:2)

    c.   The Master's response: back to the Bible (6:3–4)

    d.   The Master's claim: Lord of the Sabbath (6:5)

2. The Danger to Follow: Intent to Kill (6:6–11)

    a.   The setting: challenged on the Sabbath (6:6)

    b.   The opponents' reaction: watch closely (6:7)

    c.   The Master's response: do good or evil? (6:8–9)

    d.   The Master's action: up to the challenge (6:10)

    e.   The conclusion: opponents mad enough to kill (6:11)

3. The People to Follow: The Twelve (6:12–16)

    a.   The setting: prayer time (6:12)

    b.   The Master's action: choose twelve apostles (6:13)

    c.   Conclusion: list of the twelve (6:14–16)

4. The Teaching to Follow: Identifying the Blessed (6:17–49)

    a.   The setting: on a crowded plain with healing power (6:17–19)

    b.   Blessed or cursed like the prophets (6:20–26)

    c.   Love the hateful as God does (6:27–36)

    d.   Judge not and be not judged (6:37–38)

    e.   Blinded about being blind (6:39–42)

    f.   Good fruit and bad (6:43–45)

    g.   Confessing or obedient (6:46–49)

C. CONCLUSION: NO NEED TO WORRY

VIII. ISSUES FOR DISCUSSION

1. What conditions would make it wrong to help someone in dire need?

2. As Lord of the Sabbath, has Jesus done away with all rules and regulations about keeping the Sabbath holy? Do these apply in any way to the Christian Sunday?

3. Does Jesus really expect us to try to be poor, hungry, mournful, and rejected? Why or why not?

4. Name one person who is in some way your enemy. What are you doing about that relationship?

5. What person or group of persons are you most apt to stand in judgment over? Why? What does God want you to do about this?

6. How do people who are not believers judge you: to be a follower of Christ or a normal citizen of the world? Why?

7. In what ways are you hearing Christ's words in this chapter and putting them into practice?

Luke 7

The Savior's Call for Faith (Part III)

I. **INTRODUCTION**
Apply Without Qualifications

II. **COMMENTARY**
A verse-by-verse explanation of the chapter.

III. **CONCLUSION**
Righteous Judges or Humble Sinners?
An overview of the principles and applications from the chapter.

IV. **LIFE APPLICATION**
Traditions Face African Mission
Melding the chapter to life.

V. **PRAYER**
Tying the chapter to life with God.

VI. **DEEPER DISCOVERIES**
Historical, geographical, and grammatical enrichment of the commentary.

VII. **TEACHING OUTLINE**
Suggested step-by-step group study of the chapter.

VIII. **ISSUES FOR DISCUSSION**
Zeroing the chapter in on daily life.

"*The Christian church is the only society in the world in which membership is based upon the qualification that the candidate shall be unworthy of membership*"

Charles C. Morrison

Luke 7

IN A NUTSHELL

Luke 7 introduces us to the way Jesus screened people for admission into his kingdom. He often seemed to search for people who did not meet qualifications to become part of the Jewish temple worship of his day—people defiled by living in Gentile territory outside Israel, people needing help rather than being able to help the cause, people like John the Baptist who lived outside the limits and customs of the establishment, sinners shamelessly showing their love knowing forgiveness was their only hope in life. Jesus set up no qualifications people like this had to meet for membership. He showed compassion to those society scorned and called them to follow him.

The Savior's Call for Faith (Part III)

I. INTRODUCTION

Apply Without Qualifications

My son rashly answered an ad seeking a computer troubleshooter for a commercial real estate firm. He carefully filled out their questionnaire and sent in his resume. His loving father laughed the effort off. How could a young person never having had a full-time job and never having had computer training of any kind become the major computer person for a sophisticated urban real estate firm? But the amazing result was that my son got the job and has been widely praised by his employer.

Similarly, Jesus called people to follow and become his disciples, people who had no qualifications for the job. Many of these people were outsiders, snubbed and ostracized by society's leaders. Criticism faced Jesus at every stop. Compassion, healing, and call to discipleship were his responses. The church must hear the message of Luke 7. As we call out leaders and invite people to follow Jesus, we too often check their resume before we check their hearts.

II. COMMENTARY

The Savior's Call for Faith (Part III)

> **MAIN IDEA:** *The Savior's call for faith reaches out to people whose resumes bring only scorn and rejection from society's proper members. But the church must meet their needs for help, forgiveness, and acceptance as Jesus did.*

A The Savior's Call for Faith Reaches Outside Israel (7:1–10)

> **SUPPORTING IDEA:** *Jesus recognizes faith even in people whose occupation brings them into opposition to God's people.*

7:1. Teaching time was over. It was time for renewed action. All the people had heard the teaching. Now they could see Jesus' response to people in need. Would his actions prove his words true? So he returned to his ministry center, the city of Capernaum (see 4:23,31).

7:2. Capernaum with its bustling business required Roman soldiers for two reasons: to guard the populace against illegal business and criminal activities and to collect customs from traders who crossed the borders of Palestine. The centurion would command a unit with one hundred solders at full strength. His office commanded respect. So did his actions and attitudes. A household servant of a centurion became ill. Quite possibly the servant held a position of high responsibility. Still, he was a servant with no rights except what the centurion gave. He could easily be replaced. The centurion, however, saw him as more than a replaceable cog in the machine that ran his household. The centurion cared for his servant and did not want to lose him.

7:3. Daily gossip brought the centurion news of Jesus. Daily business brought Gentile commanders and Jewish leaders into contact. Such contacts led to doing favors for each other in crucial times. The centurion called in his chips and asked the Jewish elders to help him. They, of all people, relayed his message to Jesus. Used to issuing commands, the centurion phrased the message bluntly: Come! Cure!

7:4–6a. Jewish elders who normally argued with Jesus showed another side. They had little doubt he could heal. Their question was would he? They begged him and persuaded him to come. Why should Jesus interrupt his business to take care of theirs, especially when theirs dealt with a Gentile soldier whose troops might any day turn on the Jewish people and annihilate them? The elders had the answer. This centurion is different. He cares for the Jews. He used his own resources to build a synagogue for us. Yes, a Gentile soldier built a Jewish worship center. He was not alone. Early inscriptions show other Gentiles admiring the Jews and funding synagogue construction. Jesus' response was unusual and unexpected for Jews, but not for Jesus. Seeing the need, he went to meet it.

7:6b–8. Jesus got close, and the centurion acted in another surprising fashion. Not only did this Gentile soldier fund a synagogue and send for a nomadic Jewish rabbi to heal his servant; he recognized that Jesus, the rabbi, outranked the centurion. He sent a second delegation, this one made up not of people with authority but people whom he trusted as **friends**. They called Jesus *kurios*, a Greek word that can mean "sir," "lord over the servants," or "Lord over heaven and earth." Exactly what the friends meant, we will never know. Luke intends us to hear that this Lord was over heaven and earth, divine Master.

These people had no commands for Jesus, just the plea not to defile himself by entering a Gentile home and not to put himself out any further. Simply say the word so the servant will live, they asked. Jewish elders claimed the centurion deserved all Jesus would give him. The Gentile centurion said he deserved nothing, not even a visit from Jesus. He respected Jesus' authority and wanted him to exercise it in the way the centurion exercised his authority in his realm of expertise and power. Speak, and the cause of terminal illness will vanish!

7:9. Luke did not report how Jesus cured the servant. This was not the point. Jesus responded to the centurion's words in the same way crowds responded to his miracles—in amazement. Such words showed a unique kind of faith—a faith far beyond the Jewish elders who knew Jesus could heal but refused to follow him. This was a faith beyond the crowds, who often followed hoping for another miracle or sign. A faith like this was found in no one in Israel, not even the disciples. Being Israelite, being in authority, being a religious or political leader . . . none of these qualifications mattered. Jesus looked for only one quality in people—faith, the ability to believe God would do what he promised.

7:10. Jesus and the centurion never met. Jesus did not have to bend rabbinic purity rules to effect a cure. The friends returned, and the ill servant was well. Why? Because of faith in Jesus from a Gentile soldier.

🅑 The Savior's Call to Faith Reveals Divine Compassion (7:11–17)

> **SUPPORTING IDEA:** *Jesus' compassion brings life to the dead, awe to the living, and a call to compassion to his disciples.*

7:11. Luke does not provide a daily diary. He sketches out imprecise time notes: **soon afterward.** Capernaum was the center of Christ's ministry, but he extended his work to other places. Nain was on the southern border of Galilee twenty-five miles from Capernaum in the plain of Jezreel on the northern slope of the hill of Moreh. Large enough to have a city gate, it evidently had surrounding defense walls into which the gate allowed entrance. We do not know why Jesus would choose to go to such an isolated, out-of-the-way place. But he went, and his disciples followed. So did a crowd of spectators.

7:12. A funeral procession greeted him as he entered Nain. The age of the dead son is not known. The term of address in verse 14 may indicate he was a young adult over age 25. The focus is not on the dead but on the living. The mother has only one son (Gr. *monogenes*, the same word used of Jesus in John 3:16). One dead son meant one lonely life even amid a large crowd of friends and mourners.

7:13. Jesus immediately recognized the situation. Compassion flowed from the Son of God to the sonless widow. Words say so little in such a time. Jesus tried to brush away her tears and catch her attention. He had more than empty words to give.

7:14–15. His touch on the coffin brought the funeral procession to a halt. Focus shifted to the dead. Would he hear the compassionate Savior's words?

Get up. The dead son heard and obeyed. Silenced lips pronounced words. Wordlessly, Jesus restored the only son to his mother.

7:16. Family response is not reported by Luke, but crowd response is. Jesus came not just to do individual favors. He came to bring the kingdom of God on earth and to let people recognize it. This crowd took a step forward in responding to Jesus. In fear and awe they gave God the glory He deserved, knowing that only God at work could bring a dead son back into his mother's arms. In Jesus they saw a prophet sent from God, a divine messenger at work in their midst. They saw more. They saw God coming to visit and care for his people (cf. 1:68,78; Acts 15:14, where the same verb appears). Why would God visit at this time when the people of God had endured four hundred years without a prophetic word? Did they have more to learn about Jesus? Do we?

7:17. At least they told what they knew. Throughout Judea to the south, the actions of Jesus in the north were revealed. People saw a God-sized work in the raising of the dead and told others what had happened. The fame and glory of Jesus grew.

C The Savior's Call to Faith Provides Reasons to Follow (7:18–23)

SUPPORTING IDEA: *Jesus answers John the Baptist's question about whether he is truly the Messiah.*

7:18–20. News about Jesus reached John in his prison cell (see 3:20). Even in prison John maintained loyal disciples who looked to him for spiritual leadership and kept him informed about the outside world. John sent two of these disciples to Jesus. Things had not worked out quite like John expected. Confusion about Jesus began to set in. Was this really the deliverer who came to harvest God's crop and throw away the chaff (see 3:15–17)? Or should they look to someone else to fulfill the role of the Messiah that God had revealed to John? Faithfully, John's disciples fulfilled their commission, finding Jesus and posing John's question.

7:21. No immediate answer came from Jesus' lips. Rather, he continued his ministry—healing, exorcising, and giving sight. Evidence of Messiah in action should be more compelling than personal testimony about himself.

7:22. Having acted, Jesus spoke. Picking up snippets of Scripture from Isaiah (26:19; 29:18–19; 35:5–6; 61:1), he described his ministry to John's two disciples. Three types of action typify what Jesus did—healing, raising the dead, and preaching good news. Now we are ready for the rest of John's story. How did he react? Did he accept Jesus' testimony? How does one who looks for judgment of the chaff respond to one who cures and brings good news? Luke ignores our questions. He concentrates on Jesus.

7:23. Jesus solidified his case with a beatitude, a statement of blessing on people who act in a certain way (see 6:20–22; Matt. 5:3–11). This beatitude centers on response to Jesus. He called for people not to fall away from God because of how Jesus acts. Do not let their expectations of Messiah lead them to miss God's true Messiah. He may not be what they expected and wanted—a general to lead armies against Rome, a king to rule in a new state of Israel, an end-time prophet to bring final judgment on the world and inaugurate the kingdom of God. Still, he fulfills Scripture and continues God's purpose from creation onwards, to bring good news to all people in need. Are Jesus' actions and teachings enough to convince us he is the Messiah of God? Will we look for another?

Ⅾ The Savior's Call to Faith Is One Choice among Others (7:24–35)

> **SUPPORTING IDEA:** *Jesus' call to faith in him as Messiah of God comes among many calls to follow, but too often people criticize those who call and follow no one.*

7:24–26. John asked about Jesus. The crowds were asking about John. So Jesus told them about John. He was the one they had flocked to the Judean wilderness beside the Jordan River to see and hear. Did he meet their expectations? He was not a weakling, like a reed blowing in the wind. You do not go all the way to the wilderness just to see a reed. He was not a fashionable preacher, showing off his new clothes as much as his new message. You would have to go to the royal palace for such a display. You flocked to the desert to see a prophet. Your hopes were not disappointed. You saw a prophet and much more.

7:27. What is John's "much more"? He fulfilled Scripture about the coming of the Messiah. A combination of Exodus 23:20 and Malachi 3:1 proves this (cf. Mark 1:2). John was God's **messenger**, who prepared the way for the Messiah. No wonder people flocked to see him. The question was: Did they walk in the way he prepared (see 3:9–14)? Did they repent and change their lifestyles? Did they give to others rather than greedily hoard for themselves? They had seen John. Had they heard John?

7:28. Jesus had even more to say about the prophet John. He was the greatest person ever born in the normal human way. Name your religious heroes: Abraham, Joseph, Moses, Joshua, David, Hezekiah, Josiah, Hosea, Amos, Isaiah, Jeremiah. None matched John's stature, for John faithfully prepared the last step before Messiah came. His rank among God's heroes of faith came through his role—the task to which he was called—not by his person or his human achievements. God gave him the most honored of callings—to introduce Messiah to the world. And John completed the task as God expected.

John's period of greatness had come to a halt. His role was complete. The One bringing the kingdom was here. Following John was preparing for the kingdom. Following Jesus is participating in the kingdom. Where does that leave John? In prison awaiting his final sentence. Outside present participation in the kingdom, asking questions about it. Any person who followed Jesus and thus entered the kingdom played a more significant role now than did John. They were greater kingdom members. This is not to say John stood outside the eternal kingdom, condemned with those who rejected Jesus. It simply means John was not a participant in Jesus' kingdom ministry. Rather, his ministry had succeeded wonderfully but is now past.

The present call is not to follow John. To follow John correctly is to leave John in prison and follow Jesus. Following Jesus requires the radical choice. Leave all that was dear in the past behind. Come now, and follow the Christ.

7:29–30. Praise for John divided the people. The common people had flocked to John to be baptized and wait for the Messiah. The religious leaders had ignored John and certainly had not submitted to his baptism in that dirty river. Luke tells us the ultimate meaning of these opposing responses. The people had literally "justified God," that is they had seen God's ways in John's ministry and had agreed that what God was doing was right. They saw John as the continuation of God's ways of redemption begun in creation and started in new directions through Abraham and David. John introduced still another milestone in God's path of redemption. Even the despised tax collectors saw this.

Not the religious leaders. Experts in God's law and God's word, these teachers of the nation missed out on God's purposes. They missed the big picture because they were busy finding out how to live and how to insure others knew the precise meaning of every jot and tittle of the law. They did not see God at work in their world. They rejected God, the greatest of God's religious heroes. They fought and eventually crucified God's Messiah. Experts in fine points, they missed the major point and thus faced eternal punishment. How many people are so busy becoming experts in religion and teachers of God's Word that they do not find a personal saving relationship with God and they do not discover where he is at work in his world?

7:31–34. Parables and comparisons provided the central content of Jesus' teaching style. He tried to bring every teaching down to an everyday level that people could understand. He wanted to be sure the religious leaders did not miss his point. They were spoiled kids playing a game. One group of kids gave signals for another group to act out the appropriate response. They played the flute for the wedding dance, but the second group did not dance. They sang a funeral song, but the others refused to cry. No matter which way

IV. LIFE APPLICATION

Traditions Face African Mission

Sixteen-year-old Christina surprised us all by joining our mission group that was tromping the dusty roads of western Kenya sharing our faith with anyone we could find. A few days into the mission she surprised us even more. She and her seventeen-year-old interpreter had led a Muslim man to Christ. Then they had turned to talk with another man. This man wanted to talk to them about Jesus but could not physically utter the word *Jesus*. Christina asked Stephen, her interpreter, what was going on. "He has a demon," Stephen replied. "I will have to cast it out."

So Stephen prayed for the man to be relieved of the power that refused to let him speak the name of Jesus. Suddenly, the man praised God, asked to say the sinner's prayer, and received Jesus as his Savior. Joy and awe filled Christina and Stephen's hearts. That same joy and awe soon filled twenty-nine more hearts as Christina shared with us at the dinner table that night. Our theological mind-set raised all sorts of questions. We had never seen God work that way before. He did it differently in our church in America. Anyone there who wanted to cast out a demon might be ostracized or sneered at. Our church theologians would certainly not send an untrained sixteen-year-old girl to talk to a Muslim. Yes, here we have our ways and customs. Here we know the church's tradition, both written and unwritten. We have God's ways down pat. We do not expect him to work in any other way. Nor do we really want him to.

The mission field teaches us that our Savior's call to faith comes in unexpected ways to unexpected people. He uses us in unexpected ways that force us to decide between tradition's ways and God's ways. On the mission field God forces us to see our dependence on him, our unworthiness, our need of salvation, and God's greatness in providing salvation to sinners.

V. PRAYER

God our Savior, we admit our unworthiness today. We play the religious game so well. We know all the ins and outs of what our church teaches. We know who is acceptable and who is not. We know how you have always worked to bring people into our church. We do not really expect to see a new perspective on your ways. We do not expect to learn more about your ways. We are content to be as we are. Forgive us, God. Open our hearts to the new ways that you are using to reach new people. Take away our condemning hearts and unbelieving minds. Let us hear anew your call to faith, and let us join you in new ways of acting to win all people to you, no matter their social class, their race, their place of residence, their occupation, or their reputation. Amen.

VI. DEEPER DISCOVERIES

A. Roman Centurion (7:2)

A centurion was a Roman military officer who commanded about one hundred men. We get uniformly favorable impressions of centurions mentioned in the New Testament. Centurions were usually career soldiers, and they formed the backbone of the Roman military force.

B. Jewish Elders (7:3)

From its beginnings as a nation coming out of Egypt, Israel looked to its experienced, wise men for leadership in various areas of life. They led in religious celebrations (Exod. 12:21–27; cf. 18:13) and witnessed God's saving acts (Exod. 3:16,18; 4:29; 19:7; 24:1; Num. 11:16; cf. Num. 16:25). At one time Israel had seventy elders (Exod. 24:1; Num. 11:16). Elders were apparently the leaders who occupied the special judicial office, relieving Moses of everyday duties of deciding internal disputes (Exod. 18; Deut. 1:9–18).

As Israel became an urban community, elders took over local political, judicial, and social responsibilities (Josh. 9:11; 20:4; Judg. 8:14–16; 9:2; 11:5–12; 1 Sam. 16:4; Ruth 4; 1 Sam. 30:26–31). Elders continued to function on the tribal level and on the national level as well (1 Sam. 4:3; 8:4–5; 15:30; 2 Sam. 3:17; 5:3; 9:11; 17:4,15; 19:12; 1 Kgs. 8; 12:6; 20:7–8; 21:8–11; 2 Chr. 5; 10:6). During and after the Exile, elders remained leading figures in Jewish affairs (Jer. 26:17; 29:1; Ezek. 8; Ezra 10:14).

About 200 B.C. the Sanhedrin began to function with its seventy members that was called a council of elders (cf. Luke 22:6; Acts 22:5). Gradually, the term *elder* was reserved for the aristocratic lay members and not for the priests on the council. The lay elders lost influence as the priests and scribes gained more and more control. Elders could also refer simply to agents or representatives as the related verb does (2 Cor. 5:20). In Luke 7:3 these could be Jewish messengers or agents rather than official members of the Sanhedrin, though the latter is more likely.

C. Jesus' Raising of the Son of the Widow of Nain (7:11–17)

Nain was a hillside village in southwest Galilee overlooking the Plain of Esdraelon. It was here that Jesus raised a widow's son from the dead. Of Jesus' recorded miracles, the raising of the dead dramatically showed his power over death. The Gospels record three specific instances of Jesus restoring the dead: (1) Jairus's daughter (Matt. 9:18–26; Mark 5:21–43; Luke 8:40–56),

(2) the son of the widow of Nain (Luke 7:11–15), and (3) Lazarus (John 11:1–44).

These people were restored to life, but they later died. Jesus' power over death in their lives, however, points to his own unique resurrection. He was raised as the conqueror of death, never to die again (Rom. 6:9). Someday, those who are in Christ will also be raised to receive a new, incorruptible body.

D. Funerals in Jesus' Day (7:11)

Death was an occasion for a public display of grief and emotion in New Testament times. Crying, weeping, and beating the breasts were common expressions of grief. Some people tore their outer clothes and wore sackcloth. Some mourners threw earth over their heads, rolled in the dust, or sat dejectedly among ashes. Professional mourners, usually women, were often hired to compose and sing lamentations for funeral processions. The period of mourning usually lasted for seven days.

Burial came quickly after death. The Palestinian heat caused bodies to decompose quickly, possibly creating a health risk. Coffins were generally not used, but wealthy people cut chambers in rocks for burial. In New Testament times bodies were wrapped with linen cloths, and the folds of the cloth were filled with aromatic spices (John 19:38–42).

VII. TEACHING OUTLINE

A. INTRODUCTION

1. Lead Story: Apply Without Qualifications
2. Context: In chapters 5–7 Jesus has taught and demonstrated the Savior's call to faith. Chapter 7 concludes this section with a story of the healing of a servant of a foreign officer, the raising from the dead of a widow's son, questions from and discussion about John the Baptist, and a final dinner scene issuing in discussion apparently about party manners but ultimately about the nature of Jesus to forgive and save. The opening and closing sections illustrate faith coming from unexpected sources and Jesus' gracious response to faith. The entire chapter offers a contrast between those who should believe immediately— John the Baptist and Jewish religious leaders and those who have no background for belief but believe because of what Jesus says and does. The chapter thus becomes a description of true faith and a call for such faith responses from modern readers.
3. Transition: As we study Luke 7, the sudden switch of scenes and characters may confuse us. We may wonder what theme ties these

stories together. Listen carefully to the stories. See how the Savior's call to faith ignites the action in each story. Marvel at the wondrous faith that comes forth, but mourn that so many people reject Jesus' call to faith. If Jesus came back today, which group would you be in—the all-knowing religious leaders and heroes or the uninitiated but believing outsiders? Ones who have been forgiven much or little? Ones who love much or little?

B. COMMENTARY

1. The Savior's Call for Faith Reaches Outside Israel (7:1–10)
    a. The setting: Jesus stopped on behalf of a centurion's sick servant (7:1–2)
    b. The plot: humble centurion seeks healing without personal meeting (7:3–8)
    c. The resolution: a word of healing and of amazement at unequaled faith (7:9–10)
2. The Savior's Call to Faith Reveals Divine Compassion (7:11–17)
    a. The setting: new town, old crowd (7:11)
    b. The plot: death, burial, and resuscitation of widow's son (7:12–15)
    c. The response: awe and worship from the crowd (7:16)
    d. The result: good news is spread to Judea (7:17)
3. The Savior's Call to Faith Provides Reasons to Follow (7:18–23)
    a. The setting: questions among the forerunner's party (7:18–19)
    b. The plot: Jesus' response in deed and word (7:20–22)
    c. The result: Jesus' warning not to fall away (7:23)
4. The Savior's Call to Faith Is One Choice among Others (7:24–35)
    a. The setting: Jesus' praise and positioning of John (7:24–28)
    b. The response: opposing reactions to God's ways (7:29–30)
    c. The result: Jesus' call to action and faith (7:31–34)
    d. The teaching: the proof of wisdom (7:35)
5. The Savior's Call to Faith Elicits Faith (7:36–50)
    a. The setting: Jesus accepts a Pharisee's invitation (7:36)
    b. The scene: sinful woman honors Jesus and horrifies host (7:37–39)
    c. The test of love: Jesus' parable understood by host (7:40–43a)
    d. The test passed and failed: based on love (7:43b–48)
    e. The crowd's response: can this be? (7:49)
    f. Jesus' response: faith brings forgiveness and salvation (7:50)

C. CONCLUSION: TRADITIONS FACE AFRICAN MISSION

VIII. ISSUES FOR DISCUSSION

1. Do you know a person of power whom you regard as foreign or alien? Does that person believe in Jesus? How can you issue the Savior's call to this foreigner?
2. What unique needs do widows have? How can Jesus use you to minister to widows? How can such ministry bring forth praise and reverence to God?
3. How do you understand verse 32? Do you know people who are so critical they will never believe anything or get involved in any purpose? How can you issue Jesus' call to faith to such people?
4. What would your church do if you showed Christ's love to a person with the kind of reputation the sinful woman had? How can your church be sure it ministers to the people Jesus sought out rather than just to people who are just like you socially, economically, religiously, and racially?

Luke 8

Committed to Listen, Obey, Testify

Quote

"*If* someone in our family were missing, we would pay whatever was required. At that point money would not be the concern. What we needed, we would get. Time would not be an issue either. We would spend the time necessary to complete the search. Our only focus would be find the one who was lost. . . . Only in spiritual search and rescue do we alter these expectations. We want evangelism that does not demand time and church outreach that does not cost money."

John Kramp

IN A NUTSHELL

Luke 8 shows Jesus embarking on a nomadic lifestyle while describing and illustrating the Christian lifestyle. That lifestyle is one of commitment: to listen and follow God's Word, to obey Christ over all earthly commitments, to testify of what Jesus has done for you to the people you know best, to believe Jesus can do what he promises and what you need. The chapter is a call to commitment for us. Study to see what commitments Jesus demands of you.

Committed to Listen, Obey, Testify

I. INTRODUCTION

Big Man with Big Commitments

*H*e was a big man, six foot four or more, at one time over 300 pounds, wearing size 16-D shoes laced halfway up his calves. He had a big voice. Metropolitan opera people invited him to New York to sing. He had big talents. The world's largest seminary invited him to teach. Conference centers waited for him to come and direct games and music as well as teach. The largest religious publishing house in Protestantism hired him as a worldwide consultant. But Sibley Burnet ignored all that. He lived by his favorite phrase, "A man is biggest of all when he stoops to help a child." So he relinquished his dream to sing opera in New York. He gave up his goal of seminary teaching. He limited his conferences. He devoted himself to one thing—teaching children and teaching people how to teach children. To do this, he made another commitment, a commitment to God's Word. It is still wonderful to pick up his worn-out Bible and read the notes he made in the margin of nearly every page. At his retirement, churches and church groups around the nation honored him with dinners and plaques and praise. But the happiest days of his life came when he stood before a Vacation Bible School full of children, told them how much Jesus loved them, and greeted them as they came to say they wanted to live for Jesus.

Jesus called for big commitments from all people, big and small. Luke 8 illustrates some of those big commitments and makes us ask where our commitments lie.

II. COMMENTARY

Committed to Listen, Obey, Testify

MAIN IDEA: *To follow Jesus is to make big commitments to listen, obey, testify, and believe.*

𝔸 The Commitment to Listen (8:1–18)

SUPPORTING IDEA: *To follow Jesus is to listen to what God teaches in his Word.*

8:1–3. Luke's orderly account of Jesus' ministry (1:3) does not always locate Jesus precisely. In chapter 7, he was in Capernaum (v. 1), Nain (v. 11) and in a Pharisee's house in an unnamed locality (v. 36). Now he begins a nomadic ministry through the towns and villages, presumably of Galilee, fulfilling the purpose of his ministry explained in 4:43–44: preaching the kingdom to other towns. What follows in this chapter and beyond are examples of how Jesus and his followers preached the kingdom so everyone could hear. Luke has one specific emphasis. Jesus did not select men exclusively as his followers. A central core of women also accompanied him. They did more than the feminine household tasks. They provided much of the financial support Jesus needed to lead such a squad of followers from town to town. (For further notes on women followers of Jesus in Luke's Gospel, see "Deeper Discoveries.")

Mary Magdalene (from the unidentified city of Magdala) had good reason to follow Jesus. He had exorcised demons from her, transforming her life from a person totally possessed to an individual totally pursuing committed discipleship. She would be among the first witnesses at the empty tomb (cf. Matt. 28:1,9–10; Mark 15:40,47; 16:1; Luke 24:10; John 20:11–18). Joanna appears elsewhere only in Luke 24:10 at the empty tomb. Married to a major official in Herod's government, she may have supplied much of the means for Jesus' ministry. She apparently was a person who left home for the sake of the kingdom (18:29). Mention of her husband's position also provides contrast to the response of Herod himself (9:7–8). Susanna appears only here in the Bible.

8:4–8. Crowds play an important role in Luke. Leading Jews may have rejected and crucified Jesus. Recognizing his power and the uniqueness of his teachings, the crowds flocked to him.

Jesus did not disappoint. He stirred their interest with a parable (see 4:23; 5:36; 6:39). The meaning of the parable has tested the abilities of the best Bible students. Perhaps we have tried too hard to find one central meaning rather than letting the parable open a vast new understanding of the nature of God's kingdom and Jesus' ministry. Others have so analyzed Palestinian farming techniques they have missed the simple, obvious truths of the parable. A few lines cannot hope to unravel the depth and breadth of its meaning. The story itself is a simple lesson from everyday life. Farmers sow seeds with different results. All the seeds thrown out by hand do not hit the target, nor is every seed left alone to enjoy its home in the warm soil. Much of the seed never germinates. But seed in good soil brings abundance.

The parable indicates that if we hear God's Word, believe it, and hold fast to it, we can be "good ground" in which the Word of God multiplies and bears fruit abundantly. Make sure you are "good ground."

8:9–15. Listen as they might, the disciples did not understand. At least they had the faith and trust to speak up and ask Jesus. Jesus singled them out. Only they were supposed to understand the parables. In them lay the secrets or mysteries of God's kingdom. Those who did not follow Jesus must suffer what God described as the result of Isaiah's ministry (Isa. 6:9). Hearing and seeing, people would not truly see and understand. Words and sights would never make sense to them and lead to changed lives.

So Jesus turned to the disciples to give them the inside knowledge prohibited for outsiders. His reference was far wider than a small Palestine farm. The reference was to God's redemptive work throughout his universe. The problem was seeing and hearing. God gives his Word, but people respond in different ways. Some hear, but immediately Satan robs them of the word, replacing it with his evil words. They miss the opportunity to hear and be saved. Some people hear with joy, excited at the new information and opportunity. But soon some other joy appears before the joy in God's Word can take root and grow. Tough times come, and joy alone is not enough to endure. God's Word must bring more than good feeling.

Others hear the Word but never go back to meditate on it and absorb it deep into their lives. They get caught up in the worries of daily life and the search for material success. Pleasure seeking overcomes eternal pursuits. They have no time for God's Word. They do not mature in God. Note that Jesus attended enough parties to be labeled a "party boy" by the Pharisees (7:34), and Jesus depended on women for material resources (8:3). Jesus does not call for hermits seeking refuge from life in the world. He does seek people who have a perspective on the world that puts the Word of God far above all worldly cares, interests, and activities.

Some seed hits the target. Good soil welcomes it, encourages its growth, hides it in their heart for times ahead, to persevere through testing, temptation, and the complexities of daily life. Mature disciples represent only a fraction of those who hear and initially respond to God's Word. Mature disciples represent those who listen for, meditate on, absorb, and follow God's Word along the twisting paths of life.

8:16–18. Jesus used the obvious to teach hidden truths. No one went to the trouble of filling a pottery lamp with oil, fixing the wick, and getting it to burn, only to hide the burning lamp in an opaque pottery jar and under a bed. The lighted lamp has one purpose: to light a room. The same is true with the Word of God. God does not give his Word to be hidden among a secret few or to be the cause of concern because no one can understand it. What God speaks and what God teaches, he will explain to the right people at the right time (see v. 10). So listen to God's Word in such a way that he can open it up to your understanding, not in such a way that you will find only what you look for.

Do you think you have heard the Word and grown? Be careful. If you listen faithfully to God and hear his teaching, you will receive even more. Failing to listen to him will cause you to lose even what you think you have. Hearing the Word of God brings change. You either mature or go backward in your Christian experience. Do you have ears to hear? Only one type of soil produces maturing Christians. That soil is a good heart attuned to God as he reveals the meaning of his Word to you.

These sayings, like the parables, have a depth and width of meaning beyond the present context. Luke reused each in another context (see 11:33; 12:2; 19:26). But in this context the sayings relate to how a person listens to the Word of God.

B The Commitment to Obey (8:19–21)

SUPPORTING IDEA: *To follow Jesus is to obey what God teaches in his Word.*

8:19. Wherever Jesus went, the Twelve followed him. So did the faithful women. His own family did not. They came occasionally to check on him. They found someone else following Jesus—crowds so dense you could not penetrate them in any way to get to Jesus, even if you had family credentials.

8:20–21. Someone did pass the signal. Jesus learned of his family's presence. His response shocked them and us. "Have you been listening? Blood relationship does not prove you are listening to God's Word. My sole task is to make people listen to the Word of God and live it out. These people do not qualify. I must keep teaching those who do. I follow my own teachings. I forsake family for the sake of the kingdom (18:29). I form a new family around the Word of God. Those ties are stronger than any physical ties can ever be. My relatives imitate me in obeying God." For us this is a freeing comment. Nothing in our physical birth or environment determines our relationship to God—only our response to his Word.

C The Commitment to Jesus, the Lord of Nature (8:22–25)

SUPPORTING IDEA: *To follow Jesus is to know he is Lord of nature and thus the divine source of salvation*

8:22–23. Luke omitted much of Jesus' ministry and gave precise dates and places for only a few events. His attention was on who Jesus is and what Jesus called for, not on everything Jesus did and said. Constantly ministering to the crowds, Jesus often found need for a time away. What better place than in an isolated boat, presumably on the Sea of Galilee near Capernaum? Time away can quickly turn to disaster. It did for the disciples in the form of a storm. Would they and their Messiah die in a squall on the lake? Panic set in, but not for Jesus. He slept on.

8:24. His desperate disciples awakened Jesus with the news they were drowning. He spoke not to the fearful disciples, but to the raging winds. They heard the word of Jesus and obeyed. Calm. Still. Clear skies. No rain. No danger. The God who could command the powers of the sea to swallow Jonah could also still the power of the seas to save his Son and the disciples. The God who could divide the Egyptian Sea and Jordan River to give his people freedom and land could also rebuke the storm to reveal his ultimate source of salvation.

Now a word for the disciples: "Where is your faith?" Certainly, their faith did not approach that of the centurion or the faith of the sinful woman with an alabaster jar of perfume. Were they thorny soil where the Word of God was choked out by the cares and worries of life? Or would they listen to the Word of God?

How could Jesus question the faith of men who had followed him so faithfully throughout his ministry, men who had forsaken occupations, family, and security for the nomadic, homeless life of their Master?

8:25. Fear gripped the disciples, fear of the storm, but much more a reverent fear in the face of one who feared no storms. Who could this be (see 5:21; 7:20,49; 9:9)? Messiah! King! Savior! If nature obeys him, does anyone have equal power? Who would not obey such a one? But the one who obeys is the one who listens and knows and practices the Word. Who were these men called the Twelve? Jesus' question shows who they were. They were men marveling at someone they loved—someone they could not understand completely. They were men willing to follow this man to find out what he was up to, but not having a real clue as to the ultimate end they faced.

The disciples were men seeing Jesus' marvelous power at work in new ways every day—but men not expecting what was coming. They were men of strong character but *men* nonetheless. Times of crisis saw them reverting to the emotions of common humanity, ignoring and forgetting the power of the one they followed. Jesus looked to the day when danger would no longer bring fear but expectation of divine intervention. At this point, that day had not yet come. The disciples still tried to figure out exactly who Jesus was and where he was going. They tried to confront earthly peril and danger with earthly means. They let human fears rule their lives. Only crucifixion, resurrection, ascension, and Pentecost would change that.

D The Commitment to Testify (8:26–39)

SUPPORTING IDEA: *To follow Jesus is to testify to what he has done for you.*

8:26. The boat ride continued. Destination: Gentile country among the Gerasenes or the Gadarenes or the Gergasenes, depending on which Greek manuscript one follows. The exact location is not central to our understanding. Whatever the precise place was, it was in the midst of the Decapolis, the collection of Gentile cities beside the Sea of Galilee. In this region, pigs could be raised, sold, and eaten—something unimaginable in Jewish territory.

8:27–28. Jesus' welcoming committee consisted of one man, but what a man! Totally possessed by demons, he lived in the cemetery, never bothering to wear clothes. Seeing Jesus, he fell down in the normal posture of reverence and worship. Then he shouted at Jesus, begging to be ignored. The demon inside him was talking, not the man.

8:29–31. The demon knew what he was talking about. He knew who Jesus was—Son of the Most High God. He had already heard Jesus' demand that he leave the possessed man. He knew his power over the man, a power that defied all efforts to restrain him. Jesus recognized the demon's presence and addressed him directly, asking his name. Jesus' power forced the demon to reveal his identity and thus submit to Jesus' demands. His name was really a number; a legion was a military unit of five or six thousand soldiers. A whole army of demons had invaded the possessed man. No wonder he suffered so severely and displayed such strength. Aware that Jesus knew their name and so controlled them, the demons sought to name their own punishment. Anything but the Abyss! The Abyss was the underworld, the place of the dead, but especially a place where demons and evil spirits were kept in prison. Even demons want freedom. (See "Deeper Discoveries.")

8:32–37. The viewpoint shifted to the hillside, where pigs were eating. For Gentile country this represented nothing unusual, just a standard way of making a living. For Jewish readers, this brought immediate revulsion. Pigs were unclean and despised (Lev. 11:7; Deut. 14:8). A Jew never touched a pig, much less ate one. Such a viewpoint made pigs the proper receptacle for demons. But this situation also made it the perfect platform for one of Jesus' miracles. He paid attention to what came from the heart of man, not what a person might touch outwardly. He gladly entered the world of demons and pigs, whereas the Jewish religious leaders regarded them with hate and disdain.

Continuing to determine their own punishment, the demons asked for the pigs as their new residence. Why pigs? Scripture gives no reason. Perhaps they were the only form of life visible at the moment.

Jesus let them have their way for the moment. Bad news for the pigs. Demon possession meant unrest, uneasiness, and thus movement among the pigs. Such movement roused by the demons stirred the pigs to panic. They rushed over the cliffs, into the sea, and drowned. Bad news for the pig farmers. Those "shepherding" the pigs ran off to tell the owners the bad news. It spread throughout the town. Everyone had to see what was happening—a new type of crowd for Jesus. Everyone knew the man who had been possessed. Now they saw him in a new light—clothed, settled in front of Jesus, perfectly lucid. The crowd's reaction? Fear, almost panic! Who could this be? What would happen next? Eyewitnesses explained the scene.

They reacted differently than other crowds. People who saw a healing or exorcism usually crowded Jesus with still more people to heal and help. Not the Gerasenes. They demanded that Jesus leave their region immediately. The cares of the world and the world's riches were too much with them. Their livelihood took precedence over human need. They expelled the most powerful and most caring person the world ever knew without seeking his help for any of their friends and neighbors.

8:38–39. The cured man had an entirely different attitude. He wanted to answer Jesus' call to follow. Jesus surprised him. Following for this man meant going back home and telling the fearful friends and neighbors what Jesus had done for him. The man obeyed instantly. He took the good news to a town that had expelled Jesus, telling everyone exactly what Jesus had done for him. Following Jesus on the nomadic road would have been easy compared to that assignment. The call to faith is a call to commitment to the mission Jesus defines for us, not a call to a task we want to do. Have you heard the mission Jesus has for you? Are you committed to testify where he leads you?

E The Commitment to Faith in Jesus (8:40–56)

SUPPORTING IDEA: *To follow Jesus is to believe in his power to heal and save.*

8:40–42. Jesus returned, apparently across the sea to Capernaum, to the crowds he normally faced (see vv. 4,19). These crowds were eager to see him, view his miracles, and find healing for their sick family and friends. Ironically, the first to meet him as he returned from pig and demon country was a synagogue ruler. He was responsible for arranging the synagogue for meetings and probably leading the council of elders in the synagogue. Jairus had no time to see if all was kosher. Jesus' state of purity was not a priority with him. Only one thing mattered: his dying daughter. Falling at Jesus' feet in humility, respect, and reverence, Jairus was transformed from a respected leader to a desperate beggar. He joined the widow of Nain in focusing all attention on a twelve-year-old girl, his only child. Jesus joined Jairus on the way to the sick girl. The crowds became an impediment, barring the way.

8:43–48. One woman, in particular, stopped him, without meaning to. Having bled as long as Jairus's daughter had lived, this desperate woman saw Jesus as her last hope. She demanded no attention from him, just the opportunity to touch his clothing. So she did and healing came. She was ready to slink away, but Jesus interrupted her plans. He had power to heal without consciously doing anything, but he also controlled his power, so he knew when he healed. The woman had not counted on this. Jesus asked, "Who touched me?" Then Peter laughed it off. Who could possibly know in this mob? Everybody was elbowing their way in and touching him? How could he limit it to one person? Jesus knew one person had taken special healing power from him. He wanted to talk to that one person in this big crowd.

Fearfully, the woman edged forward and admitted her action. She testified to Jesus of her need and his deed. How would Jesus react? Was he angry because someone had sneaked off with some of his power? Of course not! Jesus cared for people and wanted them to have wholeness and healing. So he bid her to go in peace, knowing her faith had healed her. Touching the Master led to a new life for her. Now she had a testimony of faith to tell how she came to know Jesus and his saving healing.

8:49–50. Time to focus on Jairus again. Before Jesus could start, a messenger from Jairus's house stopped him: "Jairus, no need to trouble the Master. Your dear daughter died." Jesus had another message for Jairus: "Have faith. She will live." Who should the Jewish leader believe, his longtime servants or this nomadic rabbi? Jairus went with Jesus.

8:51–52. Arriving at the house, Jesus motioned for the three members of his inner circle of disciples to enter with him and the parents. Already mourning rites had begun as neighbors and professional mourners put ashes on their heads and cried and wailed to God over the child's death. "Stop this," Jesus demanded. "You mourn the living. She is simply asleep." Again a moment of crisis for the parents: Believe the neighbors and friends or believe Jesus. Was their child asleep or dead?

8:53–56. The neighbors made their choice clear, laughing at Jesus. They knew a dead child when they saw one. Jesus turned to the child's place, reached out for her hand, and said, "My child, rise up." This command can be read in at least two ways: "Wake up from sleep" or "Be raised from the dead." Vital signs returned. Life appeared in the lifeless. The girl stood up. Jesus handed her to her parents and told them to feed her. This proved she was alive and well, not a spirit returned from the dead. Astonishment captured the parents. How could this be? Who can we tell? Oh, what wonderful news!

Unexpectedly, Jesus gave them their witnessing command: Do not tell. These people will see and not see, hear and not understand. They may talk about a miracle, but they will not recognize the one who performed the miracle. They are not ready to believe the Son of God is in their midst. Miracles were not the center of his ministry. They needed to see the end before they could tell about this one incident.

MAIN IDEA REVIEW: *To follow Jesus is to make big commitments to listen, obey, testify, and believe.*

III. CONCLUSION

First Things First

Roy Angel (*Shields of Brass,* 41) tells the story of a missionary woman who came home to place her three children in American schools and then prepared to return to her mission field in Africa. A well-meaning friend watching her pack commented, "I am sure you are anxious to get back to your mission field." Frowning for a moment, the missionary replied in a solemn tone: "No, I am not anxious to get back. The place to which I am going is dirty. There are no electric lights, there are no modern conveniences whatsoever. There is no pure water, and I will be cooking on my wood stove, and while I cook I will be weeping because my children are so far away. I will be desperately lonesome for them and wondering if any of them are sick. When I remember that it will be three years before I see them again, I will be tempted to tell the Lord that I cannot stand it and I am going home. No, I am not anxious to get back, but I am more anxious to do the Lord's will than to do anything else. I would be more miserable here than there."

The missionary showed the kind of commitment Jesus demonstrated in his own personal life and the commitment he demanded from those who would answer his call to faith. Jesus did not remain safely at home and wait for crowds to come. Jesus went to as many towns and villages as possible. He crossed into Gentile country with pigs and demons. He ministered to a bereaved widow and a bereaved civic leader. He ignored physical family to minister to spiritual family. He calmed fears and brought peace to his disciples and to a woman whose life had been dominated by fear, pain, and frustration.

Everywhere Jesus went, he looked for one thing: faith. Such faith brought healing. It also brought commitment—commitment to listen, obey, testify, and believe. As he sought faith that brought commitment, Jesus had one request: listen to the Word of God. How a person listens determines his or her growth and commitment. Growth and commitment determine a person's relationship to God and eternal destiny. Only those who truly listen to, hear, and obey the Word of God retain this Word in their heart, live it in their lives, and persevere through all temptations to produce a good crop.

PRINCIPLES

- Jesus' ministry depends on people sharing their resources to support his ministry.
- To follow Jesus is to listen to his Word, retain it, and persevere in producing a good crop for him and receiving more of his Word.
- To follow Jesus is to venture into unlikely places where Jesus sees opportunity for mission.
- To follow Jesus is to trust him in the storms of life.
- To follow Jesus is to care for people more than for possessions.
- To follow Jesus is to reach out to him for help when hope for human help has vanished.
- To follow Jesus is to believe in him when such belief brings laughter and scorn from friends and neighbors.
- To follow Jesus is to testify to what he has done for us so people can see who he is and have faith in him.

APPLICATIONS

- Study God's Word every day, seeking to find where and how he wants you to show your commitment to him.
- Be ready to go places that people see as insignificant but where God is at work.
- Be prepared for life's storms by building your faith in Christ that he will guide you through each storm.
- Do not guard your possessions at the price of your faith.
- Begin today telling people in your town how much God has done for you.
- Base your faith on the teaching of God's Word, not on simple expectations of miracles.

IV. LIFE APPLICATION

Committed to Overcome

Jane Merchant offers hope to all who fear they cannot commit themselves to God's work and succeed. Jane never attended school, unless children's Sunday school at the church counts. At two years of age she was confined to a wheelchair. By twelve she was bedfast with brittle bones that broke whenever she was moved. At twenty-three she became deaf. Then she developed an eye disorder that required daily treatment.

While her brothers and sisters were at school, Jane taught herself. At age five she could read. Her father often took her driving over the green, lush countryside, where Jane was all eyes. A local librarian noted Jane's incessant reading and proclaimed her "the best educated person I know." One day, Jane read in a magazine of a poetry contest. She worked and reworked poems she had been writing. Finally, she submitted them. Back came news she had won a cash prize for honorable mention. She began to write in earnest, submitting poems to any magazine she could find that published poetry: *Good House-keeping, Saturday Evening Post,* and such.

Eventually, Jane published over a thousand poems and won many national prizes. Then two books of her poetry were published. Her editors did not know this lovely nature poetry came from the pen of a young lady who was stretched out on her back in bed, unable to move for fear of breaking bones and unable to hear the beautiful sounds she poetically described. Asked why she kept on when all was against her, Jane answered, "Faith in God kept me going."

In Luke 8, Jesus sought out people with faith that would keep them going, in spite of life's difficult stresses. Storm, demon possession, disease, and death were not deterrents to people who had faith in Jesus. The natural world, the world of spirits, the world of suffering and frustration, the underworld, and even the world of death proved no match for Jesus. He still calls for such faith as we walk through the daily stresses of life. Can we listen to God's Word and obey it? Do we have faith to follow when the path seems to lead nowhere? Are we so committed to Jesus that all other commitments fade into nothing? Will we listen to his Word so intently that we grow in it? Will we believe in him when life's storms frighten us speechless? Will we obey him even if it means ignoring family, friends, and business commitments? Will we testify to him among people who drive him away in fear and desperation? Will we trust him to help when the rest of the world laughs him to scorn? Jane Merchant let nothing blur her commitment of faith. Will you follow in her footsteps?

V. PRAYER

Son of the Most High God, we commit ourselves to you and to you alone. We will listen to your word until it has a home in our hearts. We will obey you even when this means disobeying people we love and respect. We will trust you no matter how dark the storms. We will testify to what you have done in our lives even when the audience is fed up with any talk of God. We will reach out to you in faith when life is its most frustrating and hopeless.

Yes, we will believe in you when the rest of the world laughs. Accept our commitments to you, and show us where to join you in your work. Through our faithful Lord Jesus Christ. Amen.

VI. DEEPER DISCOVERIES

A. Women in Ministry (8:2–3)

Luke spotlights women in ministry for Christ. Often he shows a pair of events, one with a man and the other with a woman: Zechariah and Elizabeth, Joseph and Mary, Simeon and Anna, a man with an unclean spirit and Peter's mother-in-law (4:31–39), the centurion's servant and a widow's son (7:1–17), the sinful woman and Simon the Pharisee (7:36–50), the Twelve and the women who supported Jesus (8:1–3), the woman with a hemorrhage and Jairus (8:40–56), the crippled woman and the man with dropsy (13:10–14:6), the parable of the shepherd and that of the woman (15:3–10), the unjust judge and the persistent widow (18:1–8), the scribes who devour widows' houses and the widow who gives her all (20:47–21:4).

Women play significant roles in Luke's Gospel. Mary and Elizabeth are the heroes of the infancy narratives. The women followed Jesus just like disciples and provide his material support. Jesus commended Mary for sitting at his feet and learning like a disciple (10:38–42). Jesus cared for the dignity of the crippled woman over against the Pharisees (13:10–17), let a sinful woman touch his feet (7:38), defended a woman in argument with a Pharisee (7:44–48), uses women's work as a parabolic example (13:21), showed his sorrow over the sufferings women would be forced to endure because of him (21:23; cf. 23:27–29), had his final rites cared for by women (23:49,55–56). At the tomb women first heard the news of resurrection (24:1–12).

Thus it is significant in a world dominated by attention to men that Luke pays so much attention to women. He does not immediately change any of their roles in society, but he shows Jesus' care and concern for them and the way Jesus let them participate in his ministry. His Gospel begins and ends with focus on women and their part in the coming of Jesus and in the death and resurrection of Jesus.

B. Falling Away from Jesus (8:13–14,18)

Jesus' parables describe people who fall away from Jesus. They hear his word for a while. Then comes testing. Daily life renews devotion to worldly cares and pleasures. The person thinks he has the word, but then ignores it in the midst of daily life. In some way the word is taken away from such a person.

Is this a central example of apostasy, of losing one's salvation? If so, it goes against the rest of Scripture. Such parables represent a call to disciples to realize what discipleship is all about. Discipleship is a call to faith in Jesus—a call that leads to devotion to the Word of God above all other priorities. A person does not become a mature disciple in a few days or weeks. A mature disciple devotes a lifetime to listening to God's Word, retaining that Word in his heart, and continuing throughout life to listen to the Word so that it becomes more and more a part of life.

People who are enthusiastic for a brief period and then trail away into the world's occupations and pleasures show they have not become disciples. They did what they enjoyed, what brought them enthusiasm and good feeling until something "better" came along. Following that "something better" reveals who they have been all along. They have not been devoted to God's Word. They have not been disciples of Jesus Christ. They have been experimenters. They have been putting God to the test. They have been trying this out until "something better" comes.

Nothing "better" ever comes along for a disciple of Jesus. The disciple never looks for or expects "something better." Thus Jesus is warning us not to get too secure too quickly. Just because you had one good feeling one time or made one statement that you believed Jesus and wanted salvation, you do not have it made for life. Receiving salvation from Jesus is a life-changing experience that stays with you for a lifetime. We must be on board for the long haul. We must seek maturity in discipleship for life, not just good feelings for a brief spell.

C. Gerasenes (8:26)

The early copyists and interpreters had difficulty locating the place where this action occurred. Many manuscripts read *Gergasenes,* while several others read *Gadarenes.* This refers to three cities or regions near the Sea of Galilee.

In Mark 5:1 and Luke 8:26 textual evidence points to Gerasenes as the original reading. *Gerasenes* refers to inhabitants of the city of Gerasa (modern Jerash). Gerasa was a prosperous trading center in Transjordan halfway between the Dead Sea and the Sea of Galilee. Over twenty miles southeast of the Sea of Galilee, it appears to be too far from the sea for the story to have occurred there, unless the term is a general reference to the region surrounding the city. Otherwise, a different city of Gerasa would have to be meant.

The Gadarenes were inhabitants of the town of Gadara (modern Umm Qeis). Textual evidence points to this as the reading in Matthew 8:28. It is five miles south of the Sea of Galilee.

Gergesa appears in later manuscripts. This is usually identified as modern Kersa or Kursi. Its location near the cliffs of the Sea of Galilee fits the story best, but its textual evidence is the poorest of the three locations. This is a textual problem that plagues scholarly textual study, and no satisfactory solution is available. What is clear is that Jesus intentionally headed for

Gentile territory. What occurred there would not have happened in territory controlled by pious Jews.

D. Demon Possession (8:27)

The New Testament assumes that demonic powers are active in the world. It gives little information about their origin or nature, concentrating on their power to control people and their lack of power in the face of Jesus' power. Eight major episodes illustrate the conflict between demonic powers (also called evil or unclean spirits and angels). Satan tempted Jesus (Matt. 4:1–11; Mark 1:12–13; Luke 4:1–13). Jesus enabled a demon-possessed mute to speak (Matt. 9:32–33). To a blind and mute man Jesus gave sight and sound (Matt. 12:22–23; Luke 11:14). Jesus healed the demon-possessed daughter of a Canaanite woman (Matt. 15:22–28; Mark 7:24–30). An evil spirit was exorcised from a man in a Capernaum synagogue (Mark 1:23–27; Luke 4:31–37). Jesus sent the legion of demons away from a man among the Gerasenes (Matt. 8:28–34; Mark 5:1–20; Luke 8:26–37). Jesus healed a boy with epileptic seizures caused by a demon (Matt. 17:14–20; Mark 9:14–29; Luke 9:37–43). Jesus silenced the demons (Matt. 8:16; Mark 1:32–35; Luke 4:40–41).

Elsewhere in the New Testament Mary Magdalene had seven demons exorcised by Jesus (Luke 8:1–2), and Satan controlled Judas (John 13:27). The disciples (Luke 10:17–20) and an anonymous exorcist (Mark 9:38–40) cast out demons. The early church also faced demon-possessed people (Acts 5:15–16; 8:6–7; 16:16–18; 19:11–12; 19:13–17).

Demons made people suffer sickness, experience seizures, and act in socially unacceptable ways. Belonging to the world of spirits, demons had exceptional spiritual knowledge. They were able to recognize the divinity and role of Jesus long before the disciples were totally convinced (Mark 1:23–24; 5:7; Luke 4:40–41; 8:28). Demons could even give humans the power to fore-tell the future (Acts 16:16). They could deceive (2 Cor. 11:15), blind a person's mind (2 Cor. 4:3–4), lead away from the truth (2 Tim. 3:13; 1 John 2:26; 3:7), and tempt people into sinful pleasures and sexual activities (Eph. 5:6; Col. 2:8; 2 Thess. 2:3).

Against the church, demons use false doctrine (1 Tim. 4:1; 1 John 4:1–4) and false signs (2 Thess. 2:7–11; Rev. 16:14). An angel of Satan physically harmed Paul (2 Cor. 12:7). Church members are warned not to let Satan gain a foothold in our lives (Eph. 4:26–27) and to be aware of Satan's plots (2 Cor. 2:11). We must be ready for Satan's attacks (2 Cor. 11:3; 12:7; Eph. 6:10–12) and determined to resist him (Jas. 4:7; 1 Pet. 5:8–9).

Jesus repeatedly exercised control over demons, casting them out by his simple word rather than through elaborate rituals. In so doing he can be said to heal, cure, save, and release a person. He gave this power to the Twelve and others (Matt. 10:1,8; Mark 9:38–41; Luke 10:17–20; Acts 16:18). Such miraculous power was not automatic and was not available to those who did not pray (Mark 9:28–29).

Satan cannot win the final battle with the church or individual Christians, however, for Christ has won the decisive battle on the cross (John 12:31; Col. 2:14–15; Heb. 2:14–15).

E. Son of the Most High God (8:28)

The legion of demons knew who Jesus was. Their title for him was "Son of the Most High God." They combined several divine titles: Son of God, Son of the Most High, and the Most High God. (See "Deeper Discoveries" on 1:31–35.)

F. The Abyss (8:31)

This is the prison for evil spirits and for the dead. The Greek term appears in the Septuagint to translate Hebrew *tehom,* the deeps, in reference to the primordial ocean of creation (Gen. 1:2), the depths of the oceans (Job 28:14; Jon. 2:5), the symbol-laden Red Sea (Ps. 106:9; Isa. 51:10; 63:13), waters under the earth (Gen. 7:11; 8:2; Ps. 78:15; Prov. 3:20), and apparently the living quarters of the dead (Ps.71:20). In the era between the Old Testament and the New Testament, *abyss* came to signify the place of torment for sinners and fallen angels (1 Enoch 10:13; 18:11; Jubilees 5:6). The New Testament describes the Abyss as the prison for demons (Luke 8:31; Rev. 9:1–2; cf. 2 Pet. 2:4, where Gr. uses *Tartarus*). A person cannot escape its closed doors, but smoke rises from it (Rev. 9:1–2), and it has its own ruler (Rev. 9:11). From there comes the beast (Rev. 11:7; 17:8). There Satan is bound during the millennium (Rev. 20:1,3). In Romans 10:7–8 *abyss* (*deep,* NIV) appears in a quotation from Psalm 107 (cf. Deut. 30:12–14), describing the realm of the dead into which Christ descended.

VII. TEACHING OUTLINE

A. INTRODUCTION

1. Lead Story: Big Man with Big Commitments
2. Context: Luke 8 begins the nomadic phase of Christ's ministry as he entered the towns and villages and ventured forth beyond Israel. In so doing he found unexpected examples of great faith and called his followers to great commitments. At the same time he called people to understand who he is. Thus Jesus interacted with his own followers, with sick, demon-possessed, dead, and dying as he called them to

commitment and demonstrated the nature of faith and the nature of Messiah.

3. Transition: We live in a too-often-closed environment of faith. Most of our activities outside office hours are shared with church members, often in church settings. Talking about faith and the work of the church is normal and even habitual. The question is, Do we understand the true nature of faith, of being a follower of Jesus, and of committing ourselves to the Messiah? Luke 8 calls on us to reexamine our commitments, to find the depth of our faith, and to consider anew who Jesus is and what he is calling us to be and do.

B. COMMENTARY

1. The Commitment to Listen (8:1–18)
   a. The setting: Jesus' preaching tour amid large crowds (8:1–4)
   b. The Master's teaching: listen to the Word (8:5–8)
   c. The Master's explanation: failure and success in listening (8:9–15)
   d. The Master's summary: the listening rule (8:16–18)
2. The Commitment to Obey (8:19–21)
   a. The setting: a family visit (8:19–20)
   b. The Master's summary: to be family is to obey (8:21)
3. The Commitment to Jesus, the Lord of Nature (8:22–25)
   a. The setting: natural disaster during Jesus' lake tour (8:22–23)
   b. The action: stilling the storm (8:24)
   c. The questions: where is faith? who is this? (8:25)
4. The Commitment to Testify (8:26–39)
   a. Meeting the demon-possessed on alien ground (8:26–27)
   b. The plot: determining the demons' punishment (8:28–32)
   c. The result: drowned pigs, fearful owners, expelled Jesus (8:33–37)
   d. The mission: testify to all that is done for you (8:38–39)
5. The Commitment to Faith in Jesus (8:40–56)
   a. The setting: amid welcoming crowd, Jewish leader pleas for healing (8:40–42)
   b. Sandwiched scene: bleeding woman secretly healed (8:43–48)
   c. The Master's response: who touched Me? I felt the power (8:44–46)
   d. The result: trembling confession brings faith and forgiveness (8:47–48)
   e. Main scene revisited (8:49–56)

C. CONCLUSION: COMMITTED TO OVERCOME

VIII. ISSUES FOR DISCUSSION

1. How did Jesus pay for his food, clothing, and other material needs? Does this have anything to say about how the church should support its ministers? Its impoverished? Its sick?
2. In what way were the mysteries or secrets of the kingdom given to the disciples if they did not understand what Jesus was teaching?
3. How many of the groups of people whom Jesus described in his parable of the soils were actually saved?
4. What priority does Jesus place on listening to him? Why?
5. Are you part of Jesus' family? How do you know?
6. Why would people ask a miracle-working teacher to leave their territory? Do you or your church in any way ever ask Jesus to leave you alone for a while?
7. How many times is faith spoken of in this chapter? What does it mean here and in the ministry of Jesus?
8. What does it mean that Jesus has power over death?

Luke 9

Committed to the Cross

Quote

"*Choosing to suffer means that there must be something wrong with you, but choosing God's will—even it if means you will suffer—is something very different. No normal, healthy saint ever chooses suffering; he simply chooses God's will, just as Jesus did, whether it means suffering or not.*"

Oswald Chambers

Luke 9

IN A NUTSHELL

Luke 9 continues Christ's call to commitment. Christ calls his disciples to committed action and demands more than simply a confession of faith. Christ's kind of commitment is the commitment he lived—commitment that leads to the cross. Such commitment centers on Christ in all his glory, but such commitment is based on humble faith in God, not on inherent miraculous powers. Such faith aims to be the least, not the greatest. Such faith sticks close to Jesus despite family crisis, racial prejudice, or employment pressures.

Committed to the Cross

I. INTRODUCTION

How Easy to Believe

A brief slight of Stalin sent Aleksandr Solzhenitsyn to prison for eight years. His prison life was worse than anything we can imagine. In an Arctic wasteland he labored as a mason from dawn until dark. This world-famous author had no pen, no paper, and no permission to write. He had no family to visit, since his parents were dead and his wife divorced him.

Surely such unjustified suffering would drive this gifted, sensitive man to insanity. Instead, it led him to self-analysis. He looked at his own vanity, superficiality, and selfishness. Asked to describe his time in prison, he blessed the prison for having become part of his life. Shortly before leaving prison, he penned a famous prayer later to be published in *Vogue*. He praised God and confessed how simple it was to live for him and how easy to believe in him (Redding, *A Rose Will Grow Anywhere*, 67–69).

How could a man with such social consciousness and such awareness of the injustice of life in his country be so simple in his analysis of life in prison? Such a response to his situation came only because he was committed to his God, no matter what. In Luke chapter 9 we find Jesus calling and illustrating such committed faith while the disciples struggle to understand what Jesus meant and to discover how to live life that way. Your study of this chapter will challenge you to examine your own commitment and how it measures up beside Christ's demands for a commitment that leads to the cross.

II. COMMENTARY

Committed to the Cross

> **MAIN IDEA:** Commitment to Jesus Christ leads us far beyond a simple statement of belief in Jesus as Savior to a life that astounds normal humans and to actions that glorify Jesus and lead us to the lowest place.

A Commitment in Actions: Power for Followers (9:1–6)

> **SUPPORTING IDEA:** Christ has committed his kingdom work to his disciples, whom he expects to carry on the ministry he started.

9:1–2. Again Luke gives no details about the time or place of this significant event in Jesus' ministry. One day Jesus called the twelve disciples and sent them on the most important part of their ministry training. (Note the continuation of such training and commissioning in 10:1–11; 22:35–38; 24:48–49; Acts 1:6–8.) They had seen him at work ministering to people. Now it was their turn. Just as he had come preaching the kingdom of God (see 4:43; cf. 6:20; 7:28; 8:1,10), so they would go preaching the same message. As he had so often healed the sick (see 4:18–19,38–40; 5:12–13,15,17–25; 6:6–10,19; 7:1–10; 8:43–55), so would they; and as he had cast out demons and evil spirits (4:41; 7:21; 8:2,27–36), they would also.

What a task they faced! They knew the response that Jesus' preaching and healing had received, bringing curious crowds and indignant religious leaders. Could they expect any different treatment? And how could they heal and exorcise? They were simple lay people with no formal training. Simple yes, but without training? Oh, no. They had been with the Rabbi, with Jesus the Master Teacher and Healer. And now he gave them the same authority he had to carry out his mission to points he would never reach.

9:3. They went as he did—without material provisions (see 8:3; 9:58). As they trusted God for authority and power to heal and exorcise, so they must trust him for daily strength and provisions. As the kingdom of God belonged to the poor (6:20), so they must display their own poverty.

9:4. Each town offered different circumstances. Again they were to accept what they got, not searching around for the best house or the kindest, most generous host. The first place they found to stay in a town was to be their residence until they left.

9:5. Rejection awaited the disciples—the same kind of rejection Jesus experienced. Entire villages would refuse to accept the visiting disciples. Jesus made provision for this, too. The disciples were not to see or feel this as personal rejection or as personal failure. They were to see people rejecting God's kingdom. When this happened, they were to symbolize God's rejection of the village. Shaking the dust off their feet showed that they separated themselves entirely from every particle that had to do with the village.

9:6. What Jesus said, the disciples did. Healing undoubtedly included casting out demons as well. Here is the mission God's people are to follow from Christ's first earthly appearance until his last. Christ's followers hit the highway with the good news of the kingdom. They invite people to accept the good news and become part of the kingdom. Christ's disciples are interested in far more than simple evangelistic success. They are concerned for the people who are lost. They show such concern in a concrete manner, curing physical illnesses. Such curing powers show the world the power of God to heal the physically sick and the spiritually destitute.

B Commitment Withheld: A Perplexed Authority (9:7–9)

> **SUPPORTING IDEA:** *Commitment does not mean finding answers to personal questions for personal advancement.*

9:7–8. Herod is example number one of a person who rejected Jesus. His intelligence system kept him advised of everything going on in his kingdom and beyond—even the rumors and interpretations. John the Baptist had been the most powerful person many of these people knew. Many remained his disciples. When they heard and saw the power that Jesus and his disciples exercised, they concluded: John is back. If not John, then one of the great prophets of old such as Elijah (see 1 Kgs. 17–2 Kgs. 2). Had not Malachi promised Elijah would return before Messiah (Mal. 4:5)?

News of Jesus' mission brought fear and perplexity to those who rejected him. Herod thought he had adequately protected his throne by doing away with John the Baptist. Only here does Luke inform us of John's death (see Matt. 14:1–12; Mark 6:14–29; cf. Luke 3:19–20; 7:18–23). Now a greater power than John was at work.

9:9. Knowing this could not be the dead John, Herod pondered: Who is this? He wanted to see Jesus to get firsthand testimony, but we know what happens to the heads of those whom Herod interrogates. People with no commitment to Jesus often gain no access to Jesus. Even the king of the Jews could not command an interview with Jesus. Who can this Jesus be? How have you answered Herod's question? This is the most important answer you will ever give in your life.

C Commitment to Human Need: Pride or Practice? (9:10–17)

> **SUPPORTING IDEA:** *Power in mission must be accompanied by care for human need.*

9:10. Excited with success, the disciples reported to Jesus. Luke reports no reply from Jesus, just action. He took them on the next step in their training mission to a city called Bethsaida. This was apparently the hometown of Philip, Andrew, and Peter (John 1:44; 12:21). Herod Philip devoted attention to building up this city and named it as his burial place. It was located on the northern end of the Sea of Galilee five miles east of Capernaum about an eighth of a mile from the Jordan River. There Jesus performed his healing of the blind man (Mark 8:22–26). Only Luke among the Gospel writers places the feeding of the five thousand at Bethsaida (see Matt. 15:32–39; Mark 6:32–44). Jesus lamented over Bethsaida's refusal to repent (Matt. 11:21;

Luke 10:13). Going to Bethsaida was intended as a withdrawal, a time for private prayer with God and private instructions for the disciples. The crowds would have none of that.

9:11. Though they interrupted his privacy, Jesus turned to the crowds and followed his general pattern of ministry among them, teaching about the kingdom of God and healing the sick.

9:12. The Twelve had not yet comprehended what Jesus was about. Jesus saw the needs of the crowd, had compassion, and met the need. In contrast, the disciples saw the need and wanted to send them away so the crowd could provide for themselves. The phrase, **remote place**, shows they were not actually in the city but in the region for which Bethsaida served as the chief commercial center.

9:13. Jesus put the burden of ministry back on the disciples' shoulders. These men had just returned from working miracles, casting out demons, and preaching under the power and authority of Jesus. Now they claimed they had no power to minister to a crowd that needed food. Their only solution lay in a commercial venture—buying food for the multitude, something beyond their financial means. Jesus wanted them to find something other than the world's way to meet needs. He wanted them to call on the power they had depended on during their mission tour. Instead, they complained, "We cannot do such an impossible task." Luke continually shows the wavering quality of the disciples' faith.

9:14–15. The disciples' bewilderment is easily understood. Feeding five thousand people—or even more if only men are literally intended here—represented a tremendous undertaking. The disciples having failed, Jesus took over. First, he acted as an administrator by organizing the throng into manageable groups of fifty. Then he had them sit down, ready to eat and out of one another's way.

9:16. Taking the resources the disciples claimed to be the only ones available, Jesus dedicated them in prayer to the Father. He sent the disciples to distribute them among the multitude. In breaking and blessing bread, Jesus followed the customs of Jewish families at mealtime. He also did what he would later commission the church to do as they celebrate the Lord's Supper. As the church reads and studies this narrative, it cannot help but remember the Lord's death, his broken body, until he comes again.

9:17. Five individual loaves of bread and two fish provided the entire meal for more than five thousand people. What Jesus provided was not meager subsistence. What he gave filled them, totally meeting their needs. Twelve baskets of leftovers remained. Could this mean one basket for each of the disciples? Or one for each of Israel's tribes so that whoever came could be sure of being satisfied. John would say that Jesus continues to be the Bread of Life for all people, no matter their number or their need. He continues to commission his disciples to meet these needs. But contemporary disciples, like the original twelve, may be too busy celebrating past works for the Lord and neglect to ask for power to accomplish present work. They may be so proud of what they have accomplished for God that they fail to see that more must be done. But when the hungry are filled, can the kingdom be far away?

Ⓓ Commitment Described: Self-Denial to the Cross (9:18–27)

SUPPORTING IDEA: *Commitment to Jesus has no shades or degrees, for such commitment has only one symbol—the criminal's cross used by the Roman government for capital punishment.*

9:18–19. Finally, a moment of privacy for prayer (see 3:21; 5:16; 6:12; 11:1; 22:40–41,44,46; 23:46) and teaching. Jesus taught by asking questions. "What is the crowd's opinion concerning me?" Several ideas were floating around! "John the Baptist has come back to life. Or Elijah? Or another prophet?" All those named shared one thing in common: they were dead. Jewish people had no problem thinking of God bringing a hero of old back to life to carry out his plans and directions. This time the Jewish people did not aim high enough with their search for understanding of Jesus. Yes, he was a prophet, but so much more. John was the returning Elijah figure (Mal. 4:5). He pointed to one far greater than himself, but how do you describe this far greater one? The crowds had seen the miracles and the feedings, but they had not understood the mystery of the kingdom—the identity of the one in whom the kingdom was present.

9:20. Jesus wanted more than the crowd's response. That was only a background introduction to the real issue. "Who do you say I am?" The crowds had not understood. Had the disciples? As usual, Peter beat all the other disciples to the draw in answering. While they sat stunned or thoughtful, he spoke: "You are God's Messiah" (*Christ* being the Gr. translation of Heb. *Messiah*, "anointed one"). What a great insight! Jesus was the one the Hebrew Bible kept pointing to. He was the one for whom all Israel hoped. He was the source of deliverance from all that opposed God's people, even the Roman government. Peter waited for Jesus' affirmation. Something else came and surprised him.

9:21. Jesus warned the disciples not to tell this to anyone. He used strong language of rebuke previously used for demonic spirits (4:35,41), fevers (4:39), and the natural forces (8:24; see later uses in 8:42,55; 17:3; 18:15,39; 19:39; 23:40). He added language of warning and command (see 5:14; 8:29,56). How could this be? "We have discovered God's Messiah, Israel's hope, the source of deliverance and salvation, and we are not to say a word about it!" They did not understand.

9:22. Jesus had a simple but horrifying answer. Messiah in your mind is not what Messiah is in my mind or in God's mind. You look for deliverance, salvation, military victory, and national domination. You look to Messiah to lead you to war. But he is Prince of Peace. He has methods radically distinct from those of the world. He will not become messianic king of the world through war and fighting. He has another way, God's way, the way of suffering. Yes, he will stand against leadership, both Jewish and Roman, but they will win the first battle. Indeed, they will seem to have won the final battle, or they will kill him. Did you hear the last part? But on the third day he will be raised. Ready for that? First, you endure his suffering. And something else!

9:23. Many of you have followed me from place to place waiting for healing and miracles, Jesus continued. You are seeking the wrong thing. Yes, I provide healing and miracles to those in need. Those are signs of God's power as he brings his kingdom to earth through me. But that is not where this earthly ministry leads. The final road you travel as you follow me leads to a criminal's cross. Not a gold cross on a chain that enhances the beauty of the wearer. Not a piece of art in a museum that enhances the reputation of the artist or brings awe to a young art student. Not a massive cross atop a cathedral that marks off a holy place. No! This cross is among the world's cruelest instruments of torture. You cannot wear this cross. You must bear it. You bear it to the government's place of capital punishment. It becomes for you the gas chamber, the electric chair, the lethal injection all rolled into one.

What does all this mean for us today? Self-denial. Quit looking for miracles and healing. Quit centering your attention on things that enhance and please you. Focus on Christ. Let him create a daily relationship with you. Find out what he wants you to do every day. Do it! Do not expect to win popularity contests, fame, fortune, or success. Be ready to suffer the rejection, pain, and death he suffered. His lifestyle leads to that. Only as you lead this lifestyle can you learn who the Messiah really is. Only this lifestyle leads to eternal life in heaven. Take up your cross and follow him to the death. Then you will find he is the life.

9:24–26. Looks deceive. The soldier who hears the command to march and then retreats is the one shot by the enemy—not the one who advances against the enemy. You do everything you can for self-protection and advancement. You may even become CEO or president or whatever goal you set out to achieve in life. Then comes the end. You look back. All is for naught! None of this has brought meaning for the present or hope for the future. Then you look at the person you laughed at and scorned, the person who accumulated nothing in this world, no money, no position, no prestige, no honors. Suddenly, you discover this person has meaning and hope that you only dream of. Why? He was willing to lose life, to let loose of life. Life itself and the accomplishments life could bring did not comprise his goals or dreams. Pleasing Jesus is all that mattered. And pleasing Jesus brought meaning here and hope beyond.

Yes, the world works for profit, gain. The person of the world may amass great profits and wealth. If in so doing he loses meaning, purpose, and hope in life, what is accomplished? He has lost self in return for wealth. Is that a fair trade-off?

Jesus finally applied the clincher. This world is not the focus. The final judgment is the focus. The world's judgment does not matter. The local newspaper's epitaph is not the final word on your life. The final word comes from the Son of Man returning to judge the world, revealing his glory and the glory of all heaven's inhabitants. If you spend your time in this world trying to hide the fact that you really believed some things Jesus said, then Jesus will hide all the glory from you. Is that the price you are willing to pay? Worldly glory? Heavenly glory? Which matters most to you—the world's ways or God's ways? Which are you following—the world's wealth or Christ's reward? Which will you receive?

9:27. Jesus shocked his disciples and everyone else who heard this statement. He also shocks us with it. Two thousand years later, we have not seen the kingdom of God. Or have we? The disciples expected the kingdom to bring victory and political domination. We expect the kingdom to bring final judgment and reward. Jesus showed his disciples a preview of the kingdom glory in his transfiguration, which will follow immediately. He let them see the kingdom at its beginning point, not at its climax. This kingdom came when he was exalted on the cross, when he was glorified in the resurrection, and when he was enthroned in the ascension. This kingdom came when Pentecost brought previously unknown kingdom power to bear on earth and reaped an unprecedented harvest into kingdom membership.

Peter's confession of Messiah did not bring the kingdom. The disciple's successful preaching and healing mission did not bring the kingdom. Only the suffering, death, and resurrection of the Son of Man brought the kingdom into view so people could see its power and glory—a power and glory that will be even further magnified when the Son of Man comes in the glory of the Father and his angels to judge the earth. Who sees that kingdom and participates in it? Those who follow the Son of Man on the path to the cross.

Ⓔ Commitment's Center: The Chosen Son (9:28–36)

SUPPORTING IDEA: *Commitment to Christ is commitment to the chosen Son of God and his mission, not to a memorial where people can glory in what they have experienced.*

9:28. Luke places the transfiguration about eight days after the confession of Peter, a somewhat unusual precision for Luke. Matthew and Mark refer to six days. Both are ways of saying "a week later." There may be differences in Jewish and Greek calendars at work or different ways of relating Jesus' transfiguration to Moses' ascension of the mountain to see God in Exodus 24 after God's glory rested on Mount Sinai for six days. Luke knows his reckoning is approximate.

Jesus took his three closest followers (see Mark 5:37; 13:3; 14:33; Luke 8:51) with him up a mountain (cf. Exod. 24:9). Identifying the mountain is impossible, since the text gives no clues. Tradition links it with Mount Tabor, but this is uncertain. As he often did (see 9:18), Jesus turned aside to pray. He taught prayer by example.

9:29–32. In communion with God, Jesus suddenly took on an otherworldly appearance. Divine glory shone through the earthly Son of Man. Jesus' uniqueness is further underlined by his companions—the great lawgiver and deliverer Moses and the great prophet and sign of end times Elijah (see Mal. 4:5). Those hailed by the Jews as the originator of their nation and as the one who would return to usher in the end time joined Jesus on the mountain. As Moses introduced Israel to God on the mountain (Exod. 19; 24) and as Elijah showed the uniqueness of God over all other gods on the mountain (1 Kgs. 18), so Jesus revealed the true nature of God and showed that he was one with the Father. Together the three discussed a new exodus, the Greek text using the term "exodus" or "going out" to refer to Christ's death. Thus Jesus received new assurance that his journey to Jerusalem was part of God's plan for his life.

The disciples almost missed the greatest moment of revelation in Jesus' earthly ministry prior to the cross. They slept while Moses and Elijah came. Eventually, they awoke and saw clearly that Jesus belonged in the company of the two great heroes of Judaism. They saw his glory. Jesus had said he would return in glory (9:26). Later he would enter his glory after his suffering on the cross (24:26). This is glory that belongs to the heavenly realm, to the Father and his angels (9:26). Thus the three disciples got a preview of the reigning King and Judge before he fully entered his glory. This confirmed for them Jesus' divine nature.

9:33. Can such a moment just appear and disappear, come and go? Peter thought not. We must continue the moment. How better to do so than to build places of worship? Like Moses built the tabernacle in the wilderness, so Peter wanted to build a tabernacle for each of the three heroes of the faith on the mountain, providing an eternal memorial to these men and to this moment. But as Moses received no burial monument, so Jesus and his colleagues received no transfiguration memorial. Commitment to Jesus is not commitment to a sacred place with its sacred memories. Commitment to Jesus is commitment to a mission that never lets a follower remain in one place. Luke notes that Peter made the suggestion but really did not understand its full import. Building tabernacles is not kingdom business. Following Jesus to the cross is.

9:34. Suddenly a cloud enveloped the mountain where Jesus and the three disciples stood. A cloud had led Israel away from the holy mountain and into and through the wilderness. Now a cloud led the disciples away from the Mount of Transfiguration and to Mount Calvary. The cloud assured God's people of his presence while preventing them at the same time from seeing his full face and glory. The cloud enclosed the disciples so they could no longer see the glory but could be reassured that God was present among them.

9:35. In the Exodus narrative (Exod. 18–24), God spoke from a cloud to reveal his nature and his will. The transfiguration ends as the disciples hear the divine voice from the cloud. The Gospel poses the question, "Who is Jesus?" Taking up Old Testament language (Ps. 2:7; Isa. 42:1; cf. Luke 3:22), God answers the question. Jesus is the Son of God, chosen by God to complete his plan of redemption and salvation. He completes that plan by being the suffering servant (cf. Isa. 53). God's people must listen to him. There is no need to build tabernacles and hope Moses and Elijah will return. Their day has passed. Their voices are drowned out by the voice of Jesus, the chosen Son. Commitment to God means listening to his Son.

9:36. Silence followed the divine proclamation. Moses and Elijah had left at some point. The disciples also left the mountain, not telling anyone of the experience until the cross and the resurrection validated it. Visions and holy moments in God's glorious presence are not the essence of religion. Walking to the cross after Jesus is. He wants to teach you this. Listen to him.

F Commitment's Characteristics: Suffering and Serving (9:37–50)

> **SUPPORTING IDEA:** *Commitment to Christ is not commitment to worldly greatness but to suffering with Christ and serving the most insignificant people among the world's population.*

9:37. Life cannot be lived on the mountaintop. The most sublime experience with God must end. You must face life again in the valley. There the crowds come clamoring for action.

9:38–40. One voice rose above the crowd—a father begging for help for his only child, a victim of epileptic seizures. Not just epilepsy, though. Demon-caused epilepsy. Personhood-destroying epilepsy. Epilepsy from demons so strong and powerful that it withstood all efforts of the Twelve even after their successful preaching, healing, and exorcising mission tour. Neither Peter's confession nor the trio's transfiguration experience enabled the disciples to cure this one. Why not?

9:41. Jesus had the answer. This entire generation, including the disciples, were unbelieving and rebellious—twisted, perverted, crooked. They had become a burden that Jesus had to endure. His endurance would not last forever; he was headed to the cross and then into his glory. Even in his frustration with his disciples, Jesus did not lose his compassion for those who needed him. He called for the son.

9:42. In one last show of power for the demon, he knocked the son to the ground and threw him into convulsions. Jesus took charge, commanding the demon to depart. Then he took the boy, now in control of his life, and gave him back to his father.

9:43. The crowds and the disciples stood amazed. They might be unbelieving and rebellious, but they knew the power of God at work when they saw it. This was a God-sized work that no one else could do. Followers of the goddess Artemis, with her greatness and magnificence, would be destroyed (Acts 19:27). Peter testified to the greatness of Christ, his majesty (2 Pet. 1:16). These are the only other places in the New Testament where the Greek word for *greatness* occurs. Jesus' greatness or majesty in healing brought amazement to the people. He had unique power no one else had. He had God-given power.

9:44. Jesus had something more amazing for them. Such great power would be harnessed. Mere human hands would capture the Son of Man. How? By human trickery and betrayal. Do not commit yourself to Jesus just because he has amazing, magnificent power. Commit yourself to the Son of Man/Son of God about to be betrayed and crucified. Do not grasp for greatness. Grasp for a cross so you can follow Jesus to Calvary.

9:45. From the top of the world over their mission success, the disciples fell to the bottom. From the mountaintop experience of the transfiguration, they fell to the valley of despair. Those to whom the mysteries of the kingdom of God were revealed found something hidden from them. After long months spending every hour of every day with Jesus, they still did not trust him enough to express their fears to him.

9:46. So they argued. Having seen the greatness of God, they wanted to experience the greatness of men. Who was the greatest among the disciples? Each had a candidate. Himself! All forgot that to be great means to be the least. To be great was to serve with deepest humility.

9:47–48. Their fear to tell served no purpose. Jesus knew without hearing. He knew their inner thoughts. This power of deity he did not surrender in the incarnation. Unable to get through to the disciples in words, Jesus tried a symbolic act. He placed a child among them. Then came the lesson. This simple, unassuming child held the key to the kingdom. Practice hospitality toward the child for Jesus' sake. What would happen? In welcoming and ministering to the child, you welcome and minister to Jesus. Not only that, you welcome the one who sent Jesus as his chosen Son. Yes, by helping a child, you will encounter God. Then you can begin to talk about taking up a cross.

9:49. Interruption. Continue the lesson on greatness later. Urgent matter. "We saw someone who does not belong to our group. He was using Jesus' name to cast out demons. What shall we do with the heretic? You know what we did. We went right up and tried to stop him, but we could not." What a frustrating night for the disciples. They had lost all their powers. And outsiders seemed to have those powers. What were they to do?

9:50. Jesus had the answer. "Leave them alone. If they are carrying out our mission in our name and not doing anything to oppose us, then they are part of us, too. They just belong to that other flock that we have never met." Yes, Jesus is the greatest. He does God-sized work. He calls you to greatness in another way. You do child-sized work. Then you will be called great. But do not try to exclude others from the same greatness. Greatness is not a race with winners and losers. It is not a fight where one person stands above all others. Greatness is open to all of us, if we will humble ourselves in service.

G The Savior's Commitment in Action (9:51–56)

> **SUPPORTING IDEA:** *Jesus demanded commitment to his mission from his followers and he demonstrated that commitment to them through his own dedication to his destiny, providing salvation for all on the cross.*

9:51. Here the center of Luke's Gospel begins—Jesus' exodus from this world. The road to Jerusalem and Calvary dominates everything Luke wants to say and teach. Jesus, having shown his openness to all people who would commit themselves to his work, now turned to Jerusalem to complete his work through the predicted betrayal, death, and resurrection. Luke notes that his ultimate destiny is to be taken to heaven (see Acts 1:2,11,22; 2:1), but Christ's road to heaven led through Golgotha, Calvary, and the open tomb.

9:52–53. Crowds did not gather for Jesus everywhere. Racial prejudice met him in Samaria. They refused hospitality to anyone who was headed for Jerusalem. Josephus even tells us of an incident later in the first century when Samaritans massacred Jewish pilgrims, causing such unrest that the Romans removed Herod Antipas from office.

Just as people of Nazareth expressed prejudice against the hometown boy when Jesus opened his ministry (4:16–30), so the Samaritans expressed opposition as Jesus closed his public ministry and turned to Jerusalem. The disciples must learn from the Master that commitment to the mission brings rejection from some people.

9:54. Prejudice and revenge grabbed the disciples. "We will do unto them as they did unto us. Let us show how much power we have. Jesus, remember Elijah called fire down from heaven on the army units of the king of Samaria (2 Kgs. 1). We just saw you with Elijah on the Mount of Transfiguration. Show us you have as much power as he had."

9:55–56. The Son of Man had not yet come in judgment. It was not time for such radical action. The disciples had not yet learned how to concentrate on the mission of preaching the kingdom and healing the sick. They had not learned to depend on God to empower their mission. They had not learned to love all people as Jesus did. So Jesus rebuked the judgmental disciples (cf. 18:15), just as he had rebuked demons and cast them out (4:35,41; 9:42), just as he had rebuked fevers and caused them to leave the sick (4:39), just as he had rebuked natural forces and brought the wind to a standstill (8:24). With the same language he had admonished the disciples not to tell anyone that he was the Christ (9:21). (For other Lukan uses of the Gr. word *epitimao,* "rebuke," see 17:3; 18:15,39; and the thieves on the cross in 23:40.)

Jesus had told the disciples before they went on mission that some villages would reject them. He told them to kick the dust off their feet and go on. He followed his own instructions, moving on to the next village on the way to Jerusalem and Calvary.

⊞Dedication Means No Looking Back (9:57–62)

> **SUPPORTING IDEA:** *Commitment and dedication to Jesus and his mission leave no room for other commitments or for thinking about what might have been.*

9:57. Commitment in words often appears to be just what Jesus ordered. Any commitment in words calls for further examination. Have you counted the cost? Do you realize what you are setting yourself up for? Are you ready to cut past ties and depend absolutely on the commitment to God in the future? What do you really mean when you say I will follow you wherever you go? Are you following to see miracles, be where the action is, and gain God's blessings? Or are you following because you are devoted to the mission and ready to take up the cross?

9:58. Jesus knew the cost. He did not have a resting place as secure as the fox's den or the bird's nest. He owned nothing and had no assurance of a place to sleep. Is that what you are ready to commit yourself to—Jesus' dedication to the Father's mission? Is it your dedication to preaching the kingdom and healing the sick?

9:59–60. In verse 57 a man declared his commitment to Christ, and Jesus told him what this commitment meant. Here Jesus initiated the action, inviting the man to follow as he had invited his original disciples (see 5:27). This man hesitated. He had parents who were dependent on him. He would follow after they died, and he could bury them. He would commit the uncertain future but not the present concrete moment.

Jesus' answer shocked the man. You are not responsible for the dead, but for the living. People with no commitment to me—people dead spiritually—can bury those who die physically. Leave the burying task to them. Commitment to me takes precedence over all commitments that earthly traditions would place on you. Yes, caring for parents in their final days is important. But you are not the only one who can do that. You are the only one who can answer the call Jesus gives you. When he calls, you must answer here and now and follow immediately wherever he leads even when it means leaving very dear and important tasks and people behind. The kingdom of God is more important even than family obligations. Come! Follow! Now!

9:61–62. Another man declared, "I will not be long. I am not looking as far into the future as that man was. I just want to run home a minute, let Mom and Dad know where I am going, and then I will come follow you."

Again, Jesus' answer shocks. The job is now. The harvest is ripe. Do not start to work and then find something else with more importance, even if for a minute. The call to follow is a call to follow without excuse, without delay. Come. Follow. Now. Once you answer the call, you have a permanent job. No looking back.

MAIN IDEA REVIEW: *Commitment to Jesus Christ leads us far beyond a simple statement of belief in Jesus as Savior to a life that astounds normal humans and to actions that glorify Jesus and lead us to the lowest place.*

III. CONCLUSION

Hearing God's Call Elsewhere

The most intelligent student I ever taught—Jim—also comes to mind as the example of commitment. The first paper he ever submitted to an Old Testament class should have been published in a professional journal. It demonstrated methods and conclusions no one else had ever seen as far as I could tell. Studying in Europe, Jim could finish studies there, continue on for a doctorate, and find an influential position in a seminary back in the United States. None of this was for Jim. He had heard God's call elsewhere!

Having married a beautiful girl from Yugoslavia and having joined her in ministering to churches there, Jim was more interested in his people in Yugoslavia. He was writing textbooks so seminary students there could study in their own languages and learn to pastor churches there, some of which had never had a full-time pastor. Graduating from seminary, Jim remained true to his call. He took no time to look back and to see if another road looked more promising. He refused to listen to advice from well-meaning friends who saw a brighter future for him. No, Jim had heard Jesus' call: Follow me to Yugoslavia. So he went to Yugoslavia, preached, pastored, taught, and wrote. Sadly, a winding Yugoslavian road proved too much for his driving abilities, and he died in an auto accident.

Jesus gave his disciples a mission of their own. They came back rejoicing at how God's power had worked through them to heal and help. Meanwhile, in high places, Herod wondered who Jesus was. Jesus taught and fed the hungry crowds, showing the disciples that mission was not a one-time affair but an ongoing work, depending on God's power and presence. Testing time came to see how far the disciples had advanced in understanding who Jesus was. They had identified him as the God-sent Messiah. Jesus had to take them another step.

They had to see that Messiah meant something different from their political dreams. Messiah would face betrayal, death, and resurrection. Disciples must follow with their cross to Calvary. This forced decision on them. Did they believe that Jesus' mission was worth more than life itself? Did they want to sit on thrones in this world or see the kingdom of God? Jesus helped them make the decision by letting three disciples see him transfigured into heavenly glory along with the two major heroes of Israel's faith: Moses the law-giver and the prophet Elijah, who preceded end time. They heard God's voice saying, "This is my chosen Son."

Still, knowing their accomplishments in mission and knowing Jesus was Messiah, they could not cast a demon out of an epileptic boy. Jesus expressed his frustration at their lack of belief. Committed faith was more than just saying words. It was commitment to action in faith in God's power.

Having seen the greatness of God, the disciples still could not understand Jesus' teaching about the necessity of his betrayal and death, so they argued about greatness in this world. Jesus settled the issue, saying hospitality to a child—not victory in politics or war—marked true greatness. Unable to find a way to be great, the disciples tried at least to confine their number to their own group. Jesus opened it to all who obediently work out his mission to the glory of his name.

Finally, Jesus set out for the final journey to Jerusalem and Calvary. Again, the disciples learned that following Jesus did not always mean having crowds applauding their work. Commitment to Jesus also meant rejection, betrayal, and death. Commitment to follow Jesus is commitment to do what he said, to join his mission, now, with no looking back.

PRINCIPLES

- Committed followers of Christ have God's power to do God's work.
- Committed followers of Christ are willing to surrender earthly goods and comforts to do God's work.
- As Messiah, Jesus had to face the cross rather than seek the throne his followers expected.
- Committed followers of Christ value suffering for him more than what the world values.
- Jesus is the chosen Son of God validated by God himself.
- Committed followers of Christ do not automatically have God's power to do his work without prayer and commitment.
- Committed followers of Christ do not have to be part of our group.
- Committed followers of Christ must expect to face rejection.
- Committed followers of Christ allow no other priorities to keep them from following Christ.

APPLICATIONS

- Ask for God's power and expect him to do his work through you.
- Take your eyes off the world and follow Jesus, no matter what it costs you.
- Look for God to do his work in his cross-carrying ways rather than in the world's fame and power-producing ways.
- Forget the desire for greatness and find those whom you can help in the name of Christ.
- Study the life of Jesus to see what it means to be Messiah, Son of God, and the Coming One.
- Spend time in prayer telling God how great you think he is.

IV. LIFE APPLICATION

A Normal Christian

Each day he walks the long, twisting halls of the major corporation for which he works. He uses crossovers to reach the three city blocks of buildings. Into each office he brings the daily mail and picks up outgoing mail. Nothing special, you think. Then you ask what is up? Or, how are things? Or, what is the good news today? Immediately you get the answer—Jesus saves. This is not just a slogan for David. It is a way of life. Everyone he sees hears a word about Jesus. Everyone who looks at his mail cart finds signs about the love of Jesus. Notice closely, and you will hear him quoting Scripture to himself as he rolls his cart, not just random popular verses. He quotes whole chapters, sections, or even books. He learns Spanish so he can witness to the Latino population of our community. While the rest of us fight to get on top and make the big bucks, David quietly lives out the mind of Christ in daily contact with stockers in the warehouse and with the corporate executives. Most would see him as one of the least of the world's population. Christ most likely places him among the greatest.

Is this example too bland for you? You want a story of real sacrifice and commitment, a story of someone facing ordeals you never expect to experience. You want to marvel at what a real religious hero has done, knowing it lies far from where you live. Perhaps that is not what you need at this stage of your life with Christ. Do you need to think about a person much like you faced with the real choices of life: the world's way to success or Christ's way to the cross? You may never face the situations of Dietrich Bonhoeffer or Mother Teresa. You often face the choices David exemplifies. Do you spend time devoted to Jesus and talking to others about him? Do you spend time in prayer seeking how to lead others to know him? Do you really expect to see God's power in your life?

Luke chapter 9 forces you to measure your commitment to God. Is it a cross-carrying commitment? Is it a world-sacrificing commitment? Is it a commitment that sends you out on a mission among the least of the world's population? Are you prepared to accept rejection from the world as you minister to the needy of the world? Are you ready to reject world loyalties as close as Mom and Dad in order to follow Jesus?

V. PRAYER

God, show me the way to the cross. It is still hard to understand why the Son of God would let mortal men condemn him to such a horrible death. What love you demonstrated. Show me how to demonstrate that same love to the world's needy. Give me your power to do your work as I set out on your mission. Help me understand who you are. Help me be and do what you want me to do. I will take up my cross and follow you to death. Amen.

VI. DEEPER DISCOVERIES

A. Kingdom of God (9:2)

The angel told Mary that her son would be king over the house of Jacob in a kingdom without end (1:33). So Jesus came preaching the good news of the kingdom of God (4:43; cf. 8:1; 9:11). He prepared his disciples and sent them out with the same proclamation (9:2; cf. 9:60; 16:16). But this kingdom did not belong to the privileged nobility. It belonged to the poor and helpless (6:20; 14:12–15; 18:15–17), admittance of the rich and famous being almost impossible (18:22–27). Its most insignificant member was greater than John the Baptist, because he came before the kingdom was established in Jesus (7:28). The coming of the kingdom was a subject for the disciples' prayer (11:2). That kingdom was established during the generation in which Jesus lived (9:27). Its approach became visible as Jesus' followers healed the sick and rejected those who rejected them (10:9,11). Spirits submitting to Jesus showed the presence of the kingdom (11:20). But its presence did not mean it had come in all its fullness. Those expecting an immediate climax to the kingdom would have to wait.

In the meantime, Jesus, the King, has disappeared into a far country, having given kingdom responsibility to his servants (19:11–27). He entered the kingdom from the cross, taking the penitent thief with him (23:42–43). Definite signs will witness to its approach (21:31). There the true fulfillment of Judaism and all its festivals will occur, God's plan of redemption being complete (22:18). Then the disciples will gain positions of responsibility and power (22:28–30), but only after they have occupied the menial position of servants who endure trials for Jesus (22:24–28).

What did Jesus mean when he spoke of God's kingdom? The disciples wanted to know, and Jesus said he was revealing the mysteries of the kingdom to them and to them alone. Thus the kingdom is not something visible and easy to understand but something within a person's heart (17:20–21). It comes only in the language of parables (8:10). It is a reality slowly growing without being seen (13:18–21). It includes the Old Testament saints, but it will not include many who think they have it made (13:24–30). Surprisingly, it will include people from all corners of the earth, not just pious Jews (13:28–30). It comes from God's pleasure and grace (12:32). God chose to give it to Jesus, who gives it to his disciples (22:29). It demands absolute priority and obedience (9:60–62). When worries vanish in the face of the certainty that God is present in his kingdom and self-sacrifice becomes the habit of life, then rewards will come (12:31–34; 18:29–30; cf. 23:52). Such life habits include caring for those whom the world ignores as unworthy (14:12–15).

B. Messiah of God (9:20)

The Old Testament pointed to a coming king who would deliver Israel (Gen. 48:8–12). The king was called God's anointed one, in Hebrew God's *Messiach* or Messiah. In the Old Testament priests were also anointed when they were dedicated to their office. The king can be addressed as God's anointed one (1 Sam. 2:10; Pss. 18:50; 20:6; 28:8; 84:9; 89:38,51; 132:10,17;

Hab. 3:13) and his son (Pss. 2:7; 89:26–27). The anointed Israelite king was expected to see himself as God's servant carrying out God's plan for his people, but early on God warned Israel of the dangers of kingship when human pride and greed took precedence over divine calling and mission (see 1 Sam. 8:10–22).

Israel's kings proved God's warning true. God's pledge to David always to have a member of his house ruling over Judah (2 Sam. 7) stood in tension with God's continuing judgment on Davidic kings who refused to be God's servants. Finally, God's judgment came on the kings of Judah, resulting in the destruction of Jerusalem and the exile of the king (2 Kgs. 25). Alongside the warnings and eventual downfall came God's promises for the future of a peaceful messiah (Isa. 9:2–7; 11:1–16) born of a virgin (Isa. 7:14) in Bethlehem (Mic. 5:2–5a). This would be the suffering Servant of the Lord (Isa. 53). He would establish God's righteous rule among his people (Jer. 23:5–8). The new David would be a protecting shepherd for the people (Ezek. 34:23–24). He would renew God's covenant with his reunited people, creating an obedient, righteous people, and restoring God's presence with them in his new temple (Ezek. 37:15–28).

Luke took up this messianic hope of a new king, announcing to the shepherds the birth of Christ the Lord, Christ (Gr. *Christos*) being the Greek equivalent of Hebrew *messiach,* "anointed one." Thus from the start of his Gospel Luke paints Jesus in messianic colors. Simeon found the baby in the temple to be the fulfillment of God's promise to him that he would see the Lord's Messiah before he died (2:26). The people thought John the Baptist might be the Messiah, but John pointed them to Jesus (3:15–18). Demons knew Jesus was the Messiah, but Jesus did not want this title publicized because of the false expectations of military and political power built around it in the people's minds (4:40–41).

Likewise, Peter identified Jesus as the Messiah, but had to learn that to be Messiah was to be rejected by the people and suffer on a cross prior to being raised from the dead (9:18–27). Jesus dealt in secret with the people who thought he might be the Messiah (20:41–44). Finally, his claim to be Messiah or Son of God led to his crucifixion (22:66–71; 23:2; cf. 23:35). The people and even the criminal crucified with him could not understand how a messiah could show such weakness as to endure capital punishment rather than to use his remarkable power to save himself (23:35,39). Finally, Jesus explained the situation, saying his suffering as Messiah fulfilled Scripture (24:25–27,44–49).

Thus, *Christ* or *Messiah* is a key term for Luke in understanding who Jesus is. But it is a term that had dangerous associations in the minds of people and had to be redefined in terms of self-sacrifice and suffering in light of

Scriptures like Isaiah 53. Luke sees the baby Jesus promised as Messiah fulfilling his messianic role by dying for all people on the cross.

C. The Call to the Cross (9:23)

Crowds followed Jesus because they sought miracles and healing and food. They saw him as the man of God who had come to save the nation and relieve their physical and material needs. Jesus shocked them by defining messiah in terms of suffering. He extended the shock when he said his disciples must join him in suffering. He defined this suffering in terms of bearing a cross. This looked forward to the moment when a Roman official would sentence him to the most horrible death imaginable—being nailed in public view to a cross until he suffocated to death. Part of that punishment was having to carry the cross through the public roadways to the crucifixion site, enduring the ultimate in humiliation.

He set two options before his disciples—make earthly life the most important thing and lose everything you dreamed of and accomplished, or make Christ's kingdom the most important thing in life and eventually gain true life. Making Christ's kingdom paramount in life meant giving up material goods and becoming dependent on God to supply daily needs. It meant going on mission when some people would reject them. It meant surrendering all earthly ties, relationships, and responsibilities in light of Jesus' call to discipleship. It meant knowing that the ultimate earthly destination was not a throne or an executive office or a military command. The ultimate earthly destination for Jesus and for his committed followers is rejection by earthly authorities. It is total humiliation. It is capital punishment. It is death. Each day was a day further along on Jesus' road and on the disciple's road to Calvary.

Many modern followers want to shove this back into history. We want to modify it to meet the realities of modern life. We want to delay it until we are able and ready to meet the demands, having met earthly demands first. That is precisely what Jesus opposed. He makes the most radical claim possible on our lives. Make a decision now—self or Christ, earthly success or Christ's cross-bearing mission. Then walk down the road you take, knowing you have rejected the other. This is Jesus' definition of faith—self-denial in favor of following Jesus on mission.

D. Will Not Taste Death (9:27)

History seems to declare this statement invalid. All those who lived in Jesus' day died, waiting for his return and his establishment of the eternal kingdom on earth as it is in heaven. Scholars labor to explain the seeming contradiction here. Several views are offered.

Some say Jesus expected to establish the kingdom almost immediately but was wrong. Our understanding of the nature and person of Jesus does not allow us to accept this viewpoint. Neither does adequate exegesis of the text.

A second view sees Jesus appearing at the transfiguration with Moses and Elijah as a glimpse of the kingdom by three disciples. It is doubtful that 9:27 limits the participants to three, and certainly this view does not give time for any to taste death before the fulfillment. The kingdom is certainly more than a brief sight of Christ's heavenly glory.

A third view sees the Roman government's destruction of Jerusalem in A.D. 70 as a foretaste of final judgment and thus of the kingdom, but this in no way revealed the kingdom of God any more than did the Babylonian destruction of Jerusalem in 586 B.C.

Another view says Jesus referred to the fulfillment of God's plan for establishing the kingdom in Christ's lifetime on earth—a fulfillment climaxed in the death, resurrection, and ascension of Jesus and perhaps including the coming of the Spirit at Pentecost. In this view Jesus is now reigning as king, having been seated at God's right hand (22:69). The transfiguration gave a few disciples a confirming moment preparing them for the establishment of God's saving purpose in cross, resurrection, and ascension. The preaching of the early church in Acts declared the reality of the kingdom of God. Many of Jesus' audience in Luke 9 saw these events. Still, all these ultimately pointed beyond themselves to a still more definite establishment of the kingdom in the second coming of the Son of Man.

VII. TEACHING OUTLINE

A. INTRODUCTION

1. Lead Story: How Easy to Believe
2. Context: Chapter 9 represents a transition in the ministry of Christ. It concludes Jesus' demonstration of the commitment he expects of disciples by explicitly defining commitment as cross bearing, self-denial, following, and losing. It continues Luke's interest in showing who Jesus is by silencing Peter's confession of him as Messiah until messiah could be defined in terms of suffering and rejection, by looking forward to the glorification of the Son of Man when he comes in final judgment, and by reporting the divine approval of the chosen Son of God. The commitment section ends by showing that the disciples had not gotten there yet. They still argued about greatness rather than following in self-denial and showing concern for the least of these. They selfishly guarded their position with

Jesus rather than sharing it willingly with whomever God empowers to do his work.

Then Luke turned the corner. Time to go to Jerusalem, so that 9:51 introduces the longest section in the Gospel—a section devoted to Jesus' teaching and work on the way to the cross. The commitment he demanded of his disciples he would now demonstrate in the most radical way. In so doing, he expected his disciples to duplicate his radical devotion to mission by giving up all other devotions and priorities.

3. Transition: Our study of this chapter demands concentration, or we will miss the central teaching of Jesus and of Luke on the commitment demanded of a disciple. This lesson forces you to decide to be or not to be. This chapter shows us who Jesus is, what his mission is, and how we fit into that mission. This chapter requires us to volunteer for mission or reject mission in favor of earthly goals. Is Jesus' mission too hard for you? Do not try to water it down and think you are still on mission with Jesus. This chapter defines what mission is. Do you have a cross over your shoulder weighing you down? Or are you fulfilling earthly responsibilities until the right moment comes to try to catch up with Jesus on the road to Jerusalem?

B. COMMENTARY

1. Commitment in Action: Power for Followers (9:1–6)
   a. The setting: Jesus empowers and commissions followers (9:1–2)
   b. The commission: go where you are welcome (9:3–5)
   c. The result: preaching and healing (9:6)
2. Commitment Withheld: A Perplexed Authority (9:7–9)
   a. The setting: Herod's perplexed questions (9:7–9a)
   b. The result: desire to see Jesus (9:9b)
3. Commitment to Human Need: Pride or Practice? (9:10–17)
   a. The setting: crowds find a withdrawing Jesus (9:10–11a)
   b. The Master's response: teach and heal (9:11b)
   c. The followers' response: send them to dinner (9:12)
   d. The Master's reaction: feed them (9:13a)
   e. The followers' counter response: we cannot (9:13b)
   f. The Master's counter response: miraculous feeding (9:14–16)
   g. The result: more than enough (9:17)
4. Commitment Described: Self Denial to the Cross (9:18–27)
   a. The setting: solitary prayer and questions for disciples (9:18)
   b. The popular reaction: prophet's returned (9:19)

    c.   The follower's reaction: the Messiah is here (9:20)

    d.   The Master's reaction: be silent and suffer (9:22–26)

    e.   The result: see the kingdom (9:27)

5. Commitment's Center: The Chosen Son (9:28–36)

    a.   The setting: prayer retreat (9:28)

    b.   The scene: Jesus' transfiguration (9:29–31)

    c.   The followers' reaction: building program and fear (9:32–34)

    d.   The divine response: listen to chosen Son (9:35)

    e.   The followers' counter response: silence (9:36)

6. Commitment's Characteristics: Suffering and Serving (9:37–50)

    a.   The setting: return to hear a father's plea (9:37–39)

    b.   The followers' reaction: cannot do it (9:40)

    c.   The Master's response: frustrated anger (9:41)

    d.   The demon's reaction: attack (9:42a)

    e.   The Master's counter response: rebuke and heal (9:42b)

    f.   The crowd's reaction: amazed at God's greatness (9:43)

    g.   The Master's teaching: remember the cross (9:44)

    h.   The followers' reaction: understanding failure, fear, search for prominence (9:45–46)

    i.   The Master's reply: humble greatness (9:47–48)

    j.   The followers' diversion: pretender caught (9:49)

    k.   The Master's teaching: for us if not against (9:50)

7. Commitment in Action (9:51–56)

    a.   The setting: determined to reach Jerusalem (9:51)

    b.   The scene: preparing to lodge in Samaria (9:52)

    c.   The Samaritans' reaction: prejudiced rejection (9:53)

    d.   The followers' reaction: burn them up (9:54)

    e.   The Master's response: purpose to save (9:55)

    f.   The result: on towards Jerusalem (9:56)

C. CONCLUSION: A NORMAL CHRISTIAN

VIII. ISSUES FOR DISCUSSION

1. Can a modern Christian expect to have the same miraculous powers Christ gave his original disciples on their first mission?

2. What does it mean to say Jesus is the Messiah?

3. Why did Jesus constantly tell people not to report about who he was and what he had done?

4. What does it mean for a person today to take up his or her cross and follow Jesus?

5. Do you think Jesus would look at your church and call it an "unbe-lieving and perverse generation"?
6. How can you illustrate, testify to, or describe God's greatness?
7. Do you ever experience rejection because you are a Christian? Why or why not?
8. What conditions do you set before you are willing to follow Jesus as a radical cross-bearing disciple?

Luke 10

Dedication at the Crossroads

Quote

"The Christian community does not live from itself and for itself, but from the sovereignty of the risen Lord and for the coming sovereignty of him who has conquered death and is bringing life, righteousness, and the kingdom of God."

Jurgen Moltmann

Luke 10

IN A NUTSHELL

Chapter 10 shows dedication in action. Jesus takes disciples, who have been arguing about greatness, prominence, and exclusiveness, and sends them on a mission to the wolves. They discover anew how God's power can operate through them. In so doing they find a new revelation beyond even what the prophets experienced. They also find Jesus has a new definition of the requirements for eternal life and the expression of love for a neighbor. He concentrates all of life on one thing and challenges us to focus on that one thing and nothing else.

Dedication at the Crossroads

I. INTRODUCTION

A Crossroads at Sea

*G*od brings a crossroads to every life. The great English founder of Methodism, John Wesley, reached his crossroads among Moravians in America. While at sea, they encountered a horrendous storm. Winds galed. Rains drenched. The ship floundered and threatened to come apart. John Wesley wondered what would happen next. Then he noticed the Moravian Christians sitting quietly, watching the storm. He asked how they could be so at peace when the world of nature seemed to have declared war. Their serene answer caught him off guard: "Why be disturbed? God will take care of us all."

This experience led John Wesley to a Moravian prayer meeting in England. The sermon described the change God brings when a person truly trusts Jesus as Savior. Wesley faced his crossroads. Would he continue the life of fear and uncertainty? Or did he truly want that peace and serenity the Moravians demonstrated. He chose the latter, accepting Jesus as his Savior and heading down the road to becoming one of history's great evangelistic preachers and leaders.

Luke 10 places Jesus' disciples at the same crossroads. Can the commitment demanded in chapter 9 become reality in their lives? This is tested in several ways: on mission, in responding to Jesus' revelation, in deciding whom they will love and minister to, and in deciding between the affairs of normal life and the demands of Jesus for cross bearing, self-denial, and Christ-focused discipleship. Studying Luke 10 may bring you to a crossroads like John Wesley faced. Which road will you take?

II. COMMENTARY

Dedication at the Crossroads

MAIN IDEA: *Jesus demands more than listening to his teaching and agreeing with what he says. He places us at the crossroads of life and forces us to decide to live his way or the world's way.*

⒜ Dedication in Action: Representing God (10:1–16)

SUPPORTING IDEA: *At life's crossroads, we face mission opportunities that call for immediate action: will we represent God or the world?*

10:1. Jesus was on mission, preaching the kingdom of God in the towns and villages (4:43–44). He was also on the way to Jerusalem to meet death (9:51). Time limitations prevented him from accomplishing the mission by himself. Even the Twelve could not do it all. That is why he had trained disciples. Now was the time to see how effective they were. He sent out seventy-two (or seventy, if other manuscripts are right), each with a partner, to prepare the way for his coming. That is what Christian mission is, preparation for Christ to come into lives, into towns, and finally to come again into this world. The first person sent to prepare the way for Jesus was John the Baptist. Herod executed John. Could others preparing Christ's way expect better treatment?

10:2. Even seventy-two followers of Jesus could not complete the task. As Christ had told them to accept anyone in ministry who did not reject or oppose them (9:50), so he now asked them to pray for others to join forces with them to reap the harvest. Already in Christ's ministry, the soil had begun to produce, and the harvest was ready (8:8,15). Does this imply the mission of the Twelve had borne fruit (9:1–6)? Harvest does not wait. Either you reap it now, or it is ruined by weather or by withering. Not just anyone can harvest this field, though. God must select and send out the workers. He is the owner of the field who controls its destiny. His followers ask him to send help to finish the task. By this they imply they will accept whomever God sends. God sets the standards and job requirements. Disciples cannot be choosy about those whom God selects and sends.

10:3–4. Jesus did not promise the task would be easy. Rather, his command placed disciples at the crossroads. A warning accompanied the command. Wolves, wild animals known to prey on helpless lambs, awaited them. Did they trust God to protect them from such danger? Or did they have a more pressing task (see 9:57–62)? They would have to show such trust. The essential items for travel are prohibited: No money, no extra clothes or provisions in a bag, not even an extra pair of sandals for the long walk. God would provide their needs. One final requirement was that there would be no time for socializing. The mission must be central. The harvest must be reaped while it was ready.

10:5–7. Advance lodging reservations would not be needed, either. Enter a city and find a family to stay with, Jesus instructed. Bless the house with God's peace. Pray that God will bring wholeness and blessing and harmony to the house. The result of the blessing will depend on the head of the household. A peace-loving, hospitable host will receive God's peace and blessing. Then what God promised at Christ's birth will start to become reality (1:79; 2:14,29; see 19:38). The person who rejects you and makes life difficult for you will not receive God's blessing, Jesus said. Thus, the coming of the messenger brings the host to the crossroads as well. Response to Christ's messengers determines the nature of a person's life. The messenger must stay put, however, and not go looking for better rooms. Again, the focus must be on mission—not on personal needs and desires. The host is responsible to take care of your needs. You are working in God's harvest and should be paid for your work. But do not try to up your pay by looking for a better place to live. Living arrangements are not important. Gathering the harvest is.

10:9. The mission was simple: heal and preach (cf. 9:1–2). The kingdom of God is near. In the simple ministry of Christ's messengers, people find themselves in the midst of God's kingdom. The kingdom is not something far away in space and time. It is present reality for those who see God's power at work.

10:10–12. Popularity, like pay, was not the focus. Workers in God's kingdom harvest should expect rejection. The demands of kingdom service are too great. The reality of kingdom presence is too unbelievable. The comfort of worldly security is too strong. Yes, the city stands at the crossroads of decision: accept God's message of the kingdom or lose your life (9:24–25). The messengers were to use the symbolic act of wiping dust from their feet (9:5) to make vivid the kingdom demand for decision. Rejection means the kingdom has come, but you have chosen the road that leads away from the kingdom. God lets you do that, but you must suffer the consequences. And what consequences—punishment worse than that of the city burned by God for unspeakable sins (Gen. 19:24–28; cf. Isa. 1:9–10; 3:9; 13:19; Jer. 23:14; 49:18; 50:40; Lam. 4:6; Ezek. 16:46–56; Amos 4:11; Zeph. 2:9; Rom. 9:29; 2 Pet. 2:6; Jude 1:7; Rev. 11:8). Rejecting God's kingdom is accepting the eternal destiny of Satan's children.

10:13. Prophetic woes, acting out funeral mourning, are due those cities that do not accept the messengers. For Bethsaida, see 9:10. Chorazin is a small village whose location is uncertain, possibly two or three miles north of Capernaum. Nothing special happened in these cities for history to remember. But one major thing did *not* happen. They did not accept Christ's demands. Thus they received horrible condemnation. Tyre and Sidon, the great cities of Phoenicia, heard Isaiah's woes against them (Isa. 23; cf. Ezek. 28; Jer. 47:4; Zech. 9:2). Cities that once had heard God's woes would repent and follow Jesus if they had the chance that the two cities near his Capernaum headquarters had. But those two cities stubbornly rejected Jesus and thus invited destruction. Sackcloth and ashes represented mourning rituals associated with funerals and penitence.

B Dedication Rewarded: Opportunities Beyond the Prophets (10:17–24)

SUPPORTING IDEA: *Persons who dedicate their lives to following Jesus find rewards in service and in eternal life far beyond the dreams and hopes of the prophets.*

10:17. Jesus' chosen messengers returned ecstatic. They exercised powers beyond their dreams. Even evil spirits obeyed them. Could anything be better than this! Next assignment, please.

10:18–20. Jesus surprised them with his answer. Satan had fallen from heaven. God had won the victory. When Jesus' followers dedicate themselves so totally to him that demons respond to their demands, then the kingdom of God is near. Satan may continue to work in this world, but his ultimate defeat is assured. He has no place in heaven and no more power for victory. The kingdom is at hand. The victory is certain. All that remains is God's timing for the final battle and total victory.

Christ promised the disciples more power over everything that symbolized evil in this world. Evil has no hopes of victory. The work of Christ on the cross and the cross-bearing faithfulness of the disciples prove that the heydays of Satan and his henchmen are gone forever. Temptation, suffering, rejection—even the death symbolized by the cross—may buffet Christ's followers. But in the final hour, Christ is the victorious judge who rules over the world, judging evil and rewarding his faithful disciples.

How did the disciples react to this? With great joy—the same joy promised Zechariah at the birth of his son John the Baptist (1:14). The same joy announced to the shepherds at Christ's birth (2:10). The same joy with which you welcome God's Word (8:13). The same joy heaven expresses when one sinner repents (15:7,10). The same joy the news of Christ's resurrection brings (24:41,52). The greatest source of joy has nothing to do with earthly events. The greatest joy comes in knowing your name is written in God's heavenly book, that you are assured a place in his eternal kingdom.

10:21. Jesus expressed his own joy—a joy caused by the Father's work and inspired by the Spirit's revelation—for God is the source of all joy. The Spirit showed Jesus what God had hidden. God hides things from people who think they are wise and understanding. He reveals the things to youngsters. Why? Because that is the way God planned it. He uses the world's most innocent to testify to his greatness and encourages them to share his word with others.

10:22. The Jesus who devoted his life to helping the weak, who never had a home, who died on a criminal's cross—this Jesus may seem weak to the world. One thing proves he is not weak: the gifts the Father has given him. Everything that God the Father has, he has placed in the trustworthy hands of God the Son. This is not obvious to the world, for the world knows neither the Father nor the Son. True knowledge of the Son belongs only to the Father. True knowledge of the Father belongs only to the Son. They do not, however, keep this knowledge selfishly to themselves. The Son has come from the Father into the world to reveal who the Father is. The Son has chosen to give this revelation to the world's innocent. Why? They will accept the knowledge that the wise ridicule. When they become messengers of this knowledge to others, the glory will go to God and not to humans (for similar teaching see Matt. 28:18; John 1:18; 3:35; 5:21–22; 10:29; 13:3; 14:6–7; Rom. 10:9; 1 Cor. 12:3).

10:23–24. The disciples were the first ones to whom Jesus revealed the great secret of the Father's nature. He pronounced an indirect blessing on them, telling them that they had received what the great prophets and kings of history had hoped for. They saw the climax of God's plan of revelation and salvation. David, Hezekiah, Josiah, Elijah, Isaiah, Jeremiah, and Daniel had all looked forward to this day but had not been allowed to see it. This placed great responsibility on the disciples. They had revelation no one before them had received. How would they handle this blessing? How would they share it with others? In weakness or in strength? They are the good soil in which Jesus has planted God's Word. The time is coming for them to produce a hundred fold. Are they up to it? Would they take care how they listened? Would they hear and do the Word of God?

C Dedication's Goal: Love for Eternity (10:25–37)

> **SUPPORTING IDEA:** *The goal of a person who dedicates himself to Jesus is the gaining of eternal life—a goal that is reached as we fulfill the law's commands to love God and to love our neighbor.*

10:25. A man with excellent religious credentials stood among the crowd. He studied God's law continually and interpreted it so the people would know how to obey it. He tried his best to obey the law himself. He helped administer justice within the Jewish system. People respected his expertise and his life. He had a question for Jesus. He thought it would reveal the weakness and falseness in Jesus' teaching and lead people away from him back to the Pharisees and the teachers of the law, the qualified religious leaders. God had given Israel an inheritance, namely the land of Israel. They had forfeited this inheritance through disobedience. Now they looked for a new inheritance, one that would last forever. The rabbis debated exactly what this inheritance was. The lawyer gave Jesus opportunity to provide a new definition.

10:26. Instead, Jesus bounced the question back to the lawyer. Both agreed the answer must be found in Scripture, particularly in the Law of Moses. So Jesus asked, What does the law say? Both knew the Law had to be interpreted for modern times, so Jesus asked for the lawyer's own interpretation. Now the lawyer was being tested, not Jesus.

10:27. True to his profession, the lawyer quoted Scripture. Interestingly, in Matthew 22:37–40 and Mark 12:29–31, Jesus quotes the same Scriptures (Deut. 6:4–5; Lev. 19:18). Thus, both from the Jewish leaders' viewpoint and from Jesus' unique teaching, these Scriptures stand at the top of all other Old Testament teaching. Love God. Love neighbor. Then you will be and do what God expects in the Old Testament. Such love must not be half-hearted. It must be all-encompassing. Every part of you—thoughts, emotions, feelings, actions—must be controlled by love for God and for others.

10:28. For once Jesus agreed with a Jewish religious leader. Again, he emphasized the nature of this answer—not just an idea of the mind, but an action of one's strength, a feeling of one's soul, an emotion of one's heart. Love must control the entire person.

10:29. The leader tried to take the offense again and put Jesus on the defensive. One more trick question: Who is my neighbor? That is, how far does my love have to extend? Jewish legal interpretation sought to govern every situation and every relationship: Jew and Gentile; Jew and Roman; man and woman; free man and slave, priest and laity, clean and unclean, righteous and sinner. Every relationship was clearly defined, and the definitions determined how and when a person could participate in Jewish worship. The question was vital to Jewish identity.

10:30–35. Jesus answered with a parable—a type of story dedicated to teaching the mysteries of the kingdom to the disciples and keeping them hidden from unbelievers. He described a normal trip a person would take, seventeen miles from Jerusalem down to Jericho through a mountain pass that fell almost 3,300 feet in elevation. Herod had built New Testament Jericho as his winter palace on the same spot Hasmonean rulers had earlier built their palace. Herod included three palaces, a swimming pool, and a sunken garden. Thus, government officials frequently made the trip from Jerusalem to Jericho as did Jewish religious and political leaders. Criminals took advantage of the upper class's need to travel this winding, crooked road through dangerous passes. They hid behind the large rocks above the narrow passes and preyed on travelers. Jesus told the story of one victim without identifying the man by race, occupation, or reason for traveling.

Fellow travelers soon happened on the situation. A priest, the highest of Jewish religious officials, hurriedly stepped to the other side of the road and continued on his important business, even though rabbinic law expected him to bury any corpse he discovered. Similarly, a Levite, who carried out the more mundane tasks of temple worship and operation, passed quickly by. No reason why, except not enough love for this "neighbor."

Next we expect a member of the Jewish laity, the clergy having failed the love test. Instead, we get an unexpected Samaritan, one who in Jewish eyes had little reason to be in Jewish territory and who would be the last person to qualify as a neighbor to be loved. Such qualification is made from the lawyer's worktable interpreting the law. From the dying man's ditch, anyone who will offer first aid and emergency assistance qualifies as a loving neighbor. Thus, Jesus uttered shocking words for a Jewish audience grilled in legal interpretations and prejudiced judgments. The Samaritan had *compassion*—a Greek expression built on the word for a person's inner parts, the seat of emotions and feelings. It expresses Jesus' feeling for those in need (Matt. 9:36; 14:14; 15:32; 20:34; Mark 1:41; 6:34; 8:2; Luke 7:13). It is the feeling and attitude of a master who cancels a servant's massive debt (Matt. 18:27). This is true neighborly love—a love that goes beyond anything society or religious law expects and acts simply because of the extreme need of another.

Thus, the Samaritan took the dying man from the ditch and gave him life under supervised care without cost to the suffering man. The Samaritan representing everything the Jews hated became more than one they should love as a neighbor. The Samaritan became the hero of the story, the person showing love, the individual whose love Jews should imitate.

10:36. Jesus had the lawyer set up for the obvious question: Who among the three was the loving neighbor?

10:37. The lawyer gave the only possible answer: the one who showed mercy to the traveler. Again, this Greek term is often applied to Jesus, who responds to calls for mercy (Matt. 9:27; 15:22; 17:15; Mark 10:47–48; Luke 17:13; cf. Mark 5:19). Jesus promised God's mercy to those who show mercy (Matt. 5:7). So Jesus told the lawyer to go and show mercy like the Samaritan had done.

DDedication in Daily Decisions: Choosing Your Master (10:38–41)

SUPPORTING IDEA: *Dedication to Jesus takes precedence over all other responsibilities and obligations.*

10:38. The long journey to Jerusalem continues. John 11:1 and 12:1–3 locate Mary and Martha in Bethany. Luke simply placed them in a village. Location was not important for him. Response to Jesus is. Martha responded in the typical homeowner's way: fulfilling the social obligations.

10:39. Sister Mary responded in a different way. The rabbis had taught people to listen to wise men or teachers but not to talk much with women. Jesus, the wisest of men, welcomed Mary to his audience of learners.

10:40. Social obligations finally got the best of Martha, especially when her sister proved to be of no help. Rather than inviting her sister to help, Martha went straight to Jesus for authority to force her sister to work.

10:41–42. For once a person in need did not receive Christ's blessing. The need was out of focus and misplaced. Martha was too stressed out about earthly things. Her life was out of focus, dedicated to fulfilling the world's expectations rather than Jesus'. Life has one essential need: to hear and obey the Word of God (see 8:18–20). Mary made the right choice. Jesus would not take away from her the blessing and opportunity. At the crossroads of decision making, Martha had opted for worldly expectation and social obligation; Mary, for hearing Christ's Word. Martha needed to change her priorities. When the Word is taught, listen. All else is secondary.

> **MAIN IDEA REVIEW:** *Jesus demands more than listening to his teaching and agreeing with what he says; he places us at the crossroads of life and forces us to decide to live his way or the world's way.*

III. CONCLUSION

Which Way?

A mission trip to Kenya taught me many things. One morning we walked through miles and miles of dirt paths that connected settlements, each containing four or five grass huts. Finally, lunchtime came. We stood where two of the narrow paths crossed. I asked my interpreter if it were not time to get back to the rest of the group for lunch. He agreed and asked which way I wanted to go. He smiled as my face reflected the confusion I felt, looking down one road and then the other. I had no idea which road to take.

In chapter 10 of Luke, Jesus sent out the larger group of followers to carry on his mission until he could get to the villages. Their work showed the kingdom of God is at hand, for Jesus sees Satan falling from heaven, all chance for victory gone. Jesus rejoiced that the followers had learned the things of God that Jesus came to reveal. Having learned from Jesus, the disciples still found themselves at the crossroads, for Jesus had another lesson for them—the lesson of love. Were they willing to follow a Samaritan's example and love a needy stranger with self-sacrificing love? Were they willing to forego the duties of the social order to listen to Jesus' teaching?

Yes, even the disciple who has won so many victories in Jesus' name remains at the crossroad of dedication. The call to self-denial and cross carrying continues. This time the call is not to suffer physically, but to suffer emotional rejection as we follow Jesus down the road of helping others and listening to God's Word rather than following the road of self-interest and social obligation. Luke wants us to hear his call to follow Jesus in mission, winning victories over Satan, but also to follow him in daily life, taking opportunity to show love to others and to show love for God by listening and obeying his Word.

PRINCIPLES

- Workers for God's harvest come when God's people pray for them.
- Dedication on mission means depending on God for one's needs.
- God's people on mission show the presence of God's kingdom and the end of hope for Satan's victory.
- Rejecting God's messengers is rejection of God himself.
- The goal of life on earth is to have your name written in heaven.
- Jesus is the only way to know and experience God.
- Eternal life comes through perfect love of God and neighbor.
- A neighbor is anyone who sees a need and moves to meet it.
- Love for God is shown by devotion to his Word in the midst of life's demands.

APPLICATIONS

- Find where God is at work and join him in his mission.
- Depend on God to meet your needs rather than let worldly cares distract you from his mission.
- Know that judgment comes on those who reject Jesus.
- Look to Jesus to find what God is like.
- Love God with everything you are.
- Show love for your neighbor in concrete ways that meet his needs.
- Focus your life on God's Word, not on social obligations and duties.

IV. LIFE APPLICATION

Take My Room

Roy Angel (*Shields of Brass*, 50–51) tells the story of a man and his wife who searched over Philadelphia late into the night for a hotel room. Finally, they trudged into a third-class hotel. The man asked the night clerk if he could please find them a room. They were too tired to search further. The young man thumbed through all his records and checked each room. All were filled with sleeping guests. "Not a single room," he reported, "but I do have a small room on the top floor. It is my own room, but I have to work tonight. You could sleep there."

Grateful to God and to the clerk, the couple took the elevator to the top floor and slept peacefully for the rest of the night. Next morning, they came down and sought out the young clerk. The young man sat at their table as they ate breakfast. "Hope you had a good night's sleep and the room was big enough," he said.

The elderly guests assured him it was just what they needed and thanked him again and again. Then the man astounded the young clerk. "Son, I want you to come work for me. You are too good for a small hotel like this. I want to build a luxury hotel in the middle of New York City and hire you to manage it for me. I'm Jacob Astor."

The young clerk faced a crossroads in his life without knowing it. He made the right choice. He loved with his complete heart, soul, strength, and mind. He made the self-sacrificing decision because that was his nature. The one small decision to show love to a couple in need changed him from a clerk in a third-class hotel to manager of a world-class luxury hotel.

Jesus invites us to make a choice between the world's selfish ways and his loving, self-denying ways. When we choose his self-denying ways, he gives us his most precious gift. He reveals the Father to us. He places us in God's loving presence and lets God reward us with his salvation. He shows us Satan's defeat and the kingdom's presence. He promises us eternal life. When decision time comes in your life, God will be looking for love in action. Do compassion and mercy so fill your life that you can be sure when God comes that he will find you faithful?

V. PRAYER

God, thank you that you have a mission for me and that you have written my name in heaven. Thank you that you have chosen to work with weaklings like me to show people your kingdom and to reveal the Father's nature. Show me where you are at work, and give me faith to join you there. Let me see the kingdom present in our world. Let me see your victory over Satan. Let me so love you and my neighbor that I may be assured of eternal life. Let me so concentrate on your Word and your ways that I do not place social obligations and physical wants above you and your kingdom. In Christ's name. Amen.

VI. DEEPER DISCOVERIES

A. Seventy(-Two) (10:1,17)

Greek manuscripts differ as to whether Jesus sent seventy or seventy-two of his followers. Similar manuscript variance occurs with the same numbers in Genesis 10, where the Hebrew text has seventy nations but the early Greek translation (the Septuagint) has seventy-two names. In Numbers 11:24–25 the Spirit falls on seventy elders and then on Eldad and Medad, to total seventy-two. Local Jewish councils apparently had seventy-two members, but the Sanhedrin had seventy. Textual evidence may slightly favor seventy-two as the more difficult reading. If we could prove that Luke and Jesus were attempting to use the number symbolically or typologically in relation to the Genesis or Numbers accounts, then we might have a basis for choice, but neither symbolism is really carried out in the passage. The point here is that Jesus trained and used many more than just the twelve disciples. He called for dedicated discipleship from all who would bear their cross in self-denial and gave them an opportunity to join in God's kingdom mission.

B. Fall of Satan (10:18)

Jesus described one result of the seventy-two followers' victorious mission: the fall of Satan like lightning from heaven. The language suggests Isaiah 14:12, which originally described the fall of a pompous king but came to be interpreted as a symbol of Satan's fall. Job 1–2 pictures Satan as part of the heavenly council roaming the earth to find evidence to accuse people of sin before the heavenly throne. Jewish writings from the period between the Testaments expected Messiah to come, resulting in Satan's defeat. This is particularly seen in Qumran writings and in the Testament of the Twelve Patriarchs (cf. John 12:31; Rom. 16:20; Rev. 12:7–10; 20:1–10). The coming of Christ brought God's kingdom near. Satan has no place in God's kingdom. When Jesus exercises God's power through the nucleus that will become his church, then the victory is sure. Satan has no hope. The text does not try to answer where Satan fell to, what he did there, and how this relates to his end-time activities. The emphasis here is that with God exercising his power through the followers of Jesus, Satan has lost.

C. Authority to Trample on Snakes and Scorpions (10:19)

Satan's fall from heaven is related to authority that Jesus gave his followers. This is authority that overcomes the power of the enemy. Many interpreters want to take this verse as authority to demonstrate their ability to handle snakes and scorpions without harm or injury. Jesus never used his power in such exhibitionist, sensation-seeking ways. Connected so closely to the fall of Satan and the overcoming of the enemy, the language here appears to be an all-encompassing symbol for all evil forces that would represent Satan and oppose Christ. Satan is often symbolized as the serpent (Gen. 3:1–14; Num. 21:6–9) or as a scorpion (1 Kgs. 12:11,14; Rev. 9:3; cf. Deut. 8:15; Luke 11:11–12). The followers' victory over demons and evil spirits indicated the authority they had received from Jesus—authority over everything that represented Satan.

D. Names Written in Heaven (10:20)

The power over demonic powers can easily go to a person's head and bring pride in personal accomplishment. Jesus warned against this. Personal accomplishment is not the issue. All comes from the authority and power that God gives. The issue is eternal destiny. One way the Bible describes eternal security of the believer with God is through the imagery of a heavenly book with the inhabitants of heaven present and future engraved (see Exod. 32:32–33; Pss. 69:28; 87:6; Isa. 4:3; Dan. 12:1; Mal. 3:16–17; Phil. 4:3; Heb. 12:23; Rev. 3:5; 13:8). Two different types of books are referred to. The one here appears to be a city registry with all citizens' names included. Other times the image encompasses a book of deeds recording the good and bad works of the people whose names are inscribed. When Satan has fallen and God's followers have authority over evil powers, then our residence in heaven is secure. Here is the reason to rejoice: God knows us and has a place prepared for us in his heavenly palace.

VII. TEACHING OUTLINE

A. INTRODUCTION

1. Lead Story: A Crossroads at Sea
2. Context: In 9:51 Luke began the longest section of his book: Christ's journey to Jerusalem to be betrayed by Jewish religious leaders and to be crucified as a criminal on a Roman cross. Chapter 10 shows that this journey to Jerusalem represents a crossroads for the disciples. Will they carry their own crosses and face execution, or will they become part of the betrayers?

   Two scenarios are painted. The first consists of victorious disciples casting out demons, exercising authority over evil powers, and thus ensuring the fall of Satan to eternal defeat. Such victory by Christ's followers may lead either to rejoicing over personal powers exercised and victories won or to rejoicing over the assurance that one's name is written in the book of life in heaven. This is possible because God has revealed himself exclusively to the Son, and the Son has chosen to reveal the Father to his selected followers. The other scenario is the attempt to gain eternal life through the law. Here a person can know the verses that summarize all the rest of the law—verses on loving God and loving neighbor. Still, this does not bring eternal life if a person does not quit separating humanity into various categories and groups and starts showing love where need is evident. You do not choose your neighbor and then love him. You find a person needing love and love him like a neighbor.

3. Transition: This chapter places us at the crossroads of faith in two ways: (1) Will we give God credit for what he has done through us and rejoice because he has chosen us to be part of his kingdom? (2) Will we try to find a legal way to justify our inclusion in the book of life, or will we simply love those in need as God does? As you study, examine your own life to see if you are exercising Christ's love for others, or if you are legalistically doing things and expecting eternal rewards in return.

B. COMMENTARY

1. Dedication in Action: Representing God (10:1–16)
   a. The commission: pray, go, and stay (10:1–7)
   b. The mission: heal and announce (10:8–12)
   c. The curse: woe on unbelievers (10:13–15)
   d. The lesson: you represent God (10:16)
2. Dedication Rewarded: Opportunities Beyond the Prophets (10:17–24)
   a. The scene: return and report of the followers (10:17)
   b. The Master's response: kingship priority (10:18–20)
   c. The Master's praise: revelation to the children (10:21)
   d. The Master's lesson: know the Father through the Son (10:22)
   e. The Master's conclusion: greater reward than prophets and kings (10:23–24)
3. Dedication's Goal: Love for Eternity (10:25–37)
   a. The setting: opponents test Jesus (10:25)
   b. The Master's response: interpret the law (10:26)
   c. The opponent's reaction: love God and neighbor (10:27)
   d. The Master's counter response: do what you know (10:28)
   e. The opponent's self-defense: who is my neighbor? (10:29)
   f. The Master's lesson: who proved neighbor to crime victim? (10:30–36)
   g. The opponent's answer: merciful one (10:37a)
   h. The Master's response: do what you know (10:37b)
4. Dedication in Daily Decisions: Choosing Your Master (10:38–41)
   a. The setting: on the way to Jerusalem (10:38a)
   b. The sisters host the Master (10:38b–40a)
   c. Martha's request: make Mary help! (10:40b)
   d. The Master's response: make the right choice (10:41)

C. CONCLUSION: TAKE MY ROOM

VIII. ISSUES FOR DISCUSSION

1. Do you see ripe harvests in today's world? Are you willing for God to send you there, even if it means leaving family to go across the oceans?

2. What does it mean for the kingdom of God to be near? Is it still near today?

3. Is God's judgment more severe on those who have had the greater opportunity to hear his Word? Who faces severe punishment from God today for not obeying him and carrying out his kingdom mission?

4. Are you sure your name is written in the book of heaven? How do you know?

5. What must a person do today to inherit eternal life? How are the two love commandments connected to this?

6. Who is your neighbor? Are you being neighborly?

7. What choices do you face between the good and the better? Which choice are you making?

Luke 11

Dedicated to What?

"*If* man is not free, prayer is folly. For then uplifted hands are but antics of a marionette, and sacred words only the turning of a phonograph. . . . Prayer is selfhood aflame— the more because it is lost in God."

George Buttrick

Luke 11

IN A NUTSHELL

*D*edication involves prayer, kingdom obedience, repentance, and love of God. Prayer reverences God, calls for his kingdom, asks for daily bread, petitions for and promises to practice forgiveness, and seeks guidance through temptation. Dedication expects the Father to give good gifts and so asks for them. Jesus' power and obedience show the kingdom has come. Repentance means changing one's lifestyle and letting the light of God shine through. False dedication brings only God's judgment. True dedication like Jesus' brings rejection and revenge from those dedicated to falsehood.

Dedicated to What?

I. INTRODUCTION

Busy Making Every Day Count

Toyohiko Kagawa was a frail teenager in Japan. One pretty day he decided to go swimming. After frolicking and enjoying the invigoration of a good swim, he slowly stroked his way back to the beach. Reaching it, he reached down to pull himself up on his feet and out of the water. Instead, he collapsed. Fortunately, friends saw his plight, rushed to him, and pulled him from the shallow water. Minutes later a doctor stood over him. A quick examination was all it took. "This young man has an advanced case of tuberculosis. He has less than a year to live."

Told of the prognosis, Kagawa looked up with a calm smile: "Then I must get busy immediately. I shall have to make every day count." The dedication to make life count did not prove easy. He lived in a poor fisherman's hut. Friends steered clear of him, afraid they would catch the disease. One man came—Dr. Myers, a Christian missionary. He even slept in Kagawa's hovel for four nights. "Aren't you afraid of me?" Kagawa asked. "No," Dr. Myers replied. "Your disease is contagious, but love is more contagious."

That day Kagawa dedicated his life to love the poor of Japan in their hovels as Dr. Myers had loved him. Preaching on the streets, he chanced to meet a former convict who pointed him to a "haunted house" where a murder had been committed. At least the rent was cheap. For fourteen years Kagawa lived there, even bringing his young bride there. Drunks beat him up several times. Still, he dedicated himself to live the life of his poor countrymen. As he preached Christ, he organized labor groups among the poor. This brought him a prison sentence. In prison he began writing books, forty in all. Finally the people realized what stood before them. "How like this Jesus he preaches about is Kagawa," they said. God gave him more than one year to live, and he lived each of them as if it were the last, bringing new hope to the poor of the land.

Such dedication is what Jesus demonstrated in his ministry and what he called for in his teaching. Luke 11 is filled with the words of Jesus that show the meaning and direction of a life dedicated totally in faith to God.

II. COMMENTARY

Dedicated to What?

> **MAIN IDEA:** *Prayer, obedience, love, repentance, and consistency characterize the dedicated life.*

A Dedication in Prayer: Praise and Petition (11:1–13)

> **SUPPORTING IDEA:** *Prayer praising God and persistently asking him to meet one's needs represents an integral part of the dedicated life.*

11:1. Seeing Jesus at prayer made the disciples want to imitate him. They knew John's disciples had learned to pray from John. They wanted to learn to pray from Jesus. They saw that his actions each day came out of his prayer life with God. They desired that same dedicated prayer life.

11:2–4. So Jesus taught them a model prayer. This prayer contains the essence of all prayer. Any other prayer is simply an application and amplification of this prayer.

The prayer begins with the direct address. It is aimed at the Father. This means prayer is an intimate talk between people who love and trust one another. Interestingly, Jesus did not surround the Father with all sorts of intimidating descriptive adjectives. The address does not try to flatter God, pass a theology exam, or gain God's favor. The address simply establishes contact between two persons who are committed to each other in close family ties.

Those close ties are not between equals. As I pray I recognize the holy nature of the Father. I pray that the innate nature of the holy God be concretely realized in our world. This realization or manifestation of God's holy nature may come in two ways. God may act in such a way that he shows the world his holy nature. People may respond to God in awe and reverence. The prayer may contain both elements, asking God to act so people will respond. That response is partial now but will one day be complete when the kingdom comes. So the prayer for God to establish his kingdom on earth in some ways duplicates the call of his holiness to be made known. In Jesus and his preaching, the kingdom has been seen on earth. We pray that the day will soon come when the kingdom will be seen in its fullness and its permanence.

Prayer is not just concerned with the large picture of recognizing God and establishing his kingdom. Prayer is also individual and personal, asking for the most basic necessities. Such prayer recognizes that we cannot provide these ourselves but are dependent on the Father for all we have. Even the personal cry for food is issued in the plural. Prayer never becomes individualistic and selfish. The most intimate requests are made as part of the worshiping community of God's people. We pray not just for ourselves but for all God's people.

Finally, prayer deals with anything that might separate us from God. We depend on God to take away our sins. In so doing, we know that forgiveness is not simply an activity of God. We are also responsible to forgive those who treat us wrong. We should not expect God's loving action if we are not willing to practice the same kind of love toward others. This does not turn prayer and forgiveness into a business transaction in which I forgive in order to be forgiven or one in which God can forgive only after I forgive. Rather, I pray that God will truly transform my nature so that I become like him. I pray that my focus will be on godliness and not on worldliness.

Prayer is not simply concerned with past sins and restoration of relationship with the Father. Prayer also seeks to maintain this relationship as a permanent experience. To do so, prayer deals with everything that would lead us to sin. We ask God to direct our lives in such a way that they will not come near the people and powers that would tempt us away from God and toward temptation. Only as God leads us away from temptation can the intimate Father-child relationship be maintained.

11:5-7. Jesus illustrated his brief prayer with a parable. The situation described is uncommon but not out of the question. A friend comes to dire needs and knocks on your door late at night asking for bread. What will you do? You see the desperate need. The friend will be dishonored if he cannot set bread before a traveling friend.

The other side of the picture is a one-room sleeping quarters for an entire family. To get up and get bread is to wake up the whole family, probably including some animals. This is a most undesirable situation. Friendship might not be strong enough to force the sleeper to awake and meet the visitor's needs. One motive is strong enough, especially in the biblical world. That is shame and honor. The person would be shamed and dishonored if he did not help a friend in need. Rather than the traditional "persistence" or the NIV's "boldness," the proper translation of the Greek term here is probably "because of his being put to shame."

11:9-10. Jesus got to the point of his parable: Ask God. Seek something from God. Knock expectantly at God's door. Admit you are in a position of need and helplessness. Depend on the Father's goodness and love. If a human fearing shame will open the door, certainly the loving Father you pray to will open the door and provide what you need. The person who truly prays the model prayer will find his prayers answered even when those prayers are petitions for personal need.

11:11-13. Jesus used a farfetched illustration to make his point. No human father of any worth would listen to a son asking for something to eat and reach down into a snake pit to give the child a dangerous animal. The father meets the child's need rather than scaring or harming him. Similarly, a request for an egg is not met with the gift of a stinging scorpion. Compared to God, we all stand as evil sinners. We cannot compare our love and goodness to God's. Still, we know how to give what our children need. We can be good to them. How much better will the divine Father treat us! His better gift surprises us. It is a concrete gift of the Holy Spirit. That gift ensures we get anything else we need, for the Holy Spirit becomes God with us, directing us to where we need to go to serve God and to meet our needs. Thus, pray to God in the spirit and words of the model prayer. Expect to receive what you ask for if God is your Father. And ask especially for the Spirit so that all your petitions will be answered.

B Dedication's Driving Force: Satan or Kingdom Obedience (11:14–28)

> **SUPPORTING IDEA:** Dedication is driven by a motivating force—either from God or from Satan and his worldly forces.

11:14. Demon possession affects people in different ways. Jesus found a man whom a demon had robbed of speech. Dealing with the demon, Jesus restored the man's ability to speak. The witnessing crowds stood almost speechless in amazement.

11:15. How did he do that? they asked. The only way to do that is through the power of the strongest demon of them all, Beelzebub (see Matt. 10:25; 12:24,27; Mark 3:22). This is apparently a transliteration into Greek of a Canaanite divine name—Baal, the Prince. In 2 Kings 1:2, Hebrew scribes have intentionally changed the name to Baal-Zebub, which means "Lord of the flies." The Jewish world apparently used Beelzebub as a synonym for Satan or the devil.

11:16. Healing a demon-possessed speechless man was not enough. Others wanted a miraculous sign from heaven to prove who Jesus was (cf. Deut. 13:1–2; 2 Kgs. 20:8–11; John 6:30–31).

11:17–19. Jesus as Son of God knew their hearts. This is one divine attribute he maintained even as he limited himself to become human (4:23; 9:47; see Phil. 2). Their logic was faulty. A king did not fight his own army, or the entire war would be lost. A family feud brings ruin for all in the family. Satan would never use his power to exorcise demons, for the demons were a major part of his forces. Jesus explicitly told them he knew what they were thinking and whispering about. Then he turned the charge on them. They claimed to have people in their company with power over demons (Mark 9:38; Acts 19:13–14). Did this mean they were allied with Satan? Oh, no! Their people exorcised demons in God's name. Well then, why could Jesus not do the same? Go let your exorcists be the judge and address the issue: Who has power to cast out demons?

11:20. Your exorcists will say only God can cast out demons, Jesus said. This means I am casting out demons with God's power, by his finger (cf. Exod. 8:15). God casting out demons on earth is proof that God's kingdom is present among you. That means I am the representative of God's kingdom. What are you going to say to that?

11:21–22. Another parable illustrates the point. A muscular, powerful man may use the latest weapons and technology to guard his house, ensuring the safety of all his possessions. The strong person always has a fear. Someone stronger will come and take away all he owns. Thus, Satan has set up a strong dynasty on earth with no one able to threaten him. In Jesus, God has shown himself to be stronger than Satan. He has taken away all possessions and power of Satan. The victory is sure.

11:23. The presence of the kingdom of God overthrowing the power of Satan does not call for an impartial audience enjoying the battle. Everyone must take sides. You must join one camp or the other. If you do not come over to my side, Jesus said, then you have joined the enemy. No "wait and see" attitude. Join the fight and be on the side of either the winner or the loser. I am here to gather a flock of sheep to be God's people. You must choose. Will you help me gather the flock, or do you belong to the enemy so that you are working hard to scatter my flock over the hills where I cannot gather it back together? You are doing one or the other. Are you dedicated to Jesus and God's kingdom or to Satan?

11:24–26. Jesus told another parable to show that defeating Satan and casting out demons is not the point of life. You must do more than get rid of the bad. The demon cast out does not remain inactive. It may return to its natural haunt, the arid desert land (see Lev. 16:10; Isa. 34:13–14), but it will not stay there long. It likes the dwelling it had far more than the desert, so it goes back "home." Without the demon occupying it, the house looks clean, neat, and inviting. The demon goes off seeking company. Seven more demons join him in settling down in the house he first left. The house they settle in is, of course, the man from whom the demon was originally cast out. That man finds his condition worse than ever. Why? Because he was content to have a nice, orderly life without demons. He did not bother to fill that life with something to replace the demons. He should have listened to Christ's words, filled his life with the practice of those words, and had a future to look forward to with Christ. Not having done that, he has no future—only the worse condition of possession by eight demons (cf. 2 Pet. 2:17–20). Life must be lived in the kingdom of God with Jesus, or it is lived as a servant to the evil strong man. Take your choice.

11:27–28. A woman in the audience interrupted. She pronounced a blessing on Jesus' mother (cf. 1:42–48) for bringing him into the world so he could do all the good he was doing. Jesus turned attention away from his mother and from the woman who may have expected blessing or commendation for her words. Rather than giving special homage or attention to his physical family, he turned attention to those who inhabit God's kingdom. True blessing comes to those who hear and obey God's Word (see 8:1–21). Dedication to Jesus involves more than saying good things about him. Dedication to Jesus means listening and obeying.

Ⓒ Dedication's Goal: Be a Light to the World (11:29–36)

SUPPORTING IDEA: *Dedication to Jesus means repenting of one's sins and becoming an example of Christ's light in the world.*

11:29–32. Now Jesus returned to the issue raised by the people who were testing him in verse 16. They wanted a spectacular sign from heaven. But they were out of luck. Only a wicked generation of people makes such demands on God. This is just the opposite of the faith road of dedication. They already have a sign and will see it realized soon in the life of Jesus. This is the sign of Jonah. Jonah represented a call to repentance and faith to the people of Nineveh. When they believed and obeyed his brief sermon, Jonah brought the people of Nineveh away from the verge of disaster to faith and repentance (Jon. 3). Jesus brings the same sign to his generation—a sign that God is calling the nation to repentance.

The queen of Sheba traveled a long distance to hear and see Solomon (1 Kgs. 10:1). Certainly, Jesus' healings and teachings have shown that his wisdom, power, and nearness to God far exceed that of Solomon. Everyone in the world should be rushing to see and hear Jesus. If Nineveh repented at the preaching of poor, comical Jonah—a prophet who tried to run away and escape the call to preach to a nation he detested—what should the present generation do? One far greater than Jonah preached to them. But this generation turned deaf ears on Jesus. They would face judgment. The men of Nineveh would be among those pronouncing this judgment. Yes, foreign enemies would be on God's side against the great Jewish leaders who taught obedience but did not know how to practice it.

11:33–36. Lamps were very precious in Jesus' day. Made from clay, they contained liquid olive oil with a wick. These oil lamps gave off a small amount of flickering light. They were certainly not made for indirect lighting. You had to put a lamp on a clay stand in the middle of the room and let its rays filter out into the dark corners. No sensible person placed it in a hidden place. You do not hide light. You use it for your benefit. Now to the point: Your eye provides light for the body. This may reflect an actual Greek understanding that the eye literally produced light. A good eye thus provided light within the entire body. Conversely, a bad eye robbed the body of any hope of light and cast it into utter darkness. Take care, then, Jesus said. Make sure your eye is good and your body full of light.

How does a person do this? Let the word of Jesus enter your life and illumine your body. Your body will be full of light. The dark deeds of evil will find no place. You will be listening to, obeying, and practicing the word. You will be part of the kingdom. No chance for demons to find a place to live. They love darkness rather than light.

Ⓓ Dedication's Goal: Love, Not Law (11:37–54)

SUPPORTING IDEA: *Dedication in itself is not the goal, for a person may be dedicated to the wrong thing. Jesus calls for dedication to love and ministry, not to law and slavish obedience.*

11:37. Luke repeatedly pictures Jesus in confrontation with the Pharisees, especially at meal scenes (5:29–32; 7:36–50; 14:1–24). Here, in spite of Jesus' harsh conflicts with the Pharisees, the Pharisee actually extended the invitation. Jews normally ate two meals each day, one in mid-morning and one in late afternoon. The Greek word here apparently refers to the mid-morning meal. Following Jewish custom, Jesus lay down on his elbow beside the low dining table.

11:38. The host watched astonished. Jesus prepared to eat in a Pharisee's house without following pharisaic practice and washing his hands ritually before eating. And he had just been in the presence of demons and crowds. He had to be ritually unclean. Such pharisaic practice was another of their ways of updating the law rather than following an explicit biblical command.

11:39–41. Jesus responded with no thought of being a polite guest. He attacked the host and his companions. You scrupulously wash the outside of the cup which never touches anything you eat, he said. Then you ingest food into a body dominated on the inside by greed and wicked thoughts and actions. How foolish can you be! Our Creator made both the inside and the outside. Spend more time checking up on your insides rather than the cup's outsides. Dedicate yourself to what the law is all about, seeking to make you qualified as a member of God's covenant community, being the people of God. Quit dedicating yourself to legalistic actions in which you take pride but which do no good for anybody.

11:42. Jesus launched into a series of woes expressing grief over the Pharisees' actions and attitudes and predicting calamity for them if they did not change (see Matt. 23).

The first woe contrasts emphasis on a normal religious duty with total neglect of God's central teaching. The Old Testament clearly taught God's people to tithe—to give 10 percent of their income, particularly their agricultural crops, to God through the temple and priests (Lev. 27:30–33; Num. 18:12; Deut. 12:6–9; 14:22–29; 26:12–15; Neh. 10:37–38; 12:44; 13:5,12; 2 Chr. 31:5–12; Mal. 3:8,10). The Pharisees pointed out to everyone that they counted every leaf of the smallest plants they grew in their gardens and gave a tenth of these to God. They even included wild plants like rue for which rabbinic custom apparently did not demand the tithe.

Old Testament teaching emphasized the centrality of love and justice for other people and love for God (see 10:27–28; Lev. 19:18; Deut. 6:5; Amos 5; Mic. 6). Correct religious practice has no meaning if one's daily life does not reflect love for God and constant attention to insuring justice and hope for other people, especially those whom society tends to oppress or ignore.

11:43. Religious leadership should help other people to grow and mature in their relationship with God. Religious leaders should devote themselves to worship and study of God's Word. The Pharisees went to worship to be seen by others and went to the town's business center so other people would lavish praise on them as they greeted them. This meant the Pharisees continually sought the public spotlight for themselves without concern for others. They were in love with themselves rather than being in love with God.

11:44. Biblical law taught that contact with the dead or anything connected with the dead made a person ritually unclean and thus disqualified for worship (Lev. 21:1–4,11; Num. 19:11–22). Every Jewish grave was supposed to be clearly marked, so no one would unwittingly touch the grave and become unclean. Jesus claimed the Pharisees were unmarked graves—they were unclean and made anyone who touched them unclean without the victim knowing it. The Pharisees must have drawn back in horror at such a thought! They perceived themselves to be the cleanest of the clean, and so did their fellow Jews. Jesus said they were clean in regard to their own legal system, but they were unclean in regard to items at the top of God's list—love and justice.

11:45. One of the scribes—a group closely associated with the Pharisees (7:30; 10:25; 14:3)—came asking for trouble. He complained that Jesus must have been applying the same woes to them as to the Pharisees. For once, Jesus agreed with a scribe.

11:46. Woes came down on these teachers of the law as well as on Pharisees. These legal experts were just as guilty. They studied the law and wrote the modern interpretations that the people were obliged to fulfill. Then they looked down scornfully on the common people and condemned them for not fulfilling the entire law. Meanwhile, these legal experts never lifted a finger to help the people. They never showed the people how to keep the law. They never tried to make obedience easy. They just kept heaping more regulations on the people along with renewed condemnation. Thus they, too, showed neither love nor justice.

11:47–48. Sarcasm seems to creep into Jesus' words here. Jewish leaders, especially the teachers of the law with their expertise in Scripture, honored the prophets in every way possible. They built elaborate monuments to the prophets, honoring their memory. Jesus interpreted the action in a different way. Their fathers had rejected, ignored, or killed the prophets (1 Kgs. 19:10,14; Neh. 9:26; Jer. 2:30; 26:20–24). The current generation's memorials only honored their fathers' murderous deeds. The current generation thus perpetuated the attitude of their ancestors, refusing to obey the prophets' teachings and honoring those who killed them. In other words, Jesus declared, you do not honor and celebrate who the prophets were and what they taught. You honor and celebrate your fathers for rejecting the prophets' messages and killing them.

11:49–51. Jesus promised that the current generation would have their chance to repent of or repeat their ancestors' sins. God would send Christian prophets and apostles with new teachings from God—teachings concerning Jesus the Messiah. How will this generation act? Just like their fathers, Jesus declared. They will kill and persecute God's messengers. Having celebrated the ancestral prophetic murders and participated in killing Christian prophets and apostles, this generation could take credit for it all. They were responsible for killing all the prophets since the creation of the world. What an accomplishment! They could read their history in the Bible beginning with Abel in Genesis 4, the Bible's first book, clear through to the killing of Zechariah in 2 Chronicles 24:21, the Hebrew Bible's last book. The verdict for this generation: Guilty of murder in the case of every prophet of God. Can you imagine what God's sentence must be?

11:52. Experts in the law should have more knowledge than anyone else, particularly knowledge of God and of his salvation. Jesus said these experts had so reinterpreted, overinterpreted, and misinterpreted the law that the key of knowledge was no longer in use. The scribes did not use the key to know about God. They used it to burden the people. When the laity tried to open the door, find the necessary knowledge, and enter God's kingdom, the legal experts hindered them. This will become a key theme in Acts where the progress of the gospel is charted as the removal of hindrances (Acts 8:36; 10:47; 11:17) until Paul can preach the gospel in jail unhindered (Acts 28:31). These experts in God's law were practicing their profession in such a way that they accomplished exactly the opposite of what God intended for them. What could they expect when they faced God's judgment?

11:53–54. The result of Christ's confrontation with Pharisees and scribes was predictable: plots against his life. The rest of the journey to Jerusalem shows determined dedication of these religious leaders to trick Jesus, shame him, show him up, trap him by his own words, and eventually kill him. Still, Jesus in his dedication to God's mission moved resolutely to Jerusalem and the cross.

MAIN IDEA REVIEW: *Prayer, obedience, love, repentance, and consistency characterize the dedicated life.*

III. CONCLUSION

Authentic Discipleship

In his determined dedication to God, Jesus stopped to teach his disciples, cast out a demon, teach the crowds, and pronounce disaster on the Jewish religious leaders. In so doing, he created a contrast between dedicated discipleship and dedicated opposition to God. Dedicated disciples seek to know how to pray, to ask God to meet their daily needs, to trust God as one who loves them and provides for them, to desire the Holy Spirit to direct their lives, to hear and obey the Word of God, to repent of their sins, and to let God's light shine through their lives. Dedicated opponents of Jesus give Satan credit for what God does, are divided among themselves, scatter God's flock, let evil spirits control their lives, seek signs from God rather than responding to the signs God sends, refuse to repent, are full of darkness and evil, and self-righteously create religious demands on the people with no love for the people or for God and with no intention of helping the people meet the demands or of showing love to God.

Thus, by the activities they use to become clean in God's sight, they have become unclean. Thinking they are honoring past religious heroes, they are actually honoring their murderous ancestors and getting ready to repeat the killing of God's messengers. Proud of their place as God's righteous, they will find they do not have the knowledge that leads to salvation in God's kingdom and they actually hinder those who seek such knowledge. They continued their practice of dedicated opposition to God as they sought ways to trap and kill Jesus—the greatest prophet of all.

PRINCIPLES

- Prayer is an essential part of the life of one who follows Jesus.
- Prayer praises God, seeks daily needs, asks for deliverance from temptation, and promises to forgive others in seeking forgiveness for oneself.
- A dedicated follower of Jesus will ask God for the Holy Spirit to lead his life.
- Jesus is united with his Father in opposing all demonic powers.
- Jesus' miracles show the kingdom of God is active on earth.

- Dedicated followers need not fear Satan, for a Stronger One has come and is defeating him.
- Persons must not only seek relief from Satan's opposition but also the teachings and demands of the kingdom of God to fill a life so the demonic forces cannot return.
- Hearing God's Word and obeying it is the chief source of God's blessings.
- People who will not accept Jesus and repent at his preaching face God's eternal judgment.
- Dedicated followers of Jesus are lights, letting others see God's light and living out an ethical example of light in their lives.
- Dedicated followers of Jesus love God and work for justice in the world rather than following man-made ritualistic laws.
- Dedicated followers of Christ are the source of help for others, not the source of making them unclean and unrighteous.
- Religious leaders are responsible to lead others to know God and enter his kingdom.

APPLICATIONS

- Pray to God every day, praising him and seeking his provisions for your life.
- Ask for the Holy Spirit to guide your life every day.
- Trust God to overcome all satanic powers.
- Listen to God's Word and obey it.
- Let God's Word lead you to repentance and salvation.
- Let God's righteousness and love shine through your life.
- Do not be a hindrance to people who are seeking salvation.
- Help other people as they seek to enter God's kingdom.
- Do not in any way join the dedicated opponents of Jesus.

IV. LIFE APPLICATION

Where Have You Been Since 1958?

The mission volunteers wearily rounded another curve in the dusty Kenyan road. There they met another Kenyan man and his family. One more time they shared the simple gospel message. They never expected his reaction. "Where have you been? In 1958 God showed me a vision of missionaries coming to tell me about Jesus. I went out here to the corner of my field and dedicated a place to Jesus. See the stone I set up? We will build a church here. Why did you not come sooner? I have been praying all these years for you to come. But thank God you have come. I do want to accept Jesus as my Savior. So does my family. Tell us how."

God's kingdom is present in places you sometimes least expect. Prayers are being raised as people sincerely ask God to provide their deepest needs. In the midst of Satan's territory, the Stronger One is at work overthrowing Satan and establishing his kingdom. Meanwhile, God's church is often sitting on its heels, complaining about something not going just like it always has or just as we expect it to. We are busy impressing one another with our religiosity rather than sharing God's good news. We are busy compiling tests of goodness and acceptance in the church rather than helping people come to know and serve Jesus. Has our love for the Word of God shown itself in big words and loud proclamations rather than humble obedience? Luke 11 indicates that church people should beware, for Jesus has many more problems with religious people who do not repent than with sinners who do. Where is your dedication? In love of God and justice for all people? Or in fulfilling your religious rules and gaining glory for yourself on earth?

V. PRAYER

God of justice and love, so often I have been a follower of rules and rituals. I feel secure in going to church and having church people tell me how fine I am. My prayers fall on appreciative ears in the church but never rise to you. May my life show your holiness. May I forgive other people rather than condemning them. May I recognize how faithful you are in supplying daily needs. May I live as a light for you to the world. Make me a dedicated follower of Jesus, not one of his dedicated opponents. In his loving name I pray. Amen.

VI. DEEPER DISCOVERIES

A. "Lord, teach us to pray" (11:1)

Prayer was a major part of Jesus' life, and Luke emphasized this in his Gospel. In Jesus' day, disciples of rabbis often asked for instruction about specific practices. The disciples, aware of its importance to their Master, made this request of him. The model prayer contains the components and attitudes that Jesus' disciples should exhibit in their lives. The first half of this model prayer focuses God-ward while the second half focuses us-ward. The elements of God's kingdom, our provision, the need for forgiveness, and dealing with temptation are parts of the believer's daily experience. The model prayer is an example of the kind of prayer that God honors.

B. "Give us each day our daily bread" (11:3)

The use of the word *bread* here is an example of a figure of speech known as *synecdoche* in which a part represents the whole. In this case, a part (bread) represents the whole (food). In this context, bread becomes a request for the basic necessities of life, not its luxuries.

C. Boldness, Persistence, Being Ashamed (11:8)

The Greek word *anaideian* is a key expression in helping us understand Jesus' teaching on prayer, but its precise meaning is difficult. It is related to the term *aidos* that refers basically to a feeling of shame caused by defeat or wrong action. This can then be turned to refer to the respect and consideration owed to other people, originally those who brought defeat on us. It also comes to refer to a restraint, a sense of modesty that prevents us from acting excessively. This also becomes a sense of personal honor and self-respect. From another perspective it describes a feeling of fear, then of reverence before a royal figure or even God. The term in verse 8, *anaideia*, is an impudence that will accomplish its goals by any means. It is what Louw and Nida (66.12) call "a lack of sensitivity to what is proper"—an insolence that keeps on knocking or asking because it lacks a sense of what is proper.

The term apparently applies to the man asleep who does not want to get up for the neighbor but does so to avoid losing face, being ashamed, and dishonored.

D. The Beelzebub Controversy (11:14–23)

Beelzebub is a name for Satan in the New Testament spelled differently in Greek manuscripts. The term is based on the Hebrew word *Baal-Zebub*. On occasions, Jesus' opponents accused him of being linked with the devil. Jesus answered them by pointing out that it was God's power at work through him, not the devil's. God used the casting out of demons to press his sovereign claims on those who saw these things.

E. Woe (11:42–52)

The word *woe* (*ouai*) denotes a grieving, giving up to judgment. Grammatically, it is an interjection of grief or denunciation and is often rendered "alas!" Jesus used the word *woe* here not as a curse but as an expression of deep regret. Jesus' purpose for these woes was to expose the sins of the Pharisees and lawyers to try to help them and the people adversely influenced by them.

VII. TEACHING OUTLINE

A. INTRODUCTION

1. Lead Story: Busy Making Every Day Count

2. Context: Jesus stopped on his way to Jerusalem to teach his disciples, the crowds, and his religious opponents. The disciples followed out of their dedication to Jesus without knowing what that meant. The crowds followed because they wanted to find new signs to gossip about, help for sick friends, or free meals for themselves. Jewish leaders followed because they were dedicated to a religion of tradition and obedience and searching for a way to trap or kill Jesus. In this situation, Jesus showed the disciples how to pray and gave them encouragement to do so. He cast out a demon, evoking questions from the crowd. These gave him opportunity to teach the difference between the kingdom of Satan and the kingdom of God.

Another interruption from the crowd gave Jesus opportunity to underline again the nature of his family as the family of the obedient before explaining what sign the people would receive and its consequences when they rejected it. Next, he defined discipleship as obedience that let the light of obedience shine through a person's life rather than the darkness of evil. Finally, Jesus confronted his opponents, directing funeral woes against them because they faced judgment for hindering rather than helping those who sought to get into the kingdom.

3. Transition: Today, we stand before Jesus. As we do, we must assume three poses. First, perhaps we are disciples wanting to know how to pray. Second, we may be members of the crowd, following Jesus to see what we can get out of it and wondering when the really big moment is coming when he will show his power. Finally, we could be religious people with pride in our religion and contempt and prejudice for those who do not do religion just like we do. Dare we learn the awful truth that most of us really are all three of these types of people? Dare we listen to let Jesus bring light to our life? Dare we dedicate ourselves to being the type of disciples Jesus seeks rather than the opponents he condemns?

B. COMMENTARY

1. Dedication in Prayer: Praise and Petition (11:1–13)
   a. The setting: Jesus at prayer asked for lessons (11:1)
   b. The Master's response: model prayer (11:2–4)
   c. The Master's explanation: dedication trusts and asks (11:5–13)
2. Dedication's Driving Force: Satan or Kingdom Obedience (11:14–28)
   a. The setting: Jesus casts out a demon (11:14)
   b. The opponents' reaction: the devil did it (11:15–16)
   c. The Master's response: divided you fall; I am united with the Father (11:17–26)

    d. The crowd's reaction: blessed is your mother (11:27)

    e. The Master's counter response: blessed are the obedient (11:28)

3. Dedication's Goal: Be a Light to the World (11:29–36)

    a. The setting: larger crowds (11:29a)

    b. The Master's response: no sign but Jonah's (11:29b–32)

    c. The Master's lesson: be filled with light (11:33–36)

4. Dedication's Goal: Love, Not Law (11:37–54)

    a. The setting: a Pharisee's dinner invitation (11:37)

    b. The opponents' surprise: Jesus ignores ritual (11:38)

    c. The Master's response: try merciful not ritual acts (11:39–41)

    d. The Master's woes: doomed by neglecting love and justice (11:42–44)

    e. The opponents' reaction: we are insulted (11:45)

    f. The Master's woes continued: doomed for not practicing your teaching and not helping your pupils (11:46–52)

    g. The opponents' conclusion: trap him (11:53–54)

C. CONCLUSION: WHERE HAVE YOU BEEN SINCE 1958?

VIII. ISSUES FOR DISCUSSION

1. In what way do verses 2–4 give us a model prayer? a sample prayer? the Lord's Prayer? How do you use this in your prayer life?

2. Why can you confidently pray to God? Why does God answer prayer?

3. What fills your life so demons cannot take up residence there? What evidence does your life give that your answer is really true?

4. What evidence can you give that you are obeying the Word of God?

5. What is "the sign of Jonah" in this chapter? Who is the one greater than Jonah? Have you listened to his preaching? How have you reacted? Why?

6. Is your body completely lighted, or do corners of darkness still remain to harm your witness and hinder God's gospel?

7. In what ways are you and your church like the Pharisees and experts in the law? How would Jesus address you today? What are you doing to avoid the Pharisees' mistakes?

8. Do you quietly try to trap Jesus so you will not have to obey all he says?

Luke 12

Dedicated and Dependent

"*Worry* makes you forget who's in charge. And when the focus is on yourself . . . you worry. . . . With time your agenda becomes more important than God's. You're more concerned with pleasing self than pleasing him. And you may even find yourself doubting God's judgment."

M a x   L u c a d o

Luke 12

IN A NUTSHELL

Fear controls too much of life. Afraid that we will not please others, we become hypocrites. Afraid of those in power, we forfeit our integrity. Afraid of ridicule, we deny Jesus. Afraid of poverty and want, we deify our wealth. Afraid of death and suffering, we lose trust in God. Afraid we have missed our opportunity, we are not ready when God calls. Afraid we will not get all that is coming to us, we take things into our hands rather than waiting to accept the reward God has prepared for us. Afraid of what our family will think, we let family loyalty override loyalty to God. Jesus seeks to lead us to trust God and overcome all fear.

Dedicated and Dependent

I. INTRODUCTION

A Prison Habit

*D*avid Redding tells of a dear friend of his son who became a top investment counselor. He had more money than he could use and seemed to have it made. He didn't need to depend on anyone, since he controlled his own destiny. Then he began using his resources to try some of life's exciting experiences. Soon he was totally dependent on drugs. His large income could not pay for his habit. Crime became the source of income to buy cocaine. Soon he was in a prison cell dependent on hardened criminals just to stay alive. He suffered pain, embarrassment, shame, and humiliation beyond description. Still, this dependence was not as bad as his drug dependence had been.

Using brute strength and determination, Bob soon climbed near the top of the prison pecking order. Still, the hurt was too much to bear. He had to find help. He retreated to the darkest corner in the cell and bowed before God. Gradually, this became a nightly habit. Soon an inmate with deep psychological problems began asking, "Bob, aren't you going to say a prayer for us tonight?" Gradually, others joined in until fifteen of the inmates were on their knees with him each night. Bob concluded: "Even if I could be paroled right now, I'd refuse. I'm having the best time I've ever had in my life. I've never imagined being so close to God. Don't worry about me. I'm praying for you" (*A Rose Will Grow Anywhere*, 154–155).

Luke 12 forces us into the same kind of decision. Which life do we want? A life dependent on things of this world, or a life with no guarantee of any of the world's goods but close to God? The financial counselor turned drug addict turned prison inmate turned friend of God made many choices— dependence on money, on drugs, on other prisoners, on his own strength and determination, on God. This chapter asks you to see where you are in your pilgrimage through life. What do you refuse to give up to be close to God? What will it take for you to trust God more than you trust something or someone in this world?

II. COMMENTARY

Dedicated and Dependent

MAIN IDEA: *You can declare your independence from fear and from dependence on anything the world offers by trusting God fully.*

ⓐ Dedication as Dependence: On the World or on God (12:1–12)

> **SUPPORTING IDEA:** *Fear need not control your life if you are willing to rely on the Holy Spirit.*

12:1. Crowds pushed, shoved, kicked, and trampled to get near Jesus. Ignoring them and thus illustrating his independence from them, Jesus turned to teach his disciples. They must make up their minds. Did they want to please the prominent religious authorities of their day, or would they display their trust in God? To please the Pharisees a person had to pretend to please God while living a self-sufficient life of pride in self and contempt for others. This was hypocrisy—a dangerous hypocrisy. Like yeast it gradually worked its way through all of a person's life and relationships.

12:2. The hypocrite tries to cover up his life, not letting others see who he actually is. Jesus warned that this was impossible. God would bring their secret lives into the open. Hypocrisy faces God's judgment. Do not go the hypocritical way of the Pharisees.

12:3. Hypocritical Pharisees plotted together in secret meetings to decide what to demand of the laity and how to gain prominence and a following for themselves. They judged people in secret councils and poured contempt on them. They thought no one would find out what they were doing. Jesus reminded them that God knows all and at the final judgment, if not before, he will reveal all. You cannot hide hypocritical acts or words.

12:4–5. Jesus was on the way to Jerusalem, knowing he would be betrayed and crucified. He was thus illustrating what he taught here. The hypocritical religious leaders would get him. They would kill him. But they could not stop God's plan in his life. He called his disciples to take up their cross and follow him to death. If they remained true to Jesus, the religious leaders would kill them, too, as we see in the Book of Acts.

Fear should have another object. Who can do more than kill the body? Who can bring eternal punishment in Gehenna? (See "Deeper Discoveries.") Behind this stands Jesus' basic assumption. Life on this earth is not what is important. Eternity should be our focus. Anything or anyone whose power is limited to this world deserves no attention. The one with power to determine your eternal destination deserves your focus. That is very limiting. God alone has authority over eternity. So, fear God and ignore everyone else.

12:6–7. Let us illustrate the point from the opposite perspective. Think not of the most powerful force on earth. Think of the weakest thing on earth. Can anything be weaker or less significant than a few birds worth maybe two cents? Literally, they are worth two small coins, each of which is worth one sixteenth of a denarius. A denarius was the ordinary wage for a full day's work by a day laborer.

But look at God! He knows every one of the sparrows and cares for the daily fate of each one. Compare this to yourself. God knows how many hairs are on your head. Yes, he cares for you in this world and in the world to come. You are valued! Fear and reverence the one who values you, not the one who opposes you.

12:8–9. What happens when you fear God? You have no fear before men. You will tell every person you meet that Jesus is the Son of God, the promised messianic Savior. When you do this, Jesus, as the Son of Man, will recognize you before the heavenly angelic counsel as belonging to his kingdom. This means your eternal victory is assured. What happens when earthly fear takes charge? Religious hypocrites come after you like they came after Jesus. Will you join their hypocritical line and say you never knew Jesus? Or will you confess that Jesus is your Lord? Now make your decision: fear human persecution—or fear not being included in Christ's eternal kingdom.

12:10. Here Luke inserts a saying that is difficult to interpret. (See "Deeper Discoveries.") Jesus contrasted rejecting the Son of Man and blaspheming against the Holy Spirit. This appears to place the Spirit in a position superior to that of Jesus. Closer examination shows, however, that the contrast is not between the Spirit and the Son. The contrast is between deserting Jesus in his earthly ministry in one particular situation and rejecting the ongoing work of the Holy Spirit in bringing salvation.

Readers of Luke's Gospel could easily read the previous verses and remember some moment in their personal history when they did not stand up and confess Jesus. They might then read verse 10 and decide they could never be forgiven. This verse tries to correct such a feeling. It wants to say that everyone has denied Jesus at some time. They can be forgiven. Peter could deny Jesus during his trial and still be forgiven and accepted back (John 21). A person who has the Holy Spirit wooing him to salvation and who constantly rejects him cannot be forgiven. Thus, if you know the Spirit is inhabiting your life and guiding you, then you know you have not committed this unforgivable sin.

12:11–12. Another problem arises for the reader. What historical context is addressed here? Is this truly an address only to the Twelve (or an extended group of disciples) in Jesus' day (see v. 1)? Or does this have meaning for contemporary readers? Many commentators want to limit verses 11–12 only to Jesus' day. To be consistent in such interpretation, they need to place the same limitation on verses 1–10 also. My personal understanding is that all Scripture retains meaning for the original audience to whom it was spoken, to the audience which first read it in written form, and to the ongoing generations of readers who continue to read Scripture as God's Word.

Under this interpretation, I am supposed to accept persecution and capital punishment judgments and still confess Jesus. What do I say in such an awesome situation? How do I testify to Jesus in the face of persecutors and judges? No fear, says Jesus. When you need to testify, the Spirit will show you what to say. You are not responsible for figuring out what to say. You are responsible for saying what the Spirit tells you to say. Do you have faith and courage to obey the Spirit in the face of persecutors? This is the ultimate test of your dependence on Jesus.

B Dedication to Riches: Redefining Wealth (12:13–21)

SUPPORTING IDEA: *Fear of financial failure should not control your life, since wealth can buy nothing in eternity.*

12:13–14. An anonymous member of the crowd interrupted Jesus. He set Jesus up as a human judge deciding inheritance rights. Jesus denied that he had any right to act in such a position. That belongs to the nation's court system.

12:15. Not making a legal judgment, Jesus did make a moral one. Your request shows how greedy you are, he told the man. Lay aside your greed. Think about life. What is most important to you? Money or relationship with God? Surely, your life is more important than what you own.

12:16–19. Jesus illustrated his teaching with a parable. A farmer overcame all agricultural odds and achieved great success. But this brought a new problem. What do you do with your riches? How do you store it until you can sell it or use it? How can you keep it from rotting and ruining? The answer is obvious. Build bigger barns. This is a great short-term solution, but can you afford the capital investment in relationship to what you normally expect? Sure I can, the farmer declared, for this crop is so good it will support me for years to come. I will be on easy street. I can eat, drink, and party with my friends. I don't have to worry about money and work any more.

12:20. But God has another perspective: you must die tonight. Then what happens to all your wealth?

12:21. This is not an exceptional case. It applies to anyone who trusts in riches. Riches have one major weakness. They have no purchasing power after death. They cannot buy the currency needed to get to heaven. Do not try to be rich in regard to the bank or barn. Be rich in relationship to God. Through prayer, study, obedience, and practice of the word, be sure you are part of the kingdom of God.

C Dedication in Daily Life: Present Service and Future Readiness (12:22–40)

SUPPORTING IDEA: *Christian dedication is to kingdom service, not worldly goods, and to preparation for Christ's return, not personal pleasure at the master's absence.*

12:22–23. Worry occupies too much of our lives. Jesus told the disciples clearly: Do not worry about life's necessities, food and clothing. The central core of life is much more than eating and clothing. Now this is not intended to dismiss the pleas of someone deep in poverty. Such a person needs to trust in God, but he or she also needs to be able to trust in us as God's instruments to care for his needy people. The verse is directed at people like the man planning to build a new barn who have sufficient earthly goods and spend their time scheming and fretting how to get more. Let God take care of the essentials, Jesus declared. You be sure you are prepared to face God's final judgment. Certainly, if you are not going to worry about the basics, do not worry about the rest of it either. Worry is not a part of God's menu for living. Let the Holy Spirit lead in your decision-making process, and trust him to lead you to meaningful life. Trust eases worry out of your life.

12:24. Jesus illustrated his point from nature. Ravens cannot farm. A raven will never grow and harvest a crop or build a barn. This means they never know where today's food is coming from, much less tomorrow's. Still, they live a good life and seldom miss a meal. God provides for the ravens. Cannot you trust him to provide for you? After all, who is worth more to God—a raven in the skies or a person made in his image and entrusted with caring for his universe?

12:25. What do you accomplish by worrying? We are not certain precisely what Jesus meant by his example. The Greek word for "single hour" can mean either eighteen inches or one hour. Jesus may have been talking about adding to one's height or to one's time on earth—probably the latter. Whichever is meant, worrying accomplishes nothing. Rather, worrying slumps the shoulders and stresses the body so much that it may actually subtract hours or years from your life.

12:26. Jesus concluded almost comically. If you cannot do such a small thing as create an hour, why worry about anything else? You certainly cannot accomplish the rest. Worry is not worth the effort.

12:27–28. Need another example? Look at the wildflowers in the field. Not one of them ever picked up needle and thread to make beautiful clothes for themselves, Jesus pointed out. Yet who has clothing as beautiful as theirs? Not even the fabulously rich Solomon (see 1 Kgs. 10:4–6,23)! What is going to happen to these beautiful flowers? They will dry up and be burned for fuel in a day or two. If God does such an elaborate job for such fleeting flowers, what will he do for you? You are worth so much more than fragile flowers. Where is your faith? Trust God for what you need. Quit worrying!

12:29–30. The sum total of it all: Do not spend so much effort and worry on things God has promised to provide. Do not fret over what might happen. Do not let radical mood swings control your life. God will take care of you. Trust him.

12:31–32. Freed from worry and stewing over material things, what are you to do? Set up one goal and accomplish it. Be part of God's kingdom. Do the work he gives you to do. Concentrate on being God's instruments to establish his kingdom here on earth. As he provided for the mission of the Twelve and of the seventy-two, so he will provide for you. Surrender your fear. Do not let anxiety rule your life. Trust the Father. The delight of his life is to find ways to give not just daily needs but his whole kingdom to you. Kingdom heirs don't have to worry about the small stuff.

12:33. We must go one step further. Dedication to Jesus is more than becoming worry-free. It is loving and living like him. So do not depend on your money. Give what you own to the poor. Do not even be tempted by your moneybags or purses. These will just grow old, rot, and be ruined. You need purses that can never be ruined. Such are not earthly, but heavenly. Obey God, practice his word, follow with him to the cross. Trust him. You will store up your heavenly treasures. Treasures here bring fears of thieves and robbers. Such people do not exist in heaven. Nothing can destroy or rob you of your treasure there. Earthly treasures you will constantly worry about. Heavenly treasures give no cause for worry.

12:34. To summarize the matter: Choose where you want to store up treasure. Your heart, the center of emotions and mental activities, will concentrate on where you have your treasures. Your identity is determined by where your heart is. Ignore God, and spend all your physical, emotional, and psychic energy on the world's goods and earthly success. Or trust God, and spend all your efforts on kingdom matters. To worry or not to worry—that is your question!

12:35. But how do you do all this? Tuck the bottom of your robes into your belt and trim and light your lamps so you are ready to serve God. A servant of the kingdom is always on call. He has no time for delay. No time to go out to buy oil. No time to get the wick fixed right in the oil. No time to light the lamps so they will keep on burning. No time to adjust your clothing so you can run to the duty the Master assigns. Time only to hear the "all to service" and set out to complete the task. This is especially true in light of the coming judgment. You must be ready to move when Christ returns. Do not think you can make preparations for his coming then. Do not think you can change your position from worrying about material goods to serving the kingdom then. When Christ comes, be ready to move with him.

12:36. The Master is away celebrating. Wedding celebrations may last four to seven days. Matters not how long. When he returns, he does not want to have to rouse you from your bed to open the door. He wants you at the door ready to open and to carry out the tasks he has planned for you.

12:37–38. For those who are ready, what a surprise. No barking of commands. No extra burden of work. Instead, it is role reversal. The slaves will lie down at the table ready to eat. The Master will put on the servant's clothes, prepare the food, and serve the servants. What a reward for being ready and for storing up heavenly treasures! Just remember: Be alert twenty-four hours seven days a week until he comes. No slack time allowed. He may come when you least expect him, in the middle of the night. Be alert, and be blessed.

12:39–40. Need reinforcement on this point? Think about the man down the street whose house was broken into and robbed. What would have happened if the thief had set up an appointment to come rob the house? The owner of the house would have had guards ready to nab him. Christ, the Son of Man, is coming back just as unexpectedly as the thief came to break in and rob the house. So be ready.

ⅅ Dedication with Responsibility: Do What You Know (12:41–53)

SUPPORTING IDEA: *Christian dedication involves the responsibility to do what you already know you should do.*

12:41. Jesus' parables taught the mysteries of the kingdom to the disciples, keeping them from the crowds (8:10). Now Jesus seemed to be addressing the crowds. Peter was confused, and he blatantly expressed his confusion. Who did Jesus intend this for?

12:42–48. Jesus answered a question with a parable. The parable centers on an administrator who is both wise and faithful—one who can make good decisions and who also carries out the task to completion in a trustworthy manner. Such a person the master gives a large responsibility—making sure the household staff has adequate food. Note that Luke moves from slaves to Lord and household staff language. Then he moves (v. 43) immediately back to speak of slave, the chosen administrator being a slave to the master. If he is faithful, then he will be blessed. That blessing is defined as greater responsibility, not just food allotments but manager of the entire estate.

Not all slaves meet the qualifications. Some seize responsibility as opportunity to show personal power and to take advantage of those for whom they have responsibility. They use the added access to the master's goods to indulge their own hungers and vices. Such abuse of other people and self-indulgence do not win the day. The master finally returns and catches the administrator-slave in the act. With a sudden twist, Jesus applied the illustration not to the world of business but to the dedication of discipleship. The person who pretends to be a disciple but is unfaithful in doing so—the one who appeared to hear the word gladly but soon forsook it (see 8:1–15), the one who refuses to take up his cross and follow Jesus without worrying about material needs—this one is cut in two and given an eternal place with the unbelievers. Fake discipleship—discipleship without dedication to Jesus—does not fool the Lord. He will exact the punishment deserved. The servant unprepared for the master's return finds himself suffering the flogging and punishment any unfaithful servant would endure.

Some servants, however, have no assignment. They do not know what the master wants of them. He apparently does not even know the rules by which the master runs the house. This unknowing servant breaks the rules, but does so unintentionally. The judicial system would seem to demand severe punishment for him. Jesus lightens the sentence to only a few blows. The principle of Christ's kingdom becomes clear: we are responsible in proportion to the task given. The more God gives you opportunity to do, the more he requires of you and the harsher the punishment for not being faithful.

Thus, Peter's question finds something of an answer. The parable is spoken to everyone, or at least everyone who belongs in some way to God's household. All are servants in this household. But some servants have more responsibility. They have become leaders over others. They must pay special attention to the parable. They face greater punishment should they not be wise and faithful in carrying out their leadership responsibilities. Everyone is responsible before God. Leaders of God's people carry a heavy responsibility.

12:49. Jesus positioned himself within the situation just described. His coming will bring severe judgment. John the Baptist had said the Messiah would baptize with the Holy Spirit and with fire (3:16; cf. 3:9,17; 9:54; 17:29). Baptism with fire is a picture of judgment on those who do not accept the Prince of Peace. Jesus' coming as Savior included the punishment of those who would not dedicate themselves to his mission.

The last part of the verse surprises us. Jesus was ready to set the fire and let the unbelievers face their punishment. This apparently is not a statement of frustration, with Jesus wanting to get the whole thing over with. Rather, it is a statement of dedication to the mission and readiness to complete the task even though it involves his own baptism.

12:50. This baptism differs radically from what Jesus experienced from John the Baptist. This is why he is headed to Jerusalem. This baptism comes from betrayers. This is the baptism of death, of crucifixion. Having set his face toward Jerusalem, he was focused on completing this baptism and thus showing himself to be the faithful servant of his Father. He is ready to be the Savior on the cross for the rising and falling of many people.

12:51–53. Jesus again knew what the disciples were thinking. They saw him as a man of peace, perhaps the king who would win the war to end all wars and create the messianic kingdom of peace (see Isa. 9; 11). They still had much to learn about Messiah. Jesus came to divide families and friends. He was the dividing line. Dedication and faithfulness to him set a person apart from family and friends. The coming of Jesus the Messiah left no room for neutrality. You choose to be for him or against him. Your choice brings strong opposition and separation from those closest to you who make the other choice.

E Dedication to Common Sense: Judge for Yourselves or Pay the Penalty (12:54–59)

SUPPORTING IDEA: *Christian dedication is often a matter of commonsense knowledge, making the only logical and reasonable choice.*

12:54–55. Jesus reminded the crowd how much they knew. They could easily predict the coming of a rainstorm. Similarly, when the wind turned suddenly to the south from the direction of the desert, they knew a scorcher was on the way. No one had to tell them these things. They just knew them.

12:56–57. Common sense should give you more knowledge. You should be able to understand what Jesus teaches on the judgment and recognize the signs of the times. You should see in Jesus the power of the Son of God. You should understand that only Messiah can do the things he does and teach the way he teaches. You have no reason not to be prepared when the Master returns. Yet you are not ready. You hypocrites! Why are you not ready? Use your common sense and prepare for the coming storm of judgment.

12:58–59. A somewhat enigmatic story concludes the section. This is not a parable, for the characters are the audience addressed. Your enemy comes and drags you off to face the king. The enemy wants the king to convict you of crime and make you pay reimbursement to the enemy. Now what does common sense say: Settle as quickly as possible or I will be in jail. Then I will stay there until I am able to pay the last penny that the enemy claims I owe. That could be forever. No, not that! Let us find a way to settle this before we reach the judge and it is too late. That is commonsense business. Well, the judge of all the earth is coming to judge the earth. You had better settle with him before it is too late. His prison has no parole and no release for served time. Every sentence in his justice system is eternal. Do not be unfaithful, too late, or unwise. Use your common sense and find a way to settle accounts with God. Then he can place you among the saved to live with him in heaven rather than among the lost where you now abide. You know their destiny. You do not want to share their fate.

MAIN IDEA REVIEW: *You can declare your independence from fear and from dependence on anything the world offers by trusting God fully.*

III. CONCLUSION

Know Jesus. No Fear.

As I write this, I am three weeks away from going to Kenya on a mission trip for the third time. I have encouraged many people to go with me. The most common answer I get is: "I am afraid to." The fear comes from different directions. Many are simply afraid to fly. Others fear to be gone so far from home for two weeks. Others are afraid of witnessing in an unknown land to people of an entirely different culture. Of course, many of these people are afraid of witnessing at all, since they do not witness at home either. Then I tell them I have someone special going with me this year: my new bride of one month. Then they really prick up their ears. You are going to take your new wife to Africa? Both of you are going to leave her ten-year-old daughter back here? You are going to take your wife to an African crossroads you could never find again by yourself and let her go off into the trees and cornfields accompanied only by two Africans? How can you not be afraid you will never see her again?

Fear and worry are so closely tied together. We find so many things to worry about in every activity of life. I can honestly say, I have no fear of flying. I have no fear of witnessing. I have no fear of going to Africa. I have no fear of leaving a beloved ten-year-old. I have no fear of letting my wife tread off through the African fields without me or any other American. Why? Because in each of these activities, I am not alone. God has called us to Africa for this mission adventure. God will take care of us. He will provide what we need. If he chooses not to, then he may choose to give us our final blessing. Whatever he chooses, I trust him to lead my life in much better ways than I can ever do.

Such testimony is not braggadocio, saying I am a better Christian with more faith than anyone else. It is simply one of thousands of testimonies to those who have tried to live out Jesus' teachings and who have found they work. My fears and worries have never accomplished anything. Jesus said they would not. My adventures of going on the road I choose rather than the road God chooses have resulted in several disasters and no victories. Finally, he has taught me to follow him. This requires a dedication that does not let fear and worry become part of the daily menu.

This is what Luke 12 is all about. God has shown his care for the creatures of nature. Surely, he cares for me more. He says to live life in expectation of coming judgment. To do so, I must go where he shows me he is at work, even if that is in the most isolated places of Kenya. He has shown me not to depend on material goods. In Kenya I learn again how happy Christians are without knowing where tomorrow's food comes from. God says seek his kingdom. That search has led us to Kenya. There God has given responsibility and opportunity. There we try to manage the opportunity with the best wisdom, faithfulness, and common sense we have received from him.

PRINCIPLES

- A Christian has no reason to fear or worry.
- Possessions are not a help in dedicating oneself to God. They may actually be a hindrance.
- Human plans eventually fail in light of divine decisions.
- God alone has the power to determine our eternal destiny, so he is the only one to be feared.
- Refusal to respond to the Spirit's urging brings eternal judgment.
- Christ will return to the earth in judgment over those who are not dedicated to him.
- God's kingdom should be the only focus of one's life.
- Christians with greater responsibility and opportunity must be ready to face stricter judgment.
- Kingdom choices separate earthly relationships.
- Common sense should make you get ready for Christ's return so you will not face his fiery punishment.

APPLICATIONS

- Quit trying to please people when this keeps you from pleasing God.
- Fear God, but trust him to provide all your needs.
- Take every opportunity to tell people about Jesus.
- Answer the Spirit's call, and dedicate yourself to Jesus as your personal Lord and Savior.
- Rely on the Spirit in life's hardest times.
- Do not let possessions become the focus of life, replacing God and his kingdom.
- Do not worry about daily needs, but focus on Christ's kingdom and trust God to provide daily needs.
- Sell your excess possessions to help the poor and needy have the necessities God wants them to enjoy.
- Get ready now for Christ to return.

IV. LIFE APPLICATION

Dedicated in Life and Death

Fear, rage, and demand for revenge swept through the Western world in January of 1956. The first news filtered out of Ecuador, where missionaries made headlines. Five dedicated men with their families had planned for years the best way to reach a new people group with the gospel. The Auca Indians had never heard of Christ. Finally the day to put planning into action. With their small missionary plane, they flew over the territory and dropped gifts for the people. Finally, one group placed a parrot in the bucket they dropped on a string from the airplane.

Encouraged, the five missionaries landed the plane. A few Auca men approached the plane and accepted the gifts the missionaries extended. They even took a ride in the missionaries' strange plane. A look at the faces of the first flying Aucas revealed their delight. The missionaries radioed back home how well the plan was working.

The next day the missionaries prepared to carry out step two of their plan. They began to walk to the Auca village to tell them about Jesus. The village men walked out to greet them. Suddenly, they lifted their bows and shot arrows into the men's bodies until the five missionaries lay dead.

Why would five highly educated and intelligent men leave the quiet comfort of America to try to tell an isolated tribe in the mountains of Ecuador about Jesus? These five men had heard the call of the kingdom. Worldly fears did not deter them. Worldly fortune did not allure them. They depended on God and on him alone. Later the wife of one of the dead missionaries would lead the first Auca convert to Christ. A Christian beachhead was established. The purpose of the five missionaries was accomplished. The price was insignificant. They had their reward in Jesus and needed no earthly rewards.

This seems an extreme example that none of us would be expected to follow. In reality, these men simply took up their cross and were baptized with the baptism Jesus experienced. The world would say they should have carried out their plan with greater care. They should have worried about the possible consequences. They should have feared what the Aucas might do. The missionaries did not listen to the world. They listened to God. He said, Go. They went. They became rich toward God.

Luke 12 describes Christian dedication in contrast to earthly dedication. The world is dedicated to riches, personal power and influence, safety, individual rights, food and clothing, manipulation and abuse of others, parties and pleasure, and freedom from imprisonment and suffering. Christ's kingdom is dedicated to trusting God for all needs, holding God in awe and reverence, witnessing to Christ's salvation, forgiveness, heavenly treasures, bringing in God's rule on earth, caring for the poor, being ready for the return of Christ, and carrying out God's work with wisdom and faithfulness. Luke 12 calls us to decide. To what are you dedicated? How you answer determines how you will experience the last judgment. Are you ready for it? It is coming when you least expect.

V. PRAYER

God, my judge, send your Spirit to guide me as I try to get ready to face your judgment. Take away worry and fear from my life. Take away my concentration on the world's goods and the world's way of power. I dedicate myself to you to seek your kingdom. I want you to rule my life and our world and universe. As I wait for your kingdom to come, show me the task you have for me to work with you. Let me be faithful in accomplishing the task. Amen.

VI. DEEPER DISCOVERIES

A. Yeast of the Pharisees (12:1)

Jesus reserved his harshest criticism and condemnation for the Pharisees. To the Jewish people these seemed the least likely objects for such ridicule. The Pharisees exerted great efforts to know God's will and to do it. They knew more about what the law taught and how the rabbinic tradition said it should be interpreted for modern life and culture. They were always visible in the temple and on the street corners as they recited their prayers and let people know what was right and wrong. The Pharisees were the most pious of all the pious people.

Jesus had a different perspective on the Pharisees. They knew a lot. They prayed a lot. They told others how to act. But was piety defined by obedience of law, especially ritual and cleanliness law? Jesus declared that the important thing was love and justice. The attitude of the Pharisees showed no love for anyone. They were too busy judging those who did not come up to their standards. Justice might be on their lips, but its application was too narrow to meet the prophetic demands. Thus, the Pharisees in the name of carrying out God's will actually turned people away from God's will, since they offered no love and no justice. Jesus claimed that to follow their leadership would be to follow them to eternal judgment.

B. Hell (12:5)

Luke warns people of God's judgment by declaring that God is the only one who can send the dead into *Gehenna*, the Greek word translated "hell" in the NIV. The term appears only here in Luke. Originally, it was built from two

Hebrew words meaning "Valley of Hinnom." This valley ran southwest of Jerusalem, and it served as the boundary between the tribes of Benjamin and Judah (Josh. 15:8; 18:16). It was used as the city's garbage dump. Here Canaanite gods were worshiped, and here children were sacrificed to the gods (Jer. 7:31; 19:4–5; 32:35). Isaiah used the high place (Topheth) of the valley to describe burning judgment (30:33; cf. 33:14; 66:24). In Jewish literature written during the time between the Old Testament and the New Testament, a strong belief in the underworld developed, with the Valley of Himmon becoming seen as the place of fiery judgment. The word **Gehenna** appears twelve times in the New Testament, each referring to fiery judgment of the wicked (Matt. 5:22,29–30; 10:28; 18:9; 23:15,33; Mark 9:43,45,47; Luke 12:5; Jas. 3:6). Gehenna occurred before creation (Matt. 25:41), and its punishment is eternal (Matt. 25:41,46). The same idea is expressed in other language such as judgment, wrath, destruction, Tartarus, fire, lake of fire and sulfur (Heb. 10:27; 2 Pet. 2:4; Jude 7; Rev. 19:20; 20:10,14; 21:8).

C. Blasphemy Against the Holy Spirit (12:10)

This unforgivable sin has raised great discussion among Bible scholars. It appears in Mark 3:29 as well as Matthew 12:32. Mark appears to define it as crediting Satan with acts done by the Spirit through Jesus (Mark 3:22). Jesus defined blasphemy against the Holy Spirit as denying that the Spirit of God works in the ministry of Jesus Christ and those whom Jesus sends out to continue his ministry. This is a stubborn attitude of heart, not just a one-time statement of the mouth.

VII. TEACHING OUTLINE

A. INTRODUCTION

1. Lead Story: A Prison Habit
2. Context: In Luke 12 Jesus continued the journey to Jerusalem and his teaching on dedication. Chapter 12 is essentially a collection of Christ's teachings to the disciples and the crowds showing that dedicated living is dependent living. Either one is dependent on worldly values like plotting and scheming and amassing wealth or on heavenly values such as confessing Christ before people and relying on the Holy Spirit. Worldly values lead to worry and laborious work. Heavenly values lead to trust in God and dedication to his mission. Worldly values measure success in the present. Heavenly values look to the end of time when God will judge the world, reward the trusting and dependent, and punish those who rely on scheming and wealth.

3. Transition: Common sense shows the best choice. Avoid worry and frustration. Avoid hasty judgment about who is best. Do not put so much pressure on yourself. Trust God and be part of the victorious side in the end when it counts. Watch for the signs of the end times and be alert for opportunities to acknowledge Jesus and help your fellowman. Luke 12 should cause you to judge what values control your life and lead you to give up the world's fears and worries. Confess Christ, and rely on the Spirit, knowing your day of reward will come.

B. COMMENTARY

1. Dedication as Dependence: On the World or on God (12:1–12)
   a. The setting: multitudes trample as teacher teaches disciples (12:1a–b)
   b. The Master's teaching (12:1c–12)
2. Dedication to Riches: Redefining Wealth (12:13–21)
   a. The setting: crowd member wants justice (12:13)
   b. The Master's twofold response (12:14–15)
   c. The Master's teaching: what kind of wealth (12:16–21)
3. Dedication in Daily Life: Present Service and Future Readiness (12:22–40)
   a. The setting: Jesus teaches disciples (12:22a)
   b. The Master's teaching (12:22b–40)
4. Dedication with Responsibility: Do What You Know (12:41–53)
   a. The setting: Peter asks, who are you talking to? (12:41)
   b. The Master's teaching: more you know, more I expect (12:42–53)
5. Dedication to Common Sense: Judge for Yourselves or Pay the Penalty (12:54–59)
   a. The setting: teaching the crowd (12:54a)
   b. The Master's teaching: do what you know or else (12:54b–59)

C. CONCLUSION: DEDICATED IN LIFE AND DEATH

VIII. ISSUES FOR DISCUSSION

1. Can a person in this world really live without worrying?
2. What part do financial resources play in your life? What would it take for you to sell all you have and give it to the poor?
3. In what ways are you ready for Christ to come again? In what ways are you not ready? Why?
4. Can you give an example in your life of complete dedication and devotion to God in trusting for something you needed but did not have?
5. How does your faith affect your family life?

Luke 13

Dedicated to Religion or to the Kingdom?

I. INTRODUCTION
Loving Missions or Loving People

II. COMMENTARY
A verse-by-verse explanation of the chapter.

III. CONCLUSION
Religion or Reality?

An overview of the principles and applications from the chapter.

IV. LIFE APPLICATION
Lostology

Melding the chapter to life.

V. PRAYER
Tying the chapter to life with God.

VI. DEEPER DISCOVERIES
Historical, geographical, and grammatical enrichment of the commentary.

VII. TEACHING OUTLINE
Suggested step-by-step group study of the chapter.

VIII. ISSUES FOR DISCUSSION
Zeroing the chapter in on daily life.

"*G*od's Law, or his Word, is meant to penetrate the secret chambers of the heart, not merely be displayed externally like words chiseled in stone or written on parchment."

R .   C .   S p r o u l

Luke 13

IN A NUTSHELL

*O*n the way to betrayal and death in Jerusalem, Jesus met people in need physically and those in need spiritually. He kept trying to show them that their current religious practices and attitudes could not help them. They must repent or perish, produce fruit or be cut down, value humans more than traditions, laws, and animals, make every effort to enter the kingdom of God rather than keeping people out of it, and obey God rather than protecting their own life.

Dedicated to Religion or to the Kingdom?

I. INTRODUCTION

Loving Missions or Loving People

*P*reparing for our mission trip to Kenya, we listened to Mike describe what he had learned in his years as a missionary in Kenya and now on several mission trips back to Kenya. He described how to witness to people who said they belonged to a church and how to deal with people who wanted to argue. After giving us several valuable tips about how to witness in Kenya, he concluded, "Witnessing in Kenya in like witnessing anywhere else. You must not love to witness in Kenya; you must love Kenyans."

Frank Laubauch, the famous literacy missionary, learned a similar lesson. Sad and discouraged, he climbed a hill looking down from the Philippine countryside to the Pacific Ocean. He began to talk to God as he walked. He admitted that he had asked God to let him take the hard job and work with the Muslim Moros in the Philippines. Now after a time of no success, he confessed that he had failed. Why? He wanted God to tell him. "I might as well go home," he prayed. "They will not listen to me. What more can I do? Send me home, Lord."

God had an immediate answer. "God spoke to me on that hillside," Dr. Laubach reported. He told me I had failed because I did not really love those Moros, and that I felt superior to them. He told me they would respond when I began to love them."

With renewed devotion and dedication, Laubach went down the hill, found a Moro leader, asked to be taught their language in its still unwritten form. Devoted to the task, he gained the confidence of the people, learned the sounds of the language, and wrote them down. Eventually his work expanded into teaching literacy in over two hundred languages—all because he learned to love the people rather than the mission.

Similarly, Jesus confronted Jewish religious leaders who loved their position and their religion, but had no regard for people. He rebuked them and illustrated to them what true love means. His ultimate illustration came as he headed for Jerusalem, knowing he would die there.

II. COMMENTARY

Dedicated to Religion or to the Kingdom?

MAIN IDEA: *Dedication to God's mission shows in one's love for people, not in one's protection of a religious system.*

A Dedication Through Repentance: A Call to All (13:1–9)

SUPPORTING IDEA: *Dedication to God's mission begins with repentance from sin for every person.*

13:1. God works in history for the benefit of his people. This is the testimony that God's people have given through the centuries. Out of the crowd came the subtle request for Jesus to apply this theological theme to a contemporary event. Apparently Pilate, the Roman administrator, had some religious pilgrims from Galilee executed as they came to the temple to offer sacrifices, probably at one of the three annual Jewish festivals—perhaps Passover. We know nothing more about the incident, but it was fresh in the memory of religious Jews. Perhaps such an outrage might bring God's Messiah to deliver his people.

13:2–3. Jesus turned the theological issue around. Is this punishment for sin? Do persecution and death prove the victim to be a greater sinner than those who do not suffer? The one who was looking suffering square in the face as he marched to Jerusalem denied such a theological outrage. He reminded them that everyone has sinned (see Rom. 3:23). All deserve to die. Each person has only one hope in face of personal sin. Each must repent, turn from sin, and turn toward God in obedience and dedication. "Do not try to create a hierarchy of sin," Jesus declared. "Do not try to make others greater sinners than yourself. You have sinned. You deserve to die. You must repent."

13:4–5. Jesus added his own illustration: "Take another recent tragedy down at the corner of the south and east walls of Jerusalem at the water reservoir called Siloam or Shiloah. Eighteen people died in an accident on the tower there. Were these the worst sinners in Jerusalem, punished for their horrible sin? Of course not! So hear me again: Repent or perish. This means you."

13:6–9. Jesus finished his teaching with a parable. A man went out to his vineyard to get figs to eat. He found a tree but no figs. This was too much. Three years looking for figs on the tree, but never any figs. Cut it down. It's taking up valuable space and soil. Plant something productive there. "One more chance, please," begged the man who kept the vineyard and had come to love his trees. "Let me try everything possible for this one year. If we have no success, then you can cut it down."

The parable added a strong note to Jesus' call for repentance. Repentance is not something you put on a list of things to do some day. Time is short. You are in the midst of a desperate effort to save your soul. Repent now, or perish now. God's grace has given you another chance.

B Dedication to Human Need: People or Programs? (13:10–17)

> **SUPPORTING IDEA:** Dedication to God leads to meeting human need, while dedication to religion protects the tradition even at the cost of human life.

13:10. Despite the antipathy the religious leadership held for Jesus, he still found ways to participate in their Sabbath worship in the local synagogues. He even assumed the role of the synagogue teacher.

13:11. Among the worshipers was a handicapped woman. Her back had been bent for eighteen years. An evil spirit controlled her. She had no way of escape.

13:12–13. Jesus' loving, caring eye picked her out of the crowd. He called her forward, taking the initiative to heal her. This time he healed by placing his hands on the sufferer. As usual, healing came immediately. The woman recognized the ultimate source of her healing and praised God.

13:14. Everything but praise came from the man who had allowed Jesus to teach in the synagogue. Filled with righteous indignation, he called Jesus' hand: "How can you dare break our law? You know we cannot work on the Sabbath, and the rabbis have long established that healing is work." The crowd got a piece of his mind, too: "Quit bringing people here to be healed on the Sabbath. You have six days to be healed. Live this day for God's work." Sadly, the religious leader missed the whole point of what God's work is.

13:15–16. This was an obvious teaching moment for Jesus, filled with emotion. "You religious leaders are all alike," he declared. "Look how you treat your beloved farm animals. Every Sabbath you go untie the animal from its feeding bin. Then you lead the animal to get a drink of water. Now compare your dear animals with this poor woman. She is a descendent of Abraham. She is a victim of Satan. Do I not have as much right to untie her from the affliction she has suffered for eighteen years? Is she less important than your animals?"

13:17. Hushed silence fell over the crowd. Jesus had humiliated the synagogue and religious leaders. Then praise and joy broke out. The crowd recognized what he was doing for people, especially the little people who had no other defender against the religious system and the political maneuvering.

They liked to see someone beat the system. Even more, they liked to see someone who cared for and helped the little people in society. They recognized that the things he was doing were glorious, which seems to indicate they knew these were divine acts (see 7:25; cf. Exod. 34:10).

Ⓒ Dedication to the Kingdom: See How It Grows (13:18–21)

13:18. Jesus the teacher always sought common, everyday events and objects to compare to the kingdom of God. He taught heavenly truths with earthly objects.

13:19. This time he reached for the smallest object imaginable to make his comparison—a mustard seed, barely visible on the end of your finger. The tiny seed placed in the right soil and given the right climate emerges into the sky as a mighty tree. This was probably a *sinapis nigra* or black mustard tree. Normally a four-foot-high shrub, it may reach nine feet tall. Other interpreters think it was a *salvadora persica,* which can reach twenty-five feet. Birds of the heavens come to its branches to make their homes. Note the contrast to Ezekiel 17:22–23, where the kingdom is compared to the giant cedar trees of Lebanon.

In Jesus' day, if a person defined the kingdom by the truly dedicated followers of Jesus, it looked as small as the mustard seed on your finger. "Just wait. The day is coming," Jesus declared. "The kingdom will grow beyond your imagination. But the main point is, do not judge by what you see now. The Jesus movement may be small, but this does not mean it is insignificant. What you see in its atom-like origin is just as much the kingdom as will be the full-blown reality when it reaches maturity. Look now not for the full-grown tree but for the sprig from which God promised to grow the tree" (see Ezek. 17:22–23).

13:20–21. Again, the teacher sought a model for his teaching. Again, he went to the world of the small, a bit of yeast. For Israel, this was a small clump of old, fermented dough added to a new dough mixture. Yeast often represented uncleanness or evil, as when Israel rid its community of yeast during the Passover (Exod. 12:15–16; cf. Mark 8:15; Luke 12:1; Gal. 5:9; 1 Cor. 5:7). But Jesus can take what the religious leaders see as evil and unclean—the "sinners" of society—to create the kingdom. The woman mixed, or more literally "hid," the yeast in her new batch of dough. What caused the dough to rise and grow is invisible, hidden away in the midst of the growing process. Jesus told the story in a humorous, exaggerated fashion. The woman used three measures (Gr. *saton* from Heb. *seah*). A measure is equivalent to a peck and a half of flour (13.13 liters or 4.75 gallons). Three measures of flour would probably weigh fifty pounds and make enough bread for at least 150 people. If the lady doing the baking had something to hide, she ended with something she could never hide.

Once started, the kingdom will grow by virtue of its own contents. You can no more stop kingdom growth than you can keep yeast from making dough rise and expand. In Jesus the kingdom has come near where people can see it, but the kingdom is still so small it is not obvious. One must have ears to hear and eyes to see. A person must listen for the word of the kingdom. One must begin practicing the word of the kingdom. Soon, this almost invisible nucleus will expand into the grand structure no one can miss—a structure that will eventually determine salvation or eternal punishment for the entire world.

D Dedication to Kingdom Entry: The Unlikely Way (13:22–30)

> **SUPPORTING IDEA:** *The powerful religious system and tradition is the wide way to hell, while Christ's way of love is the narrow way to salvation, reversing all ways of human thinking.*

13:22. The trip to Jerusalem continues (see 9:51). The trip was used to meet Jesus' stated purpose: Let all the villages hear the word of the kingdom (4:43). This placed a foreboding emotion over everyone who followed. What happens in Jerusalem? Will Jesus succeed in his preaching mission?

13:23. A voice from the crowd offered Jesus an important opportunity to teach. How many will be saved? People of all nations want to know. They seemed to think knowing the number would give them their odds to make it. But salvation is not based on human odds. Salvation is built on divine initiative and divine grace. If this teaching of Jesus is true, then the question arose from honest fear. A secure Judaism that equated itself with the kingdom faced a claim that the most pious of the Jewish leaders would not make the kingdom. If not, who will? Only a privileged few?

13:24. Jesus confirmed their fears. The wide gate of Pharisaism made provisions for so many people who tried to carry out the tradition's laws. It apparently paid little attention to the attitude of the heart as long as the ritual actions of the hands were clean. The only gate to heaven, however, is narrow. Many will try and fail. They think they know the secret entryway, but they do not. Their way of religious righteousness does not work. They must know Jesus, who is the only way to heaven. They must seek to hear, understand, and practice his word. This is the way of entry. Jesus' emphasis was on those who fail rather than those who succeed and how they succeed.

13:25. The moment will come when the owner of the house declares it is time for bed. Lock the doors. Do not let anyone else in. What happens then? If you have not entered the narrow door, hope is gone. You may stand and knock at the door all night. All you will ever hear is, "Get away, I do not know you. I do not even know where you come from." But these are Jews following the strictest of Jewish traditions. They are people of the Book, carrying out its most minute regulations as faithfully as possible. They have not chosen the narrow way. God knows no other way. What a shock for people who were so sure they were on the way to heaven!

13:26. Shocked, the Jewish leaders became defensive: "You came to our homes and ate with us (11:37). We listened to you teach in our streets. We have participated in all you did. Why can we not come in to the final banquet and be part of the kingdom?"

13:27. "I do not know you," Jesus replied. "You can see all you want. You can converse all you want. You can hear all I teach. You can be present with me throughout my ministry. You have not known fully who I am and what I am up to. You know me not! You refuse to believe me, practice my word, enter my kingdom. I never knew you! I never knew the way you try to travel to get to heaven. Your way of tradition and law does not work. I have been calling for you to come, follow me. Now time for that is over. I can only call, Get away from me, worker of unrighteousness. You had your chance. No more. Judgment comes. Get ready for the judge."

13:28. "The judge will send you to a place of suffering," Jesus continued. "You will see your religious heroes, Abraham and Isaac and Jacob (Gen. 12–37) in the kingdom, but you will not be part of it. You will be thrown out into utter darkness. Repent now!"

13:29. The kingdom will not be shortchanged. People will come from all directions to the final kingdom banquet. This could relate to the scattered Diaspora of Jews, spread out over the world since the exile from Israel in 721 and in Judah in 587. More likely, from Luke's perspective this coming was a coming of Gentiles fulfilling the prophet's oracles that God would save people coming from all directions (1 Chr. 9:24; Pss. 96:3; 107:3; Isa. 2:2; 25:6–9; 40:5; 43:5–6; 45:6,14; 49:12; 51:4; 52:10; 55:5; 56:7; 59:19; 66:19–20; Mic. 4:1–2; Zech. 2:13; Mal. 1:11). Those so secure in kingdom tradition would end up in utter darkness. Those so scorned by the keepers of tradition will parade into the kingdom as the religionists watch, helpless to stop them and helpless to find a kingdom place for themselves.

13:30. Jesus used a proverbial saying that is repeated several times in the Gospels (Matt. 19:30; 20:16; Mark 10:31) to close out the point. The safe and secure religion traditionalists of Judaism thought they were guaranteed a place in God's final kingdom. They thought everyone must submit to their religious rules and regulations to enter the kingdom. This automatically excluded all Gentiles who did not become Jewish proselytes. Jesus wants you, who think you are at the head of the line entering the kingdom, to know that you have another shocking thing coming. The Gentiles from across the sea will enter the kingdom before you do. You had better pay close attention to Jesus. He is the only way into the kingdom. Are you on the way?

E Dedication to Death: Fearless Advance to the Goal (13:31–35)

SUPPORTING IDEA: *Dedication to God finds its goal in death, while organized religion and politics prove they do not have the control and power they claim.*

13:31. " Leave," the Pharisees shouted. "Herod wants to kill you." What a change of heart by the Pharisees. Why? Is this a special group with some respect for and even secret belief in Jesus, similar to the man who invited Jesus to dinner or Nicodemus? Or is this a trick as they try to hide their intentions and place the blame on Herod? Or is this an attempt to make public Jesus' fear before Herod and thus make the crowds stop following him? Why have they waited until now to say Herod wants to see Jesus (see 9:9)? Luke does not answer these questions. That is not his point, and it should not be ours. The point is Jesus' reaction.

13:32–33. Fearlessly, Jesus responded. "The man is a sly old fox," he said. "He recognizes ability and power but does everything to undermine and destroy it. Tell that old fox to wait a minute. I am doing my normal work defeating the kingdom of Satan. In a few days I will be finished. Then I will have time to deal with him. I will not alter my course for him, nor will I change my time schedule. You are not in control over me. The Father is. I will complete his mission—a mission that must end in Jerusalem where prophets generally die" (see 2 Kgs. 21:16; 24:4; Jer. 26:20–23; 2 Chr. 24:20–22; Luke 11:49; Acts 7:52).

13:34. Jesus grieved over this murderous city. He would gladly sweep its citizens under his wings like a mother hen. But the chicks would not come. They scrambled away in all directions. Messiah came to Jerusalem, and Jerusalem ignored him.

13:35. Ignoring God brings disastrous results: Israel is abandoned once again as it was in exile six hundred years earlier. Their opportunity is gone. Never again will they see him until it is too late. Then he will be clearly recognized as Messiah, coming again, this time as judge of the world. Then they will sing the words of Psalm 118:26 and welcome Jesus as he comes in God's name to deliver his people. But the song of praise will be too late for those to whom Jesus is speaking.

MAIN IDEA REVIEW: *Dedication to God's mission shows in one's love for people, not in one's protection of a religious system.*

III. CONCLUSION

Religion or Reality?

You see them every Sunday. Dressed in Sunday best, they parade into the church. Dutifully they sit in Bible study and then climb the stairs to worship. They take hymnbooks or sing the words projected on the wall. They put their bit in the offering plate. They shake hands with acquaintances and tell the preacher he did another good job. Then they return home, take off church clothes, and forget God for another week. Religion has become rote. Meeting God is nothing more than listening to teachers, singing hymns, praying the same old memorized prayer if asked to lead in public, making a small offering, and waiting through one more sermon. Yet somehow this gives assurance. The preacher will preach their funeral, tell how faithful they were to attend church, and promise the family that today they are with Jesus in paradise.

What a parody on the Christ, who came warning the most dedicated of religious people that they were last in the kingdom line, probably not going to get in, because they had too much religion and not enough relationship to God, too much going to church and not enough dedication to God and his mission. Jesus came to call people to repent. Are you one of those whom he calls? Are you in danger of being cut down without another chance to respond to Jesus? Are you so busy being religious that you fail to see the kingdom growing in your midst? Has the wide door of religion accommodated you all these years so that you see no reason to answer the call to the narrow one? Have you read and talked and sung and listened to people preach about Jesus for years without meeting him personally as your Savior? Jesus went to Jerusalem to die for you. Are you dedicated enough to live for him?

PRINCIPLES

- Repentance is necessary for a person to enter the kingdom.
- You have only a limited time to repent, so do so today.
- Religious rules can prevent a person from knowing Jesus as Savior.
- The kingdom may appear small and insignificant, but it is growing quietly into the world's most significant institution.
- Entry to the kingdom comes in narrow, simple ways.
- Those who enter God's kingdom may not be the people you expect.
- Jesus called on his followers for total dedication, and he demonstrated this to them in Jerusalem.

APPLICATIONS

- Repent now of your sins and follow Jesus.
- Do not postpone your repentance until tomorrow, since the time is short.
- Give attention to human needs rather than to religious rules.
- Have confidence that God is at work growing his kingdom even when you cannot see much evidence of it.
- Enter the kingdom by listening to God's Word and practicing it, not by maintaining religious tradition.
- Realize that people you least expect may go ahead of you into the kingdom.
- Believe in Jesus' death as the way to salvation.

IV. LIFE APPLICATION

Lostology

Lostology is a word created by John Kramp as he tried to confront the Christian church anew with the realization that people are lost without Jesus. Luke tried long ago to make religious people realize that they were lost without Jesus. Aftershocks of a major earthquake continue to shake Turkey and Greece as I write this chapter. The quakes have resulted in thousands of deaths. Many people lay screaming in the rubble unable to attract the attention of rescuers.

Too often the church has claimed to be rescuing the perishing when what we have really been doing is protecting the dying. Jesus spoke to people who were proud and secure in their religion—a people who had become experts in God. They had made the rules so God had to accept them into heaven. Jesus tried to shock them into realizing that only God made kingdom rules. Religion, whether it is the legalistic Judaism of Jesus' day or the anemic, seeker-friendly Protestantism of today, cannot assure people a place in God's kingdom. Those who think they are ahead of the religious herd often find themselves shocked and in last place when Jesus calls. The kingdom is growing steadily and unobtrusively. It may be growing without you. Have you repented of sin, trusted Jesus for salvation, practiced his Word, cared more for the needy than for yourself and your religious repetitions? The Bible calls for dedication to Jesus, not dedication to the ongoing security of your church's practices. Study lostology. It might describe you.

V. PRAYER

Father God, ruler of heaven and earth, I want to be part of your kingdom. Deliver me from my religion of self-satisfaction, practiced by people in a mutual admiration society. Deliver me from the tame repetitions of hymns and sermons and prayers that I have substituted for dedication to you and your kingdom. I repent of my sins. I give myself to follow you to the cross. I surrender my religious security for a pure relationship with you. Only then can I be sure I belong to your kingdom. In the name of my king, Jesus Christ. Amen.

VI. DEEPER DISCOVERIES

A. Repent or Perish (13:3,5)

Jesus faced a crowd of finger pointers. They loved to proclaim their own righteousness and everyone else's guilt. He challenged them to look the other direction and see what guilt they could discover in their own lives. Jesus also issued an ultimatum: *Discover your own guilt and repent, or you will perish.* Exactly what did he call them to do? What threat did he make?

The word *repent* (Heb. *shub*) means to turn away from one thing and turn toward another. The prophets challenged the nation of Israel to renew its personal relationship with God, renew its covenant with God, and live the way God had directed (see Amos 4:6; Hos. 5:4; 6:1). The Jewish group behind the Dead Sea Scrolls also called on members to turn away from evil and to turn again to the commandments of Moses.

The Greek word for repentance (*metanoieo*) means to change one's mind and purpose and thus adopt a new direction in life. Repentance was a new thought for the Greek-speaking world. Thoughts of a new lifestyle and sorrow for the present way of living did not appear in the Greek philosophers and writers prior to the New Testament. The New Testament call to repentance is more than an intellectual idea, calling for new thought patterns or new philosophies of life. It is a call for a change in daily living habits. It is a change of masters. Sin, evil, and the world master most people's lives. Jesus and the New Testament writers called people to let Christ or God the Father or the Holy Spirit become life's master. Repentance is turning from mastery by the world to mastery by God.

Jesus' invitation was to a new life in personal relationship to him as Master. His alternative was dire, indeed—perish. The Greek term *apollumi* means to destroy and thus to cease to exist. Yes, people who think they are God's chosen race, who believe God has chosen them to show everyone else the deep meaning of his Word—these people face ultimate destruction. They will face all the judgment sinners receive in this life and beyond. Repentance is more than a mere alternative. It is a basic necessity of life for those who take God seriously.

B. The Fig Tree (13:6–8)

The common fig tree had a short, stout trunk and thick branches. Its rounded fruit would ripen during the summer. In his teachings, Jesus referred to figs and fig trees several times, using them as object lessons. The owner of a fig tree had a right to expect it to produce fruit within three years. If it failed to do so, it became a liability, since it was taking up valuable desert soil. In this parable, the owner decided to cut down the tree. But the vine-dresser asked to give the tree one more opportunity to produce. He offered to leave it alone for one year, dig around it, and fertilize it. If the tree failed to bear fruit the next year, then he would cut it down. This parable emphasized the point that although God is patient, continued refusal to repent will result in doom.

C. The Synagogue Ruler (13:14)

The ruler of the synagogue was in charge of synagogue worship. He was the president of the organization, often being its founder. He led the meetings of the organization. In Jewish society this official was highly respected and esteemed. He chose the persons who led in worship and assigned them their role in the worship service. He was in charge of building the synagogue and keeping it in order. At times this meant the ruler of the synagogue had to bear the financial burden for the building.

D. Mustard Seed (13:18)

The mustard is a large plant that grows quickly. Its seeds were once thought to be the smallest in the plant world. Jesus used the mustard plant to symbolize the rapid growth of the kingdom of God (Matt. 13:31–32), and its seed as a simile for faith (Matt. 17:20). In his commentary on Luke's Gospel, I. Howard Marshall gives this insight: "The stress is not so much on the idea of growth in itself as on the certainty that what appears tiny and insignificant will prove to have been the beginning of a mighty kingdom" (*The Gospel of Luke*, 561).

E. Herod a "Fox" (13:32)

Why did Jesus call Herod a "fox"? He may have had a fox's renowned cunning in mind. If so, he was discounting Herod's death threat as a strategy to try to frighten Jesus away. In that day, "fox" also meant an insignificant person, as contrasted to a "lion," a person of true greatness.

VII. TEACHING OUTLINE

A. INTRODUCTION

1. Lead Story: Loving Missions or Loving People
2. Context: Luke 13 continues Jesus' teaching on the way to Jerusalem. Jesus turned more and more aside from the disciples to confront the issues and questions of the crowd and of his opponents. The opening and closing sections of the chapter raise political issues. What was Jesus going to do to a Pilate who kills pious Jewish worshipers coming to Jerusalem from Galilee? How would he react to Herod's efforts to kill him? Jesus ignored the political implications of the first question to address the question of who was in danger of sin's consequences. He stated clearly that he controlled his destiny and Herod did not.

   Jesus also forced his audience to face one question: Am I too secure in my religion to become a part of God's kingdom? Do I love religious rites and rules more than I love people in need? In this context Jesus calls every person to repent and seek his narrow way to God rather than following the broad, legalistic way of the Pharisees. He offers assurance the kingdom is now present and is growing even when we cannot see the evidence. The problem is not the kingdom's presence. The problem is our definition of the kingdom: We place ourselves first in it, when God places us last. Who is first then? Those whom we exclude as totally disqualified. This is the real kingdom. It comes soon. Will you rejoice at God's glorious acts, or will you participate in the weeping and gnashing of teeth?

3. Transition: We gladly join in Jesus' condemnation of the Pharisees and their religion of rite and rule over people. We fail to notice that our religious practices tend to follow the Pharisees' model much more than Jesus'. Luke 13 calls us to examine our religion and to compare it to the call of Jesus to repent, hear his word, and practice it. It forces us to see that our security in our religion may be preventing us from dedicating ourselves to Jesus and entering the narrow door to his kingdom.

B. COMMENTARY

1. Dedication Through Repentance: A Call to All (13:1–9)
   a. The setting: political maneuvering (13:1)
   b. The Master's response: you are guilty; repent (13:2–5)
   c. The Master's teaching: one more chance (13:6–9)

2. Dedication to Human Need: People or Programs? (13:10–17)

    a. The setting: Jesus teaching on Sabbath and seeing a disabled woman (13:10–11)

    b. The Master's response: healing (13:12–13a)

    c. The woman's response: praise God (13:13b)

    d. The opponent's reaction: anger at ritual breaking (13:14)

    e. The Master's counter response: who's worth the most? (13:15–16)

    f. The opponents' counter response: public humiliation (13:17a)

    g. The crowd's response: delight in God's acts (13:17b)

3. Dedication to the Kingdom: See How It Grows (13:18–21)

    a. The setting: Jesus' questions on the kingdom (13:18a,20a)

    b. The Master's teaching: the kingdom (13:18b–19,20b–21)

4. Dedication to Kingdom Entry: The Unlikely Way (13:22–30)

    a. The setting: teaching on way to Jerusalem (13:22)

    b. The scene: crowd member wants kingdom census (13:23)

    c. The Master's response: enter unlikely way or be left out (13:24–30)

5. Dedication to Death: Fearless Advance to the Goal (13:31–35)

    a. The setting: opponents advise Jesus to flee Herod (13:31)

    b. The Master's response: on to Jerusalem (13:32–35)

C. CONCLUSION: LOSTOLOGY

VIII. ISSUES FOR DISCUSSION

1. What does it mean to be lost? Are you lost? How do you know?

2. Have you repented of your sins? Do you know Jesus has saved you?

3. In what ways is your church in danger of loving rites and rules more than people?

4. In what ways do people today show the same self-righteous attitude of the Pharisees? What is the result?

5. What evidence do you have that the kingdom is growing?

6. What group of people today would compare to the Gentiles of Jesus' day? Do you see any way they could be entering the kingdom before you? Why? Why not?

7. Do you have the same dedication to ministry that Jesus showed when Herod wanted to kill him?

Luke 14

Dedication and Humility

Quote

"*T*he meek man is not a human mouse afflicted with a sense of his own inferiority. Rather, he may be in his moral life as bold as a lion and as strong as Samson; but he has stopped being fooled about himself. He has accepted God's estimate of his own life. He knows he is as weak and helpless as God has declared him to be, but paradoxically, he knows at the same time that he is, in the sight of God, more important than angels. In himself, nothing; in God, everything."

A . W . T o z e r

Luke 14

I N A N U T S H E L L

*D*edication to the kingdom reverses life's values and expectations. Finding identity and personal meaning from God, you take the back seat in human affairs. You do not look for honors and reward in this life, knowing you will receive them at the resurrection. You know kingdom people are most often found among the world's ignored rather than among the noble. The dedicated disciple thus gives up all claims to worldly goods to carry a cross and follow Jesus.

Dedication and Humility

I. INTRODUCTION

Successful in Kingdom Business

$\mathcal{H}e$ has it made. That's what people say about my friend as they see him drive his luxury car into a new subdivision of lovely houses. After all, he has just taken a marvelous new job that lets him travel, pays him well, and lets him do what he most enjoys doing in life.

Most people do not see the other side of my friend, the side that suffered through the loss of his wife to debilitating illness. They do not see the hours he spends as a deacon and Bible study teacher. They do not follow him to the hospital as he ministers to the sick. They do not tune in as he finds other men who have lost their beloved wives and counsels with them. Yes, he is successful in business, but that is only second place in his life. First place goes to his Lord and his humble ministry behind the scenes helping young couples in his Sunday school class, helping lonely bewildered widowers, conferring with church staff, and visiting the sick. He has found the way to be first comes not from money but from humble ministry.

That is the lesson we find in Luke 14. Jesus tries to teach the crowds and his disciples that dedicated discipleship involves carrying one's cross, inviting the uninvited, being last instead of first, persistently finishing the course Jesus has set before you. Only the crucified life will lead to resurrection of the dead.

II. COMMENTARY

Dedication and Humility

MAIN IDEA: *Dedication to the kingdom reveals itself in a life that reverses the world's values, surrendering self and position for persistent obedience to Christ and confident hope in the resurrection.*

A Dedication Without Excuse: The Kingdom of the Humble (14:1–24)

SUPPORTING IDEA: *The kingdom of God belongs to those who are humbly dedicated to him, not to those in control of the religious institutions and other power structures.*

14:1. On the way to Jerusalem, Jesus stood under scrutiny. Still, members of the opposition invited him to dinner (see 7:36). Just to watch him? To spy on him? To satisfy their curiosity about him? Because they wanted to believe in him? Luke does not answer this question. He is interested in the Sabbath question and Jesus' way of dealing with the religiosity of the Pharisees.

14:2. A misformed, gravely sick man appeared in front of Jesus. How he got there we do not know. How Jesus and the Pharisees responded to him we do know. We also know that Jews often viewed this condition of dropsy as the judgment of God on sin and refusal to obey the rabbinic laws.

14:3. Jesus knew what the Pharisees were thinking: Will he heal on the Sabbath and thus break the Sabbath laws? Before acting, Jesus involved his opponents in the decision. Would they make a ruling? Is it legal to heal on the Sabbath?

14:4. They refused to answer, so Jesus acted on God's authority. He healed the man and dismissed him. The Pharisees remained in a dilemma. To allow healing on the Sabbath violated the tradition they so zealously taught and practiced. To forbid such healing made them appear without compassion and care for a person in need. Obviously, these people did not believe Jesus' teachings on the kingdom. They remained fast in their ritualistic, legalistic ways but were afraid to show their hand in front of the crowd of witnesses.

14:5. Before they could attack Jesus, he questioned them again: "What would you do if a son or a valuable farm animal fell into a well? You'd go and pull him out, wouldn't you?"

14:6–7. They remained silent again, so he told another parable. He selected the contents of the parable on the basis of what was happening in the banquet. Most guests always sought out the best seat nearest the host.

14:8–10. The parable is actually in the form of an advice column: "You are invited to a wedding reception. You are among the early arrivals. How do you choose where to sit? Normally, you take the best seat, the one closest to the host, don't you? Listen to me. Do not do that. Why? You have not seen the entire guest list. Someone with VIP credentials may show up later. The host will have to seat that person in the choice place. He may ask you to move down the table to make way for this important guest. All the places being occupied, you will have to move to the worst seat in the house. What an indignity! You will be humiliated."

"Listen! Here is a better strategy," Jesus continued. "When you arrive early, seek out the worst seat in the house. Then the host will come and ask you to move up closer to him. You will gain honor in front of all the guests."

14:11. The meaning of all this is simple. If you try to gain honor for yourself, you will be humbled and humiliated. But if you show humility, then you will receive great honor. So act with humility, not pride, in every situation.

14:12–13. Having taught the guests a lesson, Jesus turned to the host: "Here is how to give a party. Plan a different kind of guest list. Do not look to see who invited you and thus invite them. Do not look to see whose guest list you want to be on and invite them. Try an entirely different approach. Forget those who are able to pay you back party for party, honor for honor. Invite those who cannot help themselves, much less do something to honor you. Find the names of the poor, the injured, the crippled, and the blind. No one ever honors them with a dinner. They cannot even enter the temple to worship (Lev. 21:17–23; 2 Sam. 5:8). You should reverse the world's way and invite the needy to your banquet."

14:14. "Why would you do something so ridiculous?" Jesus continued. "They cannot repay you, and you are not doing it to be repaid. Instead, you are doing this for God. When you do things his way, he repays you, for you will be part of the resurrected righteous whom he rewards on the day of judgment. Will you trade momentary honor here for eternal glory there?"

14:15. Jesus' teaching drew comment from the crowd. A dinner guest pronounced a blessing on those who joined the heavenly banquet (cf. Isa. 25:6; Pss. 22:26; 23:5). His meaning and motive is not clear. Was he simply agreeing with Jesus, saying, "Amen"? Was he trying to draw attention to himself? Was he trying to defend the Pharisees and say it mattered not where you sat as long as you were included in the final banquet? Luke again does not concentrate on the man or his motive. Jesus remains center stage.

14:16–24. Another parable ensued, also with a banquet theme. The host issued invitations. Then according to custom, at banquet time with the meal ready, he sent servants to remind the invited guests. Obviously, the gossip line had found something amiss with the banquet. Everyone quickly found an excuse not to come. The host was thoroughly snubbed. No one came. The excuses were ridiculous. You do not make financial deals of such magnitude without having assessed the value of the property purchased. You do not accept an invitation to a banquet in conflict with a wedding. Jesus was showing how easy and absurdly finances and family matters get in the way of more important things. They can cause you to miss God's final heavenly banquet.

The host's response was predictable: rage. He would show those people. They got no more second thoughts or second invitations. They would never participate in his banquet. Still, he said, we will have a glorious banquet. Go out in the streets and get anybody you can get to come. Those people in rags invited as second thoughts are the very ones Jesus had earlier instructed the host to invite (v. 13). Inviting them robbed the host of any social standing in the community or with his family. He placed himself on the same social plane as the new invitees.

He could not immediately find enough of this class to fill his banquet hall. So he sent a second invitation. The upper class required two invitations to the banquet. The simple people on Jesus' list came immediately. The second invitation was issued only in order to find more people. This may hint at

Luke's constant emphasis that Gentiles as well as Jews get an invitation to God's banquet. The conclusion shows Jesus' understanding of the banquet and of his kingdom. The banquet host must represent God. The banquet is the inauguration of his kingdom. The original hosts are the upper-class Jews who were so tied to their social status, financial business, and family matters that they snubbed God. God rejected them and turned to the very ones the Jewish leaders looked on with contempt to find adequate guests for the heavenly banquet. Those who think they have a place reserved and assured in the heavenly feast find themselves on the outside looking in just as the poor and needy previously stood at their windows looking in on their banquets.

B Dedication Defined: Give Everything (14:25–35)

SUPPORTING IDEA: *Dedication to God has no limits; cross bearing means total sacrifice of everything.*

14:25–27. The more Jesus isolated the Jewish leaders, the larger the crowds who followed. Jesus taught them as well as his disciples (cf. 8:10). Following Jesus has consequences. It isolates and separates you from those closest to you. Dedication to Jesus means rejection of any who are not dedicated to him. Dedication to Jesus means rejecting self-interest and personal fortunes. Discipleship is a full-time commitment. Nothing should modify, interrupt, or compete with it. (On hatred of family and self, see "Deeper Discoveries.")

Jesus again (see 9:23) used the image of cross bearing to illustrate what he meant by absolute dedication. Dedication to Jesus is a life-long commitment to follow the road that leads to death. Persons in the crowd who sought power, responsibility, food, health, fame, or fortune could quit now. Earthly rewards were not in view. Dedication to Christ is dedication to crucifixion. Rewards come only in the next world, with the resurrection (see 14:14).

14:28–30. Discipleship is not a hasty decision. You become a disciple only after you have carefully analyzed the changes it will bring in your life. It is like starting a building project. You must budget for it and see that you can finish it. No one wants a half-finished tower. If you have what it takes, go for it. Otherwise, do not subject yourself to the disappointment of starting the discipleship journey and having to turn back when you are only halfway there. People will laugh and ridicule you. Those whom you thought you could leave behind, you now return to, only to find they have rejected and made fun of you. Count the cost. Be ready to pay the cost. Take up your cross.

14:31–32. Here is another example: Consider a king ready to fight another nation. What's his first action? He does not call up a single soldier until he has analyzed the odds. He considers his own resources and those of the enemy. Is he willing to fight the enemy with what he has? If not, then the battle is off. Send a peace delegation to make an agreement even if it involves surrender. Do not subject yourself to total defeat when you can foresee it from the beginning.

14:33. What does this mean when applied to the dedication of disciples? "Sit down and count the cost of discipleship," Jesus says. "You must leave home and family and travel on mission for me. You must depend on those you meet and witness to for your food and necessities. Every material possession is left behind, with no thought of ever returning to reclaim it. Dedication is not to possessions. Dedication to Christ is dedication to life without material resources to fall back on. Ready to leave everything and follow? Give away your money? Say good-bye to family and friends? Pick up your cross."

14:34-35. To sum it all up, you are called to be the salt of the earth, giving the flavor of Christ's life and mission to everyone. If that's not how you taste, they will never catch the flavor. Do not count on catching the flavor after you start the journey. Being salty like Christ is a prerequisite for the journey. If you do not have the salt flavor now, do not try to be a dedicated disciple of Christ. You are not even fit for the manure pile. You are useless to yourself, to Christ, and to everybody else. First, let Christ make salt of you. Then take up your cross and follow.

> **MAIN IDEA REVIEW:** *Dedication to the kingdom reveals itself in a life that reverses the world's values, surrendering self and position for persistent obedience to Christ and confident hope in the resurrection.*

III. CONCLUSION

Dying to Live

What is the aim of life? Every philosopher tries to answer this question. Each comes with a well-reasoned argument based on long experience—experience often with the failure of another system rather than the success of one's own. Jesus taught a simple answer to the question. The aim of life is death. This death comes in many forms. It is death to long-held religious convictions. Such long-agreed-upon doctrines as the requirement for Sabbath rest must die, replaced by a commitment to love people more than rules. Social rules like climbing the ladder to the highest place on the social register must die, replaced by the humility of going to the back of the line and being honored only when others choose to do so. Rules of etiquette such as reciprocating to those who invite you to dinner must die, replaced by a commitment to provide for the needy rather than entertain the wealthy. Religious expectations such as everyone like me is going to heaven must die, replaced by understanding that God determines who goes to heaven and he is on the side of the needy, not the rich. Traditional loyalties to such things as social status, family, and personal achievement must die, replaced by absolute commitment to Jesus—a commitment that will lead to rejection and crucifixion. If the aim of life is death, then you must count the cost. Are you willing to die for Christ, or must you live for self, family, and fortune?

PRINCIPLES

- Meeting people's needs is more important than keeping traditional rules.
- Personal humility marks the person who is dedicated to God.
- God calls you to minister to the needy.
- Look for rewards from God in the resurrection, not from people on the earth.
- Devotion to goods and family may cause you to miss God's heavenly banquet.
- Dedication to Jesus replaces dedication to everyone and everything else.
- Discipleship is never cheap or easy.

APPLICATIONS

- Learn humility as a style of life.
- Care more for others' needs than for your own desires and reputation.
- Trust God to provide your needs now and your rewards later.
- Make participation in God's kingdom your only desire.
- Count the cost of serving Jesus before you become a disciple.
- Be prepared to surrender everything and every relationship you have to follow Jesus.
- Start on the road toward death if you want true life.

IV. LIFE APPLICATION

Operating in a Hen House

Does he rank among the world's greatest men or among its greatest fools? He has appeared on lists of both kinds. Why?

His talents put him on both lists. He was the chief academic officer of one of Europe's elite schools. He was a world-famous musician. His pen produced many books and papers. His church regarded him as one of its most eloquent preachers and most insightful New Testament scholars. What did he choose to do with such gifts? He enrolled in medical school and became a doctor. Then he packed his medical supplies and left for the Congo in Africa. There he began operating in a hen house. Yes, from the days he learned at his father's feet, Albert Schweitzer knew he wanted to do something for God. He gave up the ease of being talented and famous in Europe to bring healing to some of the earth's poorest people.

This kind of humble service reverses all the world's values. It is precisely the kind of dedication Jesus asked for in Luke 14. Long after his death, Albert Schweitzer lives on as an example of one who counted the cost and then took up his cross. His academic and artistic peers regarded him as a fool because he was ready to die for Christ among the people whom Christ paid the most attention to while he was on earth. Jesus continues to call his people to forget earthly rewards and honors and reach out to the poor, the lame, and the blind. What have you given up in the name and service of Christ? In what specific ways can you say that you have taken up a cross with Christ and are marching resolutely to death with him?

V. PRAYER

God, who protects the needy, provides for the poor, and helps the helpless, help us get our values and goals straight. We strive too much for the rewards that men can give. We work too hard for human honors. We plan too intensely for ways to impress other people and maintain our status in society. Forgive us. Help us see the cost of discipleship. Give us the faith to pay the cost. Place our cross before us. We forsake all other ties. We will follow you even to death. Amen.

VI. DEEPER DISCOVERIES

A. Dropsy (14:2)

The condition known as *dropsy* was one of the maladies of Jesus' day. It is *edema*, a disease characterized by fluid retention and swelling. Dropsy is a symptom of disease of the heart, liver, kidneys, or brain. The condition involves the accumulation of water fluid in the body cavities or in the limbs.

B. Places of Honor at the Table (14:7)

At banquets and dinners, distinguished persons were given seats, or places of honor. A group of three cushions or couches were used for reclining. The chief seats were the first reclining places at the table. A. T. Robertson notes, "On a couch holding three the middle place was the chief one. The place next to the host on the right was then, as now, the post of honour" (Robertson, *Word Pictures in the New Testament*, vol. 2, 195).

C. Hate (14:25)

Our modern-day understanding of the word *hate* pigeonholes it as the opposite of love. It is the language of exaggerated contrast. In the context of Jesus' story, however, hate had the meaning of "loving less," not the absence of love.

D. Hate Family and Self (14:26)

Jesus said that dedication to him meant hating family and even life itself. The church has spent much of its history trying to avoid or redefine the meaning of this term. The Greek word for hate (*miseo*) is a strong word that means to detest, persecute in hatred, abhor. Horst Seebass (*NIDNTT*, I, 555) says *miseo* "connotes not only antipathy to certain actions, but also a permanent and deep-seated hostility towards other men or even the deity." Jesus had already taught his disciples to "do good to those who hate you" (Luke 6:27). Later John would write, "Anyone who hates his brother is a murderer" (1 John 3:15). How then, could Jesus command us to hate our brother?

To understand, we must see the assumptions behind what Jesus said. First, he assumed a conflict between what he wanted done and what the family wanted done. He saw a similar conflict between personal self-interest and Christ's interests. Second, he used hyperbole to make his point. This means he expressed something in the most radical language possible in order to get us to hear what he said and to think it through. When conflict arises between personal desires or family desires and Christ's mission, the disciple has no problem in knowing what to do. Christ's mission always takes precedence, no matter how serious the need of family. Nothing can be used as an excuse to refuse to do what Christ has called you to do.

VII. TEACHING OUTLINE

A. INTRODUCTION

1. Lead Story: Successful in Kingdom Business
2. Context: Chapter 13 ended with the Pharisees warning Jesus to leave so Herod would not kill him. Ironically, chapter 14 begins with Jesus eating in the home of a Pharisee. Chapter 14 then describes the conflict between Pharisees and Jesus and between the crowds of the world and Jesus in regard to the purpose of life. The Pharisees saw life as abiding by the rules that God had set out. The crowds saw life as pursuit of fame, fortune, acceptance, and family ties. Jesus used the banquet image to show that the aim of life is to die and participate in God's heavenly banquet. Such death involves death to self, religious tradition, family, and worldly values. It calls for humility to live life in service to the needy, preparing for fellowship with them in

the kingdom banquet. Dedicated disciples count the cost of rejecting worldly values. Then they take up the cross and march with Jesus toward death.

3. Transition: The world's values have changed little. We still calculate our actions on the basis of what other people will think and how our actions will gain reward and repayment from others. As we try to impress others, Jesus tries to impress on us the need to count the cost and follow him. As you study Luke 14 you may be shocked at the radical sacrifices it calls on you to make. Remember, if they seem too radical, then you have not counted the cost and have not truly taken up a cross to follow Jesus.

B. COMMENTARY

1. Dedication Without Excuse: The Kingdom of the Humble (14:1–24)
   a. The setting: Sabbath meal with sick man under Pharisees' watchful eyes (14:1–2)
   b. The Master's response: is Sabbath healing lawful? (14:3)
   c. The opponents' reaction: silence (14:4a)
   d. The Master's counter responses: healing and questioning (14:4b-5)
   e. The opponents' reaction: silence (14:6)
   f. The crowd's action: seeking places of honor (14:7)
   g. The Master's teaching: humility, reward, blessing, excuses (14:8–24)
2. Dedication Defined: Give Everything (14:25–35)
   a. The setting: traveling with large crowds (14:25)
   b. The Master's teaching: surrender all for the kingdom (14:26–33)
   c. The Master's conclusion: keep your flavor (14:34–35)

C. CONCLUSION: OPERATING IN A HEN HOUSE

VIII. ISSUES FOR DISCUSSION

1. What religious habits, rules, traditions do you put in the place of ministering to human need in Jesus' name?
2. How often do you eat with someone whose needs you can meet rather than with someone who can repay you? Why?
3. What excuses do you use not to do kingdom work?
4. What loyalties and relationships have you surrendered to follow and obey Jesus?
5. What is the cost you must pay to be a disciple of Jesus?
6. Can you give specific examples of how your life is flavoring the world with a taste of Jesus?

Luke 15

Dedication to the Lost

Quote

"*From* a spiritual perspective, getting lost is unavoidable. Human nature is fundamentally flawed by sin. If people live their lives apart from God and follow their intuitions, they stay lost. That is because getting lost—physically or spiritually—is easy."

John Kramp

Luke 15

IN A NUTSHELL

Sinners followed Jesus eagerly. Self-righteous religious leaders constantly chided Jesus for associating with such sinners. Finally, Jesus told three stories to show what it means to be lost and how a loving Father waits for the sinner to come home and be saved.

Dedication to the Lost

I. INTRODUCTION

Rich Man, Poor Woman, but Just Alike

The European tailored suit fit in perfectly in this large, white stone house nestled among the trees on a hill overlooking Lake Zurich. The man conversed comfortably in three languages. An executive with an international company headquartered in Switzerland, he calmly discussed that day's unexpected fall in the market. Obviously, it had cost him at least six figures, if not seven. Still, he remained unconcerned. He had more where that came from and knew how to make even more. When I tried to turn the conversation from finances to eternal riches, he turned cold. He had heard as much about God as he wanted. God played no hand in his world. Intelligence and quick action were all that mattered.

From her ragged mat spread in front of her mud two-room house, she looked helplessly up at this strange white man. Could we tell her about Jesus? Sure, but first would we pray for her husband? He had crossed the Kenya border into Uganda and set up housekeeping there with his other two wives. This left her almost destitute, but that was not her prayer request. She wanted her husband to come back and spend more time with her.

One could continue the stories on and on. One thing unites these people who live in totally different worlds. They are lost. They do not have a saving relationship with Jesus Christ. The destitute African woman was at least willing to listen to the story.

Jesus told three parables illustrating what it means to be lost, heaven's joy when the lost are found, and how the loving Father looks to save people. The final parable also implicated the Pharisees as those who did not share the Father's joy over the salvation of the lost because it was not done their way. Are you like the sinners seeking salvation and finding a Father's love, or are you standing aside watching and wondering how in the world the Father could do that for such unworthy, unclean, sinful people? Reading Luke 15 raises one question for you: "Am I lost?"

II. COMMENTARY

Dedication to the Lost

> **MAIN IDEA:** *Sinners are lost until they repent of their sins and find salvation. This will set off a joyful celebration in heaven beyond all their earthly experience or imagination.*

A The Joy of Seeing Sinners Saved (15:1–2)

> **SUPPORTING IDEA:** *Jesus attracts sinners who need salvation, but religious leaders are too self-righteous to associate with sinners.*

15:1. Jesus had just described heaven as a banquet for the poor, crippled, blind, and lame. He had told the rich banquet hosts to invite such people to their feasts, not seeking repayment. Naturally, such people found Jesus and his teaching attractive. They wanted to hear more and to see what Jesus would do for them.

15:2. Meanwhile, the religious experts also maintained their watch, hoping to trap Jesus (11:53; 14:1). They continually chided him: Why do you associate with these kinds of people? Do you not know their reputation? They will ruin you. Get away from them. You are becoming unclean.

B Kingdom Joy over Repentant Sinners (15:3–10)

> **SUPPORTING IDEA:** *Jesus associated with sinners because he knew they recognized their need of salvation and would respond, bringing joy to heaven.*

15:3–6. Jesus' parables, at first meant to reveal the mysteries of God's kingdom to the disciples and to conceal them from the crowds, have now become tools to teach the opponents (cf. 14:15–16). This parable retains its character as a story, but it is placed in the interrogative mood. The listeners become participants, characters in the story, and must choose a course of action. The story turns the self-righteous, ritually clean scribes and Pharisees into dirty shepherds involved in an occupation that constantly makes them unclean (see commentary on 2:8–12). The rabbis regarded shepherds—along with gamblers, tax collectors, camel drivers, and sailors—as despised, evil, thieving occupations.

As a shepherd, you care for one hundred sheep. One night one lone sheep wanders from the fold. When it comes time to count the sheep, you find one missing. What do you do? You leave the ninety-nine to fend for themselves in the relative safety of the open field and begin an immediate search-and-rescue mission for the lost sheep. Having found the sheep, what do you do? Party! Celebrate! Rejoice! Gather all your friends and neighbors and share the good news with them.

15:7. That is what heaven is like. Ninety-nine self-righteous people who keep all the rituals, festivals, and rules bring no joy to heaven. One sinner confessing his sin and repenting sets off party time in heaven. God is concerned about the lost who will admit they are lost and turn back to him. He wants people to put the sinful life behind them and follow him. Pharisees never do this. Why? They never realize they are lost! They always count themselves among the saved, even though they have never repented of their sins. Start the party in heaven today. Repent of your sins and be saved.

15:8–9. Jesus gave another perspective, hoping his hearers would get the idea. A woman had saved her small wages and amassed ten silver coins, her wages for ten days. Tragedy struck. She lost one coin. Now she faced the same dilemma as the shepherd: "Do I spend time and energy on the one when I still have nine?" Of course she does! She instigates spring housecleaning far out of season. She sets out the brightest lamp she can find, lights it, takes her broom, and sweeps the floor. She watches carefully to discover everything the broom reaches. Finally, there in front of her lies the coin. She reaches down, snatches it up, calls her friends and neighbors: party time. Rejoice! I found it!

15:10. Jesus repeated the message of verse 7. A repentant sinner brings celebration and joy to heaven. The question lingers: Does it bring the same joy and celebration to you? Do you share God's feelings of love and pity and care for sinners. Is your heart so heavy for them that their repentance—their being found for the kingdom—swells your heart with joy? Hopefully, this week the results of your witness will flood heaven with joy.

C Kingdom Celebration over Restoring the Lost (15:11–32)

SUPPORTING IDEA: *God's love restores sinners to right relationship with him.*

15:11–12. Jesus turned to the family setting for his concluding parable to illustrate why he associated with sinners. The story was told succinctly with only the points Jesus wanted to make elaborated. A younger son demanded his share of the estate and got it. There is no indication of why he wanted it or why the father so quickly gave it to him. Later we will see the older brother's attitude and surmise sibling rivalry here, as in the Old Testament stories of Jacob and Esau and of Joseph and his brothers. The younger brother's portion was only a third of the estate if the entire estate were divided. By law, the older brother got a double portion (Deut. 21:17).

15:13–14. The younger son wanted to be on his own. He distanced himself as far as possible from the family. He also took up a new lifestyle. Untrained and inexperienced in money matters, he quickly had many expenses and no income. The result came quickly: no assets. Then a famine hit the land. No one had food or work.

15:15–16. He was fortunate. He found a job, but what a job for a Jew! He fed pigs in a pigpen. Destitute of other resources, he longed to eat what he fed the pigs. How repulsive for a law-abiding Jew. But he had not authority to eat pig food. So he fattened pigs and starved himself.

15:17–19. Finally, his mind went to work again. Humans have the capacity to change. We do not have to remain in the pigpen. We do not have to continue to live as sinners. We can become responsible for our lives. We can quit our riotous living. We can come home.

The younger brother came to his senses: The day laborers on his dad's farm had enough to eat. "And I am about to die from hunger," he said. "I will go back to Daddy and tell him I have sinned against him and against heaven." Note how this ties the story back to the beginning of the chapter and the theme of sinners. No longer are we using animals or objects to talk about the lost. Now we have gotten down to basic facts. People are lost. People need to realize their lost condition and admit it. The younger son's first step is saying, "I am a sinner."

What is a sinner? An unworthy person. One who deserves nothing. Yet a sinner wants something. So the sinner searches for someone who loves the unworthy, who is willing to help the undeserving. The sinful younger brother had forfeited his position as son. He had no more claims on his father, so he applied for a new job—day laborer.

15:20. Focus shifts from son to father. Son is on the move. Father is standing still, waiting to see his son. Here is the poignant portrait of a busy man who has lost one of his chief helpers, taking himself away from his work to wait for a son who may never appear. It is certainly no given that a sinner will repent.

The father did not stay still long. There he was—the son had returned. What joy! What love! What tender compassion filled the father's heart. The old legs started churning. Arms stretched out. Lips reached for a kiss. The family feud was over and forgotten. A son was home.

15:21. Even the joyful welcome did not deter the son from his determined course. He repeated the plea he had rehearsed. Somehow the last line never came out; the job application as a day laborer was never made.

15:22–23. The father never heard his lost son. He had business to attend to. Party time! The son must be properly dressed for the party. Servants dashed off as they were commissioned to get the best robe, a ring, sandals—

things all lost long before the pigpen. Other servants ran to the kitchen to prepare the menu the father ordered. Nothing but the best for the son.

15:24. How could the father act like this? Did he not know what the son had done? Of course, but the son had been given up for dead. This was resurrection time. He was lost. We found the precious treasure for which we have hunted. The lost sheep is back. Certainly a lost and found son is worth much more than a coin or a sheep. Celebrate!

What a picture of the Father in heaven. How he does celebrate when the lost are found, when sinners repent. What compassion and love he shows. Why does Jesus associate with sinners? Because heaven loves them and waits patiently for them to return and repent so the celebration can begin. Heaven's citizens are repentant sinners.

15:25-27. The silent family member appeared. This man had two sons (v. 11). Here is son number one appearing as the last on the scene. Dutifully working for his watching father, the older son heard music and dancing, an unusual event around his home. What in the world was happening?

No one had informed him of his brother's return. He had to ask one of the hired hands. "Did you not know?" they asked. "Your brother's back home. Your father has killed the best calf in the lot to celebrate because he has your brother back safe and sound. Are not you coming to the celebration?"

15:28. Sullen anger set in. The older brother stood his ground and refused to budge. No party for him tonight. Even his dad's pleading would not win him over. The older brother was staying by himself tonight.

15:29-30. "This is not fair," he told his father. "Look what I have done for you all these years. Worked like a slave. Always obeyed. Never disobeyed. What did I get for it? Not even one small goat for a party with my friends. No. No parties around here, until now when this ingrate shows up again. He went out partying, had a wild time, spent all your money. Now here he is again, and what do you do? Party! Not a goat for junior. No, the best calf on the lot—one we have been feeding and grooming these months. And he gets it!"

15:31-32. "Listen a minute, my beloved son," his father replied. "You are with me forever. I can count on you. Everything I now have will go to you. You will never have to worry about having a fatted calf to party with. If you want one, it is yours. Take it. But a celebration was in order. After all, look what happened. Your younger brother was dead, but now he is alive right here with us. He was lost. Now I have found him. Resurrecting the dead. Finding the lost. That is party time! Come celebrate with heaven."

The elder brother does not respond. We are left to our imaginations to determine his final response. We are also left to determine how we would respond. Are we the younger brother, needing to repent and seek reconciliation and forgiveness? Are we the father, who was sinned against and who must have been tempted to respond in hatred and alienation? Are we the elder brother, the self-righteous Pharisee refusing to have anything to do with the sinful younger brother? Are you lost? Do you share God's mercy and compassion for the lost? Are you part of Jesus' mission, coming to seek and to save that which is lost?

MAIN IDEA REVIEW: *Sinners are lost until they repent of their sins and find salvation. This will set off a joyful celebration in heaven beyond all their earthly experience or imagination.*

III. CONCLUSION

God's Priority

What does God have to do with lost sinners? He focuses his attention on them. He pours his love on them. He waits patiently for them to come to their senses, repent of their sins, and come back to him. God has centered his whole plan for creation on one expectation: Sinners will see the error of their ways and turn back to him so he can bring to fruition his plan of salvation and redemption.

When a sinner repents and becomes a part of God's kingdom mission, heaven erupts in joy. It is party time in heaven. Celebrate! Sadly, it does not always work that way on earth. We are too busy establishing our in-groups and defining who is in the out-group. We are afraid to sully our reputation or to be seen with people who do not belong or measure up. Somehow, we always classify ourselves as God's saved people, even though a quick look at God's Word shows we do not act like God or like he tells his people to act. We may be fooling ourselves thinking God has joy in us. Am I a grouchy older brother refusing reconciliation and upset at imagined slights? Am I lost? Do I need to repent? Can I bring wondrous joy to heaven?

PRINCIPLES

- God and his people pay attention to sinners, seeking to find the lost and bringing them to repentance.
- Heaven is populated with the lost who were found and the sinners who repented.
- A repentant sinner floods heaven with joy.
- The church's task is to find the lost, not protect the saved.
- The church joins heaven in rejoicing over the lost when they are found.
- Self-righteous religious people bring no joy to heaven.

- No matter how sinful you are, God waits patiently and lovingly for you to return to him.
- Unforgiving, selfish spirits show a person to be a sinner even if he does not think so.

APPLICATIONS

- Follow Jesus' example and minister to sinners instead of spending your whole life with the "righteous."
- Search for the lost and bring them back to Jesus.
- Share God's joy when sinners repent.
- Do not give up on people when they turn away from family and from God.
- Show God's patient love when family members and friends desert for a while and then return.
- Practice forgiveness, as you want God to forgive you.
- Be careful not to be jealous and selfish.

IV. LIFE APPLICATION

Waiting for My Son

I will never forget the man's face that June afternoon as he sat there on those hard bleacher seats in the high school football stadium. The hot sun was constantly pulling sweat from his body and turning his face a nice shade of pink. He was oblivious. His eyes focused on one young man on the football field. "What's up?" I whispered. "I am waiting for my son. Soon he will cross the stage and get his honors diploma. Then it is off to college on a full academic scholarship. We are so proud of him."

Two years later I met the same man. He called me to go with him. We rode in silence up the interstate to the university town. We met a lawyer and walked across the street to the county jail. "What's up?" I finally asked. "I am waiting for my son," he sniffed, trying to hold back the tears. "Police picked him up for shoplifting. Afraid he is on drugs, too."

Just a few months ago, I met my friend yet again. This time I was seated in a beautiful little church. The man stood by his son at the front looking up the aisle. If I could have whispered again, "What's up?" he would have whispered back, "I am waiting for my son to get married. His beautiful, vivacious bride will be walking down the aisle toward us in just a minute. I am so proud of him. This time I have been waiting ten years, but finally the wait is over. Drugs, alcohol, and jail are all behind him. He is back in church and thinking about going into the ministry. I am so excited."

This father can read Luke 15 with special understanding. He knows what it means to wait for a prodigal son. He can identify with all the emotions that run through the father after he watched his son disappear down the long road to oblivion. Now he knows the joy of seeing the son come back, penitent and sad, seeking another chance at life. He knows the joy of running to the returning son with outstretched arms, ready to plant a big kiss on him. He truly understands party time. Now each day is a celebration as he experiences the joy of finding a lost sinner, reconciling with a lost son.

Our Father in heaven still stands at the corner looking for another lost child to come home. He still leaves the flock and goes off into the hot desert to find a stray lamb. He still sweeps the house clean looking for a lost coin. You have a heavenly Father who loves you that much. His open arms wait for you to see that you are a lost sinner needing to come home to Abba, your daddy in heaven. The party can be ready in a flash if you will come. Having come home and enjoyed the party, then you can join the Father at the corner watching for more lost children to come home. You can go for him into the wilderness looking for lost sheep. You can sit beside the elder brother and show him how much the Father has always loved him even if he never got around to party time. You can let the joy flow as you seek the lost and watch as the Father saves them.

V. PRAYER

Loving, compassionate Father, my daddy in heaven, how long you stood waiting for me to come back from the far country. How long it took me to realize how sinful I was and what I had left behind when I deserted you and declared my independence. What joy when I came home and found you waiting for me. Thank you, dear Lord, for loving me and waiting for me even when I was lost. Oh, Father, show me where to go for you, seeking the lost and inviting them to party time with you. I want others to know the joy I have found in you. Amen.

VI. DEEPER DISCOVERIES

A. Divided His Property (15:12)

The younger son demanded that his father give him his share of the property. Such legal action might be taken during the lifetime of the father to determine exactly what each heir would receive, but the actual settlement of the estate was done generally only after the father was deceased. In a very practical manner, the son was declaring the father dead as far as he was concerned. Life's priorities no longer included the father's interest as far as the younger son was concerned.

The expected response failed to come. The father showed no anger. Instead, he followed the younger son's wishes, but the Greek text shows the emotional anguish involved. It says literally, "He divided to them the life." Everything the father had lived for, that which had consumed all his time and energy, now came into the hands of his sons. Apparently, the two sons acted differently in this regard. The younger son took his part and departed. The elder son received legal claim to his share of the estate—two-thirds—since he received a double portion as elder brother (Deut. 21:17). But the elder son did not exercise control over his share, as the following story makes evident. The father maintained control of his older son's inheritance during his lifetime.

The reader's natural inclination is to praise the patience and loyalty of the older son and to condemn the younger as sinner. The following verses show that judgment to be too quick. The elder brother acted correctly, but his attitude needed correction. Praise goes only to the father, who personifies the heavenly Father in his graciousness toward his sinful children.

B. Feeding Pigs (15:15)

Having disgraced himself in demanding his money from the father, in deserting his father, and in squandering his fortune, the son disgraced himself even more. Desperate for money, he hired himself out to a Gentile—not just any Gentile, but a Gentile pig farmer. Now the young man had deserted not only his family, but his race and religion as well. People of God's covenant could not touch swine, since this made them impure and unfit for worship of God (Lev. 11:7; Deut. 14:8; Isa. 65:4; 66:17). His was the most disgraceful job a Jewish citizen could possibly take. Every time he performed his duties, he carried himself further away from his Jewish heritage and his God.

C. Pods (15:16)

After spending his inheritance, the prodigal son found himself in a severe famine. Soon he became desperately in need. "He longed to fill his stomach with the pods that the pigs were eating, but no one gave him anything." These pods were *keration*, the fruit of the carob tree. They sometimes grew to a foot in length, and they served as common feed for livestock. Rabbis considered resorting to a diet of pods an indication of being in the direst need.

D. Came to His Senses (15:17)

This phrase more literally reads, "He came to himself." It means that indeed he was thinking more clearly now, having learned some hard lessons. He certainly recalled his upbringing that he had so ignored. He also "came to himself" in the sense that he faced himself—who he was and what he had done. His look "into the mirror" was a sobering reality. The result was true repentance.

E. Sinned Against Heaven and Against You (15:21)

A sinful, disgraced, disenfranchised apostate from the Jewish faith shows that theological truth can come from the most unlikely sources. The younger son knew the religious tradition of his people intellectually. He had been taught what sin was. Sin was an action taken against human beings that had heavenly consequences. Sin involved breaking relationships on earth that at the same time severed relationships in heaven. To sin against a human being is more than an earthly act. It is an eternal sin that requires both human and divine forgiveness. The younger son knew this intellectually. Now he learned the truth emotionally and spiritually. He experienced in the deepest part of his soul the feeling of separation and guilt that sin brings. He knew he could not live with such feelings. He knew further that he did not want to live in such separation from the people he had always loved. He also knew he did not deserve forgiveness. He deserved to be treated as he had treated the father. Instead, he discovered a new truth, the truth of love that forgets and forgives.

VII. TEACHING OUTLINE

A. INTRODUCTION

1. Lead Story: Rich Man, Poor Woman, but Just Alike
2. Context: Luke 15 shifts perspectives quickly. Chapter 14 described a shocking reversal of kingdom expectations. Not the righteous religious people but the needy and helpless would be invited to the final kingdom banquet. To be a part of that banquet, a person did not follow rabbinic rules. Rather, it required taking up a cross and following Jesus even at the expense of relationships and commitments to family. Luke 15 shows why such radical dedication and commitment is worth it. When that helpless sinner made the commitment, he first went back home and found a new family. The way of the cross is also the way to the Father's open arms. Joy spreads through heaven. The party begins. You are among folks just like yourself—lost sinners who decided to return home to the heavenly Father. Jesus was and is the friend of sinners.
3. Transition: We stand in an awkward place today. We read Christ's parables and wonder where to stand. With whom do we identify? Most of us who engage in Bible study have long since made that move back down the road to home. We have repented of sins and found the joy of the Father's arms. We are not lost. Are we? So we proudly plant ourselves beside the Father, waiting for the lost to come home.

But often we never have occasion to raise the cry, "Party time." We never see the returning sinner coming where we are. Why? Have we not taken up the shepherd's role and gone out looking for the lost? Are we really standing there with an older son's attitude of envy and jealousy, wondering why the lost profligate gets all the attention and we get none? Or are we in actuality the original audience for the stories, self-righteous, self-satisfied Pharisees representing the religious establishment and looking down our noses at those sinners out there, afraid they might ruin our reputation and amazed that they will not play the religious game by our rules. Luke 15 invites us to find out who we are in a world populated by sinners as heaven waits to celebrate when just one of them repents.

B. COMMENTARY
1. The Joy of Seeing Sinners Saved (15:1–2)
2. Kingdom Joy over Repentant Sinners (15:3–10)
    a. The story: finding and rejoicing over the lost sheep (15:3–6)
    b. The moral: heaven rejoices over repentant sinners, not over righteous people (15:7)
    c. The story: finding and rejoicing over lost coin (15:8–9)
    d. The moral: angels rejoice over repentant sinner (15:10)
3. Kingdom Celebration over Restoring the Lost (15:11–32)
    a. The story: the return and celebration over the lost son (15:11–24)
    b. The story continued: the jealous brother's rejection of the resurrected son (15:25–30)
    c. The moral: rejoice when the dead are resurrected, the lost found (15:31–32)

C. CONCLUSION: WAITING FOR MY SON

VIII. ISSUES FOR DISCUSSION

1. What does it mean for a person to be lost spiritually?
2. How long has it been since you talked to a lost person about the Father's love? Why?
3. With whom do you identify in the story of the lost son and rejecting brother? Why?
4. When did heaven rejoice because you were the repentant sinner who was found? Share your story with others in your Bible study.
5. How do you and your church imitate Jesus in welcoming and associating with sinners?

Luke 16

Dedication to Kingdom Living

I. **INTRODUCTION**
Poor Little Rich Boy

II. **COMMENTARY**
A verse-by-verse explanation of the chapter.

III. **CONCLUSION**
Kingdom People

An overview of the principles and applications from the chapter.

IV. **LIFE APPLICATION**
Young Man's Kingdom Living

Melding the chapter to life.

V. **PRAYER**
Tying the chapter to life with God.

VI. **DEEPER DISCOVERIES**
Historical, geographical, and grammatical enrichment of the commentary.

VII. **TEACHING OUTLINE**
Suggested step-by-step group study of the chapter.

VIII. **ISSUES FOR DISCUSSION**
Zeroing the chapter in on daily life.

Quote

"Competitive excellence requires 100% all of the time. If you doubt that, try maintaining excellence by setting your standards at 92%. Or even 95%. People figure they're doing fine so long as they get somewhere near it. Excellence gets reduced to acceptable, and before long, acceptable doesn't seem worth the sweat if you can get by with adequate. After that, mediocrity is only a breath away."

Charles R. Swindoll

Luke 16

 IN A NUTSHELL

Kingdom living requires one hundred percent dedication to God and no percent dedication to the world. Such dedication makes you trustworthy in every situation with all things, no matter how valuable they are. Entrance to the kingdom comes by listening to God's Word and obeying it. If you do not believe God's Word, you will not believe anything, even resurrection from the dead.

Dedication to Kingdom Living

I. INTRODUCTION

Poor Little Rich Boy

*H*e grew up the envy of everyone. His parents belonged to the city's financial and social elite. He went to the best schools and associated with the city's leading socialites. He traveled with his dad to exotic places in the world, hunting and fishing. Known as one of the city's leading musicians, he soon traveled the world playing for conventions and meetings and parties. He had the good life. He was even a member of one of the leading churches and often played for other churches and citywide church events.

Finally, after a couple of failures, he married a girl who truly loved him and stayed with him the rest of his life. They traveled far and wide and seemed to have the good life. They had just three problems. First, his parents forgot to die. They clung to their money and to their lives, fearful the young son, now in his sixties, would fritter it all away. This led to the second problem: no independence and no job. He spent almost seventy years totally dependent on his parents and finally on his mother for financial support. The third problem was alcoholism. Without self-esteem or confidence, he turned to drink for comfort and escape. Musical talents waned. University business degree went unused. Brilliant mind stayed unoccupied. The prominent rich boy had nothing of meaning.

In Luke 16 Jesus turns his teaching to his disciples. He changes from the banquet images of chapter 14 and the stories of loss in chapter 15 to concentrate on wealth and money management. He uses these money stories in unusual and interesting ways that require close attention and study. He shows how easy it is for wealth and social prominence to sidetrack a person from life's real values.

II. COMMENTARY

Dedication to Kingdom Living

MAIN IDEA: *Kingdom living stands opposed to worldly living. The world values wealth and possessions, while kingdom living obeys God's Word instead of the world's worth.*

⚠ Earthly Wealth for Heavenly Purposes (16:1–13)

SUPPORTING IDEA: *Kingdom living involves managing worldly goods for the good of heaven's purposes.*

16:1–4. Jesus focused his teaching back on his disciples (cf. 15:1–3). He shifted them to a place in society they had never occupied—the realm of the rich. This echelon centered attention on maintaining and increasing wealth. A poor manager raised concern. A crooked manager was cause for alarm. This one apparently managed a farm for a landowner who lived in the city. The manager managed to squander the landowner's assets much as the prodigal son had squandered his father's (see 15:13). A pink slip was in order. What did a manager without a job do? He knew he was too old and out of shape to go back to manual labor. He was too proud to beg for help from his friends, or worse, to sit on the street corner, hat in hand. Using all his managerial skills, he developed a plan. He would not have to beg. Friends would welcome him with open arms.

16:5–7. The plan was simple: a fire sale on debt. Perhaps the men he called in were tenant farmers who worked the land and gave a percentage of the crop to the landowner. The first owed one hundred baths of olive oil, a bath being about nine gallons. The manager reduced the 900-gallon debt to 450. The second tenant owed one hundred kors of wheat. The precise equivalent of a kor is not known. Scholarly estimates vary from six and one-half to twelve bushels. This debt was reduced by twenty percent. Certainly these were simply examples. Other people also took advantage of the manager's situation and his debt fire sale.

What was happening here? Another example of squandering his master's wealth? Perhaps. The manager may have been illegally reducing debt. He may have been subtracting interest that had accrued on the debt in violation of biblical teaching (see Deut. 23:19–20). He may have been sacrificing his own commission for long-term gains. Jesus did not condone the man's business practice as legal or one to be imitated by others. This was a long-term plan by the manager to have friends indebted to him when he needed them. But how would the landowner react when he heard the news or saw the books?

16:8. Ironically, the landowner praised the man. Why? Because his business plan was smart and it accomplished the purposes the manager set out for it. First, it made the landowner look good in the eyes of those who were indebted to him and who continued to do business with him. Second, it looked forward to the long term rather than being limited to the present moment. Third, it assured people would be indebted to the manager and thus honor bound to help him when he would need it, much sooner than they suspected.

Jesus put the parable in context. In this world the children of light—those who have become lamps letting God's light shine through them (11:35–36)—often are much more foolish in their dealings with other people than are the secular people who have no concern for God. God's people should be as dedicated to living out kingdom living with other people in this world as the people of this world are in living out their own values to their own advantage in this world. The world's citizens, however, are only of this age. They have no future beyond the here and now. Children of light will shine through all the ages of eternity. Live now so you are assured of eternity.

16:9. Jesus drove the point home to his disciples: "Make use of the world's resources so friends will be there to help you when you need it most. Things of this world may be unrighteous in themselves, but they can be used for good. To do so, you must recognize that such worldly resources are temporary. One day they will no longer be available. Use them while you can, but do not make them the end, only the means. Used in this way, unrighteous worldly resources can help you prepare for eternity. By being generous with secular resources, particularly by sharing them with the poor, blind, lame, and crippled, you can store up treasures in heaven. Just as the grateful debtors would welcome the manager into their homes when he needed them (v. 4), so you will be welcomed to your eternal home when you die and material resources are no longer of value. Meeting you there will be those friends with whom you shared unrighteous worldly resources. They will show you to your heavenly resources."

16:10–11. The disciples dismissed this parable as not applicable to them. They had no worldly resources, so the message of this parable did not apply to them. Jesus disagreed. No matter how few resources you have, be trustworthy with them, he said. Only as you get in the habit of generous, trustworthy use of resources can you be trusted with more. That habit will lead you to continue to be trustworthy, no matter how high the value of your resources. Look out for the other side of this truth. You may think that it does not make much difference how you handle the little that you have. You can cheat and mislead and squander such resources. After all, it is just unrighteous money, not worth anything. Again, Jesus emphasized, the habit you form now stays with you. Be faithful in little; you will be faithful in much. Be unfaithful in little, you will be unfaithful and unrighteous if you get the opportunity to manage many resources. If you are unfaithful in unrighteous worldly goods, no one will trust you with heavenly goods.

16:12. Take the picture one step further. If you cannot prove trustworthy and faithful at managing someone else's money, what will happen when you receive money of your own? Will you mismanage, squander, and be unrighteous in dealing with personal funds? Who would ever trust you with them?

16:13. Take your choice: God or money. You cannot have both. One or the other will control you. Which is it? You cannot take orders from two masters, although apparently in Jesus' day some slaves were owned by two people and tried hard to please both. You have to listen to just one master. You cannot, likewise, do what attains wealth and what demonstrates kingdom living. Attaining wealth and attaining the kingdom represent two opposing goals. You must focus either on the kingdom or on wealth. Which will it be?

B Self-Justification Does Not Work with God (16:14–15)

> **SUPPORTING IDEA:** *Kingdom living seeks to please God, not people.*

16:14. The disciples (v. 1) were not the only people listening to Jesus. Pharisees, constantly on the watch to trap him, eavesdropped. Naturally, they scoffed at such teaching. They were in the upper financial and social echelons of Jewish society and wanted to do everything by the rules. Luke describes them with one phrase: lovers of money. They tried to serve two masters and thought they were doing a fine job of this. They had no intention of being generous with their money except on those public occasions when it raised their esteem in the eyes of the public.

16:15. Their actions had one purpose—to win public approval and to make others think they were God's favorite people. The public may see you as righteous, religious, and wise. God knows otherwise. What people admire, God detests. So take your choice. Who will be your master—the people or God? In whose eyes do you want justification: people's or God's?

C Kingdom Living Calls for Obedience to God's Word (16:16–18)

> **SUPPORTING IDEA:** *Jesus introduced a new stage in God's salvation history, but entrance into the kingdom depends on obedience to God's Word.*

16:16. Jesus addressed experts on God's Word, so he based his discussion on their field of expertise. In so doing he quietly assigned his opponents to an out-of-date, invalid era. The law and the prophets ruled until John the Baptist came. They were God's method of revelation for people up until John. John introduced something, or someone, better than the law and the prophets. John introduced Jesus. Jesus introduced the presence of the kingdom of God. It was not enough any more to be an expert in explaining and in obeying God's Word found in the law and the prophets. Now one must answer the call to enter God's kingdom. Pharisees, if you want to keep up to date with God,

Jesus declared, then listen to the new Word of God—the Word taught and revealed in the life of Jesus.

16:17. Jesus came preaching the kingdom of God present in his ministry. This does not mean he discarded the written word of the law and the prophets. The Old Testament remained valid. It would be simpler to have the universe disappear from sight than to do away with the authority of God's Word. The Old Testament is incomplete and cannot be the entire center of life, as it was for the Pharisees, but its teachings are still valid. Their validity, however, must be held in light of the new revelation in Jesus. Jesus showed the spirit, meaning, and purpose of the law in a new and radically different manner than the Pharisees viewed the law. The law was not a source of threat and judgment to hold over people's heads. The law was an opportunity to express love to God through obedience and to express love to other people through seeing the centrality of the law's call to love your neighbor, to help the poor, to care for orphans and widows. The law is not a road to self-justification. It is a road to selfless ministry to God and to others.

Viewed in Jesus' way, the law will never lose its power. Not even the smallest part of one letter can be taken away, for that smallest part of a Hebrew or Aramaic letter could mean the difference between two letters and thus the difference between two words. It would be the same thing as taking the bottom horizontal leg off an E or the angular line at the bottom of an R, suddenly changing these letters to F and P. Christ brings full meaning and understanding and obedience to God's Word. He does not want to replace it.

16:18. This verse appears out of place here. Nothing in the context prepares us for a discussion of divorce and remarriage. It serves as an example of what Jesus had just claimed—the ongoing validity of God's law.

Apparently Jesus took up a rabbinic dispute concerning legitimate and illegitimate divorce. Deuteronomy 22:13–30 and 24:1–5 provided the basis for arguments about marriage and divorce. Malachi 2:13–16 gives the strong prophetic condemnation of divorce: God hates divorce. Jesus combined this with the Old Testament teachings on adultery (Exod. 20:14; Lev. 20:10; Deut. 5:18; 22:22). He then took the strongest stand possible, saying divorce is equal to adultery. In so doing he did not say everything that could be said on divorce and remarriage (see "Deeper Discoveries"). He did show that no one in Judaism had a stronger respect for the family or a stronger determination to fulfill the letter of the law. The Pharisees could hear Jesus say that his coming brought a new era in the history of salvation. They could not condemn him for making light of God's law. He stood as the law's staunchest defender.

D Kingdom Living Leaves No Hope for Unbelieving People (16:19–31)

SUPPORTING IDEA: *The Word of God is sufficient to lead us to salvation. Unbelievers cannot be helped, no matter what God does.*

16:19. With no transition statement, Luke introduced the parable of the poor man and Lazarus. Parallel to the rich landowner in verse 1, the central character of this parable is a rich man enjoying the most luxurious life possible. His dress and his food set him apart from Jesus' disciples and from the ordinary Jewish citizen. Here was the man the Pharisees wanted to be.

16:20–21. Lazarus, the other character in the story, represents the opposite side of the social ladder. He owned nothing, but Jesus honored him with a name, while the rich man remained anonymous. Lazarus was clothed with sores. He lived not in a gated mansion but on the street beside the rich man's gate, and he depended to live on. He himself seemed to offer nourishment for the wild dogs that licked his sores. The rich man had the opportunity to do all Jesus had commanded. He could invite the sick to his banquet table. He could show his generosity in using his material resources for kingdom purposes. He could restore a lost man who was basically dead to life and join in heaven's joy. He did not have far to search for this lost sheep. He could even sell all his possessions in his dedication to kingdom living. But not this man. He ignored Lazarus and went about his luxurious life.

16:22–23. Inevitably, the poor Lazarus died, perhaps from his illness, perhaps from malnutrition. The self-righteous and self-centered rich man certainly had some responsibility in his death. One day death also visited the rich man. Dying is the only thing the two men hold in common in the story. The difference Jesus emphasized was what happened after death. Lazarus died and went with the angels to heaven. Not only was he in heaven; he was positioned right next to Abraham, the father of Jewish faith (Gen. 12–17). Nothing better could happen to a Jew after death. The rich man went where his master—money—took him, to Hades, the place of torment (see "Deeper Discoveries"). From there somehow he could see Abraham—and what a shocking discovery. There beside Abraham, he saw Lazarus, the one he had been unable to see all those years at his gate.

16:24. What a reversal of fortunes! The rich man was tormented even more than poor Lazarus had been as the dogs licked his sores and the rich man ignored him. In desperation he called to Abraham for help. He addressed him as father, indicating that he considered himself to be of the seed of Abraham and thus deserving of help from Abraham and from the God of Abraham. He cried for mercy, even when mercy meant having poor, unclean, filthy Lazarus come to his rescue, although he had never helped

Lazarus. A fingertip of cool water would mean a lot in the horrible flaming torment he suffered.

16:25. Abraham could communicate from his eternal abode to that of the rich man. He continued the family terminology, acknowledging the man as a son of Abraham. The rich man needed a history lesson. In life he had enjoyed all the luxuries. Lazarus, on the other hand, enjoyed no luxuries, only bad things. Now the situation was reversed. Lazarus received the comfort he had begged for all those years. But the rich man had slipped from the comfortable life to pure agony. Yes, those expecting to be first were last, and those who expected to be last were now first, right beside Abraham.

16:26. An eternal reality needed explaining. Abraham might be able to communicate with the man in torment, but he could not come to him. A great chasm separated them. There is no description of the chasm, no location geographically—just the reality: You cannot get there from here. You are where you are going to stay, just as we are. Torment is your eternal reward, just as heavenly comfort belongs to Lazarus forever.

16:27–28. Father, remember the rest of my family and yours, the rich man prayed. If the chasm prevents Lazarus from coming here, at least send him to my five poor brothers, caught up in the life of comfort and ease just like I was. Explain the truth to them. I'd do anything to spare my family from this horrible place of torment. Let Lazarus go back from the dead and warn them.

16:29. Abraham pointed him to the Pharisees' favorite source of authority. They already had the books of Moses—the law and the prophets, which is the rest of Scripture. They give them all the information they need. They need to listen to them. Such a warning implies that the rich man had the same authorities his brothers did, but they refused to listen to them. Obeying Scripture should lead them away from torment and to the eternal kingdom.

16:30. No, father Abraham, I am prime example number one, the rich man replied. They need something more than the Scriptures. They need someone raised from the dead. Catch the irony of the rich man's words. This man, who has everything the Pharisees did, wanted a greater authority than Scripture, that in which the Pharisees were proud experts. Does this indicate Jesus was right? The day of the Old Testament alone had come and gone. God has provided something new. The kingdom of God is now present in Jesus. If one does not follow Jesus, hope for eternity is gone, no matter how expert one is in the ancient authorities. Jesus has come calling people to repent, for the kingdom is here. The rich man then saw that people like him may appear to be blessed and perfect. They may be religious leaders. They may appear righteous. But they still need to repent and enter the kingdom.

16:31. This verse contains the awesome declaration of father Abraham. A person rising from the dead cannot convince such people. Obviously, he foreshadows the death and resurrection of Jesus. Jesus came to call sinners, not the righteous, to repentance. Why? As Abraham states, those like the rich man and his brothers and the Pharisees are so convinced of their religious superiority and their righteousness before God that they will never respond to a call to repentance, even if the authority behind it is the voice of the resurrected one—Jesus. On this basis Jesus can explain that all Scripture points to him. He is the fulfillment of all the Old Testament taught. Yet, for the rich men and the Pharisees of the world, he is something radically new—something they will never accept, no matter how powerful a sign God uses to prove that this is his Son in whom he is well pleased.

MAIN IDEA REVIEW: *Kingdom living stands opposed to worldly living. The world values wealth and possessions, while kingdom living obeys God's Word instead of the world's worth.*

III. CONCLUSION

Kingdom People

Kingdom living starts in this world. Members of the kingdom must live with the same resources and challenges as the secular person. Too often secular people outsmart kingdom people in their use of the world's resources to get ahead, plan ahead, and influence other people. Kingdom people also need to use the world's resources with acumen and wisdom. Kingdom people have a clearer vision of the future; they point toward eternity, not just toward tomorrow. Thus, kingdom living means using the world's resources to help those kingdom people Jesus consistently pointed to—poor, lame, blind, crippled. Using world resources generously to help Jesus' people is wise planning for the future. It leads to meeting those people who are waiting to greet us in heaven.

Kingdom people are single-minded people. They do not hold to both the world and the kingdom. They know no one can be a slave who obeys two masters. Nor do they need to justify their kingdom existence before other people. God justifies. People do not. What people see as justification, God sees as detestable, reprehensible.

Kingdom people live out of new resources the world does not have, even the world of the religious and pious. Kingdom people have entered Jesus' kingdom, something new beyond the authority and life of Moses and the prophets. They do not destroy the old authority. They fill it full. They may interpret the law in stricter terms than even the Pharisees and rabbis.

Kingdom living often means earthly poverty and suffering. It means being ignored by those who are enjoying the world's blessings and comforts. This enjoyment is temporary. Death soon comes and cuts it off. Then you must face eternity. What will you face? Life on Abraham's side or life in torment in Hades? The question is, Have you truly believed the law and the prophets? Have you seen that they point to Jesus and his kingdom? Have you entered eternity as a kingdom person or as a self-justifying legalist? Must you have a great sign from God to believe the true purpose of Scripture? Or will you humbly believe with those like Lazarus? Kingdom living is living Christ's way. Are you living the kingdom way today?

PRINCIPLES

- God's people should use the world's resources in ways that reflect kingdom living and help others.
- Preparing for the eternal future is more important than gathering riches for tomorrow.
- You must prove yourself trustworthy in small tasks before you will be considered capable of greater tasks.
- You must prove yourself trustworthy with worldly resources before you will be entrusted with God's resources.
- You must choose between serving the world—with its focus on possessions—and serving God—with his kingdom focus on eternity.
- You must choose between being justified in the eyes of people or being justified by God.
- Kingdom living remains obedient living.
- Eternity marks a radical, unchangeable difference in the experience of kingdom people and the experience of self-righteous people.

APPLICATIONS

- Check to see if you are using worldly resources in worldly ways or kingdom ways.
- List evidence of your generosity to the type of people Jesus associated with.
- Describe the master you are tempted to serve besides Christ. Describe ways you are serving Christ instead.
- Do not become a lover of money.
- Make heaven your supreme goal in life.
- Trust the resurrected one, Jesus, to take you to heaven.

IV. LIFE APPLICATION

Young Man's Kingdom Living

James Dobson (*When God Doesn't Make Sense*, 3) tells the story of Chuck Frye, a brilliant student who graduated near the top of his high school class, excelled in college, and actually got accepted into medical school.

His first term in medical school brought unexpected decisions. God seemed to be calling him to minister to his people. These were not just any people. They were people in a far country with no material resources. He would have to have missionary support. He would forfeit all his dreams of becoming a prominent doctor. Finally, Chuck made his decision. He would follow God to the mission field.

But he never got there. Instead, at the end of that first year of medical school, extreme fatigue set in. The diagnosis came quickly: acute leukemia. By the next November he was dead.

Fortunately, Chuck had his priorities in order. He practiced kingdom living here on earth. He placed more value on the things of God than on the things of earth. He chose to follow one Master and leave the appeal of money, fame, and power behind. He now enjoys his eternal reward.

You may not face a decision as dramatic as Chuck did. God may not call you across the ocean. He may not ask you to forfeit career dreams. He does ask you to find where he has called you and to use every opportunity as a ministry opportunity. He does ask you not to depend on financial resources for joy. He does ask you to use the world's resources in kingdom living for kingdom purposes. So easily in so many ways, money takes over as master of life. Are you truly dedicated to God's kingdom, ready to use the world's goods and the world's opportunities as ways to be generous to the needy and to seek the lost?

V. PRAYER

Controller of all the universe and owner of all the world's financial resources, teach me to use what you allow me to have in ways that honor you and help your people. Place heavenly values deep into me so that they control my life. Remove all temptations to seek approval and praise from other people. I desire only to praise you with my life and to find friends I have helped waiting to greet me into heaven. Amen.

VI. DEEPER DISCOVERIES

A. Shrewdly or Astutely (16:8)

The manager in Jesus' parable was a crook. He never denied his master's accusations. He probably added to his prohibited actions as he reduced the bills of his master's debtors. Still, the master praised him for being "shrewd" or "astute." The Greek adverb *phronimos* occurs only here in Luke's writings. The related noun occurs in Luke 12:42; 16:8 (cf. Matt. 7:24; 10:16; 24:45; 25:2,4,8,9; Rom. 11:25; 12:16; 1 Cor. 4:10; 10:15; 2 Cor. 11:19). It basically means "to be sensible or wise." This is a characteristic expected of an administrator or manager (12:42; cf. Matt. 24:45). It characterizes those who plan ahead for the coming of the bridegroom in the last judgment parable (Matt. 25). People proudly project themselves as wise or sensible (1 Cor. 4:10; 10:15; 2 Cor. 11:19). But taken to the extreme, shrewdness can become conceit (Rom. 11:25; cf. 12:16). It is a characteristic that disciples on mission for Christ need (Matt. 10:16).

In Luke 16 the landowner praised the unrighteous manager for this quality and encouraged Christ's disciples to learn from the world how to exercise it in relationships with others. Such astute wisdom apparently indicates an ability to plan ahead rather than focusing on the current moment and to relate to other people in such ways that they will gladly help you in time of future need. The Christian reversal on this is that the world acts in expectation of repayment, while Christians know that the only repayment will come in the eternal home where those whom they helped will welcome them (cf. 14:12–14).

B. Everyone Is Forcing His Way into It (16:16)

Marshall (p. 650) says, "Few sayings in the Gospels are so uncertain in interpretation as this one." Interpretation becomes more difficult because Matthew 11:12–13 places the saying in a different situation with different wording and different meaning than the context in Luke.

The Greek verb here may be interpreted as a passive, "Everyone is forced into it," or as a middle voice as the NIV translates it. Some scholars see the meaning to be, "Everyone is invited into it." Most agree with the NIV, but then interpret the meaning differently. Is this a positive or a negative action? Are people using good means or evil means to try to get into the kingdom? Are good people doing the action, or is it Jesus' opponents—either Pharisees or evil spirits? Do legitimate followers of Christ use their zeal and stubborn determination to get into the kingdom?

Nolland (*WBC* 35*b*, 813) translates, "Everyone takes vigorous steps to enter it," noting that he had to supply "to enter." For Luke, entering God's kingdom is not a passive event that just happens to a person. To enter the kingdom, we must take the initiative. We must make the hard choice to serve the right master and then do that which shows we are trustworthy so that we will be entrusted with genuine riches.

Recent commentators like Fitzmyer, Schweizer, Culpepper, and Bock return to the passive meaning of the verb, interpreting its meaning as, "Everyone is strongly urged to enter it" (*HCSB*). Jesus' proclamation and efforts to persuade the Pharisees and scribes show how valiantly he urged people to enter the kingdom. Sadly, many rejected his urging.

C. Christian Divorce (16:18)

This may be Jesus' clearest and most forceful statement on divorce. The literal meaning in the context of Luke is clear. Jesus supports the law as strongly as anyone. He rejects many contemporary excuses for divorce. To divorce a wife with the intention to marry another is to commit adultery. So is marriage with a woman divorced from her husband, very possibly either lured by the man she is marrying from her husband or more likely one who enticed the new husband and deliberately infuriated the old. Abandoning marriage vows because of interest in another person is sinful, unacceptable, and not tolerated by Jesus.

This is not Jesus' or the New Testament's only statement on divorce. Mark 10:11–12 comes close to saying the same thing as our passage in Luke. Matthew 5:32 and 19:9 appear to allow divorce if the mate has committed sexual immorality within the marriage. Chapter 19 sees the source of marriage faithfulness and continuity as the creation account of the first marriage. God has joined a couple as one flesh, so no human should try to undo what God has done.

In 1 Corinthians 7 Paul joined the chorus forbidding divorce, saying if a wife did leave her husband, she could not remarry. Even those married to unbelievers could not divorce them if the unbelieving partner did not want to. The strict line on divorce and remarriage sided with Rabbi Shammai, who said divorce was permitted only in case of immorality. Rabbi Hillel on the other side permitted divorce for several reasons, many as trivial as making a mistake while preparing a meal. Jesus stands even stricter than the strictest Jewish tradition, making the man guilty of adultery against his own wife, placing husband and wife on the same level (see Marshall, 631).

Does this mean that no Christian is ever able to remarry after divorce? The debate goes on. Bock (p. 1358) notes that "the implication of Matthew's teaching (better, Matthew's report of Jesus' teaching) seems to be that if divorce is given because of unfaithfulness, the partner who was not unfaithful has the right to remarry." The argument for remarriage after divorce is complex and goes beyond specific biblical passages to the entire concept of sin and forgiveness. Divorce is a sin, and it normally involves sin on the part of both parties. Divorce with the intention of marrying another person immediately doubles the sin, adding adultery to the sin of breaking covenant with God and with the marriage partner.

Does either divorce or remarriage become the unforgivable sin? Is there no condition under which a divorced person can be forgiven of the sin of divorce, have the slate wiped clean, and be allowed another chance at a happy marriage relationship? Does the church in the name of Jesus practice grace in this area of life as well as in others?

D. Place of Comfort; Place of Torment (16:22–25)

This is one of the clearest biblical passages indicating a clear separation between the righteous dead and the unbelieving dead. The problem in interpreting the passage and then incorporating it into a doctrinal system of heaven and hell lies in the nature of the section as a parable, a story Jesus told. Were the elements of the story intended to set forth the precise description of heaven and hell, or were they simply elements taken up from common Jewish tradition and used in order to communicate with the audience? Against the latter possibility stands verse 26, which appears to be an intentional claim to teach something new.

The New Testament represents a wide advance over the Old Testament's hints, clues, and implications about the afterlife. This passage shows an instant awareness of distinct experiences immediately after death (cf. 23:43; Acts 7:59; 2 Cor. 5:8; Phil. 1:23). It also speaks of Hades as a place of torment and fire, though Acts 2:27,31 (cf. Matt. 12:40) place Jesus in the heart of the earth in Hades after his death. Is that simply an attempt to say Jesus suffered everything? Death and judgment are consistently connected to Hades (Matt. 16:18; 11:23; Luke 10:15). Some see Hades as the place of the dead parallel to Sheol in the Old Testament. This makes it the intermediate state before final judgment. This view would say that Hades has compartments, some for the wicked and others for the righteous. Our passage appears to make a greater distinction than that, seeing Hades as the place of punishment and torment shut off from the place of comfort, although admittedly no name is given the heavenly place.

The New Testament seems to make two points standing in tension with one another: The dead are immediately conscious of their eternal reward or punishment, and the dead face a final judgment with eternal separation and gradations of rewards and punishments. No matter how this tension is resolved, the doctrine motivates us to press into the kingdom, let God be our Master, and make sure that kingdom living has started here, so that it will last eternally.

VII. TEACHING OUTLINE

A. INTRODUCTION

1. Lead Story: Poor Little Rich Boy
2. Context: Chapter 15 showed the desire of God that the lost be found so heaven can celebrate in joy. Chapter 16 turns to a grim picture—judgment for the unbeliever. Believers are encouraged to follow even the example of unbelievers in using this world's resources but for kingdom purposes rather than for selfish, worldly purposes. We are to show ourselves trustworthy with worldly goods so we may show ourselves capable of being entrusted with heavenly goods. The first mark of being

trustworthy is choosing one Master and sticking faithfully to him. This can prove difficult, since money and possessions are tempting masters. Kingdom living goes beyond Old Testament living. Jesus brought something new, the presence of the kingdom of God on earth. Kingdom living involves a higher plane of obedience than did even the law and the prophets. Too often the rich miss kingdom living in their pursuit of the world's goods. The poor seem to be left out of all blessing on earth, but their day is coming. Death provides the great divide. Then the poor who practice kingdom living will find the comfort they missed on earth, while the money lovers will face Hades and torment.

3. Transition: The kingdom was present in Jesus. Kingdom living is still the way of life for Jesus' followers. The modern church seems to walk a line between the ways of the world and kingdom living. Luke 16 forces us to see the horrible consequences of trying to serve two masters. Comfort with this world leads to discomfort in the world to come. This study should be a serious call back to the kingdom and away from the world.

B. COMMENTARY

1. Earthly Wealth for Heavenly Purposes (16:1–13)
2. Self-Justification Does Not Work with God (16:14–15)
3. Kingdom Living Calls for Obedience to God's Word (16:16–18)
4. Kingdom Living Leaves No Hope for Unbelieving People (16:19–31)
   a. The setting: poor Lazarus at rich man's gate (16:19–21)
   b. Death brings separation: torment and comfort (16:22–24)
   c. Death brings permanence of condition with no chance for change (16:25–26)
   d. Plea for help for rich man's brothers (16:27–28)
   e. No hope beyond the Word of God, not even a visitor from the dead (16:29–31)

C. CONCLUSION: YOUNG MAN'S KINGDOM LIVING

VIII. ISSUES FOR DISCUSSION

1. In what ways have you acted shrewdly in behalf of the kingdom?
2. In what ways do you attempt to serve two masters? How much success do you have? Why?
3. What do you believe the Bible teaches about divorce and remarriage?
4. What chance does a rich person have of reaching heaven?
5. In what way does teaching about heaven and hell motivate you? What do you think heaven will be like? Hell?

Luke 17

Dedication to Christian Servanthood

I. **INTRODUCTION**
Dedication Is Faith to the Finish

II. **COMMENTARY**
A verse-by-verse explanation of the chapter.

III. **CONCLUSION**
Forgiveness Unlimited

An overview of the principles and applications from the chapter.

IV. **LIFE APPLICATION**
Saving Old Miss Sadie

Melding the chapter to life.

V. **PRAYER**
Tying the chapter to life with God.

VI. **DEEPER DISCOVERIES**
Historical, geographical, and grammatical enrichment of the commentary.

VII. **TEACHING OUTLINE**
Suggested step-by-step group study of the chapter.

VIII. **ISSUES FOR DISCUSSION**
Zeroing the chapter in on daily life.

Quote

"*There are times when we . . . are called to love, expecting nothing in return. Times when we are called to give money to people who will never say thanks, to forgive those who won't forgive us, to come early and stay late when no one else notices. Service prompted by duty. This is the call of discipleship.*"

Max Lucado

Luke 17

I N   A   N U T S H E L L

Do not cause someone else to sin. Rather, practice forgiveness toward all people all the time. A little faith can accomplish miracles, but still you are simply a slave for God, never able to do more than your duty. When God does something in your life, you need to thank him, knowing God was working through your faith. Quit looking for outward signs of the kingdom of God. It is within you. The Son of Man must be rejected and suffer, but he will again be revealed. Do not try to save anything on that day, for some will be taken, and others will be left.

Dedication to Christian Servanthood

I. INTRODUCTION

Dedication Is Faith to the Finish

*J*ohn Bunyan's life was changed by two books that his father-in-law gave his wife. These books led him to become a different person, join a church, and begin preaching the gospel. People came eagerly to hear Bunyan preach. The young redhead reached all people. The uneducated people marveled that they could understand his preaching. His words challenged individuals as well as the state. He proclaimed that every person had the right to believe as his conscience led. No state, no king, no church had the right to interfere with how a person practiced his religion.

Soon England's government changed. The new government supported the Church of England. Bunyan was arrested for preaching in a nonconformist church, saying things against the dictatorial practices of king and church. He lived in Bedford prison for seven years. All the while his wife Elizabeth supported him strongly while raising their four children alone. Elizabeth pleaded with the judges to release her husband. They agreed to do so if he would quit his preaching. She answered, "He dares not leave preaching, my lord, so long as he can speak."

When the judges questioned Bunyan, he always had the same answer: "If you free me today, tomorrow I will speak in the streets that all men have a right to worship God as conscience guides them, and that the state has no right to tell them how to worship." Thus, Bunyan's preaching was silenced. His voice, however, is still heard. Prison gave Bunyan opportunity to write. While in prison he produced *Pilgrim's Progress*, one of the most life-changing books ever written.

Bunyan's life illustrates the faith and dedication that Luke 17 describes and demands. It is faith that keeps the faithful going, no matter what the environment or circumstances. It is faith that finds a way to witness to the Lord no matter the circumstances. It is faith that endures to the end despite the most inhumane treatment. Through teaching his disciples, through healing unclean lepers in Samaria, and in answering Pharisees' questions about the kingdom of God, Jesus showed his own faith and demanded similar faith from any who would follow him.

II. COMMENTARY

Dedication to Christian Servanthood

> **MAIN IDEA:** Dedication to Christ expresses these truths about faith: faith never tempts another person to sin; faith forgives one who does sin; faith asks God for miracles; faith always sees oneself as a duty-bound slave; faith expresses gratitude for all God does; and faith endures until Christ's kingdom comes in all its fullness.

Ⓐ Dedication to Christian Servanthood: Faith and Forgiveness (17:1–10)

> **SUPPORTING IDEA:** Dedication to Christ means living as a servant by doing one's duty to God and in faith forgiving, not tempting, a neighbor.

17:1–2. Jesus informed his disciples of the radical nature of following him. It was a path that led to Jerusalem and the cross. Taking this path is not a life of pious isolation. It remains a path through this world interacting with other people. Such interaction begins with a strong understanding about the nature of people. One does not divide people into two camps—(1) the ritually clean, pious, obedient Pharisees and (2) everyone else, those who are sinners. All people are the same. Everyone sins and stands guilty before God (see Rom. 3:23; 6:23). This means all people face temptations and succumb.

Jesus turned to the strong language of grief and mourning to express his woe upon anyone who is an agent of temptation, who causes someone else to sin. The agent of temptation and sin would be better off committing suicide. That would be the result of the ironic and grotesque picture of placing your head through a millstone so that you wore it like a necklace. The stone would make you sink into the ocean, no matter how well you could swim. The emphasis in Luke's writings on caring for the underprivileged, the crippled, the blind, the widow, and the poor continues in this passage. It is these "little ones" in life on whom we have influence and who will follow our lead in sinning. The "big ones" or "great ones," by contrast, would be Pharisees and scribes who would not follow our leadership anyway and would not recognize themselves as sinners.

17:3–4. Be careful. Watch out, Jesus declared. Exercise your responsibility to these "little ones" in society. Protect them. This involves more than refraining from tempting them to sin. It also means confronting them when they do sin in an attempt to bring them to repentance and God's forgiveness (cf. 1 John 5:16). If the little brother does repent, then you have an added responsibility. You must forgive just as God forgives, for this is the essence of your prayer life (11:4). Do not keep score. You may have to forgive beyond your tolerance level. Just think how much God has to forgive you for. Even if the brother sins against you a ridiculous number of times in one day, forgive him. Keep on forgiving. Do not stop to test the genuineness of the other person's request. Just forgive. Thus, you help the other person to grow and do not tempt him to sin.

17:5. The disciples caught a glimpse of the price Christ was asking them to pay. No one is that patient with another person. Normal human aptitudes and abilities cannot fulfill such a command. Total faith in God and total dedication to God's way of life are required. Thus, the disciples asked for an added supply of faith to live in such an abnormal way—abnormal at least from a human perspective. They did not think they could supply such faith themselves. They knew Jesus was the source of all faith.

17:6. Jesus did not grant their request. Rather, he told them to exercise the faith they had. The smallest imaginable amount of faith, just as much as a tiny seed that you can barely see, is enough to accomplish unimaginable miracles. Who could think of speaking to an old, gnarled tree and making it jump out of the ground? Add to that asking it to jump into the sea and start growing there. No one would attempt such a feat. Yet, the smallest amount of faith can accomplish such a miracle.

What does this mean? Should God's people talk to trees and play miraculous tricks with them? Of course not! This is a call to seasoned disciples—people who have matured in Christ—to realize the potential of their relationship with Jesus. It is a call to dependent, expectant faith. The key term is *faith*. We must know who God is and trust him to do the kind of things he does in the way he does them. We must live within his will and ask for his will to be done. Then we can see marvelous things happen among his people in his world.

We do not need more faith. We need to see the faith that is already in us and exercise it. We need to understand the very nature of faith itself. It is not something we place in a deposit account until it grows sufficiently to do what we want done. Faith is an acknowledgment that no matter how long we wait, we will never be able to do anything on our own, but the moment we call on God, he can do anything.

17:7–9. Picture yourself as a landowner who employs slaves, Jesus told them. You send one of your slaves into the field to plow or into the hillside to tend the sheep. What would you do when the slave returned from doing his work for the day? Would you rush to him and invite him to sit down and eat a wonderful meal you had provided? Of course not! You would sit at the table and wait for the slave to go to the kitchen, prepare your meal, and bring your food. Only when this part of his daily work was done could the slave expect to eat something himself. Or would you rush out to the slave coming from the field and say, "Oh, thank you for working in the field today. That is so wonderful of you." You would never even think about acting in such a manner.

17:10. Finally, Jesus drove the point home to his disciples. You have gone out on mission for me, he told them. You have preached and healed and exorcised. You follow me each day, surrendering normal home life. You have done much, but remember that what you have done is simply what God expects you to do. Do not expect to get some great prize for what you do in faith. Realize God is actually the one at work, doing what you prayed for. So having done all you know to do, simply sit down and say to God, We are worthless slaves. All we have done is the task assigned us to do. Faith is accepting the role of an obedient servant without expecting great gratitude and reward. Faith trusts Jesus and so follows Jesus.

In summary, verses 1–10 depict the life of mature faith in Jesus. It is a life of forgiveness, faith, and humility. Forgiveness is unlimited. Nothing should prevent a disciple from forgiving. The true disciple realizes how difficult this is for humans, so the request is made for more faith.

Jesus rejected such a request. Increased faith is not the answer. Faith is not something measured and compared to see who wins the faith championship. Faith is either true or false. The smallest amount of faith can do the impossible. Forgiving is not the impossible; it is the normal act of faith. Jesus' followers, trusting him in faith and seeking to do the Father's will, naturally forgive people without keeping score.

How can we have such faith and offer such forgiveness? We must live in humility, knowing our place in the stream of life. God is master and we are slaves. We should not look upon a life of ongoing forgiveness as a great accomplishment. We should see it as the normal act of the life of faith. Forgiveness is what Jesus expects of us. As his slaves, we do what he expects. If we refuse to forgive or think we cannot forgive, we have the wrong opinion of ourselves. We think we are something greater and better than a servant. Do not ask for increased faith, Jesus said. Ask for the true faith that makes you a slave of Jesus who normally practices forgiveness as a faithful way of life.

B Dedication Across Boundaries: Overcoming Contagion and Prejudice (17:11–19)

SUPPORTING IDEA: *Dedication overcomes religious and racial prejudice to accomplish God's work and spread God's message.*

17:11. Jesus maintained his course: "on to Jerusalem" (see 9:51; 13:22; 18:31; 19:28). This course did not detour around Samaria, the land populated by people whom Jews considered half-breeds who were unworthy of

God's blessings or their friendship. Entering Samaria and encountering Samaritans made Jesus unclean under the Jewish law.

17:12–13. As if he were not unclean enough, Jesus met ten men who suffered from a terrible skin disease (see 5:12). The men knew their condition. Any contact with them made other people unclean (see Lev. 13:42–46). Still, they knew Jesus' reputation for healing, so they shouted from a distance. Calling Jesus "Master" (5:5; 8:24,45; 9:33,49), they begged for mercy. Mercy, in their case, would mean empathy and pity that would lead to an act of healing.

17:14. Jesus pronounced no great healing formula. He did nothing dramatic. He uttered a simple command: Go let the priests see you. Such a command demanded action from the sick men. To run to the priests meant to show them that they were no longer infected and so could return to normal human contacts. But they had to start to the priests before they were healed. All ten exercised faith in what Jesus said. They started for the priests. When they did, healing came.

17:15–16. Healing sent nine of the lepers scurrying to the priests at a rapid clip. But one of the men reversed direction; he returned to thank Jesus. He did not seek a private session to say thank you. He screamed praise and thanksgiving to God so everyone could hear. He knew what Jesus did had come directly from God. The man fell at Christ's feet to say thank you. Not only was this person an unclean leper, but he was also an unclean Samaritan. Why would Jesus deal with a person doubly unclean? Is this the nature of God, to bring healing and salvation to sinners, unclean people, rather than to the religious self-righteous?

17:17–19. Jesus responded to thanksgiving and praise with a surprising question: Where are the other nine who were healed? Did only **this foreigner** return to show what God had done and let God get the glory for it? Note that on Jesus' lips "foreigner" was not a word of scorn and contempt. It was a declaration of fact to bring to the attention of the town and especially of the disciples the identity of this man. By identifying the foreigner, he showed the "superiority" of the foreign man of faith to the Jewish men who lacked faith.

C Dedication to the Master's Return: The Eschatological Surprise (17:20–37)

> **SUPPORTING IDEA:** *Faith holds out through the normal ups and downs of life, waiting for the moment of surprise when Christ returns to earth.*

17:20–21. The focus shifts again from disciples to Pharisees. They had another question for Jesus: When will the kingdom of God come? The Pharisees had logic and reason behind their question. They knew all the apocalyptic expectations raised by the Jews as Roman oppression grew and the era of prophecy faded further into the dark pages of yesteryear. Would Jesus openly admit he was the Messiah, bringing the kingdom, and thus make himself an enemy of Rome? Would he affirm the signs and wonders of contemporary apocalyptic writings and teachings? Or would his teachings be so radically new that the people would quit listening to him?

As usual, Jesus confounded them. They wanted to know signs of the times. They wanted to be able to be the first to predict and be prepared for the inbreak of God's kingdom on earth to reestablish David's rule. You will not see anything different, Jesus told them. The kingdom stands among you right now. People do not have to go out searching for it and come back reporting that they have found it here or there. The kingdom of God is present wherever Jesus is present. It is present in a different manner than they expected. Signs such as the healing of the lepers should show them the presence of the kingdom.

17:22–24. Jesus needed to make sure his disciples understood what he was teaching. He prepared them for the long wait. One day they would want to see the kingdom. They would want the Son of Man, Jesus himself, to return to earth. They would be in such desperate straits they would think their only hope lay in the immediate return of Christ. In such desperate straits, Jesus' word was "wait a little longer."

In such times even the disciples would be tempted to follow false prophets, who would point to different events in history as signs that the kingdom of God was coming to earth. Jesus' warning was simple: ignore them. We will not have to guess where Jesus is when he returns. His return will be as evident as lightning during the night that flashes across the sky, clearly visible to everyone.

17:25. One sign the disciples could count on: Before the kingdom came with the return of the Son of Man, the Son of Man must leave. He would suffer many things and be rejected and betrayed. The disciples must give Jesus up before they could receive him back.

17:26–30. The nearest a person can come to describing the cataclysm the returning Christ will bring is to look all the way back to primeval history when Noah's generation endured the flood (Gen. 6–9). As Noah prepared the ark for the flood, the people continued in their normal daily routine. They ate, drank, and married. One day Noah boarded the ark. The rains came. Everyone except Noah and his family perished without warning.

Similarly, when the Son of Man returns to earth, no one will suspect anything until it is too late. Weddings will be interrupted. Farm routines will give way to God's judgment. The same thing went on in Lot's day. People carried out the normal routines of life. Then one day Lot quietly left the cities, and God rained fire down on Sodom and Gomorrah. The cities vanished from history (Gen. 19).

17:31–32. That will be no normal day, Jesus told them. Do not think you can see the disaster coming and go back to retrieve something before it strikes. Whether you are on the flat roof of your house enjoying the afternoon sun or out in the field working, the coming will be so quick that you will not have an opportunity to go back for something you forgot. Possessions mean nothing in the face of the kingdom. Only faith in Jesus determines your fate. Remember how Lot's wife looked back at the destruction of Sodom. She suddenly became a block of salt. Without faith in Jesus when he comes, you will be destroyed.

17:33. Let's get to the bottom of all this, Jesus continued. You cannot protect yourself in those days. If you try to save yourself from the coming judgment at that time, you will be destroyed like the people of Sodom. When the time comes, you must be willing to give up, to surrender your life, to die.

17:34–36. Past biblical examples show that in times of God's great saving action, many people are left behind, and a few are saved. So when Jesus returns, some will be left on earth and others will be taken by Jesus. Verse 36 is not found in the best Greek manuscripts and is not translated in most modern translations. It simply picks up the agricultural metaphors of the context and makes sure men as well as women are included.

17:37. The disciples had as much trouble learning about the return of Jesus as the Pharisees did. The Pharisees wanted to know when this would happen. It is already here and you do not see it, Jesus told them. The disciples wanted to know where this would happen. You do not go out searching here or there for a place, Jesus replied, for it will be everywhere like lightning across the night sky.

The section concludes with a proverbial saying based on Job 39:26–30. It was especially appropriate, since the bird Jesus mentioned seems to be the same as the eagle that appeared on the military banners of the Roman legions. You do not have to know where just as you do not have to know when, Jesus told them. It will be in plain sight and will be as natural and inevitable as eagles sensing the presence of a dead animal and gathering overhead to eat. Just as you see the eagles from afar and know what they are up to, so you will see the coming of the Son of Man and know what is happening. It is going to happen.

Are you ready? Do you have faith in Jesus, even the faith of the smallest seed imaginable?

MAIN IDEA REVIEW: *Dedication to Christ expresses these truths about faith: Faith never tempts another to sin; faith forgives one who does sin; faith asks God for miracles; faith always sees oneself as a duty-bound slave; faith expresses gratitude for all God does; and faith endures until Christ's kingdom comes in all its fullness.*

III. CONCLUSION

Forgiveness Unlimited

Jesus moved from the story of Lazarus and the rich man back to intimate conversation with his disciples. He saw the Pharisees constantly trying to tempt him and force him into self-destructive action. So he told the disciples that what was really destructive was causing someone to sin. The proud Pharisees were spotlessly clean but hopelessly mired in sin. They cared for their own reputation at the expense of making the "little ones" out to be dreadful sinners.

Jesus had another method: If a person sins, show him his sin and encourage him to repent. When he repents, forgive. And never put a limit on the process. Keep on forgiving. Such a forgiving attitude and spirit seems humanly impossible. It demands great faith. Not so, said Jesus. Any amount of faith at all can move huge trees and plant them in the Mediterranean Sea. To be forgiving, you must be obedient like a duty-bound, faithful slave. Trust God, and do what he says. When God does something, be grateful, unlike these nine lepers who were healed and left for the priest without saying thank you. Imitate this foreigner, this Samaritan. You see him as the least of the little ones, yet he has a grateful heart.

The Pharisees could not keep out of Jesus' life. They kept seeking ways to tempt him. They wanted his take on the kingdom of God. He claimed they did not have to look any further. Where Jesus is present, the kingdom is present. One day the kingdom will come in fullness, but only after the Son of Man has suffered following his betrayal and rejection. Then he will return when you least expect it. There will be no grand signs, no secret places. If you are alive, you will know it, just as you would know if you were in the midst of a violent thunderstorm. God brings judgment in the midst of daily life with no spectacular preliminaries. Just look at Noah and the flood or Lot and Sodom and Gomorrah. Their daily routine was interrupted by total destruction. So will be the return of the Son of Man to establish the eternal kingdom. When it comes, be ready. Have faith in God, not in possessions. Do not try to go back and protect something or retrieve something. Too late. You will not need anything material.

The disciples had the same kind of question as the Pharisees: Where? Jesus replied with the same type of answer: You will know—just like vultures or eagles find a dead corpse. You cannot miss it. Just be ready. Have faith to the finish.

PRINCIPLES

- All people sin, but we should never cause another person to sin.
- Forgive people who sin as many times as they ask, with no hesitation or limitation.
- Faith is not something that comes in increasing increments that allow you to do greater and greater things.
- Any faith at all can be used to accomplish God's works.
- A believer is a dutiful servant of God who does not expect commendation for anything he does.
- A person of faith expresses gratitude for everything God gives him.
- The kingdom is present on earth where Christ is present.
- The kingdom will come in its fullness when the Son of Man returns unannounced and unexpected.

APPLICATIONS

- Care for earth's most helpless people and avoid tempting them to sin at all cost.
- Never go out of the forgiveness business.
- Exercise the faith you have to do God's work.
- Identify yourself as a duty-bound slave of God who has no reason to expect reward or glory.
- Be aware of what God is doing in your life and thank him for it.
- Be faithful in serving God so that when Christ returns you will be taken with him.

IV. LIFE APPLICATION

Saving Old Miss Sadie

C. Roy Angel (*Shields of Brass*, 63–64) tells of a citywide revival meeting in a small country town. The Spirit of God moved throughout the town. It even reached Old Miss Sadie's house at the very edge of the city limits. Everyone knew Old Miss Sadie, but no one claimed to have visited her or spoken to her. Her evil ways were legendary. The worst insult you could give someone was that they were as ugly as or as bad as Old Miss Sadie.

The Spirit moved two compassionate ladies to visit Sadie and invite her to the revival. Sadie laughed, "You wouldn't have me in your church if I did come and if God did save me." On their third visit, Old Miss Sadie finally agreed to come. But she insisted on sitting in the dark beyond the lights of the revival tent. For five nights she sat there, the two ladies sitting with her. The sixth night Sadie advanced to the back row of seats. During the sermon,

God spoke to Old Miss Sadie, and she cried out, "Praise the Lord." At invitation time she came forward. Everyone rejoiced, then reacted in fear. What if Miss Sadie chose to join our church Sunday morning? Maybe she will become a Methodist.

But Sunday morning Miss Sadie came to church. Whispers floated through the pews. What will we do if she comes forward? Sure enough, she came forward to join the church. The congregation stood aghast. This woman's reputation would ruin the whole church. Then out of the choir stepped a lovely teenage girl—everything in purity, beauty, sweetness, and innocence that Old Miss Sadie was not. She walked past Dr. Angel in the pulpit, down to the center aisle. She met Miss Sadie at the fourth row, took her haggard but shining face in her lovely hands, and kissed the wrinkled, leathery forehead. Taking Miss Sadie's arm, the young girl escorted her to the front row where she filled out the forms to become a church member. Weeping replaced the resentment on the face of each member of the congregation.

This church learned Jesus' lesson of faith, forgiveness, and kingdom presence from a sinful, despised woman and a pure, innocent teenager. A pharisaical attitude gave way to a Christlike spirit of forgiveness and acceptance. One more of the world's little people came to the head of the line in the kingdom. So Jesus calls all of us to forgive the sin no matter how horrible the sinner. He teaches us to be grateful for what God is doing, even when God chooses to do something for the people we respect the least and hate the most. He calls us to exercise our faith in responding to people and give him thanks for what he does even when his action is the last thing on earth we expected. In all of this, we are not to look for his congratulations or reward. Forgiving and accepting the Old Miss Sadie's of the world into our fellowship is simply doing the expected duty of Christ's servants.

V. PRAYER

God, who forgives us every day, teach us to forgive. Forgive me where I have been the reason another person has sinned against you. Show me how to exercise my faith in joining you in kingdom work. Accept my thanks for all you do for me. I give special thanks that you have saved me and forgiven me all my sins. Thank you that I am a part of your kingdom. Help me be ready when you come again. Amen.

VI. DEEPER DISCOVERIES

A. Things That Cause People to Sin (17:1)

Jesus lived in the real world, and he taught his disciples to do the same. They will face stumbling blocks, which could lead them to sin. The literal reading in the Greek of verse 1 is, "It is impossible for *skandala* not to come, nevertheless woe to him through whom it comes."

Skandala is a plural noun meaning "something that lures, baits, or causes one to stumble." The world is full of baited traps luring you to defect from God's way of life and fall into the world's scheme. The harsh reality is that you may become such a lure to sin; then Christ's judgment lies upon you.

The point of the passage, however, is not to describe the lurid fate of those who bait you to sin. The point is to call you to faithfulness, forgiveness, and humility. Avoid the lures strewn along your path. Accept the difficulty others have in avoiding such lures. Teach them the danger of falling into such traps, but forgive them and accept them back into the community of faith. Realize that you, too, have weaknesses and will sin. Humbly ask God for forgiveness even as you forgive others. Know that such forgiveness and confession of sin is possible only when you live tied securely to Jesus in faith and clearly identified as his slave.

B. "Little Ones" (17:2)

This phrase refers to little children, but also to persons of immature faith. Jesus warned his disciples against doing anything that would lead others astray or cause them to stumble and fall into sin. A Christian leader who causes others to stray can have a disastrous impact on those who look to him or her for a Christlike example. Such a leader could cause the "little ones," or immature believers, to stray from the truth. At all times and in all circumstances, we should strive to live our lives so that we exhibit Christ to those around us. We never know when someone is looking to us as an example of our Lord.

C. Forgiving Others (17:4–5)

As a part of His teaching about forgiveness, Jesus spoke of the human dimension of forgiveness. A firm condition for the receiving of God's forgiveness is the willingness to forgive other people. In the Lord's Prayer (Matt. 6:12; Luke 11:4) and the parable of the unforgiving servant (Matt. 18:23–35), Jesus indicated that such is the case: "But if you do not forgive men their sins, your Father will not forgive your sins" (Matt. 6:15). The forgiven life is the forgiving life.

Human forgiveness reflects our experience and understanding of divine forgiveness. Love, not rigid rules, governs forgiveness (Matt. 18:21–22). Jesus demonstrated this teaching on the cross, as He asked for forgiveness for His executioners (Luke 23:34).

D. Faith That Moves Mountains (17:5–6)

The disciples asked Jesus to "increase" their faith. The word they used means to add to what is already there. They recognized their need for divine help in this area. Jesus spoke of faith that can uproot a tree and plant it in the sea. Matthew's parallel account refers to moving a mountain from one place to another. These hyperbolic expressions describe what faith can do. But in practice, Jesus was not speaking of a faith that stages a miraculous event. It is a faith that leads to healing (Luke 7:9; 8:48; 18:42; Acts 14:9), that understands the need of Christ to suffer (Luke 24:25–26), that has confidence in God's providential care (8:25), that will not fall away (8:13; 22:32), but will endure (Acts 14:22) and believe God and grow (Acts 6:5; Luke 1:45 with 1:20).

E. Samaritan (17:16)

Jews saw Samaritans as the enemy (see John 4:9). These people came from the area near the city of Samaria, which King Omri built as the capital of the Northern Kingdom shortly after 900 B.C. The Assyrians destroyed the city in 721 B.C. The territory of Samaria lay between the Aijalon and Jezreel valleys and between the Mediterranean Sea and the Jordan Valley. After the destruction of the Northern Kingdom, these people tried to maintain an identity as Israelites who worshiped the God of Israel on Mount Gerizim near Shechem. They thought of their name "Samaritan" as coming from a Hebrew word which meant "keepers of the law." They believed the great mistake in Israelite history was the move of the central sanctuary from Shechem to Shiloh in the time of Eli or before. They believed that King Darius of Persia sent Sanballat back from Babylon to build a Samaritan temple on Mount Gerizim.

The Samaritans recognized only the five Books of Moses as sacred. Their text established Mount Gerizim as the worship center with unique readings at Exodus 20:18 and Deuteronomy 27:4. They looked for a Messiah like Moses to come and restore their religion and their land.

Jews in the south around Jerusalem had a different view of the Samaritans. They saw them as descendants of foreigners whom the Assyrians brought in to replace the exiled Israelites in 721 B.C. Jerusalem saw Samaritan religion as only an attempt to learn how to worship the historical god of the region to avoid destruction (see 2 Kgs. 17:25–26).

Samaritans opposed Jews as they tried to rebuild the temple and walls of Jerusalem after the Babylonian Exile (Ezra 4:4–24). Papyri found in the Jewish settlement near the town of Elephantine in Egypt show letters from Samaritan priests as well as Jerusalem priests asking for help in building a temple shortly after 500 B.C. The Samaritans may have built a worship place some time after 400 B.C. This was destroyed in 128 B.C.

Samaritans again stirred Jewish ire by supporting Alexander the Great with troops when he invaded Egypt. During the Egyptian campaign, however, the Samaritans revolted, killed their governor, and then faced Alexander's retaliation. Alexander destroyed the rebuilt city of Samaria, sending the surviving Samaritans fleeing to Shechem. They rebuilt the city in 331, but the Jewish king John Hyrcanus destroyed it in 107 B.C.

Immediately before Jesus came during the early Roman period, Pompey forced the Jews to quit persecuting the Samaritans as John Hyrcanus had, and then Herod initiated a huge building program in Samaria. Still, Samaritans did all they could to harass the Jews. They even forced Pontius Pilate from office.

On their first mission venture, Jesus' disciples were protected by not having to go to the Samaritans (Matt. 10:5–6; John 4). But Jesus also made Samaritans heroes of his stories to show the Jews the need for forgiveness, humility, acceptance, and mission (Luke 10:29–37; 17:11–10). He himself attempted to minister in Samaria, but the Samaritans did not accept him (Luke 9:52). He did bring a Samaritan woman and her townspeople to belief in him (John 4). Jewish leaders tried to shame Jesus by accusing him of being a Samaritan (John 8:48).

About A.D. 70 Emperor Vespacian besieged Mount Gerizim for a month and then slaughtered ten thousand Samaritans. Finally, Emperor Hadrian some time before A.D. 138 constructed a temple for Zeus Hypsisto on Mount Gerizim.

Over the centuries Samaritan fortunes have varied. During the fifth century Palestine was home to almost a half million Samaritans. By the sixteenth century the Samaritan community was reduced to a dwindling number around ancient Shechem (or modern Nablus).

F. The Kingdom of God (17:20–37)

The kingdom of God was the central image of Jesus' teaching, as clearly seen in Mark 1:14–15, a summary of Jesus' preaching ministry. To the Pharisees, the time for the coming of the kingdom was of great interest. When would God establish his kingdom? However, their understanding of the nature of the kingdom caused them to miss its present reality.

Jesus taught that the kingdom was within. In this sense, the kingdom had already come. The term *kingdom*, used by Jesus, means reign, not realm. It is the reign of God as king. The official establishment of God's kingdom on earth is yet to come. The rule of God over human lives through the ministry of Jesus will be consummated, or made complete, at an unspecified time in the future.

VII. TEACHING OUTLINE

A. INTRODUCTION

1. Lead Story: Dedication Is Faith to the Finish

2. Context: In Luke 17 Jesus turned from fighting the Pharisees to teaching the disciples. The lesson was how not to be a Pharisee but to maintain dedication to the finish. Unlike Pharisees, Jesus' followers do not want others to sin. They do everything possible not to lead other people to sin. When others sin, a disciple points out the sin, but also points the way to repentance and forgiveness. The disciple leads the person to accept God's forgiveness. Followers of Jesus also practice forgiveness without limits and without hesitation. The disciple depends not on his own aptitudes and strength but on God in faith. A Christian realizes his only identity is as a slave of Christ, duty-bound to do whatever God commands without complaint and without expectation of praise or reward.

   Rather than questioning everything as the Pharisees did, the disciple of Jesus sees God at work in everything and expresses gratitude to God just as did the foreigner, the Samaritan healed of leprosy. Disciples can do this for one reason. They know in Jesus the kingdom of God is present, and they are part of it because they live and abide in him. Daily life is kingdom living, awaiting the day of ultimate surprise when Christ interrupts our daily routine to take us to be with him.

3. Transition: Luke 17 demands your close attention. It grabs you where you live every day. How do you segment society? Do you have strong people you want to impress over against little people whom you do not care for? In Luke 17 Jesus calls you to change your attitude. He offers you a new self-identity. He wants you to be sure you are a servant carrying out your duties faithfully as you live in the kingdom and wait for the kingdom.

B. COMMENTARY

1. Dedication to Christian Servanthood: Faith and Forgiveness (17:1–10)
   a. The setting: teaching the disciples (17:1a)
   b. The Master's teaching: forgive and help, not hinder, others (17:1b-4)
   c. The followers' reaction: increase our faith (17:5)
   d. The Master's response: faith and servanthood (17:6–10)

2. Dedication Across Boundaries: Overcoming Contagion and Prejudice (17:11–19)
   a. The setting: in Samaria headed for Jerusalem (17:11)
   b. The scene: ten lepers seek mercy (17:12–13)
   c. The Master's response: go as healed to the priest (17:14)
   d. The Samaritan leper's response: praise and thanks (17:15–16)
   e. The Master's counter response: the nine and faith (17:17–19)
3. Dedication to the Master's Return: The Eschatological Surprise (17:20–37)
   a. The setting: opponents ask date of the kingdom (17:20a)
   b. The Master's response: kingdom is among you now (17:20b-21)
   c. The Master's teaching for disciples: be ready for the surprise coming (17:22–36)
   d. The followers' reaction: where? (17:37a)
   e. The Master's response: where you should expect it (17:37b)

C. CONCLUSION: SAVING OLD MISS SADIE

VIII. ISSUES FOR DISCUSSION

1. How do you cause other people to sin? Why?
2. How do you respond when another person asks you to forgive him or her? Do you need to do more?
3. In what ways do you exercise faith in Jesus each day?
4. What is the basic way you understand your identity?
5. What has God done that deserves your gratitude?
6. How can the kingdom be already among you and still not yet here until the Son of Man returns?

Luke 18

Dedication to Persistent, Childlike Faith

Quote

"*Prayer is for every moment of our lives, not just for times of suffering or joy. Prayer is really a place; a place where you meet God in genuine conversation. . . . Instead of beginning with prayer, we sometimes resort to it after all other resources have been used. When we come to the end of ourselves, we come to the beginning of God. We don't need to be embarrassed that we are needy. . . . Every feeble, stumbling prayer uttered by a believer is heard by God.*"

Billy Graham

Luke 18

IN A NUTSHELL

Prayer is the permanent occupation of a believer, done in persistence but done knowing that we who pray are undeserving sinners dependent on God's grace. We are trusting, helpless children looking to our Father for help beyond our abilities. We do not trust in anything we have or own but in God alone, knowing he will give us what we need here and hereafter. God asks what we want him to do for us. We fall down calling for mercy. God answers and we respond in gratitude and praise.

Dedication to Persistent, Childlike Faith

I. INTRODUCTION

Children's Prayers

*C*harlie Shedd tells of a church where Sunday evening vespers was a service for the young only. Adults above college age were invited to come and be silent. Five-year-old Ronnie attended consistently and persistently. Then one Sunday Ronnie was absent. The company that employed most of the workers in the town had used its plane to rush Ronnie to the big city hospital. Doctors there were just as puzzled as the local doctors. No one knew what ailed Ronnie. They just knew he was critically ill. Nothing seemed to help. Doctors had no more prescriptions for Ronnie.

That Sunday vespers took on a new meaning for the children and young people. They prayed fervently for the big smile to return to Ronnie's face and for their friend to return to vespers with them. This was not just polite ritual done to start or close a service. This was a long time of children, young people, and "non-participant" adults praying in silence and then praying together for Ronnie. Shortly after the vespers service, the call came. Ronnie's mother jubilantly shared the news: "Late this afternoon Ronnie sat up and said he was hungry." Doctors examined all his vital signs. They were stunned. All was normal. Maybe one of their strong antibiotics had finally worked, although they had given up on them. Ronnie's mother had a better answer: "Doctor, this afternoon all his friends and the children and young people of the church were praying together for Ronnie."

The doctor turned thoughtful for the moment. "Guess the prayers got through, too, didn't they?" he said. "Would you tell the children thanks for me? What time was all this praying?"

"It was five-thirty this afternoon," Ronnie's mother answered. "My husband and I were thinking about vespers and everyone praying there, so we began praying with them, even though we were here in the hospital."

"That is when Ronnie got well and sat up, isn't it?" the doctor said.

Luke 18 continues Jesus' teaching on kingdom living as he journeys slowly toward Jerusalem. His teaching was on the vitality of persistent prayer in the life of the believer. In talking with his disciples and with the Pharisees, as well as in healing a blind man, Jesus showed the nature and power of childlike faith in asking God for the needs of life.

II. COMMENTARY

Dedication to Persistent, Childlike Faith

> **MAIN IDEA:** *Prayer, an essential component of life with God, involves asking God persistently for what you need, believing he will provide. Faith places no stock in personal goodness or personal wealth. Faith prays persistently even as it takes up the cross and walks toward crucifixion. Faith knows it can ask for God's mercy and receive God's rewards for a persistently faithful life.*

A Dedication in Prayer: Trust to the Last (18:1–8)

> **SUPPORTING IDEA:** *Dedicated kingdom living includes persistent prayer that trusts God to supply our needs.*

18:1. In spite of interruptions from the crowds and his opponents, Jesus consistently turned back to his disciples to teach them new truths about the kingdom. This time he augmented his teaching on prayer (see 3:21; 5:16; 6:12,28; 9:18,28–29; 11:1–13; 20:47; 22:40–46). Prayer is not one quick session of listing needs and expecting immediate results. Prayer is continuing to talk to God with persistence. Prayer is based on absolute faith in God, so it never gives up, knowing God will answer when and where he chooses. Prayer also knows that God expects us to keep on praying until the answer comes.

18:2–5. Another parable illustrates Jesus' teaching on persistent prayer. An emotionally passive judge settled cases in one town. He did so without passion, not caring for either party. He did so on the basis of his own wisdom and power, never looking to God for help, since he did not fear or believe in God. In an Israelite community where the judge was to be impartial and judgment ultimately belonged to God (Deut. 1:16–17), this judge was unfit for his job.

The judge met his match when a local widow pled for justice in a dispute with a neighbor. The nature of her grievance is of no concern for the story. The point is that she was a widow who never gave up. As a widow she should have received special protection and care from the justice system (Exod. 22:22; Deut. 10:18; 24:17–21; 27:19; cf. Jas. 1:27). No matter how long the judge ignored her or denied her plea, she returned to his court asking for justice. The judge finally threw up his hands in disgust and frustration. Religious grounds did not cause him to act. He had no religion. Social justice grounds did not cause him to act. He cared nothing for people. He simply had a job as a judge and he did it. He did have limits to his patience. So he finally gave in to the woman just to get rid of her.

18:6–8a. Jesus applied the story for his disciples. If an uncaring human judge acts like this, how much more does a loving heavenly Father care for his children. He will never put you off. He does care for you. You will get a quick answer. You will receive justice. But remember, this involves continuing to pray day and night. Your definition of quick may not equal God's definition.

18:8b. The problem is not with God. He will answer when you need it. You can count on that. The problem is with us. When Christ returns, will there be anyone here who calls out in faith day and night? Will we become so lackadaisical in our faith that we allow people of persistent prayer to become extinct? Will the second coming of Jesus find us persisting in prayer that his kingdom will come? Or will it find us trapped on the housetop trying desperately to get back into the house to find the possessions that we rely on more than we do on God? Persistent prayer, the work of the person of faith, continues on, no matter what the answer. When Christ returns, the person of persistent prayer will still be praying. Will you?

Ⓑ Dedication to Humility: The Justified Sinner (18:9–14)

SUPPORTING IDEA: *Dedicated kingdom living involves prayer that confesses one's sin and seeks God's forgiveness, not prayer that extols self and excludes others.*

18:9. The character of the two people in this parable is more important than their identity. Jesus described the Pharisees and scribes without naming them. They were religious. They kept the law. They told everyone else the requirements for being religious. They saw themselves as the perfect example of God's righteousness. They saw everyone else as ignorant sinners to be scorned and sneered at.

18:10. Two personalities take center stage in this parable. The first is a Pharisee. Hearing the word *Pharisee*, the crowd would have had two reactions. This was a religious man who kept all the rules. This was also a man who opposed Jesus and constantly heard Jesus' condemnation and ridicule. The second character was a tax collector. Hearing this word, the audience would have felt disgust and betrayal. Here was a person working for the foreign government that dominated them. *This one takes our money and gives it to Rome,* they probably thought. *This one is probably a cheat and a thief, taking far more money than Rome authorizes him to take.* One might wonder what a tax collector was doing in the temple. How could such a person become ritually clean enough to be allowed inside the temple?

18:11–12. The Pharisee prayed. That would be expected. Pharisees legalistically followed every rule. Prayer was expected several times a day. His prayer was unexpected: He prayed about himself. He did not praise God. He thanked God for making him better than other people—especially better than the tax collector. The tax collector was grouped with robbers, unrighteous people, greedy individuals, and adulterers. The Pharisee confidently asserted his superiority before God over all these people. He described all his religious acts. He praised himself in the face of God. This was not persistent prayer, depending on God for one's needs. This was self-adulation, giving all the credit to self and none to God.

18:13. An entirely different kind of prayer came from the tax collector's lips. It was a prayer of humility, dependence, and desperation. The Pharisee prayed to God; the tax collector looked to the floor but raised his voice to heaven. The Pharisee was proud and confident; the tax collector grieved over his own condition as a sinner. The Pharisee described his righteousness; the tax collector begged for mercy to escape the judgment his sin deserved. Which one of them truly prayed?

18:14. Jesus had no doubts. The sinful tax collector was justified before God. He was righteous. He was clean. He was prepared for temple worship. His sins were forgiven. The Pharisee left the temple confident he had fulfilled his religious duty but still bearing his own guilt and sins. He had not prayed, because he never addressed God. He was not forgiven, since he never confessed his sins. He was not clean and qualified for worship, because he remained separated from God by his unconfessed sin. Jesus put it succinctly: praise yourself, God will humble you; humble yourself, and God will praise and honor you.

Ⓒ Dedication to Childlike Faith: Possessing the Kingdom (18:15–17)

SUPPORTING IDEA: *Dedicated kingdom living begins with childlike faith and continues with open invitations to all children.*

18:15. In a time and environment plagued by infant illness and death, parents brought infants and children for Jesus to heal. The disciples made themselves the clearinghouse to Jesus. Too many adults needed his attention. There were already more than enough children. So the disciples sent the parents away to give Jesus time to do more important things.

18:16. Jesus put a stop to their action. He held out his arms to the children. Bring the children here, he declared. The kingdom belongs to such as these. Did you not hear me say not to cause a little one to sin (17:1–2)? Here are some of the little ones. This marks off God's ways from men's ways. God deals always with the little ones, the unknown ones, the powerless ones. The world seeks people of power, influence, and wealth. God seeks the children. God builds his kingdom on childlike characteristics: trust, love, innocence, lack of power, lack of pretension, lack of credentials. God wants children whom he can make into disciples, not power brokers whom he has to steer away from political and military expectations.

18:17. Jesus went one shocking step further. You must be like a little child to enter the kingdom, he said. Childlikeness is not just one possible way among others to be part of Christ's kingdom. Being like a child is the only way to kingdom living. If you cannot do away with your pretensions, your greed, your claims to fame, your need to dominate and control, your grasp for identity and power, you cannot be part of Christ's kingdom. Christ constantly seeks those who have no hope of power and position: the poor, Samaritans, women, children, blind, crippled, lame, tax collectors. These lack the vanity and self-assurance that keep a person from entering the kingdom.

D Dedication to Kingdom Living over Wealthy Living: A Worthy Reward (18:18–30)

SUPPORTING IDEA: *Kingdom living gives up the luxury of wealth for the rewards of Christ.*

18:18. A Jewish civil administrator interrupted Jesus with a question. The question centers on the divisive point between the two leading groups of Jews, the Pharisees and Sadducees. Sadducees, using only the first five books of the Old Testament, found in these books no reference to resurrection, so they denied that resurrection of the dead was possible. Pharisees, following all three parts of the Jewish canon—Law, Prophets, and Writings—saw definite proof of resurrection in Daniel 12:2 and many other references, particularly in the Psalms and Isaiah. Was this administrator trying to get Jesus to take sides, or was he searching for certain hope in his own life? Luke does not give us his motivation, just the question.

This man called Jesus "good teacher." This represents a common politeness of speech and recognition to some degree of Jesus' role as an intelligent, caring teacher.

18:19. Jesus caught the man's attention by challenging his description of Jesus as good. Only one person can be truly good. That is God. Thus, unknowingly, the administrator had linked Jesus to God. Jesus caught the link and brought it out into the open. He repeated traditional Jewish theology in confessing that God alone is good. In so doing, Jesus did not affirm or deny his own claim to deity. Luke expected his readers, however, to see the link that Jesus made and to affirm the obvious—that Jesus, being good, was also God.

18:20. Jesus turned to the source of authority that all Jews accepted—the Law, the Torah of Moses. He quoted part of the Ten Commandments from Exodus 20 and Deuteronomy 5.

18:21. The man with the question also had a personal testimony. He had rigorously obeyed all the commandments since youth. We must not quibble with his answer at this point and try to point out that all have sinned. That is not under discussion here. Here the issue is obedience and eternal life. This Jew apparently thought on the criteria of his religion that he deserved eternal life, but internally he felt something missing. What was the *more* beyond moral living?

18:22. Jesus had the answer. He returned to the theme that he had addressed so often—wealth and dedication. Do you trust possessions more than you trust God? he asked the man. Are you trying to put your trust in both possessions and God at the same time? Can you live without your possessions but cannot live without your God? Sell your possessions and find out (see 6:45; 12:13–21,33; 16:13). I have told you all along that your relationship to the poor and needy is of paramount importance from a kingdom perspective. Take the money you get from your sale, and give it to the poor. Then follow me with the rest of my penniless disciples and see what kingdom living is all about.

18:23. These words cut to the quick. Jesus had found the man's weak spot. He had great riches and evidently trusted in them to make life meaningful and hopeful. Grief and mourning set in. There was no way he could give up his money, even for God's kingdom.

18:24. Jesus spoke in the form of lamentation, much as a deep sigh would be used at a funeral to express grief at personal loss. The sad truth is that the rich have a hard time giving up their trust in their possessions. They cannot take the long-term look and realize that one day they will lose control over wealth. Then they will be robbed of eternal treasure, too. No wonder Jesus issued his sad lament: How hard for the rich to enter the kingdom. They have never experienced the need to trust someone or some thing outside their own intelligence and wealth.

18:25. Jesus turned to hyperbole to make a point. He described the utterly impossible. The lure of wealth overpowers the lure of the kingdom, not just in this rich Jewish administrator's life, but in the lives of virtually all rich people and many who are not quite so rich. Thus, the first step to the kingdom is not to solve the problem of putting a camel through a needle's eye. The first step is to get rid of the burden of riches so a person has nothing to trust but Jesus.

18:26. The audience was amazed. If the blessed rich cannot be saved, they declared, who can? They saw that Jesus had described an impossible situation.

18:27. God does the impossible was Jesus' quick answer. Don't try to figure out the hows and whys. Just let God do it. Trust him with your life more than you trust your riches. Place your riches in his control. Watch God work the impossible.

18:28. Blunt and to the point, Peter piped up, "We left all and followed you. Does that qualify us for the kingdom?"

18:29–30. Jesus told Peter not to worry. Those who had given up life's closest relationships, greatest responsibilities, and strongest commitments to follow Jesus had a reward coming. Luke is imprecise in describing the reward, but he puts it in two stages. In this age, the committed, self-denying follower will receive many times as much as he has given up. Is this strictly parallel to the preceding verse, so that the reward is in terms of family? The family of believers will be more important, more numerous, and more meaningful than a follower's family of origin. Or is this much more indefinite so that Jesus was calling for faith even as he promised rewards? God has a reward for you, but you do not need to know exactly what that reward is. You just need to trust God. The second part of the disciples' reward is eternal life, a quality of life beginning here on earth with Jesus as Lord and extending through resurrection to the eternal kingdom.

E Dedication to the Cross: A Call Not Yet Understood (18:31–34)

SUPPORTING IDEA: *Jesus illustrates kingdom living and fulfills God's plan as he walks to Jerusalem to fulfill Scripture. In Jerusalem he will be rejected, betrayed, mocked, insulted, beaten, crucified, and resurrected.*

18:31. Again, Jesus turned attention from the crowds and opponents to the disciples. They must know that he knew what was happening as he approached Jerusalem. He had begun to tell them about this before (9:22,44–45; 12:50; 13:32–34; 17:25). First he gave an affirmation. The entire Old Testament prepared the way for him. Everything written in Scripture about him would take place. This appeared to be a reassuring statement, but it turned out to be just the opposite.

18:32–33. What did Scripture say about Jesus, the Son of Man? Enemy Gentiles would take control of him. They would ridicule and mock him, insult him, spit on him, and beat him. Then they would kill him (see Isa. 50:6; 52:13–53:12; Dan. 7:13; Zeph. 3:11–12; Pss. 2; 94:2–7).

18:34. Repeated passion predictions by Jesus did not penetrate the dense, stubborn predispositions of the disciples. They knew the definition of Messiah, kingdom, and salvation/deliverance. They knew Scripture's teaching on God's restoration of Israel's rule. That death could come before the kingdom reigned in Jerusalem just did not compute in their brains. God was not yet ready for them to grasp all this, so he hid it from them. He was able to hide it because they were in no condition to grasp it. Here we see the connection between the electing, choosing work of God in carrying out his plan in his time and the free operation of the disciples' will as they hung on to old ideas and could not grasp Jesus' radically new teaching. The day would come when the disciples would turn the world upside down with the message of a resurrected Messiah. But at this moment they were confused about God's timing, Scripture's meaning, and their previous understandings.

F Dedication to Merciful Acts: Rewarding Persistent Faith (18:35–43)

SUPPORTING IDEA: *Dedicated kingdom living means crying out consistently to God for mercy.*

18:35–36. Jericho marked the last stage of the journey to Jerusalem for Jesus (see 12:51). One last climb up the mountain—and the fateful trip would end. But Jericho was the first stage of the journey for one man, a blind beggar. He sensed a crowd coming and wanted to know what was happening.

18:37–38. The crowd told him Jesus was coming through the town. Immediately he shouted for mercy. He used the messianic title, Son of David, identifying Jesus' royal roots and implying that this one would be crowned in his ancestor's place. Luke does not indicate how this man knew about Jesus.

18:39. The crowd had greater things in mind for Jesus than to tend to the whining of a blind beggar. But the beggar refused to be silenced. He lifted his voice again and again to Jesus.

18:40–41. Jesus illustrated his teaching that it was important to care for the poor. He turned his attention from the crowd to talk to a blind beggar. He had a question for the beggar. What did he really want Jesus to do? The blind beggar did not hesitate. He wanted to see the world.

18:42–43. Jesus did not hesitate. "Your faith has healed you," he replied (see 7:50; 8:48; 17:18). This disabled, poverty-stricken man refused to give up. He trusted in Jesus whom his eyes could not see. He gave God glory and praise, and this started a chain reaction among the crowd. Educated, religious Pharisees could not come to such faith. Even the disciples had difficulty understanding. A blind beggar joined a sinful woman, a woman who had suffered for twelve years, and a Samaritan leper in exercising healing faith. Of such is the kingdom of God.

MAIN IDEA REVIEW: *Prayer, an essential component of life with God, involves asking God persistently for what you need, believing he will provide. Faith places no stock in personal goodness or personal wealth. Faith prays persistently even as it takes up the cross and walks toward crucifixion. Faith knows it can ask for God's mercy and receive God's rewards for a persistently faithful life.*

III. CONCLUSION

Persistent, Childlike Faith

Jesus related to four different groups of people. He taught the disciples the secrets of the kingdom, hoping they would hear and become bountiful soil. He listened to the crowds, answered their questions, and healed the sick among them. He argued with the Pharisees, trying to show them the true nature of God and his kingdom. He showed mercy and care for society's "underclasses," those with no religious, social, economic, or political power. He made them the center of his statements on the kingdom. He used them as examples of what it meant to be kingdom people. Luke 18 shows Jesus' interaction with all four groups, often in contrast: the poor widow and the powerful judge; the self-righteous Pharisee and the humble tax collector; the helpless children and the disciples; the rich ruler and the blind beggar along with the uncaring crowds.

From these interactions we learn important lessons about persistence in prayer, God's desire to help, the danger of faith disappearing from the earth before the Son of Man returns, the meaning of humble prayer as opposed to proud boasting, the necessity of becoming like a child to enter the kingdom, the relationship of Jesus to the Father who is good, the danger of possessions robbing us of faith, the reward for self-denying discipleship, the inevitability of Christ's betrayal and death in Jerusalem, the hope of the resurrection, the inability of pre-resurrection disciples to understand, and the care of Jesus for the poor and hopeless of society. Luke 18 thus invites us to persist in faith and prayer, maintain a childlike attitude of trust and hope, and give up our trust in possessions and wealth for the true hope in Jesus. Such a life of persistent faith will result in rewards here and hereafter. It will bring us to praise God and give him all the honor and glory. It may guide us to sell our possessions for heavenly rewards.

PRINCIPLES

- A loving God answers persistent prayer.
- Self-righteousness accomplishes nothing.
- Humble prayer is answered and rewarded.
- Childlike trust and faith are required if you want to enter the kingdom.
- To inherit eternal life, you must depend totally upon God.
- Possessions often separate us from God.
- God rewards those who are faithful to him.
- Christ's suffering, death, and resurrection fulfilled Scripture.

- Faith expressed in persistent calling to God brings healing.
- Faith responds to God in glory and praise.

APPLICATIONS

- Never give up on God; keep praying.
- Trust God's love and care for you.
- Be persistent in faith and prayer until Christ returns.
- Confess your sin humbly to God, knowing that no one is righteous before him.
- Obey God's commandments.
- Trust in God, not in riches and possessions.
- Maintain a childlike attitude without pretense or dependence on your own qualifications in your relationship to God.
- Know that God has a reward for your faithful, self-denying trust in him.
- Imitate Jesus in caring for those who cannot care for themselves.
- Ask God for healing physically and spiritually.

IV. LIFE APPLICATION

Persevering Through Grief

For nine months I mourned the loss of my wife Mary. Seventeen chapters of a book never published chronicle my trail down Job's path of complaining, crying, demanding, and accusing. Nine months of silence came from above. I could not understand. Where was God when I needed him?

God was introducing me to a grief group, to a friend named Lewis who had recently lost his wife, and to a woman who caught my eye immediately but who was more interested in completing her grief correctly than she was in paying attention to me.

Finally, God spoke and promised his presence along the lonely path as a single adult in a married adult world. Friends gathered in support one by one. At times I barely acknowledged their presence in my search for the pool of despair. Still they stuck lovingly by me, giving God a smiling face and loving arms I desperately needed.

A year after the loss of her husband, the woman in the grief group agreed to a date. We enjoyed one another. I began to pray about the relationship. God said in a quite clear voice, "I have given her to you. Be patient." I rejoiced in the promise and ignored the admonition. Over two years went by. As Thanksgiving and Christmas approached, I decided it was time for decision. She decided it was time for separation and finding our separate ways in freedom from each other. So I moved away from her to my own condo, built lovely new bookshelves, and decided to marry myself to writing. Still, as I prayed, God said, "She is yours."

I gave up. I went in other directions seeking companionship. Suddenly, she called. She had to see me. Soon we had set a date for marriage. My prayers were answered. Her children balked. The date was postponed, then canceled. Again, I turned to God in despair. What could be going on here? Again, freedom proved not to be what she wanted. She came back, set a marriage date, and God's promise came true. On August 5, 1999, I received a new wife, a gift from God, a gift of persistent prayer even through times of doubt and despair. Friends still laugh about it as the strangest courtship they have ever witnessed. I smile, knowing God had found a way in his timetable and somehow had kept me faithful to him in prayer during the darkest hours.

My experience parallels that of the poor widow, the sinful tax collector, and the blind beggar in Luke 18. All found in different ways on different timetables that God is good and that he answers our faithful prayers, but those prayers must be faithful. We cannot pray a time or two and give up. We must pray and pray until the Son of Man returns to earth. God's rewards come in this life and in the next, but always on his timetable. God moves us away from worldly possessions and worldly sources of comfort and hope. He calls us to himself. In him as we pray and obey, we find kingdom living, the only kind that brings meaning here and eternal life hereafter.

V. PRAYER

God, who cares for me and wants justice and healing for me, I come to you trusting in faith that you will have mercy on me. I confess my sin. I have depended on my own abilities and possessions. I have trusted in my ethical lifestyle. I have seen my place in the church as assurance of my place in your kingdom. Forgive me of my false trusts. Forgive me for self-satisfaction that quits the prayer line for the bragging line. Keep me true to you. Oh, God, I will be true to you and pray persistently to you until our Lord Jesus returns. Amen.

VI. DEEPER DISCOVERIES

A. His Chosen Ones (18:7)

The term *chosen* refers on the one hand to the quality of the thing or person referred to as the finest, highest quality (see Gen. 23:6; 41:2; Exod. 30:23; Judg. 20:34). On the other hand, it refers to those specially selected for relationship, reward, or task (see Isa. 43:20). In the New Testament, Jesus is the chosen servant of God who fulfills his plan of salvation (Luke 23:35;

1 Pet. 1:20; 2:4). Matthew 12:18 shows that Isaiah 42:1 is the scriptural base for calling Jesus God's elect servant.

God chose not only a Messiah/Servant/Savior. He also chose a people to be in a loving covenant relationship with him (Deut. 7:6; cf. 10:15; 14:2; Ps. 105:6; Isa. 41:8). With the Exile and return God reduced the chosen to a remnant within Israel (Isa. 65:8–10; cf. 14:1–2).

The New Testament applies the understanding of God's elect people to those who accept and follow Jesus (1 Pet. 2:9; cf. Exod. 19:5–6). This elect group is quite select, being relatively few in number (Matt. 22:14). God protects his elect, even shortening the end time for their sake (Matt. 24:22; Mark 13:20; cf. Rev. 17:14). In the end time false messiahs and false prophets will attempt to deceive the elect (Matt. 24:24; Mark 13:22). But God will gather his elect from around the world (Matt. 24:31; Mark 13:27).

God has determined the elect, forgiven their sins, and declared them just in his sight, so no one can condemn them (Rom. 8:33). Still, the elect are responsible before God to live according to the lifestyle he chooses for them (Col. 3:12). God's ministers suffer persecution and ridicule to protect and provide role models for the elect (2 Tim. 2:10; cf. Titus 1:1). Thus, individuals can be called elect or chosen in the Lord (Rom. 16:13).

This choice of individuals and the church for salvation as God's people occurred before creation as part of God's eternal plan (2 Thess. 2:13). God's pattern and reasoning in election defies human reason and denies anyone reason to boast for being chosen (1 Cor. 1:26–31).

The chosen are thus free to cry to God for help, for they know the nature of God. He is just and will bring justice to those he has chosen as his own (Luke 18:7).

B. The Son of Man Comes (18:8)

Son of Man is a title Jesus often used to refer to himself. Its linguistic formulation comes from a Hebrew background imported into the Greek language. In Ezekiel the term frequently refers to the prophet (see 2:1). It means simply a human being (Pss. 8:4; 80:17). The Aramaic form of the expression appears in Daniel 7:13, where one like a son of man was given eternal authority in an eternal kingdom. "Son of Man" by itself is an indefinite reference to "a person" or "someone." It may or may not relate to the speaker who uses the term, and it may or may not relate to the context of Daniel. Jesus may have coined an expression using the definite article to refer to himself in a somewhat indefinite and mysterious way and to connect himself cryptically to Daniel 7:13.

The Gospels use the term seventy-seven times. It can refer to Jesus in his earthly ministry, his death and resurrection and vindication, or his rule in glory. Luke specifically uses the term to refer to the earthly Jesus' authority to forgive sins (5:24); his authority over the Sabbath (6:5); his persecution and rejection (6:22); his rejection by the Pharisees as a glutton and drunkard (7:34); his prediction of his crucifixion and resurrection (9:22); his rejection in glory of people who rejected him on earth (9:26); his function as a sign to his generation in the way Jonah was a sign to his (11:30); his acknowledging in glory of those who acknowledge him on earth (12:8); the availability of forgiveness to those who reject or speak against him (12:10); the call to be ready for his unexpected return to earth (12:40); the time when he will no longer be available to men (17:22); his appearance when his day comes (17:24); the crisis situation at his coming compared to that of the days of Noah (17:26); the normal activities of life will continue when his day is revealed (17:30); the fear that faith will disappear from earth before he comes (18:8); the certainty that the Scriptures concerning his suffering must be ful-filled in Jerusalem (18:31); his mission to seek and save the lost (19:10); his visible coming on a cloud in glory (21:27); the need to pray for ability to escape the trauma of the last days and stand before him (21:36); the question if Judas was betraying him with a kiss (22:48); his future place on the throne at God's right hand (22:69); and the necessity of his crucifixion (24:7).

Thus, Luke uses Son of Man extensively to refer to Christ's coming. This coming is certain. The question is not will he come, but will people of faith persevere until he comes?

C. "Eye of a Needle" (18:25)

A hyperbole is an exaggerated statement or figure of speech not to be taken literally. To make a point, Jesus used this hyperbolic statement to illus-trate the impossibility of a large animal, such as a camel, going through a very small opening, the eye of a needle. Attempts to understand this saying as involving a camel going through a small city gate (no evidence exists of a gate named *Eye of the Needle*) or as a mistranslation (*camel* as a mistranslation of the word *cable*) lose sight of the hyperbolic nature of Jesus' words. There is a rabbinic analogy that speaks of an elephant going through the eye of a nee-dle, which is an example of the hyperbolic nature of Jesus' saying in verse 25. C. S. Lewis once observed that God *can* bring a camel through the eye of a needle, but the camel will not be the same creature after coming through a needle's eye!

D. Bartimaeus (18:35–43)

Bartimaeus was the blind man Jesus encountered sitting by the roadside as he approached Jericho. We know the blind man's name from Mark's Gos-pel. Bartimaeus is an example of faith that refuses to give up. He showed great faith by responding to what he had heard, persisting in his request for help, and standing to his feet when Jesus summoned him. Bartimaeus then followed Jesus.

E. Jesus' Messianic Authority (18:31–43)

As Jesus returned to Jerusalem, he again displayed his authority when he predicted his suffering and healed many as the "Son of David." Jesus warned the nation that they had failed to respond to God's promise and would face his judgment. Although the Jewish opposition to Jesus resulted in his death, it resulted in something much worse for the nation. Jesus predicted the nation's defeat by Rome in A.D. 70. God's plan advanced in triumph.

VII. TEACHING OUTLINE

A. INTRODUCTION

1. Lead Story: Children's Prayers
2. Context: Luke 17 concluded as Jesus answered questions from the Pharisees and from his disciples about the coming kingdom. In chapter 18 he turns to speak of how to live while waiting for the Son of Man to return to earth. Kingdom living is life in the interval between Christ's ministry on earth and his coming again from heaven. Kingdom living centers on communication with God in prayer. Kingdom citizens pray until Jesus comes. They pray persistently for what they need, even when God's quick answer seems slow.
3. Transition: Two thousand years closer to the return of the Son of Man, kingdom living remains the same. We are called on to pray and live persistently. We are called to forsake the world's way of riches and possessions to take Christ's way of mercy and trust in the heavenly Father. Luke 18 will encourage you to decide whether you will persist in the Christ way of living or whether the allures of this world are too much with you.

B. COMMENTARY

1. Dedication in Prayer: Trust to the Last (18:1–8)
    a. The setting: Jesus' teaching on persistent prayer (18:1)
    b. The Master's teaching: God will answer (18:2–8a)
    c. The Master's conclusion: will the Son of Man find faith? (18:8b)
2. Dedication to Humility: The Justified Sinner (18:9–14)
    a. The setting: overconfident snobs with Jesus (18:9)
    b. The Master's teaching: humility leads to exaltation (18:10–14)
3. Dedication to Childlike Faith: Possessing the Kingdom (18:15–17)
    a. The setting: bringing children for Jesus' touch (18:15a)

b. The followers' reaction: rebuke (18:15b)

c. The Master's response: be children to enter the kingdom (18:16–17)

4. Dedication to Kingdom Living over Wealthy Living: A Worthy Reward (18:18–30)

a. The setting: administrator seeks eternal life (18:18)

b. The Master's first response: who is good? (18:19)

c. The Master's second response: obey the Bible's commandments (18:20)

d. The ruler's reaction: always have obeyed (18:21)

e. The Master's counter response: sell everything and follow (18:22)

f. The ruler's counter response: sorrow over wealth (18:23)

g. The Master's teaching: hard for the rich to enter the kingdom (18:24–25)

h. The crowd's reaction: who can be saved? (18:26)

i. The Master's response: God is God of impossible (18:27)

j. The followers' reaction: we left all to follow (18:28)

k. The Master's counter response: it will be worth it all (18:29–30)

5. Dedication to the Cross: A Call Not Yet Understood (18:31–34)

a. The setting: teaching the Twelve (18:31a)

b. The Master's teaching: death and resurrection fulfill Scripture (18:31b-33)

c. The follower's reaction: lack of understanding (18:34)

6. Dedication to Merciful Acts: Rewarding Persistent Faith (18:35–43)

a. The setting: Jesus near Jericho (18:35a)

b. The scene: blind beggar seeking mercy (18:35b-38)

c. The crowd's reaction: shut up! (18:39a)

d. The beggar's reaction: have mercy on me (18:39b)

e. The Master's response: what do you want? (18:40–41a)

f. The beggar's counter response: I want to see (18:41b)

g. The Master's counter response: faith has healed (18:42)

h. The beggar's reaction: follow and praise (18:43a)

i. The crowd's reaction: praise God (18:43b)

C. CONCLUSION: PERSEVERING THROUGH GRIEF

VIII. ISSUES FOR DISCUSSION

1. Recall an experience where you persevered in prayer and found God's grace.

2. What does God expect of his people when the Son of Man returns to earth?

3. In what ways are your prayers touched with pride and self-serving?
4. What childlike qualities are necessary to enter the kingdom of heaven?
5. In what ways are you tempted to stand on your works before God rather than on his grace?
6. What rewards do you expect from God? Why?
7. Why could the disciples not understand Christ's mission?
8. In what ways has God shown mercy to you and your family?

Luke 19

Dedication to Save the Lost

"*The* skeptic may deny your doctrine or attack your church, but he cannot honestly ignore the fact that your life has been cleaned up and revolutionized. He may stop his ears to the presentations of a preacher like me, or the pleadings of an evangelist, but he is somehow attracted to the human-interest story of how you—John Q. Public—found peace within. Believe me, the steps that led to your conversion are far more appealing and appropriate to the lost than a pulpit exposition of John 3 or Romans 5."

Charles R. Swindoll

Luke 19

IN A NUTSHELL

In going to dinner with Zacchaeus, Jesus showed his dedication to seeking and saving the lost rather than catering to the egos of the proud. But ultimate salvation did not break in with Jesus' first coming. That must wait until the king returns. The triumphal entry and cleansing of the temple gave a foretaste of the final coming, but Jesus also gave a prediction of what Jerusalem must soon taste. Jesus continued to control his destiny. His opponents are unable to carry out their plans to kill him until God's time.

Dedication to Save the Lost

I. INTRODUCTION

Never Give Up

James Dobson shares the testimony of his paternal grandmother Juanita Dobson. She was married to a man's man, a six-foot-four-inch railroad conductor. He had never been physically ill in his life, going to work every day and giving a hard day's work. He was ill but did not know it. He had the worst kind of illness—the deadly spiritual kind. He let Juanita go to church and participate in the activities there, but he never went and did not want anyone to try to get him to go. He was as good and moral as anyone else and saw nothing he needed at the church.

Juanita knew what he needed. She never said anything to her beloved husband. She simply prayed. Every day she prayed. Regularly, she fasted and prayed for her husband's salvation. She saw no evidence of change. Nothing gave her reason to think her prayers were being answered. Still, she prayed.

Decades passed. At age 69, he still showed no signs of listening to God. Then strokes felled him. He became partially paralyzed and bedfast. He was devastated. One afternoon, his daughter carried out her daily ritual of straightening the bed, giving him his medicines, and seeing what else she could do to cheer him or comfort him. Suddenly, she realized he was crying. No one ever remembered seeing a teardrop run down that leathery cheek before. Gulping down her shock, she bent over the bed and asked, "Daddy, what's wrong?"

"Honey, go get your mother," he replied.

The faithful Juanita ran up the stairs as fast as her aging legs would carry her. She took his outstretched hand and heard him say, "I know I am going to die, and I am not afraid of death. But it is so dark. Will you pray for me?"

Words she had waited forty years to hear! She called to heaven for her husband. He accepted Jesus as his personal Lord and Savior. Her heart sang, joining the heavenly chorus in rejoicing over a lost sinner who was saved. Two weeks later he died, saying what Jesus meant to him. Later his devoted prayer-champion wife joined him in heaven, where he was because she never gave up in her dedication to seeking the lost (Dobson, *When God Doesn't Make Sense*, 205–206).

Luke 19 introduces us to the climax of Luke's Gospel. Jesus shows that his mission is to seek and save the lost. The parable of the king and his servants shows the need for Jesus to leave for a long time before returning as *king*. It also shows the responsibility of his slaves while he is gone. Entering Jerusalem, Jesus is greeted as a king, but this is only a foretaste of the final coming. All things point to his death; only God's timing remains to be revealed.

II. COMMENTARY

Dedication to Save the Lost

MAIN IDEA: *Jesus Christ is the king whom God sent to seek and save the lost, but his coming was only preliminary to his return to heaven to wait until the final coming when he will be revealed in all his glory. Death in God's time awaited him in his first coming to earth.*

A Dedicated to Seeking and Saving the Lost: Son of Man's Goal (19:1–10)

SUPPORTING IDEA: *Jesus came to seek and save the lost, not to fulfill legalistic religious demands or to cater to religious experts.*

19:1–4. Reaching Jericho (see 18:35), Jesus continued his journey up the dangerous hills toward Jerusalem. Interruption came before he could leave the city. A short, clever tax collector was determined to see Jesus. As an administrator for the Roman government's tax office, Zacchaeus had amassed great wealth, overcharging the Jewish people and taking a cut from the taxes gathered by other tax collectors whose work he administered. His wealth could not provide the one thing he wanted more than anything else. Unable to see over or get through the massive crowd swarming around Jesus, Zacchaeus noted the direction Jesus was taking, ran ahead, found a tree, and climbed up into its branches.

19:5. The clever tax collector did get a view of Jesus, and Jesus spotted him up in the tree. Jesus even invited himself to dinner at Zacchaeus's house. Jesus said it was necessary for him to visit Zacchaeus—apparently a necessity initiated by God to show one more time Jesus' central mission on earth.

19:6–7. Overjoyed at this unexpected privilege, the short man scurried down the tree. This time he had no trouble getting through the crowd to Jesus. But as they let the tax collector through, the crowd must have complained. How can this be? they grumbled. We thought Jesus was Messiah, and he is going to eat with a sinful man, a man who represents the enemy government and takes our money to give to them. How can Jesus eat and fellowship with such a traitor? Jesus showed he was an "equal opportunity" diner with traitors. Earlier he had eaten at the home of Pharisees and showed how they were traitors to God's intentions for the Jews. Now he ate with a person whom the Jews considered a political and economic traitor.

19:8. After meeting Jesus, the tax collector/traitor was no longer the same man. He would enter the kingdom of God, but not as a wealthy man (see 18:25). He would take half of what he owned and give it to the poor. He would find the people he had overcharged on their tax bill and refund four times as much as he had cheated them. Thus, he took the Law of Moses seriously. Leviticus 5:16 and Numbers 5:7 demanded restitution plus twenty percent. Exodus 22:1 called for rustlers to repay four sheep for one (see 2 Sam. 12:6). The Dead Sea Scrolls and Roman law also contain incidents of fourfold restitution. Zacchaeus seems to have accepted the harshest penalty of the law and applied it to himself. Acceptance by Jesus made money insignificant (see 12:33). Repentance came in the form of action (see 3:12–13). He had a new lifestyle because he had a new Lord.

19:9. Jesus showed ultimate acceptance of the tax collector/traitor turned repentant sinner. Salvation had come to Zacchaeus and to his house. Jesus' mission had basically been a mission to the Jews, and this man was a Jew, participating in the covenant with Abraham, even if he acted the part of the traitor in Jewish eyes. For Jesus a repentant Jew from such a sordid background was better than a self-righteous Jew with no sense of the need for repentance (see 5:31–32).

19:10. The scene with Zacchaeus provides Luke's Gospel with its ultimate statement about Jesus. Jesus knew his purpose on earth. His purpose was not to reform the Jewish religion. His purpose was not to prove the Pharisees wrong. His purpose was not to bring in a military, political kingdom. His purpose was to bring salvation to lost people. Jesus dedicated the three years of his earthly ministry to finding people who knew they were lost and showing them God's way of salvation—the way of repentance and faith.

B Dedication to a Distant Kingdom: Serving with Patient Intelligence (19:11–27)

> **SUPPORTING IDEA:** *God's kingdom will not come in its fullness until the king returns at a time he determines. His slaves must serve him with intelligence, waiting for his return.*

19:11. Having made his way up the dangerous winding mountain road from Jericho, Jesus came to the entrance of Jerusalem. The crowds were following him and listening to his teaching. They made it clear to Jesus that they thought the moment had arrived. It was time for him to bring in the kingdom.

Evidently, they thought he would enter Jerusalem as a conquering king, ready to throw out the Roman government and take charge. He could use the miraculous powers he had shown and call on God to send the angelic army, and a son of David would once more occupy the throne of David. Jesus sought to dash such expectations. He used his normal method: telling a parable.

19:12–14. In the parable a man traveled to another country to be crowned king of the country where he had been living (see "Deeper Discoveries"). To test their responsibility, the king gave each of his ten slaves one mina. It took sixty minas to make a talent. The man entrusted almost nothing from his standpoint to the slaves, but each of them had over three months' pay. Would the slaves wait idly while the master was gone, living on the unexpected windfall? Or would they obey the master and put the money to use and earn a profit?

The man seeking the kingship had to deal with other people besides the slaves of his household. He had citizens of the kingdom. These people were not slaves. Rather, they claimed power and influence in the kingdom. They had resources of their own, independent of this king. They used these resources to send their own delegation to the far country, trying to prevent his appointment as king. They did not want this man as king.

Certainly, behind such an image stood the Pharisees and other religious leaders of Israel. God sent his Messiah to be their king. They rejected Messiah and even collaborated with enemy government officials to prevent him from gaining the kingship. They did not realize that Jesus never intended to establish an earthly kingship. Rather, God used their opposition to Jesus to achieve his plan of redeeming the world through the blood of his Son.

19:15. The opposition failed. The man became king in the far country and returned to rule. This again parallels the kingdom of God. Jesus journeyed to heaven after his death. There the resurrected Lord sits on the throne at God's right hand. He is king, but his opponents cannot see that. They think they have won the victory. Instead, Jesus is on his way back. He is coming. One day his kingdom will be evident to all the world. Then what will happen? The story tells us. He summons his slaves to whom he has entrusted responsibility. He wants to know how they have done with his resources.

19:16–19. The first slave passed the examination with flying colors. He had earned one thousand percent on his investment. Now the king rewarded him with even more responsibility and power. The least on earth, a slave, became powerful and great because he was a faithful steward, responsible over all he received. The second slave made only five hundred percent profit. Again the master rewarded him with more authority and responsibility.

19:20–21. The story does not follow each of the original ten. It simply illustrates the two extremes: great faithfulness and utter failure. The third slave exemplifies the latter. He knew the king's habits and feared what would happen to him if he should lose his money. So he gave the king back what he had received. But this was not faithful obedience. This was not responsibility. This was lazy, fearful idleness. He did not put his money to work as the king ordered (v. 13).

Verse 21 makes interpretation of the parable difficult. If God or Jesus is seen as the returning king, then this description hardly fits. It is a caricature of the king who so graciously gave the money before he left and who so richly rewarded some of his slaves when he returned. This is the only servant who attempted to describe the king, and his description was wrong. He represents the worst side of the Jewish religion of his day—a side that thought it had to obey God at any cost and in the smallest detail of the law. Otherwise, God would become the angry judge, throw the book at them, and punish them beyond imagination. This is the natural outcome of legalistic religion. It changes God from a gracious redeemer who gives laws because he knows the life that is best for us to a mean tyrant who forces us to obey laws for his own pleasure and cheats us out of what rightfully belongs to us. Legalistic religion concentrates so heavily on the religious system that it gets out of touch with the God it claims to represent.

19:22–23. The king took the disobedient slave's words at face value. This is not to say the king accepted such a description. What monarch would publicly admit to such a character profile? The king simply says, "If this is the system he is seeking to follow and this is the god he is trying to please, then he will be judged on that system." That system makes even more demands for obedience. Why did he not follow the command of the king rather than retreating in fear? If nothing else, let someone else do the work. Just put the money in the bank and receive common interest on it. Then he would have had something to give the master.

The slave's excuse makes no sense. Similarly, the judgment scene in Matthew 25 shows people totally unaware of how false their religious conceptions are and how wrong their expectations of heavenly reward. The religious system Jesus found in place in Israel did not work. It was not based on intelligent reasoning, consistent actions, or a true understanding of God. The people who practiced it faced judgment.

19:24. The judgment involved taking away what the slave had. The most faithful of the slaves got even more reward and responsibility. The evil slave was left with nothing. His whole system disintegrated. What he thought he controlled, he lost. So the Jewish religious system would face terrible judgment in A.D. 70 with the destruction of the temple, but the individuals would face ultimate judgment when the Messiah returned in all his glory.

19:25. The crowd, or perhaps the other slaves, saw this as unfair. Why take away what little the one had to give to the one who had enough? This represents the response of legalism, a system built on eye for an eye, tooth for a tooth, absolute justice. Jesus' kingdom represented an entirely different type of system. It was a system of grace to the faithful and trusting, but judgment for those who trusted themselves rather than leaning on God's grace.

19:26. This summarizes the story in proverbial form (see 8:18). Jesus divided people into two classes: those who have and those who do not. The latter class includes very religious people who think they know God and believe they have the only way to gain his rewards. In reality, they do not know God at all. They are evil. They will lose the religious power and responsibility they have and will face the king's final judgment.

19:27. The class of those who do not have includes another group. These not only think they have the way to God all locked up, but they actively oppose Jesus. Here Jesus spoke directly to the Pharisees and scribes who would soon lead him to Pilate and Calvary. They were opposing him. They did not want his type of relationship to God. They refused to acknowledge him as king. Eternal slaughter and death awaited them. Active opposition to God brings even greater punishment than refusal to do things God's way.

C The Glory Recognized (19:28–40)

> **SUPPORTING IDEA:** *Jesus is the eternal king, the promised Messiah, who comes in the name of the Lord.*

19:28. Jerusalem! The goal is attained. Now the tension mounts. How will the Messiah be received in God's holy city? Have we been listening to what Jesus said? Are we ready for the events to follow in swift order? Jesus has established himself as the king in the preceding narrative, but a king who had to go into the far country before returning in power. He has shown the nature of his kingdom—a kingdom different from that expected by the religious establishment. He had shown who would participate in the kingdom—those faithful to him, who had given up everything to follow him rather than those who had the religious system locked up in their own hands.

How would this idea of the kingdom play out? Jesus knew what would happen (9:22,44–45; 12:49–50; 13:32–33; 17:25; 18:31–34). Still, the crowds and the disciples were not ready for Jerusalem, the city of David.

19:29. Approaching Jerusalem, Jesus passed through two small villages east of the holy city on the Mount of Olives, which looked down on the city and the Kidron Valley. The Mount of Olives, the central of three peaks rising east of Jerusalem, stands 2,660 feet above sea level. Standing on it, a person faced the temple. Zechariah 14:4–5 situates the final battle on the Mount of Olives (cf. Acts 1). The king stood with the holy city at his feet.

19:30–31. The king sent two of his disciples on a mission: "Find a donkey that has never been ridden before and bring it to me. If you face questions, just say, 'The Lord needs it.'" Jesus acted in regal manner but commandeered a lowly animal.

19:32–35. Events occurred just as Jesus described. So the disciples brought the donkey to Jesus, threw their robes on it as a saddle, and set Jesus on it (cf. 1 Kgs. 1:33 for the coronation of Solomon on a mule). Zechariah 9:9 used poetic parallelism to describe the messianic king riding on a donkey to bring salvation to his people. His coming would break all instruments of war and bring peace to the city of peace.

19:36. The disciples also spread their robes on the street, signifying a royal procession (cf. 2 Kgs. 9:13).

19:37. The crowd of disciples, indicating a group beyond the Twelve, joined the procession, praising God for all the miraculous signs Jesus had given (cf. 7:22; 13:10–17; 14:1–6; 17:11–19; 18:35–43).

19:38. They praised Jesus as king, citing Psalm 118:26. Finally, Jesus' glory was openly recognized (cf. 1:32; 18:38–39). He was more than the babe of Nazareth or the Galilean rabbi. He was more than a miracle worker. He was a royal figure entering the royal city down the royal road. He came as God's representative, God's chosen king. He showed that the hopes of Israel are being fulfilled. God has sent the messianic king to bring peace, a peace that only heaven can establish, and a peace established in heaven that cannot be negated on earth. This means that the angels who rejoice over one sinner who repents now see all the heavenly glory of God's plan of salvation brought to fruition. As earthlings praise the king on a donkey, so heaven glories in God's great work of salvation.

19:39. This was too much for the Pharisees. They came to crucify Jesus, not to praise him. They asked Jesus to silence the disciples. Do not let such blasphemy continue, they said. They showed themselves to be the enemies opposing Jesus so aptly described in the previous parable.

19:40. Impossible, replied Jesus. This is the moment God ordained for me to receive praise. If human voices were silent, nature would shout its praise. The Pharisees just do not understand the nature of the God they spend so much time talking about. They are evil servants as in the parable. The king has come. They see only a false teacher on a donkey. But for those who do see the king, praise is the language of the day. Such language will lead to eternal rewards and responsibility.

Ⓓ The Glory's Results: Death of a Blind City (19:41–44)

> **SUPPORTING IDEA:** *Jerusalem's blindness to God's Messiah means absolute destruction for the city, bringing pain and tears to the Messiah who loves the blind city.*

19:41. Luke has begun the Jerusalem story (19:28), but he has not yet let Jesus reach Jerusalem. The recognition and praise of Messiah comes from disciples outside the city, not from the religious crowds or religious power brokers inside the city. Jesus knew that the city of Jerusalem and its power structure—both Jewish and Roman—would reject him. They would take him to the cross. So he wept, not for his immediate fate but for the stubborn, sinful blindness of the city. The city God loves had no love for him.

19:42. He had come with peace from heaven. They could not see or understand. They did not act responsibly and intelligently, just as the parable described. Why? It was hidden from their eyes. Here is the biblical teaching on hardening in another guise. Irresponsible use of religious power finally separated the Jerusalem establishment from God. Thus, his revelation no longer came to them. He hid his plans from their eyes. As in the parable, they would rise up in outrage: unfair! No, God was just giving them what they deserved, taking away responsibility and privilege from those who misused it because they could not learn to recognize him and how he acted.

19:43–44. Hidden revelation was only the beginning of Jerusalem's troubles. Jesus looked ahead to A.D. 70, when the Roman government would have enough of Jewish rebellions and would destroy the city. The inhabitants would not escape. Jesus made special mention of the children, since caring for the helpless was the center of his ministry. God had visited his people as he had promised. Messiah had come to seek and to save the lost. They refused to recognize they were lost. They refused to see God's glory in Jesus or to give God glory for sending Jesus. Their beloved temple and all the glorious architecture of Jerusalem would fall, not one stone attached to another, no hope for rebuilding and renewal.

E The Agent of Glory and the Place of Glory: Cleansing the Temple (19:45–46)

SUPPORTING IDEA: *The rejected king of glory condemned the gory business of the temple and restored God's place of worship to its rightful glory.*

19:45. Having viewed the temple from the Mount of Olives, Jesus finally entered the city. For Luke, the first appearance in the city comes in the temple, the place where God's Messiah would be expected to appear. Did he find worship of God and praise for the grace and mercy of the saving Lord? Oh, no! He found secular business in the sacred precincts. The religious establishment had cornered the market on sacrificial lambs and birds and on changing money into the coins that were acceptable for temple offerings and purchases. The Pharisees and Saduccees placed wealth above obedience. Jesus had to get rid of this. His Father's house must be pure and holy. Exit businessmen. Enter worshipers.

19:46. What authority did Jesus have for such actions? He had Scripture on his side. Isaiah 56:7 and Jeremiah 7:11 combine to show God's intent and the Jewish leaders' result. God established the temple as the place where his presence could be experienced and witnessed by the people. There his people could converse with him in prayer. Out of this conception of the temple grew the Book of Psalms with its prayers for all kinds of life situations.

But legalism had set in. Jewish rabbis established interpretations of laws and interpretations of interpretations. To be sure of obeying the law of sacrifice, a person felt obliged to purchase an animal at the temple. Other similar activities increased until commerce replaced conversation with God. The temple not only had commerce; it had a commercial monopoly. As usual with monopolies, prices rose to outrageous heights. Jesus described such monopolistic, price-gouging commerce as robbery. God could not stand for this. Exit commercial activities and animal stalls. Enter the royal king to reclaim his house for prayer and worship. The king had come not only to seek and to save the lost. He had come to save the temple from the thieves who occupied it.

F The Glory Overrules Human Plans: Plotting and Listening (19:47–48)

SUPPORTING IDEA: *Jesus maintained control of his future even as the Pharisees plotted his death and the crowds stood spellbound waiting for his moment of action.*

19:47. The cleansed house of prayer became Jesus' classroom. Here he taught the disciples and the crowds about God's kingdom. The Jewish leaders ignored his teaching. They had one goal—to destroy him. They revealed their true nature as people who opposed and rejected the one who visited them in the name of the Lord.

19:48. The power block's plotting could not succeed. It was not yet God's time. God used the power of popular appeal to keep the religious leaders at bay. The people hung on every word of Jesus, spellbound by his authority and his unique style of teaching. The religious leaders dared not cause an uproar among the people. Then Rome would interfere. They would lose all power just as Jesus had predicted. So the stage was set. When and how would the passion predictions of the Messiah come true? In what way would this be a victory for the religious establishment? In what way would it be a victory for the sovereign plan of God to seek and to save the lost? How would the disciples react? How would the crowd respond?

MAIN IDEA REVIEW: *Jesus Christ is the king whom God sent to seek and save the lost, but his coming was only preliminary to his return to heaven to wait until the final coming when he will be revealed in all his glory. Death in God's time awaited him in his first coming to earth.*

III. CONCLUSION

The Compassionate Savior

Why did Jesus come? Jesus made his mission clear as he invited himself to a tax collector's home. He came to seek and to save the lost. Still, Jewish religious leaders bickered with him over who was lost. They felt secure in their religious system in which they controlled all authority and power.

Finally, Jesus approached Jerusalem. He looked at the holy city in its unholy state and grieved for it, pronouncing judgment on it and its inhabitants because they had rejected him, the one who represented God's visit to the city.

Entering the city, Jesus went to reclaim the temple because it had given way to legalistic religion and secular commerce. He drove out the businessmen and restored the order of prayer and worship that God intended. The king had momentarily reclaimed his home, but soon he would go to the far country; his prophecy of destruction would come true. The religious leaders were even then plotting his death.

PRINCIPLES

- Jesus' mission and that of his followers is to seek and save the lost.
- Salvation brings repentance and change of lifestyle.
- Christ will return again to bring judgment on his enemies and to reward the faithful with more responsibility.
- Jesus is the expected messianic king who came in the name of the Lord to bring peace.
- God controls history and its events.
- Destruction and judgment come on those who do not recognize God and do not praise his Messiah.
- God's house is a place of prayer, not of business.

APPLICATIONS

- Search for lost people and tell them about the Savior.
- Check your lifestyle; do you need to repent and renew your commitment to the Savior?
- Prepare yourself in faithfulness and prayer to be ready when the Savior returns.
- Confess Jesus as king of your life and of the universe.

- Realize the danger you face if you do not accept Jesus; turn from your sins and confess him as your Savior and Lord.
- Be sure your church is easily recognized as a place of prayer, not of commerce and secular activities by people who seek to line their own pockets.

IV. LIFE APPLICATION

Is He Here Yet?

The final cluster of planes was headed into the airport before it shut its doors and hangars for the night. A small girl came skipping down the hallway, taking two or three steps for every one the woman beside her took. Tied to her arm was a long string connected to a big yellow balloon that was bobbing above the people who were rushing to meet the night's last incoming flight.

"Is he here yet?" the girl screamed. Eyes glanced her way, smiling at her enthusiasm. Then eyes turned to follow her stare to the exit leading to the plane.

"No! He is not here yet," the woman answered, seeking to calm the child a bit. Weary, bloodshot eyes lighted up as travelers caught sight of the girl and remembered their childhood experiences at airports.

"Is he here yet?" the girl cried out again and again. Each time the young mother looked down to say, "No, honey, not yet." Still the young legs pumped forward eagerly, getting as close to the doorway as possible.

Suddenly, the balloons began waving back and forth, up and down as the young girl jumped up and down, screaming. "There he is! He's here! He's here!" All eyes turned to see a young soldier walk through the doorway into the airport waiting room. Returning from Operation Desert Storm, he glanced quickly through the crowd to the leaping balloons and the small arm attached to them. Stooping down, he scooped up the running girl into his arms, welcome sign, balloons, and all.

"Daddy, Daddy," she yelped. "I found you! I found you!"

The airport crowd smiled at the little girl's happy discovery. Our smiles should be much bigger. Jesus came to earth to seek and to save the lost. He found us while we were yet sinners. He died for us. Now he rules on the heavenly throne at God's right hand, watching as we carry out the responsibilities he has assigned us. Meanwhile, we join the disciples at the triumphal entry in singing Christ's praises. We also join Christ in looking at a lost world that has rejected him and will not accept him as their Savior. Tears fill our eyes as they did his. We realize that we, too, are on a search-and-find mission with Jesus after the lost. Sadly, that mission begins in our own church, where secular business and human greed too often have taken over God's house of prayer. Jesus calls us to let revival begin at our church, purifying our church life and worship. We must let Christ's teaching once again be the central concern of our church. We must hang on every word he says, not because we are spellbound waiting for a miracle to gasp at, but because we know that obeying his teaching is the only way to meaningful life here and eternal life hereafter.

V. PRAYER

Loving Shepherd, who came to seek and save us when we were lost, seal your vision and your mission deep within our hearts. Show us how to join you in searching for the lost. Show us how to bring them to know they are lost, to accept you as Savior, and to love you as Lord of life. Amen.

VI. DEEPER DISCOVERIES

A. Salvation (19:9–10)

Salvation is a key word in Luke's Gospel. The infancy narratives point to salvation as the reason for Christ's coming (1:69,71,77). This salvation seems to have two components: physical deliverance from enemies and spiritual deliverance through the forgiveness of sins. Such salvation is for "the house of his servant David" (1:69). Zacchaeus needed such salvation. He acknowledged the deceit and fraud he had perpetrated. The Jewish people saw him as a traitor to their nation and their God. He was separated from everyone. Jesus knew precisely who he was and what he had done. Still, Jesus offered this chief of sinners his salvation because he saw that Zacchaeus had repented and changed his way of living.

Jesus argued with the Pharisees because he saw his miracles as saving life, while they saw such work as violation of Sabbath commandments (6:9). Jesus said the person he healed and restored to normal life had been cured or saved (the same Greek word *sozo* being capable of being translated as "delivered," "cured," "healed," "made well," or "saved"; 7:50; 8:36,48,50; 9:24; 17:19; 18:42). The crowd at the cross and the criminals crucified with him expected Jesus to use the same power he exercised in saving people from disease to save himself from the cross (23:35–39), but Jesus exercised his power only within the limits of God's will and purpose.

Jesus also speaks of spiritual salvation. Hearing and believing the word of God leads to being saved, but Satan seeks to prevent people from hearing, believing, and being saved (8:12). Being saved is the same as entering the kingdom of God, but only a relatively few people make it (13:22–30; 18:26).

Those few have to admit they are among the lost so Jesus can find them and save them (19:10).

B. The Kingship (19:12–27)

This story perhaps has recent Jewish history as its background. Herod the Great had gone to Cleopatra in Egypt and then to Mark Antony in Rome, where a Jewish delegation had been accusing Herod of misconduct. Herod's father Antipater had been gracious to Antony, so he persuaded the Roman Senate to make Herod king over Judea. Herod then made a habit of murdering his opponents.

Later Archelaus and Antipas, Herod's sons, traveled to Rome seeking political appointment. The Jews revolted against Archelaus and appealed against him in Rome. Caesar finally divided the kingdom, making Archelaus tetrarch of Judea, with his two brothers Antipas and Philip splitting the remainder of Herod's kingdom. Archelaus continued his cruel ways, finally forcing Rome to take away all his political power. After the time of Jesus, this pattern continued in Judea. Jesus' audience thus easily understood the situation he described and may have thought he was talking about a current political situation.

Many interpreters seek to limit this parable to earthly kingship and make its teaching a contrast to the way Jesus is king. The close relationship between Jesus' comings and goings and those of the man in the parable force us to see the story as illustrating exactly what verse 11 introduces: the delay of Jesus' kingdom.

VII. TEACHING OUTLINE

A. INTRODUCTION

1. Lead Story: Never Give Up
2. Context: At 9:51 Jesus set out for Jerusalem, knowing betrayal and death were at hand (9:44). In chapter 19 he finally reached the city. Careful Gospel readers should be prepared for this as the place and time for betrayal, death, and resurrection. The religious leaders were plotting the death and betrayal, but they found it hard to put their plans into action because of the crowd's continued devotion to Jesus. The disciples who were supposed to be learning the secrets of the kingdom entered Jerusalem oblivious to what was to come. They had failed to grasp what it meant to be king. In chapter 19 Jesus showed his mission of salvation, his role as messianic king of Israel, and his dedication to the Father's will. He again tried to show the disciples that the kind of kingship they were talking about is distant, requiring

Christ's journey into a distant land. He acted to cleanse the temple and show its priestly operators that they were not part of God's kingdom. They had become dedicated to secular business and riches rather than to kingdom worship and prayer.

3. Transition: Christ is king. Luke had spent much of his Gospel trying to show his disciples and the people what that means. Chapter 19 presents the contrast in all its boldness. To be king is to seek and save the lost, not to seek and save personal power. To be king is to face opposition and to journey into a distant land before receiving the kingship and coming back to rule. Being king is to descend the Mount of Olives on a donkey, seeking to bring heavenly peace on earth, not instigating rebellion to bring a new regime in Jerusalem. To be king is to cry over a lost city and its coming punishment, not to enter the city and declare oneself its ruler. To be king is to renew the religious life of God's people, beginning in the religious center—the temple. To be king is to teach the people about the kingdom of God until God calls you home to seat you at his right hand as king forever. Studying this chapter is an invitation to you to review all that Luke has said about Jesus as king. You need to decide if the kind of rule Jesus talked about and the kind of mission he set his disciples on will bring meaning and hope to your life.

B. COMMENTARY

1. Dedicated to Seeking and Saving the Lost: Son of Man's Goal (19:1–10)
   a. The setting: Jesus passing through Jericho (19:1)
   b. The scene: short Zacchaeus climbs tree to see Jesus (19:2–4)
   c. The Master's response: come down, I will stay with you (19:5)
   d. Zacchaeus's reaction: down the tree with glad welcome (19:6)
   e. The crowd's reaction: muttering over Jesus' company (19:7)
   f. Zacchaeus's response: give to poor and to ones cheated (19:8)
   g. The Master's response: salvation has come (19:9)
   h. The Master's teaching: Son of Man came to seek and save the lost (19:10)
2. Dedication to a Distant Kingdom: Serving with Patient Intelligence (19:11–27)
   a. The setting: listening crowd expects immediate kingdom (19:11)
   b. The story: man gives responsibility to his slaves, while opponents reject him (19:12–14)
   c. The climax: reward for faithful, judgment for idle, more reward for faithful (19:15–24)
   d. The crowd's response: unfair (19:25)

    e.   The Master's teaching: faithful get more; unfaithful lose what they have; opponents die (19:26–27)

3.   The Glory Recognized: Triumphal Entry (19:28–40)

    a.   The setting: going up to Jerusalem (19:28)

    b.   The scene: followers commissioned on Mount of Olives (19:29–30)

    c.   The followers' reaction: get donkey and put Jesus on it, spread coats on road (19:32–36)

    d.   The followers' response: praise for the king (19:37–38)

    e.   The opponents' reaction: make them stop (19:39)

    f.   The Master's response: praise cannot be stopped (19:40)

4.   The Glory's Results: Death of a Blind City (19:41–44)

    a.   The setting: Master nears Jerusalem (19:41a)

    b.   The Master's response to the city: lament over future destruction (19:41b-44)

5.   The Agent of Glory and the Place of Glory: Cleansing the Temple (19:45–46)

    a.   The setting: entering temple area (19:45a)

    b.   The Master's action: drive out robber merchants (19:45b-46)

6.   The Glory Overrules Human Plans: Plotting and Listening (19:47–48)

    a.   The setting: teaching at the temple (19:47a)

    b.   The opponents' reaction: murder plans (19:47b)

    c.   The crowd's reaction: hanging on his words (19:48)

C. CONCLUSION: IS HE HERE YET?

VIII. ISSUES FOR DISCUSSION

1.   Define the kingdom of God.

2.   How are you and your church seeking and saving the lost? What does it mean to be lost?

3.   Do you think the parable in chapter 19 refers to what Jesus was about to do or does it illustrate the kind of king that was opposed to all that Jesus was and did?

4.   How do you respond to Jesus the king?

5.   If you had been a Jew living in Jerusalem at the time of Jesus, what would have made you reject and oppose Jesus?

6.   How would Jesus react if he appeared in your church on a Thursday afternoon?

7.   What response are you making to Jesus' teaching?

Luke 20

Identifying the Glory

I. INTRODUCTION
Who Is He?

II. COMMENTARY
A verse-by-verse explanation of the chapter.

III. CONCLUSION
Growing Conflict

An overview of the principles and applications from the chapter.

IV. LIFE APPLICATION
Dying to Save Others

Melding the chapter to life.

V. PRAYER
Tying the chapter to life with God.

VI. DEEPER DISCOVERIES
Historical, geographical, and grammatical enrichment of the commentary.

VII. TEACHING OUTLINE
Suggested step-by-step group study of the chapter.

VIII. ISSUES FOR DISCUSSION
Zeroing the chapter in on daily life.

Quote

"*A*mong his contemporaries Jesus somehow gained a reputation as 'a wine-bibber and a glutton.' Those in authority, whether religious or political, regarded him as a troublemaker, a disturber of the peace. He spoke and acted like a revolutionary, scorning fame, family, property, and other traditional measures of success. . . . In the midst of such confusion, how do we answer the simple question, 'Who was Jesus?'"

Philip Yancey

Luke 20

IN A NUTSHELL

*O*pponents tried valiantly to trap Jesus into providing evidence against himself that they could use to convict him in a Roman court and to discredit him before the crowds. Jesus avoided their traps and put them on the defensive, showing that their history was one of persecuting God's prophets, that they had responsibility both to God and to Caesar, that resurrection is real because God is God of the living, and that the Messiah must be greater than simply a son of David. In all this Jesus began to identify himself as one with authority from heaven, giving his life to die for the salvation of God's people, being the first and primary example of resurrection, and being the messianic son of David who is David's Lord.

Identifying the Glory

I. INTRODUCTION

Who Is He?

$\mathscr{I}$ work in a large organization. Still most of us old-timers recognize the majority of the 2,000 plus employees who enter our buildings on a regular basis. That means we also do not have to see a stranger signing in at the front security desk to recognize that an outsider is among us. We also know that our organization draws the most famous of Christian leaders to confer with our people, to lead conferences and seminars, and to write books, commentaries, study guides, and other Christian literature for our publishing units. Often when we see someone signing in or someone walking down the hall with one of the leaders of our company, we stop and ask, "Who is he?"

It reminds me of reading comic books about super-heroes and watching their movies as a young lad. When would the bad guys finally discover the secret identity of Superman or Batman and Robin? Would the day come when the mask was removed and the identity of Bruce Wayne or Clark Kent was discovered?

Those who walked with Jesus day by day in his earthly ministry knew he was more than a poor boy from Nazareth. He could teach with authority, heal with power, and argue with clarity and cleverness against their religious leaders. In many ways, the Gospel stories have only one point: Who is Jesus? This becomes especially clear as the narrative comes to its climax in the last days of Jesus' life. Crowds, disciples, religious opponents, and even Jesus himself seem absorbed in the question: Who is he? Chapter 20 zeroes in on this question as Luke begins to reveal the glory of the Christ.

II. COMMENTARY

Identifying the Glory

MAIN IDEA: *Human wisdom cannot entrap Jesus into self-incrimination. Jesus operates from heavenly authority as the beloved Son of God/Son of David who dies for his people and will be the first example of resurrection.*

Ⓐ The Glory's Authority: Parallel to John's Authority (20:1-8)

SUPPORTING IDEA: *Jesus' heavenly authority is evident, as was John's, but religious tricksters cannot get him to speak of his authority in ways that will give them an excuse to accuse him of treason.*

20:1-2. Jesus spent much of the time during his last days in the complex of temple buildings. No longer did he confine his teaching to his disciples. He openly taught the people who gathered to listen. His teaching had one central thrust: the good news of the kingdom (for Luke's repeated emphasis on preaching good news, see 1:19; 2:10; 3:18; 4:18,43; 7:22; 8:1; 9:6; 16:16). This repeated the opening message (4:18–19,43). The uniqueness of his teaching style and method had always been evident. When he first entered Capernaum, the people were amazed at his teaching because of its authority (4:32,36). His authority extended to the power to exorcise demons (4:36) and forgive sins (5:24). It was authority he could share with his disciples (10:19).

Thus, his opponents, seeking ways to kill him (19:47), tested him at the point of authority. What authority did he claim? The scribes had authority. They had studied with rabbis. They had all the qualifications they needed to be qualified public teachers of the law. The priests had authority. They had inherited the position of priest all the way back to their forefathers Aaron and Levi. The elders had authority. Their age and experience had gained them leadership in the social and economic affairs of the community. These three groups of Jewish leaders knew that Jesus had no formal training with the rabbis, no priestly lineage, and no experience of the elders. How dare he usurp their positions and contradict their teachings. Could these Jewish authorities expose Jesus' lack of credentials and thus rob him of the authority everyone recognized in his teaching?

20:3-4. Jesus countered with a question: I will tell you if you tell me. He limited their choice of answers to either/or: Did divine or human authority undergird John the Baptist's ministry? Such a counter question was crucial to answering the Jewish leaders' question. Especially in Luke's Gospel, John's ministry and authority has been closely linked to that of Jesus (chaps. 1–3). John claimed no authority except from heaven. Neither did Jesus. Would the Jewish authorities admit heavenly authority?

20:5-7. The trappers were trapped. Again, their fear of the people hindered action. To reply "from heaven" was to cause people to ask why they did not go to John and repent and be baptized. To say "from earth" was to say that the people formed the wrong opinion of John because they believed he came from God. Thus, the experts in religious knowledge had to claim ignorance. They did not plead ignorance for lack of knowledge. They pled ignorance for self-preservation in the face of the people. A firm gap has formed between Jewish people and Jewish leaders. People hung on Jesus' words. Leaders feared the people but wanted to kill Jesus.

20:8. The leaders did not meet their end of the bargain. Jesus would not meet his. Neither question would be answered. To audience and to readers, the answer was clear. The Jewish leaders exercised self-contained, self-perpetuated authority for leadership. John and Jesus relied on heaven as their authority.

B The Result of Rejecting the Glory: Punishment (20:9–19)

SUPPORTING IDEA: *Israel's history is one of rejecting God's prophets. Rejecting the beloved Son is only the climax of a history that opposed God and brought punishment on the nation*

20:9–12. Jesus counterattacked against his opponents with his usual weapon, a parable. The language of this parable has rich associations with Old Testament language (Isa. 5:1–5; Ps. 80:8–13; Isa. 27:2; Jer. 2:21; Ezek. 19:10–14; Hos. 10:1). Usually the vineyard symbolized Israel as a people. Jesus made a subtle play on words. The vineyard became God's gift to Israel, including the gift of the covenant, the land, the political power, and the promise for future renewal.

The parable was based on the practice of absentee landlords letting hired people till their land for a commission or portion of the profits. Jesus described unexpected reversal. The tenants revolted and mistreated the landlord's messengers, refusing to pay the owner's share of the income. This pictures Israel's history with God's messengers. He sent them. They killed them. The prophetic message in Scripture they so ardently taught and argued over had its foundation in people who died at the hands of these leaders' forefathers.

20:13. The owner had Plan B. He sent his only son, the one he loved. Having no respect for messenger slaves, surely the tenants would respect the son who carried all the authority of the father. Here the real meaning of the parable shines through. Jesus is the beloved Son (3:22; cf. 9:35). He is the last of the prophets and more. Would this generation treat Jesus any better than their ancestors treated the prophets?

20:14–15. There was no respect at all for the son. The tenants saw a perfect opportunity to grab authority, power, and wealth for themselves, knowing the law allowed tenants on the land for a minimum of three years to claim property at the death of a sonless landlord. The decision appeared simple— kill the son, take over the property. So they did. Now for Plan C: What will the landlord do to these murderous tenants? They had omitted one small detail from their plan. The landlord remained alive.

20:16. Jesus had a quick answer. Plan C meant the landlord would come himself with proper backup. He would seize the evil tenants and kill them. Then he would find other tenants who would take care of the vineyard and pay him his share of the profits.

The religious leaders were clever enough teachers and students of history to realize what Jesus meant. They were the evil tenants. They faced God's punishment for shamefully treating the prophets and for their plans to kill the Son. They used a curse formula to express their reaction. No! Never let this happen. Do not upset our secure and comfortable religious apple cart.

20:17. Jesus subtly continued the battle of authority. He took the authority they held dearest, the Scriptures. He quoted Psalm 118:22. He used their methods of interpretation to push the psalm back at them. The cornerstone or foundation stone was placed at the corner of the building. It bore the weight of the two walls that intersected at the corner. It could be said that it held up the building.

Israel's leaders were supposed to be builders of God's kingdom, equipping God's people to carry out his mission. He sent his Son to them, but they rejected him. They killed him. Now what would happen? God would take Christ, the one they rejected and killed, and establish a whole new building on him. God's vineyard would no longer be in the hands of authorities who were trained by rabbis or authorities based on racial or priestly heredity, or authorities based on leadership experience among the Jews. The new authority would be directly from God through his Son Jesus. On Jesus he would raise the walls of his church. The temple would be destroyed. Gentiles would become part of God's people built on Christ.

20:18. Jesus changed the stone image a bit. The stone changes from being a support system for a building to being a freestanding stone against which you may smash something or under which you may crush something. Either way, it remains an instrument of destruction. Christ thus carries two identities. He is the cornerstone on which the entire weight of the church rests. He is the millstone on which Israel's corrupt religious leaders and religion will be destroyed.

20:19. Infuriated, the religious leaders now had to kill Jesus. They wanted to do it immediately, but a barrier remained. To arrest Jesus was to incite the crowd into a rebellious mob. What was right did not matter. Only two criteria determined their actions: what preserved their authority and what preserved their power base with the people.

◀ The Glory's Wisdom: God or Caesar? (20:20–26)

SUPPORTING IDEA: *Jesus will not fall into a political trap, but he distinguishes between the authority of government and the authority of God.*

20:20. The leaders stepped back. They hired spies to do their dirty work. The spies appeared innocent and pure, but their purpose was not innocent. They wanted to twist Jesus' words so the Roman government would sentence him to death. Surely Roman authority could deal with the authority of a lone individual such as Jesus. They used a two-kingdom question to bring Roman authority against Jesus' authority and to determine who ruled.

20:21. Flattery provided their entry to Jesus. He did not lie. He taught the truth. He ate with Pharisees and sinners, showing no partiality to anyone. He taught the way of God and showed people how to walk in God's will. With ironic flattery these spies acted like they had spied on Jesus and could describe him accurately. They did not mean to give an accurate description, but they did so, thus investing him with an authority they could not claim—the authority of truth.

20:22. Having politely set Jesus up, they asked the "innocent" question. Was it legal for a Jewish citizen to pay taxes to a pagan Roman government? Now they had set Jesus up with an either/or, yes/no answer. As with the either/or problem he posed in verse 4, neither answer was safe. To say the Law of Moses permitted taxes to Rome would be to alienate heavily-taxed people who saw Rome as the intrusive enemy. To say the Law of Moses forbade taxes to Romans would be to commit treason in the eyes of the Roman government and to face the death penalty.

20:23–24. Jesus could not be fooled. He picked right up on their deceit. He turned the question back on them: Look at the coin and tell me whose picture is on it. The spies reached for their moneybags and pulled out a silver denarius minted by the Roman government and used to pay the wages of a day laborer. On it was a picture of Tiberius Caesar and the inscription, "Tiberius Caesar, son of the divine Augustus." The Jewish spies implicated themselves and the leaders who sent them. They dealt in Roman coin. They were involved in Roman commerce and business. They had thus to some degree capitulated to the enemy.

Still, they gladly showed the coin to Jesus. Now he had to answer. No, he had further instructions for the spies. Look at the coin, Jesus told them. Tell me whose picture is on it. Who has the right to determine what is written on the coin? Simple, straightforward answer: Caesar.

20:25. Jesus had a simple retort. Give Caesar what he controls, and give God what he controls. Caesar's image is on coins. Let Caesar have coins. God's image is on people. Let people be devoted to God. This would include all people, for Jesus came to seek and to save the lost. Certainly people are more important to God than things, so Jesus placed devotion to God on a higher plane than devotion to Caesar without indicting himself as opposed to either God or government (see Rom. 13).

20:26. There were no more questions. Jesus could not be trapped. He amazed the spies, the leaders, and the people. Again, Jesus demonstrated his power and authority as he silenced the representatives of Jewish authority and taught about Roman and religious authority.

DResurrection Glory: Silencing the Opposition (20:27–40)

SUPPORTING IDEA: *Resurrection is possible and will soon be exemplified by Jesus, the Son of the living God, who is God of the living, not of the dead.*

20:27. New opponents take center stage: the Sadducees. They appear nowhere else in Luke's Gospel. One trait separated the Sadducees from all other Jewish groups: They denied the resurrection because they could not find it in the five books of Moses, the only books they accepted as Scripture. Other groups turned easily to Daniel 12; Isaiah 26:19; Job 19:26; and Psalm 16:9,11 to prove resurrection in Hebrew Scripture. Seeing their approach, Jesus must have known what to expect.

20:28. First, the Sadducees quoted the Law of Moses, specifically Deuteronomy 25:5 (cf. Ruth 4:1–12). They centered on the practice called levirate marriage in which a brother was obligated to marry his brother's widow and raise children for the deceased.

20:29–32. The priestly Sadducees took the practice of levirate marriage to absurd lengths, through seven husbands. The result: seven dead men; one dead woman; no children.

20:33. Now the clincher to stump Jesus: Whose wife would she be in this resurrection everyone talked about? The question assumed that people live in monogamous marriage relationships in the resurrection and shows how impossible this would be for a situation like they described.

20:34–36. Jesus attacked their assumptions. First, not everyone participates in the resurrection. This is the continuation of his teaching on the kingdom of God, his teaching about the punishment awaiting people like the rich man who ignored Lazarus, and his assault on the religious leaders who would be surprised at the last judgment. Second, life in the next world is not like life in this world. People do not practice marriage relationships after death. Third, since the major focus of marriage is to rear children and fill the earth as in Genesis 1, this will not be necessary for the afterlife, since no one dies there. In this respect, and only in this respect, do people become like angels.

They have put on immortality, whereas angels are created immortal. Here again, Jesus attacked the Sadducees, for they did not believe angels existed. Thus Jesus defanged the Sadducees, taking all the venom from their argument. In so doing he implied the reality of resurrection and set the stage for his own personal proof of the resurrection.

20:37–38. Jesus finished his argument by going back to the Sadducees' own authority, the Law of Moses, specifically Exodus 3:6. Moses referred to God as the God of Abraham, Isaac, and Jacob. In Moses' time, the three patriarchs were long dead. Using typical methods of interpretation of his day, Jesus drew the theological conclusion that God does not have a relationship with dead people but with living people. The implication was that if he could be the God of the patriarchs, the patriarchs must be alive. Obviously, their earthly life was long past, so the life must be one after death, a resurrection life. Only God has power over life, so the resurrected life is a life with God and under his control.

20:39–40. Earlier, the scribes had joined the Pharisees in leading the opposition to Jesus (see 5:21,30; 6:7; 9:22; 11:53; 15:2; 19:47; 20:1,19). Now some of their group complimented Jesus. Does this indicate a break in the ranks? At least Jesus had finally silenced his opponents. They had learned they could not trap Jesus. He was too smart and clever for them. They must accept his authority without determining its source.

E The Identity of the Glory: the Son of David (20:41–44)

SUPPORTING IDEA: *As Messiah, the expected Son of David is greater than David, who calls him Lord.*

20:41–44. Having passed the examination of the various groups of Jewish religious leaders, Jesus then set up a test for them based on Scripture. Citing Psalm 110:1, he used Jewish methods of studying Scripture to identify the Messiah. Israel looked for a Son of David who would occupy the Jerusalem throne and restore Israel's political fortunes. Jesus argued that they had the wrong concept of the Messiah. He is greater than David, with a greater mission than David, since this psalm showed that David called him Lord. You do not call your own son by such an honored name. Originally, David may have uttered the words as he looked forward to a successor who would complete the job he started and do it in such a way that all enemies would be subdued and all warfare would be ended. Jesus used the psalm to say that Messiah had the highest title, that of Lord, used by the Jews in place of pronouncing the divine name. If one is recognized as Messiah, then he is recognized as one greater than David and as one closely associated with God.

Such lofty language about Messiah prepares us as we walk to the cross with Jesus. We are being led closer and closer to the identity of Jesus, the Messiah, the beloved Son of God.

◧ The Glory in Contrast: False Glory Disrobed (20:45–47)

SUPPORTING IDEA: *The glory of God in Christ shows the false sense of glory and pride by the Jewish teachers.*

20:45. Jesus turned once more to teach his disciples, but he had to do so in public. The crowd eavesdropped on his teaching, still hanging on his words.

20:46. Jesus assumed a prophetic teaching role, issuing a prophetic condemnation but directing it to his disciples rather than to the ones condemned. When the going gets rough, Jesus' disciples will be tempted to turn back to the familiarity of Judaism. Jesus reminded them how false this way of life had become. The teachers wanted to be seen for their extraordinary clothing. They wanted everyone to gush over them, eager to greet them and be seen with them in the market. They wanted seats of honor during worship so everyone could see and admire them for their wisdom. At social gatherings they wanted to be seated with the honored guests. All this demonstrated one personality trait: pride ruled their lives. Pride makes a person self-centered. Do you want a self-centered person to teach you? Or would you rather have someone who has shown love and care for you and your needs? Jesus said this on the way to the cross, where he would be stripped of clothing and die for his disciples.

20:47. The Old Testament emphasizes the necessity for the people, especially the religious leaders, to care for widows. The scribes probably had authority as executors of estates for widows. Certainly they had access to funds taken for charity. They may have gone so far as to use legal tactics to rob widows of their houses and other properties. Whatever method they used, they found ways to manipulate widows and their possessions so the scribes got richer and the widows joined the poverty lines. Having so mistreated the needy, they would then go to prayer time and make a public show of their piety.

After outlining their sins in prophetic fashion, Jesus then stated the judgment. They faced greater punishment than all the rest because they had greater responsibility and had not exercised it properly (cf. 19:11–27). To whom much is given, much is required. Yes, Jesus can affirm the reality of resurrection, but not a resurrection of blessing and joy for these religious leaders. They have their glory now. In the world to come, they would face a fate far worse than they imposed on the widows.

> **MAIN IDEA REVIEW:** *Human wisdom cannot entrap Jesus into self-incrimination. Jesus operates from heavenly authority as the beloved Son of God/Son of David who dies for his people and will be the first example of resurrection.*

III. CONCLUSION

Growing Conflict

Jesus taught freely in Jerusalem as he prepared for the cross. Opponents from different directions attempted to trap him and find a way to get the Roman government involved in killing him without raising the ire of the crowd. They used questions of authority, taxation, and resurrection to trap him. Each time he turned the tables on them. Between their questions, he told stories and made prophetic announcements condemning the Jewish leaders for their role in leading Judaism down the wrong path, beating up prophets and killing the beloved Son. These experts in the law had also set a poor moral example, strutting their way through the town while enriching themselves at the expense of widows. Their religion was all show, seeking personal honor and fame. So Jesus prepared them to identify who he was as he walked the Calvary road to glory. He is the Messiah, David's Lord, the beloved Son. We must join the disciples in deciding whom we will follow: self-promoting religious leaders or the cross-carrying Christ.

PRINCIPLES

- You will never outwit or trap God with your schemes.
- God's authority lies behind all Jesus said and did.
- Israel's history of rejecting God's prophets shows why Jesus came into the world.
- Jesus brings salvation glory to those who follow and obey him, but he crushes those who oppose and reject him.
- God's people have responsibilities both to government and to God, but God has highest priority.
- Resurrection life is different from earthly life, but it is just as real under the control of God.
- Jesus is the Messiah, Lord over all, even David.
- Pride, showy piety, and cruel treatment of the poor have no place among citizens of God's kingdom.

APPLICATIONS

- Follow Jesus' authority, not the authority of self-appointed religious experts.
- Acknowledge Jesus as God's beloved Son who died for your sins.
- Be aware that rejecting Jesus leads to punishment.
- Fulfill your obligations and responsibilities to the government.
- Believe in resurrection as a life with God beyond any joyous life you can imagine.
- Confess Christ as your Lord.
- Ask God to forgive you of the sin of pride and to remove all pride from your life.

IV. LIFE APPLICATION

Dying to Save Others

In his book *Dreams at Sunset,* F. W. Boreham takes us to Glenalmond School in Scotland and points to a memorial. Everyone who passes is reminded of the heroism of Alexander Cumine Russell. Having completed his schooling, Russell joined the Highland Light Infantry as an officer. His regiment was assigned to a ship called the Birkenhead. Stormy waters sank the ship. The captain assigned Russell to guide a lifeboat to safety. He warned him that the boat was full and could take on no more passengers.

Russell found himself in deep, murky, stormy waters with a boatload of women. Suddenly, he felt a tug on the oar. A man struggling in the waters grasped the oar and would not let go. Gradually, he pulled himself up so his face became visible above the waters. A shriek pierced the darkness. "Save him! That's my husband," a woman on the lifeboat shouted.

Without hesitation, Russell jumped into the cold water and pushed the man on board. Russell was never seen again. He had voluntarily surrendered his life to save another. As Boreham says, "He had joined that illustrious company of which Jesus is the head, the company of those who, saving others, are unable to save themselves."

So as we walk to the cross, we become more and more prepared for what Jesus will do. Luke 20 shows us some of his glorious identity—led by heavenly authority, wiser and more clever than the religious leaders, assured of the reality of resurrection as a God-protected life, David's Lord and God's beloved Son ready to give his life so others may have eternal life. This is how far he went to seek and to save the lost. Now we must ask how far we have gone to make him Lord of life and to forsake the life of self-interest and pride to follow him to the cross.

V. PRAYER

Lord of the vineyard, forgive me when I have selfishly and proudly rejected your messengers and walked my way instead of your way. Forgive me that I have caused the death of your beloved Son. Help me to assume all the responsibilities you have given me, even the responsibility to support my government. Thank you that I am sure that resurrection awaits me as I walk with you, carrying my cross. You are my Lord. Amen.

VI. DEEPER DISCOVERIES

A. Preaching the Gospel (20:1)

Among all the Gospel writers, Luke emphasizes Jesus' ministry as preaching good news. The term appears only in Matthew 11:5 in Gospels other than Luke. In Luke the angel explained to Zechariah that he had been sent to tell good news (1:19). Again the angel announced good news to the shepherds (2:10). John the Baptist's ministry included telling the good news (3:18). Jesus introduced his ministry at Nazareth as being anointed to preach good news to the poor (4:18). He was constantly aware of the need to share the good news with all the towns (4:43; 8:1; 9:6; 20:1). He replied to John the Baptist's doubts with the evidence that he was preaching good news to the poor (7:22). The good news was that the kingdom of God was at hand and people needed to enter it immediately (16:16). Thus, a major identifying mark of Jesus' ministry for Luke was the preaching of good news, especially to those who were neglected by the religious establishment. This good news offered an invitation to enter God's kingdom and find God's blessing. Luke contrasted this with pious religious leaders, who had received their reward and who must await God's ultimate judgment.

B. Authority (20:2,8)

Jesus' conflict with the religious leaders came down to the issue of authority. Who had the right to teach God's ways to the people of Israel? Who was ordained to declare God's truth and interpret God's Word? What authority and power lay behind all the amazing things Jesus did?

The Greek word for authority (*eksousia*) appears 108 times in the New Testament. Its basic meaning is "power, control, permission, and exercise of authority." It encompasses the right to do something, the freedom to do it, and the ability to do it. This does not refer so much to physical strength (Gr. *dunamis*) as to power in social, political, legal, and moral spheres of life. It is applied only to people, never to natural forces. It refers to the power to give orders (Matt. 8:9; Luke 7:8; 19:7; 20:20), the exercise of such powers (Luke 23:7), or the officers who exercise the power (Luke 12:11; Titus 3:1).

God by his nature has all power. He can judge people and send them to eternal punishment (Luke 12:5). He can do what he likes with what he has made (Rom. 9:21). As risen Lord, Jesus shares God's authority and exercises it over all rivals to authority (Eph. 1:21; 1 Pet. 3:22).

Satan also has power and exercises it in controlling this world, but that power is limited by God (Luke 22:53). The earthly Jesus showed this power over Satan and the demonic powers as he cast out demons (Luke 4:36) and forgave sin (Luke 5:18–26). Jesus' authority stood apart from all earthly authority. He taught in a unique way that amazed the professional scholars and teachers (Luke 4:32). Such authority came directly from the Father and the personal relationship between Father and Son (Luke 10:22). Thus, Jesus could claim all authority and power in heaven and on earth (Matt. 28:18).

The New Testament consistently teaches the unique authority of Jesus, challenging readers to accept or deny such authority. If Jesus has the authority he claims for himself, then he is the Son of God, deity incarnate, and must be worshiped and obeyed. But as Luke 20 shows clearly, such authority was not something to be flaunted in the face of others, nor was it to be revealed to those who had no intention of acknowledging the authority or of having faith in Jesus as bearer of God's authority. To these, Jesus refused to reveal the nature of his authority (see O. Betz, "Might, Authority, Throne," *Theological Dictionary of the New Testament*, ed. Colin Brown, II, 601–611).

C. Vineyards (20:9–14)

The Bible frequently uses the terms *vine* and *vineyard* as symbols. *Vine* is often used in speaking of Israel. In the New Testament, Jesus often used a vineyard as an analogy for the kingdom of God (Matt. 20:1–16). Those who hope to enter the kingdom must be like the son who at first refused to work in his father's vineyard but later repented and went (Matt. 21:28–32). Ultimately, Jesus himself is described as the "true vine" and his disciples (Christians) as the branches (John 15:1–11).

Jesus, in his parable in Luke 20, showed that the vineyard is God's gift to Israel. This gift includes the gift of the covenant and the promise for future renewal. In this parable the tenants revolted against the owner's messengers, even killing the owner's son. It is a picture of Israel's rejection of Jesus.

D. Capstone (20:17)

Jesus used Psalm 118:22 to give scriptural authority to his claim that he must be killed before he could exercise his total authority. The quotation expressed such authority and power in figurative terms as the cornerstone. This is not a final capstone on the building but the foundation stone on which two walls intersect and from which the building gains its strength. Both Hebrew and Greek express this literally as "the head of the corner." The figure of speech comes from architecture. It refers to the building block around which the entire building was constructed. The ability of the structure to withstand attack from natural or human forces depends on the integrity of the cornerstone. God's plan for building up Israel as his eternal people on mission to seek and save the lost centered on establishing Jesus as the cornerstone on which the entire plan of salvation is built. Sadly, Israel rejected Jesus. They wanted to build a kingdom of their own based on obedience to their interpretations of the law and on their authority over the worship and life of the nation. Despite such rejection, Jesus still became the cornerstone of God's new temple, his new people, the church (Eph. 2:20).

E. The Tribute (20:22–26)

A tribute is any payment exacted by a superior power, usually a state, from an inferior power. In this case, the tribute was an annual poll tax levied by the Roman authorities. The imposition of this despised tax led to a Jewish rebellion under Judas the Galilean (see Acts 5:37). The Romans required payment of the tax with a special coin that featured the likeness of the Roman emperor.

F. Sadducees 20:27

The term *Sadducees* means "the righteous ones." They were in charge of the temple and its services, and they viewed only the Torah (Law) as their authority. They opposed oral law. Many relate the name of the Sadducees to Zadok, the high priest during the days of David and Solomon. The children of Zadok comprised the priestly hierarchy during the time of captivity (2 Chr. 31:10), and the name persisted as the title of the priestly party during the days of Christ.

Historically, the Sadducees developed from the priestly supporters of the Hasmonean dynasty during the intertestamental period. Sadducees accepted the Torah or Law as having a higher authority than the prophets and the writings in the Hebrew Bible. Smaller in number than the Pharisees, they were antisupernaturalists who did not believe in a bodily resurrection and denied the existence of spirits and angels (Mark 12:18–27). In the New Testament, the Sadducees were wealthy political opportunists who joined with any group who could assist them in retaining power and influence. They were the priestly party, and their influence disappeared with the destruction of the temple in A.D. 70.

VII. TEACHING OUTLINE

A. INTRODUCTION

1. Lead Story: Who Is He?
2. Context: Jesus finally entered Jerusalem. Ministry in Jerusalem switched from confrontation and testing by the Jewish authorities to

daily teaching and evangelizing in the temple area. Jewish leaders of all types joined forces to destroy Jesus. They sought a reason for the Roman government to put him to death and for the crowds to quit hanging on his words and start joining the chorus to crucify him. They asserted their authority over his, their knowledge of Scripture, their doctrine or lack of doctrine of the resurrection, their loyalty to God as contrasted to loyalty to Rome. They wanted Jesus to say something that alienated the people and infuriated Rome. Jesus in wisdom and craft sidetracked their questions and trapped them with counter questions. Finally, silencing them, he issued a prophetic judgment on their pride, injustice, and false piety.

3. Transition: The church stands in some ways much like the temple and synagogue of Jesus' day. It lives under financial stress and need for public image. It wants to grow and meet human expectations of success. It is tempted to use human methods to transform the meaning of Scripture to justify its actions. Its leaders face a world where leading corresponds to a big ego trip and a display of success symbols. We are tempted to measure ourselves in the same way the Bible-teaching scribes did. Luke 20 challenges us to measure our church by the cross-carrying Jesus, the beloved Son who died because of our sin.

B. COMMENTARY

1. The Glory's Authority: Parallel to John's Authority (20:1–8)
    a. The setting: teaching and preaching the gospel in the temple (20:1a)
    b. The opponents' reaction: unauthorized actions (20:1b–2)
    c. The Master's response: who gave John authority? (20:3–4)
    d. The opponents' counter response: do not know (20:5–7)
    e. The Master's counter response: I am not talking (20:8)
2. The Result of Rejecting the Glory: Punishment (20:9–19)
    a. The setting: Master teaching people (20:9a)
    b. The Master's teaching: unfaithful tenants hurt messengers and kill beloved son (20:9b–15a)
    c. The owner's response: kill and replace the tenants (20:15b–16a)
    d. The people's response: impossible (20:16b)
    e. The Master's counter response: Scripture points to cornerstone that supports and crushes (20:17–18)
    f. The opponents reaction: kill him but fear the people (20:19)
3. The Glory's Wisdom: God or Caesar? (20:20–26)
    a. The setting: opponents' spies sent to trap Jesus (20:20)
    b. The opponents' trick question: pay taxes? (20:21–22)

    c.   The Master's response: whose image is on coin? (20:23–24)

    d.   The opponents' quick reply: Caesar's (20:25a)

    e.   The Master's counter response: give each his due (20:25b)

    f.   The opponents' counter reply: silence (20:26)

4.   Resurrection Glory: Silencing the Opposition (20:27–40)

    a.   The setting: questioning Master's theology (20:27)

    b.   The opponents' question: which of seven husbands is hers in resurrection? (20:28–33)

    c.   The Master's response: new lifestyle in resurrection (20:34–38)

    d.   The opponents' reaction: no more questions (20:39–40)

5.   The Identity of the Glory: The Son of David (20:41–44)

    a.   The setting: Master teaching (20:41a)

    b.   The Master's teaching: how can Messiah be David's son and Lord? (20:41b-44)

6.   The Glory in Contrast: False Glory Disrobed (20:45–47)

    a.   The setting: crowds eavesdrop as Jesus teaches disciples (20:45)

    b.   The Master's teaching: judgment on hypocritical teachers and their false piety (20:46–47)

C. CONCLUSION: DYING TO SAVE OTHERS

VIII. ISSUES FOR DISCUSSION

1.   Describe Jesus' authority. How does he exercise authority over you and your church today?

2.   Why did God have to send Jesus to die?

3.   What responsibility do you have to pay taxes and support your government?

4.   What will be different about life in heaven from life on earth?

5.   What does it mean to you to say that Jesus is the Messiah and Lord?

6.   In what ways do you display worldly pride and success symbols rather than helping the poor and needy?

7.   How would Jesus describe your prayer life?

Luke 21

The Future Glory

"*The* believer becomes essentially one who hopes. He is still future to 'himself' and is promised to himself. His future depends utterly and entirely on the outcome of the risen Lord's course, for he has staked his future on the future of Christ."

Jurgen Moltman

Luke 21

IN A NUTSHELL

Persecution, the destruction of Jerusalem, and heavenly signs will point the way to the return of Christ to establish fully the kingdom of God. Pray that you will be ready when this happens.

The Future Glory

II

I. INTRODUCTION

The Dream Prepared Me

*C*harlie Shedd tells of a trip to Europe with a magical stop in Wolfsburg, Germany, the home of Volkswagen, where he bought his son a new car for graduation. That night in one of those immaculately clean magazine-picture bed-and-breakfast spots, Charlie had the most unusual dream of his life. Son Peter kept driving his Volkswagen in and out of the dream. Somehow, the dream placed them in Copenhagen, Denmark. There the hotel-keeper had a message: "Grandma died; please return to the States."

Now the question: what to do with the dream. He shared it with Martha, his wife, at breakfast. Then at dinner in Hamburg, Germany, he felt the need to tell his boys. Young Timothy did not like it and showed his fear. Older Peter came through philosophically with the wisdom of youth: "But Tim, Grandma is eighty-one. Let's face it. She is going to die some time."

The next day they visited Grandma's hometown. She had immigrated to Iowa at age 21 from Odense, Denmark. They saw all the landmarks of Grandma's childhood and ate with her relatives who stayed behind. Then on to Copenhagen on Saturday. There the hotel clerk did have a message: "Important. Call Mr. Petersen, Portland, Oregon, immediately."

So Charlie hurriedly called his brother-in-law. "Charlie, I am sorry to tell you that Mom died this morning. Pastor Tange said she ate a hearty breakfast, went to her room, and died."

Charlie Shedd writes, "For a long time we sat there sharing our feelings. We cried. We prayed. Especially we thanked God for three days of preparation by way of 'our' dream."

Jesus' disciples needed no dream to see the future. Jesus outlined it for them in broad strokes. His Word prepares us to get ready for his return.

II. COMMENTARY

The Future Glory

MAIN IDEA: *Christ is coming again and has given us the signs that ought to make us pray and get ready for his coming to establish his kingdom.*

A The Stewardship of Glory: Bankrupting False Glory (21:1–4)

SUPPORTING IDEA: *Stewardship is judged on what you have left, not what you give.*

21:1. In the temple, teaching as usual during these final days, Jesus noticed the rich dropping their offerings into the temple coffers. The way they did it, one could hardly fail to notice them. They did this as they prayed (20:47) for show, to be seen by others.

21:2. Jesus did not focus on the rich. He zeroed in on a poor widow. She had two lepta, each worth about one one-hundredth of a denarius, the coin used for a day laborer's daily wage. Thus, her contribution to the temple was tiny in terms of monetary value.

21:3. But her two lepta had spiritual power. They form the subject for teaching Christian stewardship to this day. Why are they so important? Jesus valued these "worthless" coins as worth more than all the rich people had put in.

21:4. Jesus' reasoning is simple. The rich gave from their abundance, leaving much more for themselves. The widow gave from abject poverty, leaving nothing for herself. They gave out of discretionary funds. She gave her bread money. Giving is judged by the degree of sacrifice.

B The Future Glory: Signs of the Times (21:5–38)

SUPPORTING IDEA: *Christ will return in glory, following the signs he listed, and he expects his people to be ready for his return.*

21:5. The Jews gloried in the beauty and wonder of their temple. In the time of Jesus, repairs continued to fulfill the dreams of Herod the Great, who had rebuilt the temple along with other massive building projects. Josephus says Herod adorned the temple with white marble stones up to sixty-seven feet long, eighteen feet wide, and twelve feet high. The special gifts or offerings that decorated the temple included silver and gold gates and doors. Beautiful Babylonian tapestries veiled the entrance to the temple.

21:6. Adamantly, Jesus repeated his warning (19:41–44) that the total destruction of the temple was eminent.

21:7. A group of Jesus' followers asked when this would happen. They wanted to know, How will we know? What signs will warn us?

21:8. Jesus was not the only person who promised big signs for the future. Many teachers of that time claimed to have more knowledge than Jesus did. They wanted to name dates and places. They wanted people to follow them as God's Messiah. They were even audacious enough to use the mysterious divine name "I Am" (Gr. *ego eimi*) from Exodus 3:14 to describe themselves. Jesus could call this "My name," for he often used it in John's Gospel.

One word described these false messiahs: deceivers. Jesus gave one piece of advice about them: do not follow. The one who called people to "follow me" now said, "Do not follow them."

21:9. Wars and revolutions always excite people. This would be especially true for people who wanted someone, anyone, to overthrow the Roman government. Jesus reminded them that such was business as usual. Every generation has its wars or at least its rumors of wars. These are not signs of the end, though they must, by divine necessity, take place before the end comes.

21:10. International disturbance and fighting will take place. This is part of history leading to the end, but it is not the end.

21:11. Nature will join in giving signs. Earthquakes, famines, and plagues around the world should remind God's people that he controls nature and he has the power to bring it all to a halt. Not only does he have the power, but he has promised to do so one day. Be attentive to nature's signs, and know the end is coming.

What is more, the heavens will join in. In the skies you will see sights that terrify you, Jesus declared. You will realize that these heavenly happenings are signs to you that the end is on its way, but not yet!

21:12. Before international warfare and natural chaos come, the church will face persecution, Jesus continued. Belief in Christ and his name will be cause enough for you to be put in jail and punished by the government. Jewish religious leaders will join force with the government to make this happen.

21:13. And how will we respond to such an ominous moment? We can use it as an opportunity to tell about Jesus. Persecution will carry us into the highest government circles to plead our case. When this happens, tell even the governor about Jesus. We are not there to defend ourselves. We are there to be sure everyone knows about Jesus. We can tell them about Jesus by showing how Jesus is responsible for our being where we are—in prison.

21:14. Talk of persecution and imprisonment may scare you, Jesus said. Do not worry. The signs of the end are not given to you so you will have some special secret knowledge. They remind you how to act as the end approaches. You do not have to write out a prepared defense before the judge. You do not have to write out your testimony and know exactly what you are going to say about Jesus.

21:15. All you need do is trust Jesus. He will give you exactly the words to say, exactly when you need to say to them. You will have God's wisdom with you. No one can contradict your testimony or refute your evidence when you are on the witness stand. No one who accuses you will have the resource of wisdom that I will give you. Trust me. Do not fear. You will be able to defend yourself honorably and wisely.

21:16. Jesus did not mean to imply that all this would be easy. Jesus told them he was about to be betrayed. You will be betrayed, too, he told them. Your best friends and your closest family members will turn you over to the enemy. They will kill some of you. This is not easy, but it is a time to build your faith and trust. Pain will last for a moment, but glory will be yours for eternity.

21:17. This is not a popularity contest, Jesus continued. You are not running for office or trying to make as many friends as possible. You are testifying for Jesus. You are being an example of faith in God and faith in Jesus. You see how the religious leaders attack me and hate me. You will face the same. Yes, you will be greatly hated. Not because of who you are, but because of who I am. Are you ready for this?

21:18. Remember, we are talking about end time, Jesus went on. You will be persecuted. You may die, but nothing will be ultimately destroyed. God is protecting you for eternal life with him.

21:19. The flip side of God's protection is your endurance, he declared. I am giving you these signs so you will not be surprised. You will remember I told you they were coming. You will not yield to temptation to join the world or the devil. You are to remain true to me through all persecution and catastrophe. Only by such perseverance can you gain your life for eternity. Remember, I warned you these things were coming. Keep the faith. Trust me through everything. Stay under God's protection.

21:20. These things will start quite soon, Jesus continued. You will see enemy armies surround Jerusalem. Do not look for deliverance. God is not planning on delivering the city that will betray and crucify his Son. Jerusalem faces destruction.

21:21. Do not think Jerusalem has some holy power to save you, Jesus warned. Do not run back into the city for security. Do not hide in the city for safety. Get out of the city. Go, hide in the mountains. Stay out of the city no matter what you do. Jerusalem will be destroyed. Do not be destroyed with it.

21:22. How can God do such things to the holy city, David's city, Messiah's city? God sees Jerusalem in a different light, Jesus pointed out. Jerusalem rejected and mistreated the prophets. Jerusalem will reject and kill the beloved Son. Jerusalem has turned temple worship into big business. Jerusalem's religious leaders practice religion for show and personal gain. The prophets have warned you over and over again what will happen to a disobedient, sinful Jerusalem. Their Scripture is now being fulfilled. Jerusalem has called down God's wrath in judgment. God will take out his vengeance on Jerusalem. The city faces imminent destruction.

21:23. Woes in Luke foreshadow disaster and suffering (6:24–26; 10:13; 11:42–47,52; 17:1; 22:22). The woe appears here unexpectedly, for it is on pregnant women and nursing mothers, those who populate the earth. These people are in fragile physical condition, and thus are more vulnerable. This woe does not represent a condemnation of these as especially wicked people, as woes often do. This represents a cry of grief and empathy for the suffering these special women will have to endure in this awful moment in Jerusalem's history.

21:24. Traditional wartime atrocities picture what Jerusalem's citizens and especially the young mothers will suffer. The sword will kill some. Long marches into foreign captivity await others. Unclean, impure, idolatrous foreigners will control Jerusalem, trampling everything left under their feet. But remember! This is the beginning part of God's signs, Jesus declared. Jerusalem's defeat will not mean God has been defeated. Nor does it mean God has lost control of history even for a moment. God has predicted this decades before it happened. He has set up a time for the Gentiles to reign over the city. Everything will follow his plan. That way you will know early on that God's Word is true as it paints the signs of the end for you.

21:25. Jesus seems here to revert to the original description in verse 11. Here he becomes more specific about the heavenly signs that lead up to the end times. He takes over Old Testament language (Pss. 46:2–4; 65:7; 89:9; 107:23–32; Isa. 13:9–10; 17:12; 24:18–20; 34:4; Ezek. 32:7–8; Joel 2:10,30–31; 3:15; Hag. 2:6,21). Sun, moon, and stars will bring warnings. This probably refers to eclipses, comets, and shooting stars. Such signs will fill the earth with fear and a sense of being trapped with no place to escape. No nation will be exempt. The whole earth will stand perplexed as seas and oceans pound their roaring waves onto the beaches.

21:26. The heavenly signs will cause people to swoon in fear. Not knowing that I have told you the signs that must come before the end, Jesus said, they will have no source to trust and no reason for hope. They will be frightened to death.

21:27. Finally the end comes, Jesus continued. The great sign of the end is the return of Jesus, the Son of Man. You will see the full power and glory of Jesus. Yes, in Jesus God's full glory will be revealed to the earth. All the earth will see. This will bring greater fear and consternation to those who are unprepared, but not for you.

21:28. How will you react when this occurs? Jesus asked. You will know this is the sign I told you about. Do not bend over with fear and trembling. Stand up straight. Lift your head high. Why? Now your redemption is near. Persecution is over. Dying for Jesus' name is past history. The Redeemer has come in full glory. He has your rewards. Now you will know for sure why you endured all you had to endure. No longer must you live by faith. Now you see the Redeemer coming to judge and rule the earth.

21:29–30. At last, Jesus resorted to his favorite teaching method to try to prepare his followers for the end time. The fig tree is a sign for us. In winter it stands bare of leaves, a stark sign of the barren winter. Then it finally puts on leaves. Now everyone can tell summer is near. These signs of nature we can read easily.

21:31. If you can read nature's signs like the fig tree, Jesus said, you can also read the signs I am describing. When these things happen, you can be sure that God's kingdom is coming to you in all its fullness. Be prepared to see the signs and know the kingdom is coming.

21:32–33. Here Jesus gave us one of his most difficult sayings to understand. He had pointed to things far beyond A.D. 70, forty years after his death. Now he said everything would take place before this generation of people died out. How do we understand this? One thing is sure. The saying is paired in contrast with the next saying (v. 33), where the strong emphasis lies. The signs point to the time when heaven and earth will pass away. Then one thing remains: God's Word. You can trust God's Word above everything else on earth. What God has said will happen. Signs he gives will come to pass. The truths he teaches are true. His demands for obedience must be obeyed, since the judgment he threatens will be enforced.

If this verse is to be believed, then verse 32 must be true, but how? Scholars have argued for centuries over this. Many views have come forward. (1) Jesus' coming to destroy Jerusalem in A.D. 70 before all that generation died fulfills the saying, but the saying in no way limits itself to that one sign. (2) Jesus made a prediction that was correct but he used hyperbole in specifying the time to get the people's attention and to make them obey. (3) The destruction of Jerusalem began the signs that continue to appear, so that that generation saw the beginning of the end times. (4) This generation means this nation, the Jews, or even the human race. (5) The statement is like so much prophecy that foreshortens history or uses one event in history as a type for a future event of greater magnitude, so that the destruction of Jerusalem in A.D. 70 becomes a type of the final catastrophes leading to the coming of the Son of Man and of the kingdom. (6) The disciples are representatives of God's people in the last generation, so this becomes a promise that all the signs will take place quickly within the lifespan of that one generation.

What can we conclude about these verses? With such a complex and divided history of scholarship, we must be humble and admit from the beginning that any conclusion we reach is tentative and far from final. Following is an approach that tries to take seriously the authority of Scripture and the difficulty of understanding the text.

The time span here corresponds to what has been said in the first part of this end-time discourse. More than just the fall of Jerusalem must be in view.

Jesus spoke here as a prophet. He sought to impress on the generation to which he spoke the need for immediate action and change of attitude. As the prophetic word often had more than one moment of fulfillment, so Jesus' word was open to subsequent fulfillments that make it relevant to each new generation. The A.D. 70 fulfillment for that generation showed the true and fearsome power of Jesus' prophetic warning. What happened once can happen again. End-time signs reappear throughout history. The final end time will fulfill the words in even more dramatic fashion than our most creative imagination can picture.

Jesus' words will never pass away. Their warning pictured events that his generation faced and saw as the most drastic moment in the nation's history and the end of the nation's hope for self-rule and power among the nations. Their warning pictured the plight of the church under the same evil government that destroyed Jerusalem. In A.D. 68–70 the church certainly saw the coming of Jesus to fulfill his words of warning. This was not the ultimate coming of the Son of Man in glory, but it was one coming to bring to pass what he prophesied.

In summary, the generation to which Jesus spoke saw a massive act of God bringing final destruction on his holy city and its magnificent temple— destruction that in many ways outdid the turmoil and terror of Babylon's capture of the holy city in 586 B.C. The church of that generation saw God's power directing them through persecution and empowering them to witness under unpleasant conditions. The believers of that generation saw the destruction of Jerusalem as a manifestation of the Son of Man coming in power to fulfill his prophecy. All of this together represented the first fulfillment of Christ's prophecy, but certainly not the last. Jesus pointed to A.D. 70 and used it as a precursor for the final end time coming in glory to bring judgment to the whole world.

As Bock (*Baker Exegetical Commentary on the New Testament,* 1675) describes Luke's emphasis: "It would seem that Luke sees in Jerusalem's collapse a preview, but with less intensity, of what the end will be like. . . . He wants to make clear that when Jerusalem falls the first time, it is not yet the end. Nonetheless, the two falls are related, and the presence of one pictures what the ultimate siege will be like. Both are eschatological events in God's plan, with the fall of Jerusalem being the down payment and guarantee of the end-time."

21:34. The conclusion of the matter is not a review of signs to be sure you caught each one, Jesus pointed out. It is an ethical commandment to be sure you prepare yourself for the days to come. Two things may easily distract you and make you forget and/or miss the signs and not be prepared for the return of Jesus. The first of these is drunken parties in which you dull your mind with alcohol until you have no capacity to think about Jesus and his coming. The second is the stress of life so that you concentrate so much on worldly matters and your position in the world that you forget that this world is not eternal and that your eternal life depends on your readiness for the next world. Jesus has given you the signs. You have no excuse not to be ready. He has warned you of ways that will keep you from being ready. Do not get caught up in drunken partying or in this world's stress. Keep your eye on the signs of the times.

21:35. If you follow the two errant ways of life, Jesus continued, you will find yourself in a trap. Also, do not think you can escape the second coming and its judgment. It comes on the whole earth. Everyone is involved and no one escapes.

21:36. Jesus' emphasis is not on knowledge but on action. Pray! Stay alert! Ask God for strength to escape the persecutions and wars and destructions. Pray that you may be one of those fortunate ones who sees the Son of Man when he returns. Then you will stand before him as he judges the world, and you will receive the reward coming to his faithful ones who maintain their faith, trust, and testimony through all the hard signs.

21:37. Having given the signs of the end times, Jesus did what he expected his disciples to do. He returned to his daily routine of faithful service to God. He taught in the temple. At night he retreated to the Mount of Olives, probably to Bethany with his friends Mary, Martha, and Lazarus.

21:38. The Jewish leaders continued to try to kill him, but they could not because of the people. They converged around him each morning to hear his authoritative teaching about the kingdom of God. A chasm had formed between the Jewish people and their leaders. The people hung on his words, but the leaders wanted to kill him.

MAIN IDEA REVIEW: *Christ is coming again and has given us the signs that ought to make us pray and get ready for his coming to establish his kingdom.*

III. CONCLUSION

Watch and Pray

It has been two thousand years, and no generation has yet seen the signs of the last times. Maybe it is time to give up on this and look elsewhere for truth about the nature, endurance, and end of our universe. Luke 21 shows that Jesus was well aware of this temptation. He constantly warned us to be alert and pray, not to be led astray by doubters. We are to be as faithful in watching as the widow was in giving. The first signs have happened.

Jerusalem has been destroyed and occupied. Have any of the other signs come? Once these begin, we can expect the other signs to follow quickly—so quickly that we will not have time to change our mind. Our preparedness now determines our place in God's kingdom at the end. Reason may say, Forget it. Faith says, Trust him. The kingdom is coming. Watch for the signs.

PRINCIPLES

- God expects us to give our best and our all to him.
- Signs of the times will help us realize the end is near so we can make final preparations for Jesus' return; meanwhile, alertness and prayer are the right attitudes and actions.
- Deceivers will always try to gain glory and power by pointing to false signs of the last times.
- Persecution is certain, but even in persecution Christians can depend on God for the right words to use in testifying to him.
- Jesus' followers can expect persecution and death in this world, but God will protect them for the next life.
- Betrayal by friends and relatives is inevitable for followers of Jesus.
- God's Word is true and can be trusted for now and eternity.

APPLICATIONS

- Count how much you can give to Jesus, not how much you can keep for yourself.
- Do not depend on fortresses or beautiful architecture for protection from the final punishment.
- Pray that God will give you strength and protection for the last days.
- Be alert to what is happening and be prepared to stand before your Judge as a faithful and true follower.
- Forgive those who betray you.
- Learn to read God's signs.
- Study and trust God's Word.

IV. LIFE APPLICATION

Making the Choice

Jim Jones . . . Waco . . . sidewalk preachers . . . people on a mountain in Tennessee . . . television hucksters . . . you add to the examples. Our time has seen so many people led astray. Charismatic leaders and smooth talkers become convinced they have read the signs of the times. They can give dates and places. The end of the world is coming. How many cartoons make fun of such predictions? How many tragedies have resulted from such predictions?

Luke 21 merits our close attention. It assures us that enough signs are there to cause us to prepare. But its emphasis is not on setting a date and getting in the right place. The biblical emphasis of its apocalyptic, end-time materials is almost always ethical. Get your life in order. Pray. Stay awake and alert. Do not get involved in drunken parties. Do not let the temptations and stresses of life encompass you. Pray that you may have strength to escape the persecution and death. Be ready to stand before the Son of Man as he brings the last judgment.

It is simple to condemn those who go off the deep end with dates and places and withdrawal from normal living. Jesus invites us back into the everyday routine of life—but back with a consciousness that this routine is not the central part of life. You must choose what is central. Does life center on drunken parties and the stresses of life in this world? Or does life center on Christ and on waiting for him to return? Are you ready? Pray!

V. PRAYER

God, who holds all eternity in your hands, thank you that you care enough to show us the signs that must come before you come again. Wake us up. Do not let us slumber. Forgive our sins. Show us how to be alert for your signs. Show us how to be prepared to stand before the Son of Man at the last judgment. Give us faith in you. Amen.

VI. DEEPER DISCOVERIES

A. The Fall of Jerusalem to the Romans (21:5)

Much to the shock of his disciples, Jesus predicted the destruction of Jerusalem. He told them that "the time will come when not one stone will be left on another; every one of them will be thrown down" (Luke 21:6). The Jerusalem in which Jesus walked was destroyed by the Roman general Titus in A.D. 70 after zealous Jews revolted against Rome. As Jesus had predicted, not one stone of the temple building remained standing on another, and widespread destruction engulfed the city. A second revolt in A.D. 135 (the Bar-Kochba Rebellion) resulted in Jews being excluded from the city.

B. Desolation (21:20)

Matthew (24:15) and Mark (13:14) quote Jesus in his end-time discourse as saying that people would see an "abomination that causes desolation" in the temple. Luke does not use this technical term. Rather, he speaks more generally of the desolation Jerusalem will suffer from besieging armies. Greek literature uses the related verb to speak of the depopulation of a city or a vineyard wasted by weeds. In a series of woes on "Babylon," Revelation 18:17 uses the verb to speak of loss of a city's wealth. Jesus thus warned Jerusalem that great danger awaited them—a danger that would destroy the city and leave it desolate.

C. The Times of the Gentiles (21:24)

Old Testament prophets pointed to times when foreign kings such as those from Assyria, Babylonia, and Persia would overthrow God's people and take them captive. Daniel took this to its ultimate depiction (Dan. 2:44; 8:13–14; 12:5–13). Jesus could point to Scripture that said Gentiles, or foreigners, would rule God's people. Among the Gospels, only Luke uses the exact phrase, "the times of the Gentiles."

The phrase apparently has a double focus. First, it underlines the totality of Israel's coming destruction, with Gentiles taking control of all of the promised land. Second, it implies that this time is limited, so that in God's time the Gentiles will be defeated and face judgment as they were instruments of Israel's judgment.

Interpreters who seek to develop a thorough eschatological chronology and framework see this as pointing to the time of Israel's millennial restoration. Such exegesis requires a fuller exposition than space permits here.

D. Redemption (21:28)

The concept of redemption is vitally related to the themes of liberation, deliverance, and ransom. The Greek word *apolutrosis* means "release for the payment of a price." In fact, the term *redemption* was used of the ransom for a slave. Luke probably used this word to mean the *consummation of the hopes and promises for God's people*. Luke's readers would have understood redemption as involving salvation in its fullest sense.

Redemption is the reason Christian's can "stand up and lift up [their] heads." As redeemer, Jesus breaks the power of sin and creates a new and obedient heart by delivering us from the power of sin, guilt, death, and Satan. Christians are a people who have been bought with a price (1 Pet. 1:18). In the last days, they can be even more encouraged because their redemption is coming.

E. "Be Always on the Watch" (21:34–36)

The verb translated "be always on the watch" means to "pay attention, be on the alert, be on guard." This verb is in the imperative mood, which is used in New Testament Greek to express a command or exhortation. Jesus will return, and when he does, he will establish his kingdom on the earth. The consequences of sin will be removed. For those who have rejected Jesus, his return will be a day that will close on them unexpectedly like a trap. Jesus' followers are always to be "on the watch." In the context of Luke 21, this phrase is best understood as revealing the means by which we can be watchful—by praying.

VII. TEACHING OUTLINE

A. INTRODUCTION

1. Lead Story: The Dream Prepared Me
2. Context: Having silenced the Jewish teachers in their attempts to entrap him and find reason for the Roman government to sentence him to death, Jesus turned to teach his disciples. Two things about the temple caught his attention and led to his most serious teaching on the difference between temporal and eternal and on the signs of the end time. The false religion of the leaders in giving their gifts to the temple contrasted starkly with the sacrificial gift of the poor widow. Her kind, the religious leaders "devour" (20:47). Then the disciples began admiring Herod's wonderful new temple. Jesus reminded them that the temple would not last forever. In fact, nothing but God's Word will last forever. This would lead them to the signs of the end and show them the way to act as the end time approaches.
3. Transition: The year 2000 choked our generation with fear, panic, and wonder. What would happen? Does the millennial year signal the year of Christ's return? Much talk about last things resulted. Thus, we have heard all sorts of theories and ideas about the end time. Luke 21 invites us to review what we believe about the end time. More importantly, it invites us to check our readiness for Christ's return.

B. COMMENTARY

1. The Stewardship of Glory: Bankrupting False Glory (21:1–4)
   a. The setting: temple offerings of the rich (21:1)
   b. The scene: widow giving everything (21:2)
   c. The Master's response: her gift most valuable (21:3–4)
2. The Future Glory: Signs of the Times (21:5–38)
   a. The setting: followers admire temple (21:5)
   b. The Master's response: a passing fancy (21:6)
   c. The followers' reactions: when will it be? (21:7)

d. The Master's teaching: catastrophes, persecution, false teachers, faithfulness (21:8–36)

e. Summary: life facing the time of redemption is time of teaching and listening (21:37–38)

C. CONCLUSION: MAKING THE CHOICE

VIII. ISSUES FOR DISCUSSION

1. What kind of giving pattern would you need in order to meet the standard set by the widow in the temple?
2. How do you answer someone who asks, "When will these things happen?"
3. What do you look for when you look for the signs that the kingdom of God is coming?
4. What does it mean that your redemption is drawing near?
5. How do you understand what Jesus referred to in verse 32?
6. What is the most important thing you have learned from studying the signs of the end time? How will this affect your daily life?

Luke 22

Opposing the Glory

Quote

"*Life's* not fair!' You hear it everywhere—on the playground, the athletic field, in the office, in the entertainment world, in medicine, even in the Bible. . . . Lawyers, spouses, children, students . . . you name it—no one has been immune from the feelings of injustice. Life's unfairness touches everyone at one time or another."

Robert Schuller

Luke 22

IN A NUTSHELL

*S*atan got to Jesus' disciple and friend. Judas betrayed him to the Jewish religious leaders. In a mockery of fairness and justice, they arrested and charged Jesus with blasphemy. Meanwhile, Jesus prepared the disciples for his death at the Last Supper and prepared himself in prayer on the Mount of Olives. Still, Peter went out and denied him three times, and the Jewish guards mocked him. The Jerusalem teaching ministry was over. The Passion had begun.

Opposing the Glory

I. INTRODUCTION

The Day the World Disintegrated

*B*illy Graham (*Hope for the Troubled Heart*, 41) introduces us to Gretchen, the lady whose sun-filled life disintegrated one day. Gretchen had everything—beauty, wealth, an attentive, caring husband. She fulfilled every girl's dream of "what I want to be when I grow up." Then one morning a drunk driver crossed Gretchen's path, launching Gretchen's car into a fatal spin. The car hurtled across the freeway and exploded in a burning inferno. Gretchen's mother died instantly. Some would say what Gretchen suffered was worse than death. The beautiful face disappeared forever. A blank socket had replaced her beautiful gleaming eye. Her nose showed signs of total reconstruction. Her blemish-free, smooth-as-silk skin was covered with scars. A missing arm gave a final reminder of the horrible accident.

In the face of such injustice, what did Gretchen do? Recovering from her coma after six weeks, she discovered her new appearance and circumstances. All she could imagine doing was hiding. She wanted no one to see her. She endured over seventy operations. She retreated solely into the world of television. There she saw a Billy Graham crusade and gave her life to Christ.

Now seven years after the horrendous experience, she was ready to come out of hiding and face the world with her scarred, mutilated face. She realized life still had purpose. Rescuing her from death, God had a reason for her life. She volunteered at a rehabilitation center. There she met others for whom life had been quite unfair. They saw her face and knew she understood their experiences. A ministry developed. Now when asked what her greatest joy in life has been, she does not have to retreat to the distant past where life was full of sunshine and dreams. She states quickly and firmly, "My greatest joy is waking up in the morning and knowing that nothing is an accident."

People who consider the events in Luke 22 might ask how these could be anything but unfair accidents. The man who had stirred up the entire nation by doing good for them saw the nation's leaders turn against him, trump up false charges against him, mock him, and get ready to kill him. He saw the leader of his own disciples deny ever knowing him. Life got down to a bitter reality. It is not fair. All that was left was his communication with the Father. God had revealed his glory, and the world could not stand its beauty.

II. COMMENTARY

Opposing the Glory

> **MAIN IDEA:** *Jesus experienced the unfair, unjust nature of earthly existence in his betrayal, arrest, unfair trial, and in his denial by the leader of his band of disciples. Still, he showed the world that he was the Son of God.*

Ⓐ The Glory Meets Opposition: Betrayal (22:1–6)

> **SUPPORTING IDEA:** *In God's timing, Jesus' teaching ministry ended and the unfair trial began as Satan used a disciple and friend to betray Jesus.*

22:1. Jesus met the world's injustice head-on at Israel's most holy moment, the Passover celebration. Israel prepared to remember and commemorate God's saving acts in Egypt that created a nation and introduced them to their God (see the Book of Exodus, where Israel's religious leaders began the process that led to a new Passover Lamb being slain for the sins of the world).

22:2. Luke reiterates what he has underlined before (6:11; 11:53–54; 19:47–48; cf. 9:22; 17:25). Jesus has carried out his entire ministry under the watchful, death-planning eyes of the Jewish religious leaders. Now that plan is about to take effect. One thing prevents its being carried out: fear of the people. The rift between leadership and populace is complete. How can the leaders' plan be carried out if they do not have the support of the people?

22:3. An old enemy reenters the picture. The devil had left Jesus "until an opportune time" (4:13). The time had come. Satan could not lure Jesus with his tempting, but he did prevail over Judas. This was more than yielding to temptation. Satan actually entered Judas, controlling him as if he were possessed by demons. Luke had already warned us in 6:16 that Judas would become a traitor. That happens here. A discontented disciple met a devilish tempter and agreed to hand over his Lord. But the battle is now on a higher plain. No longer is this simply a human plot against a leader who threatens their power and position. Now a battle ensues between the Son of God and the ultimate evil power. Jesus' passion is more than a miscarriage of human justice. It is the ultimate battle between good and evil, Satan and God. The rest of the Book of Luke must be read in light of this verse.

22:4–6. Judas held a secret meeting with the two groups that had to be involved if Jesus was to be arrested. The chief priests controlled the temple area where Jesus had been coming to teach. The officers of the temple guard or temple police were involved in the actual arrest. They plotted a strategy to catch Jesus privately when the people could not interfere and prevent the arrest. With Jerusalem overflowing with foreigners coming to celebrate Passover, care had to be taken to prevent public uprising.

Judas, the disciples' treasurer, was always interested in money. The negotiations with the priests and police determined the price Judas would receive for his betrayal.

Judas made the deal and began searching for the time when he could lead the police to Jesus without the crowds surrounding him. Again, Luke makes sure we see the word *betray*. The arrest of Jesus began with unfair, unjust practices and continued on that track until he died. The arrest procedure involved the betrayal by a friend, not the standard operating procedure of a justice department. But this was no ordinary "friend." It was a friend possessed by Satan.

𝔹 Preparing for Glory to Come: The Last Supper (22:7–38)

> **SUPPORTING IDEA:** *The Lord's Supper marks Jesus' preparation of the disciples for life in the coming kingdom, but it teaches them the lesson of humility and true greatness.*

22:7. The day of unleavened bread came (see 22:1). For Luke this is the fourteenth day of the month of Nisan. Exodus 12:18 set up the practice of beginning to eat unleavened bread on the fourteenth. On the tenth each family had determined how many would eat, how much lamb was needed, and they had chosen the lamb to be slaughtered. On the fourteenth between 2:30 P.M. and 5:30 P.M. they slaughtered the lambs in the temple court. Then the evening meal was held in an agreed-on place, either a home or other suitable building. The evening would be the beginning of 15 Nisan.

22:8–9. Jesus told the two leading disciples to get the Passover meal ready. By doing so, he created the Twelve into a family for this family observation. They had forsaken their own families (see 18:28–30) and joined a new family. Their family celebration would be quite unique—a Passover celebration with God's Passover Lamb for the world. Preparations would include finding a place and taking the lamb to be slaughtered in preparation for the meal.

This was no ordinary family preparing for Passover. They did not even have a place to lay their heads, much less a room for the family to gather around the Passover table. The disciples did not know how to find a place. They asked the Master.

22:10–11. With his supernatural knowledge, Jesus directed them to a man who would be carrying a water vessel on his head. Carrying water was normally a female responsibility, not something that a man did. The disciples were to follow this man into a house. They were to find the owner of the house and inform him of the Teacher's need for a place to celebrate Passover. The owner of the house was expected to know who the Teacher was and to be willing for his house to be used for this purpose.

22:12–14. The willing owner led the disciples to the right place, and they prepared for Passover, setting out everything needed for the guests to recline at the table and eat. By such preparations, Jesus apparently protected his disciple family from intrusive outsiders. They celebrated the supper in private. The feast approached (22:1), the day of unleavened bread came (v. 7), and the hour arrived. At the mealtime hour, they gathered in the upper room, built onto a flat Palestinian house. Each person found a place around the table to stretch out to eat. The family was prepared for Passover, but were they prepared for *this* Passover?

22:15–16. Jesus wanted to share one last Passover with his disciples. Jewish religious leaders wanted to kill him and prevent him from doing any more teaching or performing any more miracles in Jerusalem. He knew what lay ahead of him in Jerusalem. But now, safely cloistered from his enemies, he had a final opportunity to prepare his followers for the events of the future. He needed one last time to give them a symbol to teach them the meaning of who he was and what he had done for them. Thus, he ate his final Passover with his disciples, knowing they would not share such a meal together until the great eschatological banquet around God's table in heaven. Then their redemption would be complete. Then Jesus' preaching that the kingdom had come near would be complete, and the kingdom would be fully present for eternity.

22:17–18. The Passover meal began with a cup of wine, which was blessed with thanksgiving for the meaning of the day. Jesus also took a cup of wine and blessed it. Often a host would give his cup as a special honor to a banquet guest. Jesus appears to share his own cup with all the family, rather than each drinking from his own cup. This symbolized their unity in facing what lay ahead and in looking forward to the final appearance of the kingdom of God. The Last Supper is a time of looking forward to two goals: the cross and the final heavenly banquet in the kingdom. Jesus underlined that this was his last supper. He would be with the Father at the final banquet the next time he partook of the wine.

22:19. Along with lamb, unleavened bread was also a central part of the Passover meal. The family, having recited the Exodus story through questions and answers and sung parts of the traditional Hallel collection of psalms in Psalms 113–118, would give a prayer of thanks over the bread and eat the Passover meal. Jesus apparently took the role of the father of the family and gave thanks for the bread. As he did so, he replaced the Passover celebration with a new celebration of unleavened bread. This one interpreted the bread not as representing what Israel had to carry out of Egypt but the body of Jesus broken on the cross for his followers.

It is difficult to know how the disciples would have reacted as Jesus spoke of his body given for them. Later they would realize what he had done and why he wanted them to repeat this rite again and again. No longer did they need to celebrate the Passover and look back to the Exodus redemption. Now they could celebrate the Lord's Supper or Last Supper and look back to what Jesus did for them by dying on the cross. Jesus would no longer drink and eat physically and visibly with them, but each generation of disciples could remember his desire to eat this last meal and the meaning he gave to it.

22:20. Passover included four cups of wine drunk at specific intervals. The last two came after the meal and were separated by the reading of the rest of the Hallel Psalms. Jesus took the occasion of one of these cups to again transform the meaning of Passover, transforming the Jewish celebration into the Christian Easter. The cup they drank served as an eternal reminder that Jesus had spilled his blood for them. Passover celebrated the old covenant ratified on Sinai (Exod. 19–24). The Lord's Supper celebrates the new covenant of Jeremiah 31:31 written on the hearts of the people rather than on tablets of stone. As blood sacrifices sealed the old covenant (Exod. 24), so Christ's blood would seal and ratify the new covenant.

No longer would they need to look back to Egypt and Sinai for their redemption. No longer would they need to celebrate a yearly day of atonement. Now they looked to Jesus and his death on the cross as the sole and sufficient means for their atonement. Jesus would no longer celebrate Passover. His followers would no longer need to celebrate Passover. Now they would celebrate the Lord's death until he came again.

22:21–24. Quickly Jesus changed the topic. The betrayer is here at the table, he declared. What a shock for the apostles. Who could he be?

Jesus emphasized that the betrayer had not forced Jesus' hand. The betrayer did not control history. Neither did the one who had entered in to possess him. God had determined that Jesus must pass on. He would go just as God had planned it. Still, for being Satan's accomplice and choosing to reject and betray Jesus, the betrayer stood under judgment. Everyone should grieve and mourn for him, Jesus said. He would face God's wrath.

The disciples had not formed a complete fellowship of trust. They argued over which of them might betray Jesus. Deep down, they knew each one of them was capable of such betrayal.

The argument spread from who was the worst among them to who was the best. The implication of this argument rested on who would receive the highest offices in Jesus' kingdom, as the following response shows.

22:25. Jesus' kingdom was not like the earthly kingdoms they experienced. Gentile kings exercised domination, literally, "lord it over them."

Gentile authorities were called *euergetai:* "benefactors." The term literally means, "ones who do good." It was an honorary title that the government bestowed on princes, emperors, and the gods. Jesus ironically used a form of the Greek term for "called" that is probably to be interpreted as "have themselves called benefactors." These people required recognition and glory for anything they gave or did for someone else. They bestowed the title on themselves. So in reality "benefactor" described a system that promoted injustice and unfairness. It was a system of "I will scratch your back if you will scratch mine." It was a system of wealth limited to the few, and poverty shared by the masses. It was a system of a few gifts and an immense amount of oppression. It was a system where the oppressed had to praise the oppressor for any small favor. It was a system without freedom, without opportunity, and without love and care.

22:26. Jesus' system was entirely different. The senior leader with the most experience must adopt an attitude as if he were the youngest with no experience, no leadership responsibility, and no honors expected. Whoever had decision-making responsibility should make those decisions as if he were a servant totally dependent on the decision maker. You do not seek for greatness or recognition, Jesus said. You seek for opportunities truly to be a doer of good for the rest of the "family."

22:27. Jesus turned the question on the disciples. You want to determine greatness, he observed. Who is greater—the one enjoying a banquet feast or the one serving it? The world says the one being served. Jesus' perspective was different. He stood as one serving the cup and the bread, not the one reclining at the table to be served. You must make a choice. Will you accept the world's oppressive way of honoring greatness? Or will you follow Jesus' example of becoming a servant and seeking the best for the "family"? Will you be part of the last who will become first? Or must you be first now?

22:28. Jesus recognized what the disciples had endured. They had stayed with him from Galilee to Jerusalem, in spite of the plots of the religious leaders, the fickleness of the crowds, and the difficult lifestyle with no financial resources, no place to live, and no guaranteed source of food. They had not fallen away in the time of testing (see 8:13). Many of his followers had turned back and rejected him, but the disciples had remained true—except for the betrayer.

22:29. Their faithfulness would not go without reward. Jesus came saying the kingdom of God is near. That meant God had given the kingdom to Jesus (see 1:32–33), and the kingdom was near any time and any place Jesus was near. Because of their faithfulness, Jesus would give them a kingdom.

22:30. The disciples will eat at the king's table. But they must remember that Jesus has just warned that he will not again eat and drink until he does so in the kingdom of God. He has thus described an interval, perhaps a long interval, before the banquet table is ready. Are they able to remain faithful during this interval?

22:31. Again, Jesus shifted the focus. He warned Simon Peter directly. The warfare with Satan that Jesus won and that Judas lost had started again, this time for Peter. Peter stood in Job's shoes. As the prime example of the righteous of his generation, he must pass Satan's muster. Satan wanted to accuse him and show him wanting.

22:32. Peter had an ally Job did not. Jesus was praying for him. This is a foretaste of Jesus' heavenly role as our intercessor (Rom. 8:34; Heb. 7:25). Here is a prayer of Jesus that was not fulfilled. Faith did fail Peter. Jesus knew it would. So Jesus encouraged Peter to come back from failure. Failure does not have to be the last word. Satan can win a battle and lose the war. After giving in to temptation, Peter could become stronger and become a source of strength for others. Failure need not be complete. Forgiveness is readily available. Here is the good news of the gospel for everyone.

22:33. Impetuous, brash, self-confident Peter did not get the picture. He vowed his faithfulness until death. He would endure all the persecutions Jesus described as signs of the end. He would be there to take one of the twelve thrones over the tribes of Israel. He did not mention Jesus' prayers. Neither did he mention his own prayers. He was confident he could do it. Later he would, but only after failure.

22:34. Jesus brought Peter back to reality quickly. You will not be faithful as you promise, Jesus told him. Today you will deny me three times. You will refuse even to acknowledge that you know who I am, much less that I am your Lord. Be ready to face your weakness, Peter. The roosters will crow to greet the morning sun, but they might crow any time sooner. Jesus emphasized the immediacy of the denial in contrast to Peter's self-confident prediction about the future.

22:35. Now Jesus was ready to prepare the disciples for the immediate events leading to his death. He used their past history to prepare them for future actions. He had sent them on mission (9:3; 10:4) without essential supplies. They came back testifying how God had provided all their needs. They still remembered they had lacked nothing during their mission.

22:36. The present situation was quite different. Take whatever supplies and resources you have, Jesus told them. You will especially need a weapon for self-defense. Go sell whatever is necessary to get one. Satan had come after Jesus and his followers in full force. The persecution and arrests were about to begin. They must be ready to protect themselves.

22:37. The new situation was not coming because Satan had increased his power or because the Jewish religious leaders or the government of Rome had taken further control. All that would happen in Passion Week was under God's control. Scripture had already pointed to it. Persecution would come because the Old Testament prophets knew Messiah would be categorized with the out-laws and sinners (Isa. 53:12). Jesus claimed the messianic passage had to wait no longer for fulfillment. He was the one who fulfilled Scripture's messianic expectations—all of them. He would have to be seen as a criminal, an outlaw. To do so, he would have to submit to arrest, trial, and condemnation.

22:38. The disciples quietly took inventory: two swords among twelve (eleven) disciples. Jesus told them that would do; they need not go and buy others. Jesus' answer had an ironic twist. The two swords were obviously not enough to resist those who came to arrest Jesus. He used this irony to close the conversation.

C The Glory Decision: The Father's Will Wins (22:39–46)

SUPPORTING IDEA: *Jesus faced Calvary from Gethsemane, submitting to the Father's will but still having to warn the disciples to pray in the midst of temptation.*

22:39. Prayer was a way of life for Jesus. He had a special place in the Mount of Olives where he habitually went for prayer. The disciples followed, an ironic statement in light of Christ's original call to "follow me" (5:8–11,27–28; 9:23,59,61; 18:22,28). Now they followed, but only to fall asleep in Jesus' great-est moment of need and in the face of Satan's renewed attack on them. They fol-lowed, but not in the way a person takes up a cross and follows.

22:40. Jesus gave them a prayer assignment. It centered on their chief need. The renewed activities of Satan called them to pray to escape tempta-tion as Jesus had escaped Satan's tempting. Judas and Peter were not the only ones Satan wanted. He wanted all of Christ's disciples and would tempt each of them. Only prayer and Scripture can successfully fight such evil power and overcome temptation.

22:41–42. Prayer time for Jesus. Every major decision called for special prayer time for Jesus (3:21; 5:16; 6:12; 9:18,28–29; 11:2; 18:1). Jesus knew what lay ahead. The cup of the blood of the new covenant must be spilled. Yet he, as a human being, did not want to suffer. He did not want to die. He would have liked to have found another way to follow God's plan. Still, he submitted to the Father. The Father's will he would do, not his own. The Father's will he knew was best. The Father's will was what he always prayed for and did, even when the human side wanted something else.

22:43. Verses 43–44 are missing from many of the best Greek manu-scripts and may reflect the interpretation by an early Christian scribe. Christ found immediate answer to his prayer, but in a somewhat unexpected way. Rather than tell him what to do, God sent an angel to feed and encourage him. The angel's presence reaffirmed what Jesus knew. He had to face the task

God had placed before him. He had to go to the cross. But he went with heavenly presence, heavenly strength, and heavenly nourishment.

Angels played a significant role in Luke. Gabriel guided Zechariah, announcing John's birth (1:18–19). Gabriel also told Mary of Jesus' birth (1:30–38; cf. 2:21). Angels delivered Jesus' birth announcement to the shepherds (2:9–14). Angels thus prepared for the coming of Jesus and for the exodus of Jesus as he looked to the cross.

22:44. Prayer was not a small thing for Jesus. It was a time of anguish as he sought God's will for his life. Just like us, he faced a difficult decision and suffered emotional distress while he tried to make it. He became so emotionally involved that he perspired profusely. His perspiration became so heavy that it did not run in little rivulets like water. Rather, it dropped from his skin as if each drop of sweat were as heavy as a drop of blood. Herschel Hobbs observes, "With a physician's touch Luke says that his 'sweat was as it were great drops of blood falling down to the ground.' He broke out into a bloody sweat which became clotted blood" (*Life and Times of Jesus*, Zondervan, 1966, 180).

22:45–46. Jesus' prayer time came to an end. It was time to get back to the world of rejection and arrest. So he walked over to the disciples, hoping to find them in prayer. Instead, they were sleeping. Luke explains their sleeping. Finally, the reality of what Jesus said was creeping into their consciences. They realized Jesus expected to die. They began grieving his passing while he was still with them. Their grief wore them out. But while sleeping away their grief, they yielded to temptation by not praying for power to withstand temptation. Again, Satan had won a battle. But Jesus invited them to pray so temptation would not be too much for them.

𝕯 Darkness Arrests Glory: Betrayal at Work (22:47–53)

SUPPORTING IDEA: *God's plan sometimes allows the powers of darkness to win a victory over God's people, even over his Son, but the victory is always short-lived.*

22:47–50. Prayer time led to arrest time. The temple police arrived to arrest Jesus. Judas led them to identify him and to locate his private prayer spot. The betrayer approached Jesus to greet him with a kiss, a traditional sign of friendship and the sign of Judas's betrayal.

Jesus pointed out the irony and duplicity of Judas's act. Would he use the sign of affection to disaffect himself from Jesus and betray him to the enemy? This was betrayal and pretense carried to the extreme.

Armed with two swords, the disciples were ready to act. Here was the ultimate opportunity for self-defense, the chance to defend Jesus from arrest. First, they asked Jesus if this was the appropriate time to use the swords.

Not waiting for an answer, one of the disciples used a sword to sever the right ear of one of the high priest's slaves. Ironically, the high priest, while arresting Jesus, was not able to protect his slave. Again, Luke indicates that the priests were not in control. They were simply instruments working on their own decisions but carrying out the plan that God had decreed long ago.

22:51. Jesus was ready to display his power. Certainly he could call down angels if needed to disperse and disrupt the arresting crowd. Instead, he interrupted his disciples' brief stab at self-defense. Would the disciples have been willing to see this as the time to bring in Jesus' kingdom? Could this have been the start of the rebellion against Jewish religious leaders and even Rome? No. Jesus displayed his power in another way. He quieted his disciples, quelling any revolution they might think of starting. Then he used his miraculous power to restore and heal the slave's ear. Healing was his power game, not revolution.

22:52–53. Jesus turned the mob's actions around. Here was a quiet, peaceful teacher and healer. Every day he went about his ministry healing and helping people. Any time they could have easily taken him. Instead, they waited until the cover of darkness and brought the entire leadership team as well as the armed police. Did they think he was a criminal leading a rebellion? No, he had already shown they were the thieves by the way they mismanaged temple business (19:46). He saw through their pretense. They could not claim to the crowds who hung on Jesus' words that they had found him in criminal activity under cover of darkness.

They must know one thing. They were not in control. This was their hour, but they did not control history's hours. God set up the system of day and night, light and dark, twenty-four hour days. He controls each hour. He had assigned this hour to them to do their business of darkness. They operated in the dominion of darkness—under the rule of Satan. He had another victory, but only because that was God's plan.

Ⓔ Denying the Glory: I Don't Know Him (22:54–62)

SUPPORTING IDEA: *The strongest disciple of Jesus can fall prey to Satan's temptation and deny him, but such denial brings bitter sorrow and guilt.*

22:54. The arrest was made. Jesus stood at the house of the high priest. What should have been holy ground, keeping the leading religious official in Judaism holy and pure, became the scene of the most evil deed in history: the mockery of a trial that convicted the Son of God. Again, a disciple followed Jesus (see v. 39), but this time at a distance. He followed with curiosity to see what would happen, not with devotion to identify himself with the Master.

22:55. This disciple did not follow Jesus for long. He distanced himself from the Master until he had joined the crowd around a comfortable campfire. He had quietly shifted identities. No longer a follower of Jesus, he became one of the crowd, curious to see what was about to happen and eager for a good time around the fire.

22:56–61. The rugged Galilean fisherman could not hide among the group at the Jerusalem court. He stood out from the crowd. A slave girl quickly noticed him. She took a second and third look. Yes, she was sure of it. This man had been with Jesus.

Without thinking, Peter went into a defensive mode. "No way! Not me! Woman, I am not acquainted with him." Peter had denied Jesus, but what he had done did not sink in. He had successfully defended his right to enjoy the warmth of the campfire.

Another passerby noticed Peter. Same results. "You are one of them, too."

"Not so, man. Not me." Peter again moved away from Jesus and joined the crowd more intimately. A defensive reaction changed his identity without him being aware of the immensity of what he had said and done.

An hour passed, still the devil's hour. Another face in the crowd spoke up, recognizing the Galilean accent: "This man was certainly with him, since he is also a Galilean."

"I don't know what you are talking about." Peter was completely distant from Jesus. He had denied three times any knowledge of or relationship to the man. He now belonged to the crowd and to the devil. Satan had sifted him and found him wanting.

A rooster's crow, not a human voice, made Peter realize what he had done. Reinforcement came in one glance from Jesus. Jesus' words stabbed their way into Peter's memory: "Before the rooster crows today, you will deny me three times."

22:62. The brashly self-confident man disappeared. Now he distanced himself from the crowd. Outside by himself, he wept bitter tears. Grief overwhelmed him. Follow Jesus to prison and to death? He could not even follow him to a mockery of a trial. The grief was as deep as Judas's later proved to be, but the response and subsequent actions would be quite different. Guilt led Judas to suicide. It led Peter to Pentecost.

F Sentenced to Glory: Mockery of Justice (22:63–71)

> **SUPPORTING IDEA:** *Jesus was sentenced to death not because he deserved it, but because religious leaders were determined to have him dead at any price.*

22:63. Luke's trial report begins on an ironic note: guards beat and mocked Jesus. Guards should protect the prisoner and ensure fair treatment and justice. Instead, they turned on Jesus. *Mockery* is a key term in Luke's passion predictions (18:32) and in the trial (23:11,36). The justice system of Israel decided the verdict even before Jesus' trial.

22:64. Children's games replaced legal maneuvers. They blindfolded Jesus and asked him to indicate who hit him, just as children would do—but children would hit, not beat. Jesus was supposed to use his God-given powers in a game. The Prophet without parallel was ordered to prophesy who had hit him. What lack of respect for who Jesus was and for what God did in sending Jesus to earth.

22:65. The ultimate charge against Jesus would be blasphemy. The accusers practiced before accusing. They called Jesus names and tried to anger him. Their opinion of Jesus was formed before the trial began.

22:66. Daylight came, opening the way for an "official" meeting and conclusion by the Sanhedrin, Judaism's official council. Note that Mark 14:53–64 and Matthew 26:59–66 appear to describe a nighttime trial, certainly a violation of Jewish legal practice. The site in the high priest's home is irregular, for the temple was the center of Jewish justice. Jesus was not allowed to defend himself. Jesus never used the name of God and so could not be technically guilty of blasphemy. Jewish death-sentence trials were supposed to last two days, not the one day given Jesus. The trial came during the Passover festival, when no trials were allowed. Jesus' accusers allowed contradictory evidence but listened only to the part that agreed with their predetermined verdict. Jewish practice let the least experienced members of the council cast votes first, with the high priest casting the final vote. In Jesus' trial the high priest immediately pronounced a guilty verdict. Nothing can cover the fact that justice was not served, that the justice system became pure mockery.

22:67. The trial opened with one major question: Are you the Messiah? Jesus was clever enough to avoid the trap. He turned the charge back on the council. If I told you, how many would really believe me? he said. You are not asking for information. You are seeking a way to indict me and kill me.

22:68. What is more, if I had the position to ask the questions so that you had to give the answers, he continued, you would do just what I am doing. You would not answer. Why should I do any differently?

22:69. Jesus made a claim no one expected. He used the term for himself that he had consistently used: *Son of Man* (5:24; 6:5,22; 7:34; 9:22,26,44,58; 11:30; 12:8,10,40; 17:22,24,26,30; 18:8,31; 19:10; 21:27,36; 22:48). He placed himself in an unexpected position: next to God in heaven. He claimed to be planning to leave the earth, presumably through death, and to occupy heaven's throne. Moreover, he made the claim in the language of Scripture (Ps. 110; cf. Luke 20:41–44). The claim was not for some far distant time (cf. 21:27), but for the immediate present. He would get the chance to ask questions. He would be the judge. These people now asking questions proudly and presumptuously would be reduced to standing before Christ's judgment seat.

22:70. The Jewish religious leaders were outraged. Has he claimed divine prerogatives for himself? they asked. Does he have a privileged position with God that no one else shares? No one else can walk into the presence of God.

Only the high priest once a year can enter the inner courts of the temple, much less the heavenly throne room.

Jesus' response was intentionally ambiguous. He did not give his own opinion. He simply quoted them and let their statement stand without denying it. They could take the answer any way they wanted to.

22:71. Of course, they took it in the worst possible way. They claimed he had made divine claims for himself, had put himself on equality with God, and had accepted the title Son of God from the Psalms. Jesus was given no opportunity to defend himself. No witnesses were called. Jesus was allowed to condemn himself on their interpretation of what he meant by an ambiguous statement. Human Jewish judges, not knowing they actually stood before the one who would judge the universe, rendered the verdict. They sought to humiliate and abase him. Instead, they were on the way to exalting and glorifying him on the cross and in the heavenly throne room.

> **MAIN IDEA REVIEW:** *Jesus experienced the unfair, unjust nature of earthly existence in his betrayal, arrest, unfair trial, in his denial by the leader of his band of disciples. Still, he showed the world that he was the Son of God.*

III. CONCLUSION

Unswerving Loyalty to the Father

Jesus was betrayed by the kiss of a greedy friend. This friend was controlled by Satan, but so was the leader of Jesus' faithful followers, as he denied the one whose body would be broken and whose blood would be spilled in the new covenant. Jesus never submitted to the will of man, not even to his own will. He submitted only in prayer to the Father's will and so was willing to drink the cup of death, the cup of the new covenant. Arrested and tried in an unfair, illegal, unjust manner, he endured mocking, beating, game playing, and an unfair trial. In so doing, he revealed that he was the Son of God who would join the Father in exercising rule and judgment over the entire world. The hour of darkness had come. The power of darkness appeared to be in control, but only because this was the Father's plan. Nothing is done outside the Father's plan. No one exercises control but the Father. The unjust trial and conviction of the Son of Man and Son of God occurred because this was the Father's will.

PRINCIPLES

- The world does not operate on the rules of justice and fairness, because people are evil and are subject to control by the power of evil.
- Greed leads people to heinous acts.

- The kingdom of God will appear one day in all its fullness, and God's people will join him at the heavenly banquet.
- The Lord's Supper calls us to remember what Jesus did for us in dying on the cross and establishing the new covenant.
- Authority in God's kingdom is exercised by servants, not by self-seeking people.
- Self-confidence and dependence on human willpower lead to denial of Jesus.
- God's people need to pray for power not to yield to temptation and to remain faithful to Christ in the darkest hours.
- Jesus' kingdom is not established through physical means or human warfare.
- Jesus is God's Son who sits at God's right hand to judge the world.

APPLICATIONS

- Pray that God will not allow Satan to take charge of your life.
- Identify ways that you are tempted to betray or deny Jesus.
- Reflect on what taking the Lord's Supper means to you.
- Find ways to show servant greatness to the world.
- Pray for power to overcome temptation.
- Confess Jesus as your Lord and Savior at every opportunity.
- Beware of ways you may deny Jesus and ask God to help you lift him up at all times.
- Prepare yourself to stand before Christ's judgment seat.

IV. LIFE APPLICATION

Defeat Is Not Final

Dave Dravecky amazed the sports world, first by his catastrophe and then by his miraculous recovery. After much struggle and effort, Dave became a star pitcher, who headed the staff of the San Francisco Giants and who looked to lead them to the National League pennant. Then the news came. The muscle in his pitching arm had been invaded by cancer. This would not kill him, but it would end his baseball career. What an unfair way to end a promising career.

Dave did not complain. He told everyone he would come back. He went on a training program unheard of in the exercise rooms of the world. He trained his other muscles to replace the function of his deltoid. He began tossing baseballs. He began throwing baseballs. He began pitching baseballs. Then came the biggest test. He had to convince the team management that he could pitch effectively again. Words could not win that argument. Actions did.

The day came when he ascended the mound in San Francisco. He pitched effectively without a deltoid muscle. Cincinnati batters fought hard against him. He gave up a homer, but in the end Dave Dravecky won again in the major leagues. Justice appeared to be served, but later in Montreal, the bone made brittle by so much treatment gave way and broke. Dave's pitching days were over. Defeat seemed stronger than victory.

Or did it? Dave testified to the peace he had through the whole experience. Depression did not set in. Through it all, he said, "I learned to trust in God completely."

This is the story of Luke 22. Satan tried to take charge of Judas, Jesus, Peter, and the other disciples. He succeeded with Judas. He succeeded for a brief moment with Peter. He controlled the Jewish religious leaders, because God had granted him his hour of darkness. But Satan never succeeded with Jesus. Jesus prayed his way through the moments of temptation and the moments of wanting to do his own will rather than the Father's. He yielded his life to follow the Father's will even if that meant going through the pain and mockery of an unjust trial and being crucified. Through it all Jesus revealed the glory of God and showed that as the Son of God he would become the judge of the universe.

Jesus' example stands before you as you face the unfair situations of life. Will you give in, as Judas and even Peter did? Or will you resist the devil, pray your way through temptation, and endure the world's injustice to testify to God's goodness?

V. PRAYER

Mighty God in heaven, life on earth can seem so unfair. People mistreat us and harm us and mock us. We try to be true to you through it all, but it is tough to hang in there. Your kingdom can seem so far away. Help me endure and not yield to temptation. Help me hold fast to you, no matter what Satan and the world throw at me. You let your body be broken. You spilled your blood for me. I will live for you. Amen.

VI. DEEPER DISCOVERIES

A. Passover and Unleavened Bread (22:1)

Israel celebrated two consecutive holy festivals to teach their families about God's great deliverance in the Exodus (Exod. 12–13; 23:15; 34:18; Lev. 23:4–8; Num. 9:1–15; 28:16–25; 33:3; Deut. 16:1–8). Passover was celebrated beginning on the afternoon of the fourteenth day of the month Nisan with the slaughter of the Passover lamb. Blood from the lamb was placed on the doorposts of the house, reminding people how God had protected the Israelites from the passing of the death angel in Egypt. That evening, now 15 Nisan since the new day started at sunset, the family gathered to eat the Passover meal and celebrate the festival, retelling the story of the Exodus. The meal included bitter herbs and unleavened bread. Family members were to be dressed ready to travel, imitating their ancestors' actions in Egypt as they prepared the feast just before fleeing from Pharaoh.

The Feast of Unleavened Bread began on 15 Nisan and lasted for a week. During this time no yeast or leaven was allowed in an Israelite home. Pious Jews wanted to celebrate the festivals in Jerusalem, so that the holy city was packed to capacity.

The Gospels of Matthew, Mark, and Luke show that Jesus ate the Passover meal with his disciples. John's Gospel appears to picture Jesus as being slaughtered as the Passover lamb along with the slaughter of the other Passover animals. The irony of the entire account is that when Israel celebrated its greatest deliverance, they simultaneously crucified their Savior and Deliverer. They put to death the only one who could bring life.

B. "Satan Entered Judas" (22:3)

Satan "entered" Judas. What does this mean? It means that Satan took advantage of Judas's wickedness and used him as a tool against Jesus. Judas made himself available to be controlled and manipulated by Satan. It is frightening that a person so close to Jesus was controlled by the enemy. Judas is a warning for all believers to guard their hearts and minds vigorously and not give way to Satan's schemes and strategies. Peter exhorted believers by saying, "Be self-controlled and alert. Your enemy the devil prowls around like a roaring lion looking for someone to devour. Resist him, standing firm in the faith, because you know that your brothers throughout the world are undergoing the same kind of sufferings" (1 Pet. 5:8–9). We would do well to have a healthy respect for the power and strategies of Satan.

C. Passover Feast (22:7–8)

Also called the Feast of Unleavened Bread, the Passover celebrated a past deliverance—God's deliverance of Israel from Egyptian bondage. The word *Passover* indicates deliverance from the tenth plague in Egypt, the death of the firstborn (Lev. 23:4–5). The observance fell in the spring, at the beginning of the barley harvest. Along with Pentecost and Tabernacles, Passover was one of three annual pilgrimage festivals (see Deut. 16:16). Over the centuries it also came to be an anticipation of God's coming kingdom.

D. Betrayal (22:21–23)

Jesus' words of prediction regarding Judas's betrayal hold more meaning than that of a simple prediction of betrayal. The phrase "who is going to betray me" is an action that is forward-moving in its meaning. The verb *betray* is present active participle, indicating that the one betraying was "actually engaged in doing it" (Robertson, "Luke," *Word Pictures in the New Testament*, 268). We might render this phrase as "him who is in the process of betraying." The betrayal process had already begun.

E. "Take This Cup from Me"(22:42)

"Cup" is a metaphor for Jesus' suffering. He voluntarily drank the cup of suffering (Matt. 20:22; 26:39,42; Mark 10:38; 14:36; Luke 22:42; John 18:11). It is a metaphor here not only for physical death in general, but also for the particular death Jesus would suffer on behalf of mankind. As he contemplated the awful experience awaiting him, his soul drew back from the horror of the essence of sin. In spite of this "cup," Jesus willingly obeyed God's will, bearing the sins of all people so that mankind could be saved.

F. Sanhedrin (22:66–71)

The Sanhedrin was the highest Jewish court in the first century, consisting of seventy members plus the high priest. The Sanhedrin included both the main Jewish parties among its membership. They exercised authority over the religious life of the Jewish people. They also operated under the jurisdiction of the Roman authorities. Generally, the Roman governor allowed the Sanhedrin considerable autonomy and authority.

The Book of Acts describes how the Sanhedrin harassed and threatened the apostles. When the apostles continued to preach, the Sanhedrin had them arrested. The Gospels describe the role of the Sanhedrin in the arrest, trials, and condemnation of Jesus.

VII. TEACHING OUTLINE

A. INTRODUCTION

1. Lead Story: The Day the World Disintegrated
2. Context: Jesus has outlined the signs of his coming end in chapter 21. Now in chapter 22 the end begins with the betrayal and arrest of Jesus and the temptations of his disciples. Judas let Satan occupy and control his life. The disciples argued over greatness rather than contemplate the meaning of the Lord's Supper. They slept in grief rather than pray to withstand temptation. Peter denied Jesus three times as Jesus predicted he would. Then Peter sank in bitter grief and

repentance. The authorities arrested Jesus and convicted him in a mock trial. How did Jesus respond? He submitted himself to the will of the Father, taught the symbols of the Last Supper in the meaning of his coming death, and then endured the beating, mocking, and mockery of the unfair trial as blasphemous people convicted him of blasphemy. He looked ahead to the day when he would sit beside the Father judging the world.

3. Transition: If anyone endured an unfair world, Jesus did. Nothing about the way the disciples betrayed, denied, and deserted him, nor the way the Jewish religious leaders arrested, tried, and convicted him was fair. His example in submitting to the Father's will should help us as we endure the unfairness of life.

B. COMMENTARY

1. The Glory Meets Opposition: Betrayal (22:1–6)
   a. The setting: Passover approaches (22:1)
   b. The scene: fearful opponents seek to kill Jesus (22:2)
   c. Satan's reaction: enter Judas (22:3)
   d. Judas's reaction: agree to betray (22:4)
   e. The opponents' response: agree to pay money (22:5)
   f. Judas's counter reaction: seek right time (22:6)
2. Preparing for Glory to Come: The Last Supper (22:7–38)
   a. The setting: Passover sacrifice (22:7)
   b. The Master's response: prepare for Passover (22:8)
   c. The followers' reaction: where? (22:9)
   d. The Master's counter response: follow the jar (22:10–12)
   e. The followers' counter reaction: prepare Passover (22:13)
   f. Scene B: Passover meal (22:14)
   g. The Master's teaching: eating now and then (22:15–16)
   h. The Master's actions: the Lord's Supper (22:17–22)
   I. The followers' reaction: from "who, me?" to "who is the greatest?" (22:23–24)
   j. The Master's response: serve now and rule in kingdom (22:25–30)
   k. The Master's private response: praying for Simon's faith (22:31–32)
   l. Simon's reaction: prepared to die for you (22:33)
   m. The Master's counter reaction: you will deny three times (22:34)
   n. The Master's question: what did you need on mission? (22:35a)
   o. The followers' response: nothing (22:35b)
   p. The Master's instructions: take what you need for final battle (22:36–37)

      q. The followers' response: two swords (22:38a)

      r. The Master's counter response: enough (22:38b)

3. The Glory Decision: The Father's Will Wins (22:39–46)

      a. The setting: Mount of Olives (22:39)

      b. The Master's warning: pray to withstand temptation (22:40)

      c. The Master's prayer: take the cup; do your will (22:41–42)

      d. The heavenly response: angel of strength (22:43)

      e. The Master's response: prayer sweating blood (22:44)

      f. The followers' reaction: sorrowful exhaustion (22:45)

      g. The Master's counter response: wake up and pray to withstand temptation (22:46)

4. Darkness Arrests Glory: Betrayal at Work (22:47–53)

      a. The setting: Judas leading mob scene (22:47a)

      b. The scene: Judas seeks to kiss Jesus (22:47b)

      c. The Master's response: betray me with sign of love? (22:48)

      d. The followers' reaction: draw swords (22:49–50)

      e. The Master's response: healing, not fighting (22:51)

      f. The Master's teaching: hour of darkness has come (22:52–53)

5. Denying the Glory: I Don't Know Him (22:54–62)

      a. The setting: trial of Jesus at high priest's, with Peter following at a distance (22:54)

      b. The scene: Peter distanced from Jesus at opponents' fire (22:55)

      c. The crowd's response: you belong to him (22:56)

      d. Peter's reaction: do not know him (22:57)

      e. Another crowd response: you belong to them (22:58a)

      f. Peter's response: no, sir (22:58b)

      g. Another crowd response: you are a Galilean, you must belong to him (22:59)

      h. Peter's response: you make no sense (22:60a)

      I. Scene C: crowing rooster (22:60b)

      j. The Master's response: glance at Peter (22:61a)

      k. Peter's response: bitter memory brings bitter tears (22:61b–62)

6. Sentenced to Glory: Mockery of Justice (22:63–71)

      a. The setting: guards beating and mocking Jesus (22:63–65)

      b. Scene A: Jewish council tries Jesus (22:66)

      c. The opponents' question: are you the Messiah? (22:67a)

      d. The Master's response: future judgment of the Son of Man (22:67b–69)

      e. The opponents' counter question: are you Son of God? (22:70a)

      f. The Master's response: you might say so (22:70b)

      g. The opponents' response: all the evidence we need—blasphemy (22:71)

C. CONCLUSION: DEFEAT IS NOT FINAL

VIII. ISSUES FOR DISCUSSION

1. What could tempt you to betray or deny Jesus?
2. Describe the meaning of the Lord's Supper as you observe it in your church. In what ways could you do things differently so that people would be more likely to remember what Jesus did for us?
3. Describe the work of Satan in the arrest and trial of Jesus. How does Satan work in your life and that of your church?
4. Define greatness and show how people today show they are great in God's kingdom.
5. Describe the injustice in Jesus' trial. How did he respond? How do you respond to injustice?

Luke 23

Sentenced to Glory

"*It's difficult to look at a naked, beaten man and see anything kingly about him. How odd that in the fullness of time, Herod would be remembered a tyrant. The naked, beaten man he studied would rule the hearts of millions.*"

C a l v i n   M i l l e r

Luke 23

I N   A   N U T S H E L L

Accused of treason by the leaders of his own people, Jesus was proved innocent before Pilate, the Roman leader. Seeking to shirk responsibility, Pilate gained a new friend in Herod, his political enemy. Bowing to mob rule, Pilate released Barabbas, the murderer, and sentenced Jesus, the innocent one, to death by crucifixion. On the way to the cross, Jesus turned human grief for him into mourning for oneself. The convicted one who needed no forgiveness forgave his accusers and persecutors. The one mocked by accusers, soldiers, and criminals promised a believing criminal a place in paradise. His manner of death convinced even a Roman centurion of his righteousness. A nonconsenting Jewish ruler offered his tomb for Jesus' body and buried him. Meanwhile, women followers, faithful to the end, prepared to honor his memory.

Sentenced to Glory

I. INTRODUCTION

An Ambitious Vine

*J*ames Dobson tells of an "ambitious" vine that grew behind his house. Dobson and his wife Shirley concluded the plant had a secret ambition to conquer the world. Its first battle came with a 150-year-old oak tree. Gradually, week by week, month by month, the vine slowly wrapped its tendrils around the tree, inching higher and higher up the stately oak. Climbing above the tree's trunk, the vine began to attack the individual branches. Victory appeared in sight.

Then Dobson struck the mortal blow. With a sharp knife, he quickly sliced through the vine near the ground. The rest is history. Nothing changed immediately. Slowly, day by day, leaves faded, became discolored, turned brown, and then black. One by one, the leaves fell from the vine. Eventually, the only sign of the vine was a dry stick winding its path up the tree. Eventually, even the stick fell away. The glorious tree raised its leaves toward the sky, unencumbered by the worrisome vine. Blind ambition lost the day (*When God Doesn't Make Sense,* [Weaton, IL.: Tyndale House, 1993], 19).

Luke 23 introduces a cast of characters filled with blind ambition: Jewish leaders, Herod, Pilate, Roman soldiers, even criminals. Each in his own way sought to take advantage of Jesus to gain personal power and glory. Each represented a small but ambitious vine attacking an ancient tree. On Calvary's tree, Jesus found his own glory and surrendered his life to cut off human ambition. There God's plan of salvation reached its culmination. There Christ prayed for forgiveness for those ambitious politicians, religious leaders, warriors, and criminals who had a part in nailing him to the tree. There his innocent righteousness was revealed. So was the deadly ambition of his opponents. There the dying one promised paradise to one who deserved to die. There the world's Savior placed himself one last time in the Father's hands. There at Calvary, the ambitious seemed to have won, never realizing that the one they crucified had just sliced their vine and guaranteed their demise even as he provided salvation and eternal life for all who would believe in him.

No changes were immediately apparent in the world that day. But Christ's death had pronounced the death sentence on all human ambition. Sin and all its minions suffered a fatal blow from which they would never recover. Discoloring and death might come slowly to the powers of evil, but it would come surely. Those who sentenced Christ to death did not realize they had actually sentenced him to glory, where he was safe in the Father's hands.

II. COMMENTARY

Sentenced to Glory

MAIN IDEA: *The death of Jesus Christ showed his righteous innocence, paved the way to paradise for those who believe in him, and led Christ back into the Father's loving hands in glory.*

A Sentenced by Pilate's Fearful Ambition (23:1–25)

SUPPORTING IDEA: *The Roman representative sentenced the innocent Jesus to death because of his fear of political reprisals.*

23:1–2. The Sanhedrin aroused mass hysteria, leading Jesus from their meeting place to Pilate's court. Jewish religious leaders needed to rid their world of one who threatened their leadership, their popularity with the people, and their religious system. But religious charges would not do in Pilate's court. They had to have political charges. Jesus, the self-proclaimed enemy of ambitious, self-serving religion, had to be portrayed as the enemy of Roman rule in Palestine. Thus, the Jewish leaders painted him as a subversive, one leading the Jewish nation away from Rome. Such charges were not hard to believe. Jewish religious radicals frequently led revolts against Rome in the name of religion. The Jews tried to place two concrete examples of such subversion before Pilate. First came the tax issue, then the king issue. In 20:20–26 the Jewish leaders had failed to trap Jesus into opposing Roman taxation policies. Rather, they gave him opportunity to set up the principle of loyalty to government in the realm of government but loyalty to God in everything.

Then they used his title, Christ or Messiah, to charge him with political rebellion, claiming he was a king opposed to Caesar. Jesus had radically proclaimed a new kingdom, the kingdom of God. He had implied in various ways that he was the new king. He portrayed himself in messianic colors, raising expectations among the Jewish people that he would fulfill their hopes based on Old Testament prophecy. They wanted him to be the new king who would overthrow Rome. Jesus did nothing to encourage military action. He did nothing to advocate governmental change. His was a kingdom above and beyond this world. His was a glory to be realized only in heaven in the Father's hands. He had to go away on a long journey before returning to earth as king (19:11–27).

23:3. Pilate bluntly asked Jesus to answer his accusers. Would he confess to being king of the Jews as charged? Jesus' answer only created uncertainty as he said, "It is as you say." Some interpreters even see a return question on Jesus' lips: Do you say so? More likely, Jesus was suggesting a positive answer to Pilate but doing so in such a way that Pilate was construed as making the statement, not Jesus. Neither the Jews nor Pilate could take the answer as clear evidence of guilt to the charge of being a king in opposition to Rome.

23:4. Pilate gave a clear verdict: Innocent of all charges. He directed his answer both to those making the charge—the chief priests—and to the emotionally charged crowd. The priests must know their wish had been denied. The crowds must be prevented from any attempt to make Jesus king and force his hand against the Roman government. Jesus was not an enemy of Rome, no matter how much an enemy of the Jewish religious system he might be.

23:5. The priests refused to take no for an answer. They repeated their charges with vehemence. They sought to do what they charged Jesus with doing: stirring up the crowds. The priests gave witness to Jesus' far-ranging ministry in both northern Galilee and southern Judea. They recognized him as a northern boy from Galilee who came south to preach and teach.

23:6–7. Their chance reference to Galilee might give Pilate an out. He could turn the decision over to the administrator in charge of Galilee. After all, Herod just happened to be in town for the Jewish Passover celebration. So Pilate made sure he had heard correctly. Yes, Jesus was not from Judea. He was from Galilee. Let Herod hear the case. This was Herod Antipas (see 3:1,19; 9:7–9; 13:31). He had inherited rule over Galilee and Perea from Herod the Great, his father. He had married Herodias, his brother's wife. This led to John the Baptist's rebuke that resulted in Herod beheading John (Luke 9:7–9).

23:8–9. Herod knew about Jesus and his wonder-working reputation. Now Herod wanted to instigate a sideshow with Jesus as the star. Herod used provoking questions to try to force Jesus' hand so he could see a miracle. Having survived Pilate's court, Jesus wanted no part of Herod's trial. So he gave him no answer.

23:10. Jewish religious leaders used every trick they knew to get Jesus to incriminate himself. As Herod questioned him, they accused Jesus of every crime imaginable.

23:11. Unable to provoke a miracle, Herod turned to mockery. He turned the charge of kingship against Jesus and treated him as a mock king, putting royal clothes on him. Seeking to humiliate him, Herod sent Jesus back to Pilate dressed as a king.

23:12. Pilate had interfered in Galilean affairs (13:1). Philo, the Jewish historian, tells of an incident when Pilate placed shields in Herod's palace, angering Herod and the Jews. Tiberias, the Roman ruler, made Pilate relent, relegating the shields to a pagan temple. Also about this time, Tiberias' chief advisor—Sejanus—lost his power. He was ruthless, and he hated the Jews. How all this affected Pilate's relationship with Herod, we do not know. We only know Luke's report that their relationships had not been friendly. Getting involved in Jesus' trial apparently made Herod forget any past grievances and renew his friendship with Pilate. The two men joined in injustice. Their silence and refusal to act led Jesus to the cross.

23:13–16. Pilate called a high-level conference of Jewish leaders. Chief priests represented the religious leadership. The word *rulers,* used here for the first time by Luke, included all the social and political leaders, among whom were the elders and scribes.

Thus, the people joined religious, social, and political leaders in hearing Pilate's verdict. Jesus was innocent of all charges brought against him. Pilate could call on his new friend Herod for support. Jesus did not deserve death. Pilate made that clear. In an attempt to pacify the leaders, Pilate proposed a compromise action. He would submit Jesus to a Roman scourging and then release him.

23:17. This verse is absent in the most reliable manuscripts of Luke. It was apparently introduced by a scribe who missed this information in Luke since it did appear in Matthew 27:15 and Mark 15:6. The custom of the Roman ruler releasing a prisoner during the Passover festival is assumed by Luke if not explicitly written.

23:18–19. The identity of those who cried out for Christ's crucifixion is not clear. At least the rulers of Israel are meant. Most likely the crowd is included, though not explicitly (cf. Acts 3:14–15). Only here does Luke mention Barabbas by name, identifying him as a murderer and instigator of rebellion against Rome. He was guilty of the most serious crime of which Jesus was accused.

23:20–21. Pilate was a pitiful character, a man of absolute power but fearful of disappointing the people he ruled. The people felt no compulsion in overruling the ruler. They shouted him down. They were determined to get rid of Jesus. They must protect the tradition of the people.

23:22. Pilate was reduced to arguing with the people rather than making his decision stick. He invited them to offer further evidence against Jesus, to name a crime of which he was actually guilty. Pilate knew Jesus did not deserve the death penalty. He also knew the Jewish leaders would settle for nothing less. Still, Pilate tried to find ground for a compromise. He again suggested scourging Jesus and then releasing him (see v. 16).

23:23–25. The Jews knew when they had the advantage, and they pressed it hard. Crucify. Crucify. Crucify. The clamor increased. Finally, Pilate gave in. Public pressure defeated absolute government power, so injustice could prevail. Pilate let mob rule determine justice. He gave in to the crowd so they would not report him to Rome. He pardoned a murderer, who led rebellions against Rome. He let an innocent man suffer the death penalty to protect his political power and position. Jewish religious ambition had joined Pilate's Roman political ambition to sentence the innocent Jesus to death.

B The Glory Revealed on the Cross (23:26–49)

SUPPORTING IDEA: *The cross revealed the glory of Christ in his obedience to God, his care for other people, his innocence, and his control of the gates of glory.*

23:26. The crowd had their way. Jesus trudged toward the hill of execution, the crossbeam on his shoulder. Roman soldiers accompanying him apparently saw Jesus had become too weak to carry a heavy Roman crossbeam, so they forced a man from the crowd to carry Christ's cross. Mark 15:21 notes that Simon was the father of Rufus and Alexander, apparently Christians known to the church (cf. Rom. 16:13). Cyrene is part of present-day Tripoli (see Acts 6:9; 11:20; 13:1). More than likely, Simon was a Jewish pilgrim who had come to Jerusalem to celebrate Passover. On his way back to the city from a visit to the countryside, he suddenly found himself forced to carry the Savior's cross. Inadvertently, he etched his name in world history.

23:27. Some of the people joined in demanding Jesus' crucifixion (vv. 14–25), but others sadly joined the procession from Pilate's court to Calvary's cross. Women often served as professional mourners, but certainly that was not the case here. The women who had so faithfully supported Jesus (8:1–3) were probably included in this larger group. They expressed grief and anguish over the coming suffering and death of their Lord.

23:28–31. Always attentive to the needs of others, Jesus noticed the women and probably recognized some of them. He tried to change the direction of their grief. He was not the one who needed to be mourned. Later he would confess that he was in the Father's hands. They needed to turn attention inward. They faced the tragedy of the fall of Jerusalem and all the suffering connected with that. Jesus had already wept over the city and the fate of its inhabitants (19:41). These mourners needed to save their tears for their own disastrous future. What would they do when the Roman army surrounded and destroyed the holy city? Even more, what would they do when the final judgment day arrived with its tribulation and horror? The universe will be turned upside down. Barren women will be blessed (contrast the picture of blessing on Elizabeth and Mary in chaps. 1–2). Why such a reversal? Because no mother will want to see her child suffer the tortures that all the inhabitants of Jerusalem will face.

That will be the time when Hosea 10:8 is fulfilled. Jerusalem's citizens, particularly its women, will seek refuge. Even the refuge of death caused by a mountain toppling on them would be better than facing the Roman armies as they destroy Jerusalem.

Jesus closed his speech to the women with a proverb whose meaning is highly debated. It is a comparison between a lesser and a greater evil, but who causes the evil and exactly what is the evil? The image is of a green tree and its lumber that is hard to burn and dry wood that burns easily and quickly. Apparently, Jesus said the current disaster that God was allowing to happen—the joining of Romans and Jews to kill him—was hardly comparable with the disaster the women would face in Jerusalem. God would let the Roman government destroy Zion, the city of promise, the city of hope, the city of David. All Jewish political, messianic, and religious hopes would be snuffed out. The city of peace would be the scene of deadly warfare in which innocent civilians would suffer as much as defending soldiers.

The implication of this statement is that all hopes rest in the green tree of Jesus on Calvary, not in a new political leader on a Jewish throne in Jerusalem and not in a new religious priest in a purified temple in Jerusalem. Romans and Jews may think they have established their power and authority in crucifying Jesus. Romans will think they have proved their superiority to the Jews' religion and their God when they destroy Jerusalem. But before either of these events, Jesus shows that he remains in charge, knows what will happen, and confirms it as part of God's eternal plan.

23:32. Jesus had known all along that he faced a criminal's death. He looked to his participation with the lawbreakers in 22:37. Here the expectation became reality. To the uninformed bystander, Jesus' death appeared one more instance of cruel Roman justice, which took the most notorious criminals and placarded them against the sky for all to see so no one would imitate their heinous deeds. Ironically, Jesus now showed his followers what he expected of them—taking up a cross to follow him. They must lose their lives to save them just as he was doing.

23:33. Three men carried crossbeams to Calvary. All arrived at the deathly destination, aptly named Golgotha, "Place of the Skull." Modern tourists join the pilgrimage to the Church of the Holy Sepulchre to find Golgotha. Nothing proves or disproves this ancient tradition. Ironically, as Jesus was ushered into his glory on the mount of crucifixion, two criminals claimed the position on the right and the left, positions over which his disciples had argued so vehemently. Meanwhile, the disciples had fled the area, afraid of being identified with this criminal. Two thieves took up crosses and followed Jesus to Golgotha, while his chosen disciples hid in fear.

23:34. Jesus had proven his ability to forgive sins in his healing ministry (5:24). He had taught that forgiveness comes only to those who forgive others (6:37; 11:4) and that forgiveness has no limits (17:4). He had called for love of enemies (6:27–28). On the cross he practiced what he had taught. He watched those who mocked him, played games with him, scourged him, and crucified him. Then he asked the Father to forgive them. He called for forgiveness because he loved his enemies, but the explicit reason was their ignorance. Neither Jewish accuser nor Roman executor fully realized the gravity of their actions. The Jews were protecting their religious establishment against this obnoxious newcomer who pulled the crowds away from them and demanded that they look at motivation rather than simple legal action. The Romans in the person of Pilate protected their political territory against one who proclaimed the kingdom of God was at hand. Both Roman and Jew acted defensively in putting personal self-interest and political and religious institutions above the call for justice. Blinded by self-interest, they never realized that they were executing an innocent man. They certainly were not aware that they were executing the Son of God who came to save his people from their sins. Jesus went beyond the call for justice to pour out grace on those who executed him.

Jesus' prayer for forgiveness leads to a deeper question. Does God forgive sins of ignorance? This passage does not answer that question. It does show that God can forgive the most heinous crimes. It shows that God knows the complex causes of sin and the interplay of motivations that lead to the most horrible sins. It shows the need for victims of sin and crime to forgive and seek forgiveness for those who have misused, abused, and persecuted them.

As Jesus prayed for forgiveness, the Roman soldiers continued their mocking games, taking his clothes and casting lots for them. In this act they fulfilled Psalm 22:18, although Luke does not explicitly say so. Nothing the Romans or Jews did caught God by surprise. He knew his Son would die, suffering for the sins of the world (Isa. 53). He knew the Romans would gamble for his few earthly possessions.

23:35. In Luke 22 the people gathered with Pilate and called for Jesus' crucifixion. Here they became mere onlookers, part of the audience in the theater of death. The Jewish leaders, however, continued their obnoxious behavior, mocking Jesus (cf. Ps. 22:8). In so doing, they unwittingly testified to the work Jesus was accomplishing (19:10; see Matt. 1:21). While the religious leaders worked to destroy life, Jesus worked to save it (6:9). As they attempted to save their own life, they lost it (9:24). The devil had taken the word of life away from them, and they did not believe and were not saved even though Jesus prayed for their forgiveness (8:12). First in the eyes of the people, they had become last in the eyes of God (13:30).

The leaders had listened to Jesus' teachings carefully; they knew he implied he was the Christ, the Messiah, the promised Savior of Israel (see 2:26; 9:20). He claimed to come from the Father and to have the power of the

Father at work in all he did. Only in one other place does Luke use the term *the Chosen* or *elect*. Jesus had reminded them that God would not put off the prayers of his chosen ones but would bring them justice. Here in the midst of injustice perpetrated by the religious leaders and the Roman representative, Jesus finally showed the ultimate meaning of his teaching. On the cross God was answering the prayer of his people. He was bringing them salvation, assurance of eternal life. The elect were receiving more than justice. They were receiving the gift of grace. But that gift involved one person dying for the sins of the people. That one person could not save others by saving himself. He saved others by dying for them, sacrificing himself. This was the suffering Servant-Messiah, not the self-serving, all-triumphant political messiah the Jewish rulers wanted.

23:36–37. Soldiers joined the religious leaders in their mocking game. They wanted to quench Jesus' thirst, so they offered him cheap wine used by the poor. Continuing his ironic presentation, Luke shows how those involved in killing Jesus stopped for a moment to care about his thirst. Having played at helping him, they joined the Jewish chorus in challenging Jesus to prove his kingship and to save himself. Thus, mockers echoed the charges against Jesus: religious blasphemy in claiming to be Messiah and political treason in claiming to be king of a new kingdom. Both Jews and Romans saw life from one perspective: self-preservation. Neither group understood that self-preservation is fleeting. No person can preserve his or her life for eternity. Eternal life is God's gift, given by the one who died on the cross. Refusing to save himself, he provided salvation for the world.

23:38. Pilate had authorized a placard to be placed above Jesus' head to describe his crime. Jesus' crime was claiming to be king of the Jews. Again, this had both a religious and a political dimension. This mocking placard, however, proclaimed eternal truth for those who would listen. Jesus is truly the king of the Jews, the promised Messiah, and as such is the only hope for the world. Those who would be part of an eternal kingdom must believe on him as their king.

23:39. Even the dying criminals who were crucified beside him got in on the mocking act as one of them echoed the Jewish cry. The Messiah should at least be able to save himself. While he was doing that, he might as well show his power by saving those who were dying with him. Surely this criminal deserved his fate, showing his character to the end. Suffering the most insulting of deaths, he hurled insults at the only one who could save him.

23:40–42. The word *rebuked* is the same term Jesus used in casting out demons (4:35,41; 9:42), healing the sick (4:39), and calming the storms (8:24). The second thief thus followed Jesus' advice in an ironic way, catching his fellow thief in a sin and rebuking him.

The second thief confessed his sins and invited the other thief to join his confession. They deserved to die. They were guilty. As such, they stood in sharp contrast to Jesus. How this thief came to recognize the innocence of Jesus we are not told, but his statement incorporates a great theological truth: Jesus did not deserve to die. He was the sinless dying with sinners, the innocent sharing the fate of the guilty, the pure Lamb of God taking on himself the sin of the world. Certainly, the thief did not recognize all this, but it was implicit in his statement. It calls Christians to confess the great work of the innocent Jesus. The thief thus joined the Roman ruler and the Jewish tetrarch in confessing Christ's innocence (see vv. 4,14,15,22). A Roman soldier would soon join them (v. 47).

The repentant thief had rebuke for his fellow thief but a request for Jesus. He wanted to be remembered when Jesus entered his kingdom. Funeral inscriptions in Jesus' day often requested that the deceased join the righteous at the judgment. The thief shortcircuited this process, believing in some unexplained way that Jesus would survive crucifixion and establish a kingdom. This thief is the primary example of a deathbed confession. He did not know all he asked, but he had enough faith to ask to be part of whatever Jesus was up to. He had no more life ahead of him, but he sought eternal blessings beyond the cruel death he was enduring. When Jesus raised the dead, some decided to kill him. When they killed him, one decided to join him.

23:43. The time frame of the thief's request is not clear, but Jesus' response was quite clear. The thief did not have to wait even one day. His faith, whatever its source, secured him an immediate place with Jesus. He would be part of Jesus' kingdom today . . . in paradise. The expression is borrowed from the Persian language, where the word *paradise* means a park or garden. The Hebrew equivalent appears three times in the Old Testament (Neh. 2:8; Song 4:13; Eccl. 2:5).

The earliest Greek translators of the Old Testament used the Greek term for paradise for God's garden (Gen. 2:8–10). In the Apocrypha and Pseudepigrapha written between the Old and New Testaments, "paradise" takes on a new meaning in Jewish thought. It becomes associated with the blessing of final judgment (see 2 Esdras 4:7; 6:2; 7:36,123, 8:52). This meaning appears three times in the New Testament (Luke 23:42; 2 Cor. 12:4; Rev. 2:7). This ideal end-time garden was described in terms of Genesis 2; Isaiah 41:18–19; 51:3; 58:11; 60:13; Jeremiah 32:41; Ezekiel 31:8–9; and Psalm 1.

Here we see a central New Testament text on eternal life. Jesus promised this believing thief that he would share life with Jesus in paradise today (cf. Luke 16:23). Some would take this as a reference to an intermediate state where Jesus and the thief would reside—Jesus until his resurrection and the thief until the final judgment. The promise of Jesus appears to offer much more than this. The thief had asked for participation in Christ's kingdom, and Jesus appeared to grant the request.

Jesus promised the thief immediate consciousness *today* of life in the *eternal kingdom*. This promise raises questions for Christians who look to the resurrection as the time for final judgment and entrance into the heavenly kingdom. How can a person wait for the final resurrection and still be aware of immediate presence with Christ today? Does this require an intermediate state as some would teach? To say this is to say that Jesus went to an intermediate state, and that paradise means an intermediate state. Yet, we know that Jesus went to rule with his Father in heaven.

The complex answer may involve a distinction between human linear time and God's eternity with never-ending time. On earth humans live in linear time, seeing one event following immediately after another. Our experience in linear human time causes us to describe life after death as a series of linear events. But with God one day is as a thousand years and a thousand years as a day. Thus, in the view of eternity, a period of linear waiting may not be necessary. The next human experience after death, in this view, would be the final resurrection and eternal life with Christ experienced in the realm of eternity.

Christ's promise to the thief extends to all who believe in him. When we call on him for salvation, acknowledging our sin and seeking his salvation, he responds with a word for today. You, too, may experience life in Christ's kingdom today by believing in him.

23:44–45. Darkness, the symbol of Satan's power, ruled the land for three hours. The time reckoning apparently places the beginning of this darkness at the most unlikely of times: high noon. This makes clear Jesus' statement to the Jewish leaders that they had an hour, an hour when darkness rules the earth (22:53). The Jewish rulers were instruments of the powers of darkness in bringing Jesus' death. With the death of Jesus, the light of the world was gone. The times of the last days were inaugurated (see Isa. 13:9–10; 50:2–3; Jer. 15:6–9; Lam. 3:1–2; Amos 5:8,20; 8:9; Joel 2:2,10,31; 3:15; Zeph. 1:15). Death reigns in the world. Only an act of God can bring new hope. Only resurrection can bring new life into the darkness.

Darkness did not cover just the cross or Jerusalem. It encompassed **the whole land**, or perhaps better translated, the whole earth. The death of Jesus has universal implications. A world that kills Jesus must live in darkness. The sun paid its homage to Christ. When God's Son dies, the earth's sun cannot shine. It must hide its face in mourning and darkness. A sinful world cannot count on the guarantee of sunlight, for God controls all the rules and laws of nature. A world that rejects God's Son must expect signs that God has rejected the sinful world.

God rejected not only the sinful world; he also rejected the sinful religious practices of that world. His people who claimed to follow his law in his house had become instruments of darkness. At the moment Jesus died, God destroyed their entire religious system. No longer could religious leaders control the system of atonement. No longer could scribes and students of the law hold a reign of terror over the common people, dictating to them what was acceptable to God and what was not. No longer could priests claim to be the only ones with access to God. God himself tore the veil that separated the holy of holies from the rest of the worship place. God opened his presence to the common worshiper. Every believer could now go straight to God with prayers for forgiveness and atonement. As the thief pleaded directly to Jesus, so every person could now go directly to God. No religious system separated them from contact with the heavenly Father.

23:46. Jesus' final words from the cross, a quotation from Psalm 31:5, expressed his faith, his relationship to God, and his insistence that death and the cross did not represent the last word. Death led only to paradise, to protection in God's hands, to the kingdom. If death led Jesus safely into God's hands, does it not do the same for all who trust in Jesus? Death becomes nothing more than a barrier, like the temple curtain, to be torn in two to allow immediate and permanent access to the Father. But death is real. This is not some fakery, trying to fool the public into believing Jesus really died when he did not. Jesus breathed his last. He died. Life left his body. As with every other corpse, it was time for burial.

23:47. Pilate's representative at the crucifixion, the commander of the Roman solders, silently viewed the entire proceedings. He saw the Jews mocking. He saw the soldiers gambling and teasing Jesus with wine that would not help his situation. He heard the thieves arguing over the identity and power of this man on the center cross. He heard Jesus' promise to the thief and his commitment of himself into the Father's hands. He knew that Pilate, his commander, had approved the crucifixion, but he did not. An innocent victim had suffered capital punishment. The "righteous" Jesus can be described in terms used for many of Luke's heroes: Elizabeth and Zechariah (1:6), Simeon (2:25), and Joseph of Arimathea (23:50). He also joined the class to which the Jewish leaders claimed to belong, thus denying their need for repentance and excluding themselves from Jesus' ministry (5:32; cf. 15:7; 18:9; 20:20). It is the righteous who have wisdom (1:17) and who will be rewarded at the resurrection (14:14). Admitting that Jesus is righteous is more than a declarative statement. It is a form of praise, of worship, for it brings glory and honor to God. This is what proper response to Jesus always brings (2:20; 5:25–26; 7:16; 13:13; 17:15; 18:43; cf. 24:53).

23:48. The Jewish leaders and Pilate had drawn the crowds into the decision on Jesus' death. Ultimately, they had cried for his crucifixion (vv. 18–24). Now the people could survey all that happened. They left the scene mourning for the one whose crucifixion they had demanded. How far can we go in interpreting this symbol of grief? Did they simply mourn for the one who suffered so grievously, or did they grieve over their own actions and the injustice they had brought about? Or did they truly mourn over and repent of the sins they had committed in killing Jesus? Whatever the full impact of their reaction, they went away never to be heard of again in Luke.

23:49. The thieves, the centurion, the people, and finally the friends responded to Jesus' death. The simply stood at a distance, observing all that happened. Later, they would serve as Luke's sources. They would join the Pentecost group in proclaiming the message of resurrection hope. They would spread over the world as messengers of Christ. Their time for proclamation would come. For the moment, they were content with witnessing everything that happened and trying to understand it.

◖The Glory Is Buried (23:50–56)

SUPPORTING IDEA: *Jesus, who revealed God's glory, actually died and was buried in the same manner as all dead people.*

23:50. Out of nowhere a new character appears in Luke's narrative. Each of the four Gospels focuses briefly on this man. Luke not only joins him with the righteous heroes described above (v. 47), but also calls him "good." This is the only time Luke uses this adjective for a specific person. He describes the good person as a man whose heart stores up good things and activates them at the right moment (6:45). The good man perseveres in God's Word (8:15). He is trustworthy and uses his master's goods in a worthwhile way (19:17). Ultimately, Jesus, the "Good Teacher," must point to God as the only one who is good (18:18–19).

Such high praise is unexpected for any man, but especially for this one. He was no normal private individual. He was a member of the Jewish Sanhedrin, the ruling council. He was a part of the court that condemned Jesus and took him to Pilate for the death penalty. Could a man who voted to crucify now desire to pay homage to the dead?

23:51. Luke strikes down the previous assumption. The Sanhedrin was not unanimous in its decision about Jesus (cf. 22:66–23:1). At least one man voted against taking Jesus to Pilate for crucifixion. Joseph voted against his council members. Why? Because he had focused his life on God and the kingdom God had promised (cf. 2:25,38). He was the kingdom at work in the actions of Jesus. He recognized that the one crucified as king of the Jews truly was the anointed one, the king. Joseph's hometown of Arimathea must have been near Jerusalem, but the exact location is unknown.

23:52. Joseph went courageously to Pilate. The last time Jews went to Pilate, they sought to kill Jesus. Joseph wanted to bury him. But Romans controlled the crucifixion, so Roman officials controlled the body and its disposal. They could have been reluctant to release the body of a person who was charged with treason. Could he become the martyr figure that inspired others to rebellion? Joseph made the situation easier. He was not a known follower of Jesus. Rather, he belonged to the group that had demanded his death. Events at the cross seemed to dispel any fears of mob action. Not a single voice of protest was raised there by his followers or the people at large. So Pilate gave the body to Joseph.

23:53. Joseph followed the common customs of the day in preparing the body for burial. He placed it in a tomb that had never been used. In Jewish society this was important. It meant Jesus did not share a tomb with generations of Joseph's ancestors, buried on rock ledges in a cave-like tomb. It meant that Jesus' tomb had not been used previously and then emptied of its contents because a new generation needed it. Joseph had an unusual tomb, one reserved strictly for himself and his family. He gave this precious possession to Jesus, not realizing how short the occupancy would be.

23:54. Jesus' burial had to be done hurriedly. This was the day before the Sabbath. Each family had to prepare for worship, for clothing, and for food to ensure that no work was done on the Sabbath. Joseph interrupted Sabbath preparations to prepare Jesus' body for burial. Sabbath would begin at sundown. This may have meant that full preparation and anointing of the body for preservation could not be completed before Sabbath began. Burying Jesus before the new day began at sundown fulfilled the provisions of Deuteronomy 21:22–23.

23:55–56. The disciples are noticeable by their absence here. The faithful women continued to follow Jesus (8:1–3). They had provided for him in life. They prepared to provide for him in death. They watched Joseph's activities so they would know exactly where Jesus was and what needed to be done to his body.

They hurried to their residence, prepared anointing spices used to honor the dead and to hide the odors connected with death and decay. Then the Sabbath came. They observed Sabbath. Jesus and those most closely associated with him could not be condemned for violating Old Testament law. They might not follow Pharisee and scribal interpretation, but they obeyed Scripture (see Exod. 20:10; Deut. 5:14). Not disciples but women exemplified Christ's call to take up the cross and follow him. They followed to the cross and to the tomb.

MAIN IDEA REVIEW: *The death of Jesus Christ showed his righteous innocence, paved the way to paradise for those who believe in him, and led Christ back into the Father's loving hands in glory.*

III. CONCLUSION

A Righteous Man

Responding to death may be life's most difficult passage. Can I ever forget the nine months of bitterness and agony I suffered after my wife died? I wrote seventeen chapters of a proposed book, cried daily to God, huddled my grown sons around me trying to protect them from what I was suffering, and acted out the Job role in as many ways as possible. My book and my prayer diary reveal all too clearly the extreme responses I made to God as I contemplated life without Mary. Death jolted me, and the jolt continued to be felt for long months, much like the aftershocks of a major earthquake.

Meanwhile, my sons suffered much more quietly. A few friends like Lewis and Alice and Jay hovered over me, being there when I needed to talk or when I simply needed a caring presence. Other friends like Ray and Mimi invited me over once a week to eat and play with their son and try to get back into a normal routine of living. Still other friends ministered to so many needs during the last days of Mary's life, the funeral, and the following week or two. Then they silently resumed their own routines. People are related to the deceased in different ways with different degrees of feeling. Thus, they respond in different ways.

So, too, with the death of Jesus. As Jesus died, many people responded. Jewish religious and social leaders, threatened by Jesus' popularity and teaching, quietly and effectively orchestrated his death. They trumped up religious charges that angered the Jews and political charges that angered the Romans. But their evidence was flimsy. Pilate did not buy it. Neither did Herod. Both knew he was innocent, certainly undeserving of death, and positively undeserving of the humiliating and agonizing death by crucifixion.

The Jewish people had followed Jesus resolutely through his ministry. Their devotion to Jesus aroused the fears of the religious and political leaders. At the crisis point the people backed away, demanding, "Crucify him. Crucify him." Crucifixion done, the people walked away in grief, beating their chests. Somehow they recognized the death of Jesus as a sad moment.

The soldiers carried out Pilate's assignment and crucified Jesus. They gambled for his clothes, mocked him, and demanded that he prove his kingship by abandoning the cross.

The Jewish leaders wanted Jesus to fulfill his promise of salvation and his claim of messiahship. Come down from the cross and show who you are, they demanded. You had power to heal others and even raise the dead—exercise that power now.

Two notorious thieves were crucified with Jesus. One joined the Jewish leaders and Roman soldiers in mocking him. The other thief somehow came to faith as he hung dying. He rebuked the other thief, pointing to their guilt and Jesus' innocence. This believing thief asked to be remembered when he died, not just placed among the just rather than the wicked at the last judgment. He asked to be part of Christ's kingdom. He received a better surprise. He would join Jesus in paradise *today!*

Luke says nothing of the disciples. Luke focuses on the women. They represented the faithful who followed to the cross. They had faithfully provided funds for Jesus throughout his ministry. First, Jesus warned them. They need not grieve for him. He remained in God's hands, carrying out God's plan. They needed to prepare themselves for the suffering they would soon face. So the women and others who knew Jesus watched the events of the cross, ready at a later date to be faithful witnesses proclaiming the good news of Christ's death and resurrection. And they watched the burial, ready to give Christ proper burial when Sabbath law allowed.

The center of attention, however, was Jesus. He called on the women to join him in weeping over Jerusalem's fate. He called on the Father to forgive those who so ignorantly and self-centeredly crucified him. He promised the believing criminal that he would join Jesus in paradise today. And he gave himself over to the Father so the Father could care for his dead Son.

The Father responded to the cross. He shut off the sun and opened up the temple's holiest place. He showed earth how dark its evil had become and showed true worshipers free and open access to him without ritual or priest.

A Roman commander also watched. Never had he seen such a man. No sign of guilt or crime. This was an innocent, righteous man. This was certainly one of God's heroes.

A secret disciple watched. Joseph of Arimathea surprised his Sanhedrin cohorts. He went directly to Pilate as they had done to demand Jesus' death. Now he demanded Jesus' body for proper burial in his own unused tomb.

An innocent man died. God's plan of the ages was enacted. And the way to God and to paradise opened up. The death of Jesus calls on each reader to ask a simple question: How do I respond to this dying one? Do I realize he died for me? Do I reach out to him in faith and seek a place in his kingdom? Do I hear his promise of a place in paradise? Am I sure that I will rest in the Father's hands?

PRINCIPLES

- Jesus did nothing to deserve a criminal's death.
- Jesus died so we might be part of his kingdom.
- Jesus often makes friends out of enemies.
- Self-interest and fear cause good people to commit heinous acts.

- The judgment the world faces is much worse than the human judgment Jesus endured.
- Jesus has a place in paradise for believers.
- Forgiveness is Christ's way in every situation of life.
- Self-preservation is not the first value of life.
- The dead have hope in God's hands.
- Life should be lived in waiting for the kingdom of God.

APPLICATIONS

- Confess that your sins led Jesus to the cross.
- Be sure that you have trusted Jesus and have a place in his kingdom.
- Do not expect justice to prevail in this world.
- Be prepared to suffer in the judgments of this world and in the end times.
- Give up self-interest and ambition for the sake of Jesus.
- Forgive others, no matter what they have done to you.
- Recognize Jesus' innocence and know that it qualifies him to be the Good Shepherd, seeking and saving those who are lost.
- Praise God for all he has done for you on the cross.
- Live in expectation of the kingdom.

IV. LIFE APPLICATION

Mourning a Hero

As I write this, the sports pages of the newspaper provide sufficient commentary for this lesson. The Atlanta Braves roared through the regular baseball season in unequalled fashion, winners over everyone. They quickly disposed of their opponents in the postseason playoffs. They were sitting on top of the world. Then they faced the New York Yankees in the World Series. Exhilaration turned to embarrassment and agony. Swept in four games, the Braves could respond in no other way than to say: The Yanks were the better team.

Another sports headline bemoans the mysterious accident that carried a private jet bound from Florida to Texas far off course, ending in a crash in South Dakota. A world-famous golfer met an early, unexpected death.

Much of the world watched, listened, and responded to these events. Fans mourned the loss of a baseball team and the death of a golf hero. Shock and disbelief conquered all spirits. This was not fair. It was not planned for. It just could not happen that way. But it did.

Jesus' disciples could not imagine things could turn out this way. The Master, Teacher, Healer, and Exorciser lay dead in a tomb. Jewish religious leaders finally had their way. A Roman court proved him innocent but pronounced him guilty. The one who had been the center of attention—the hero beyond all heroes—now found the same crowds calling for his death and mocking him. It was not fair, but no one promised it would be. It was what God had planned for in the Old Testament. It was the only way for a perfectly innocent, sinless man to die for the sins of the world. Christ faced the choice: save himself or save the world. He chose to save us. His choice forces us to make choices.

Will we acknowledge his innocence? Do we recognize that he came to seek and save the lost? Will we accept his salvation? Are we prepared to testify to the world that a man who died represents our only hope for life?

V. PRAYER

God, our Father, we commit our lives into your hands right now. Save us. Forgive us. Prepare a place for us in your kingdom. Share with us the promise of being with you in paradise. Make us faithful witnesses to what you have done for us. We truly want to glorify your name in all the earth. Amen.

VI. DEEPER DISCOVERIES

A. The Charges Against Jesus (23:2)

Luke shows charges against Jesus from both Jewish and Roman perspectives. According to the Jewish leaders, he subverted the Jewish nation. That is, he tried to turn the Jewish people from their loyalty to Rome to loyalty to him. He tried to overthrow the Roman government in Judea so he could be king. Such a charge was built on false evidence. The Jewish leaders could point to Christ's preaching of the kingdom of God, but such preaching never invited the people to turn away from Rome. Disciples wanted to make Jesus king so they could occupy high positions in his government, but Jesus never encouraged their hopes.

The Jewish religious leaders also charged Jesus with opposing payment of taxes to Rome. This was clearly a lie. Jesus had clearly said to give to Caesar what belonged to Caesar. The Jewish leaders might have countered that nothing belongs to Caesar. It all belongs to us and our God. But Jesus never said that. He supported church loyalty above political powers.

They charged Jesus with claiming to be the Messiah and king of Israel. Jesus never denied that he was the Messiah, but he spent his entire ministry changing the definition of Messiah from rebellious king to suffering servant. Jewish leaders and even Jesus' disciples could never separate Messiah from king on David's throne in Jerusalem. His adversaries read into Christ's remarks about Messiah a claim to be king of Israel and a claim to restore the rule in Jerusalem so that Rome no longer ruled. Jesus never intended this. His Messiah had to be rejected and die. Rule would come only when he returned in the glory of his father.

The priests and other leaders backed up their claims by pointing to the wide-ranging teaching tours that Jesus took. He gained followers from all parts of the nation. Crowds followed him and hung on his words. Christ's popularity exceeded that of the Jewish leaders, making them jealous—so jealous they were willing to kill him on trumped-up charges. Christ's popularity exceeded that of Roman governmental authorities, making Pilate fearful of their reaction and ready to sentence as they chose. However, Christ never translated popularity into political power or military force.

The priests and Saduccees supported Rome to protect their own power and the wealth they gained from temple commerce. Jesus had the power to overthrow Rome, but that was his temptation, not his calling. God called him to preach, to teach, to heal, and to die. He followed God's calling, never initiating any action that could be called sedition against the Roman government. Pilate, Herod, the believing thief, and the Roman centurion in charge of the crucifixion proclaimed Jesus innocent, not deserving of capital punishment.

B. Herod's Jurisdiction (23:7)

Herod Antipas ruled Galilee and Perea from the death of his father in A.D. 4 until the Roman Emperor Gaius deposed him in A.D. 39. This meant Herod ruled over Capernaum and Nazareth and the other territory around the Lake Galilee but not the territory east of the lake. Perea included land east of the Jordan River southwards to Moab. Perea reached eastward to Philadelphia, Gerasa, Arabia, Heshbonitis and Medeba. Apparently, Perea reached to the north almost to Pella, north of the River Jabbok. The Wadi Jabis may have been the boundary line. Thus, both the Galilean and Perean ministries of Jesus played out in territory that Herod controlled. This gave Pilate an excuse to send him to Herod. He hoped Herod would make the decision and face Rome and the Jewish people afterwards.

C. Barabbas (23:18)

The four Gospels are our only source for knowledge about the criminal whose release the Jewish leaders and crowd demanded in place of Jesus. The meaning of his name is debated, although its Aramaic origin is clear. It probably meant "Son of the Father," either in reference to God, to a man named Abba or Father, or to a Jewish rabbi, the rabbis sometimes being referred to as "Father." Many manuscripts of Matthew 27:16–17 give his name as Jesus Barabbas, a somewhat ironic twist and one that later scribes seemed to have tried to eradicate.

The Gospels describe this crook as a murderer who was imprisoned for insurrection or treason. Matthew describes him as a notorious prisoner

(Matt. 27:16), while John 18:40 sees him as part of a rebellion. All of these descriptions may mean he was a bandit or a member of a gang of bandits who preyed on the wealthy Jews and Romans. They fostered unrest among the people and harassed the Roman forces that were trying to maintain peace and order.

We have no direct evidence that the Roman government regularly released a prisoner during the Passover, but the practice of clemency during religious festivals is common in various parts of the ancient world.

The Gospel portrait of Barabbas provides a clear contrast to the portrait of the innocent Jesus. The Jewish leaders, the crowds, and Pilate knew Barabbas was guilty. Releasing him invited more of the same criminal activity and unrest. They all knew Jesus was innocent, but for their own self-centered, ambitious reasons, they allowed Barabbas to go free and executed the innocent Son of God on the cross.

D. Crucifixion (23:13–49)

The Roman government acceded to the wishes of the Jewish leaders and the crowd and crucified Jesus of Nazareth. In so doing they followed ancient practice. The Persians apparently used this form of capital punishment. Less reliable sources report crucifixion in India and Assyria, as well as among Thracians, Scythians, Taurians, Celts, Germans, Carthaginians, and Britons.

Crucifixion was a favorite punishment used by Alexander the Great, particularly for survivors from cities that he conquered. Antiochus IV crucified faithful Jews who obeyed Jewish laws against his orders.

The Jews used crucifixion against their own people during their brief independence under the Hasmoneans. Around 100 B.C. Alexander Janneus, the high priest, had eight hundred Pharisees crucified. In Roman times crucifixion became a common occurrence and was used for people convicted of war crimes, treason, violent crimes, and especially for punishing slaves. Many Jews were crucified as the Roman armies captured Jerusalem in A.D. 68 to 70. Crucifixion took place at busy traffic intersections so people could see the suffering and would be encouraged to refrain from criminal or seditious activity. At times crucifixion became a form of entertainment in the various arenas built by the Roman government.

This form of punishment was the most extreme a government could enforce, and it was viewed as the worst form of death. In most cases Roman citizens and especially members of the upper classes were exempt from crucifixion.

The crosses used in crucifixion varied in shape. They could be a simple plank fixed vertically in the ground. A crosspiece could be attached at the top of the plank, forming a T, or slightly lower, forming the cross of modern art and imagination. At times two planks were crossed in an X form. After carrying the crossbeam to the place of crucifixion, victims were stripped of their clothing and nailed to the beam. Nails could be hammered into various parts of the body. Often a peg was placed on the upright plank, forming a crude seat for the victim. Ropes bound the body to the cross. In some cases the victim was placed head down on the cross. In grotesque instances the Romans sometimes let wild dogs attack the victims or burned the victims for torches at night.

Vital organs were not generally damaged as the victim was affixed to the cross, so suffering dragged on, sometimes for days, as the victim suffered starvation and asphyxiation. Jesus did not require very long to die. Apparently, the Roman scourging and beating before his crucifixion robbed him of physical strength and endurance.

Jesus thus endured the most horrible death humans knew how to inflict. He gained a reputation as a disobedient slave or a violent, treasonous criminal in his death. No greater disgrace or shame could come to a person. Jesus identified himself with the lowest of the low as he allowed the Roman government to take its cue from the indignant Jewish leaders and sentence him to crucifixion. His punishment fit the crime of sedition and treason of which the Jews accused him. It did not fit the verdict of innocence rendered by Pilate for the Romans, Herod for the Jews, the believing thief for sinful humanity, and the Roman centurion for the Roman legal system. An innocent man endured the most gruesome of deaths because he was carrying out the divine will to bring salvation to the world.

VII. TEACHING OUTLINE

A. INTRODUCTION

1. Lead Story: An Ambitious Vine
2. Context: Luke 23 moves from the flagrant violation of justice in the Jewish secret meetings that condemned Jesus to the flagrant violation of justice in the Roman trials. The chief Roman official joined with the chief Jewish official in repeatedly pronouncing Jesus innocent but then sentencing him to the most horrendous of deaths, reserved only for the most vicious criminals and for slaves. The sentence was then carried out. Various persons responded to Jesus in various ways, mocking and condemning him or testifying to his innocence. Self-interest and selfish ambition led many to mock and scorn him, but a thief and a Roman commander affirmed his innocence. The thief gained an invitation to paradise from the innocent one on the central cross. The crowds grieved for Jesus. The women and other acquaintances watched him, becoming prepared to be eyewitnesses of this

central event in the life of Christ. A member of the Sanhedrin backed his refusal to vote for Jesus' crucifixion with firm action in gaining Jesus' body from Pilate and burying it in his own personal tomb. The women prepared to give proper burial rites to Jesus.

3. Transition: The cross is central to Christianity. Luke surprises us with his lack of explanation of the cross. He tells the story in simple fashion, letting us gain several perspectives on what was happening through responses of various people and groups involved. Then he leaves us to decide. Was this an innocent man? What is the import of the death of Jesus? Does it still mean something two thousand years later? How will we respond to the cross?

B. COMMENTARY

1. Sentenced by Pilate's Fearful Ambition (23:1–25)
   a. Jesus before Pilate (23:1–7)
      (1) The opponents' action: accusation of subversion (23:1–2)
      (2) Pilate's reaction: are you king of the Jews? (23:3a)
      (3) Jesus' response: so you say (23:3b)
      (4) Pilate's verdict: innocent (23:4)
      (5) The opponents' response: stirring up the crowds throughout Israel (23:5)
      (6) Pilate's response: let Herod decide (23:6–7)
   b. Jesus before Herod (23:8–12)
      (1) Herod's hope: see a miracle (23:8)
      (2) Herod's action: question Jesus (23:9a)
      (3) The Master's response: silence (23:9b)
      (4) The opponents' reaction: vehement accusations (23:10)
      (5) Herod's counter response: mock Jesus (23:11)
      (6) The result: Herod and Pilate reconciled (23:12)
   c. Pilate's discussions with Jesus' opponents (23:13–25)
      (1) Pilate summons the opponents and people (23:13)
      (2) Pilate's verdict repeated: innocent, so beat and release (23:14–16,17)
      (3) The opponents' reaction: away with him; give us Barabbas (23:18–19)
      (4) Pilate's counter reaction: let me release Jesus (23:20)
      (5) The opponent's counter reaction: crucify him (23:21)
      (6) Pilate's reprisal: accuse him; innocent; beat and release (23:22)
      (7) The opponents' response: crucify him (23:23)
      (8) The results: Pilate relents, releases Barabbas, and surrenders Jesus (23:24–25)

2. The Glory Revealed on the Cross (23:26–49)
   a. The scene: the way to crucifixion (23:26–32)
      (1) The scene: Simon forced to carry the cross (23:26)
      (2) The followers' reaction: mourning (23:27)
      (3) Jesus' response: weep for yourselves, not me (23:28–31)
      (4) The other characters: two criminals also led to be crucified (23:32)
   b. The scene: the crucifixion (23:33–43)
      (1) The setting: the skull and three crosses (23:33)
      (2) Jesus' response: forgive them in their ignorance (23:34a)
      (3) The executioners' reaction: gamble for his clothes (23:34b)
      (4) The crowd's reaction: watch in silence (23:35a)
      (5) The opponents' reaction: mock: save yourself if you are God's Messiah (23:35b)
      (6) The soldiers' reaction: taunt him to save himself if he is king (23:36–37)
      (7) Pilate's reaction: placard him as king of the Jews (23:38)
      (8) The first criminal's reaction: save all of us (23:39)
      (9) The second criminal's reactions: he is innocent; remember me (23:40–42)
      (10) The Master's response: paradise with me today (23:43)
   c. The scene: death in darkness (23:44–49)
      (1) God's actions: darkness; torn temple veil (23:44–45)
      (2) Jesus' actions: commitment to the Father; death (23:46)
      (3) Roman centurion's actions: praise God; Jesus was innocent (23:47)
      (4) The people's actions: extreme grief; leave the scene (23:48)
      (5) The actions of his "acquaintances" (including the women): stand at a distance; watch (23:49)
3. The Glory Is Buried (23:50–56)
   a. The scene: righteous opponent asks for body (23:50–52)
   b. Joseph's actions: bury body before Sabbath (23:53–54)
   c. The women's actions: prepare to anoint body before the Sabbath (23:55–56)

C. CONCLUSION: MOURNING A HERO

VIII. ISSUES FOR DISCUSSION

1. Why did different people respond to Jesus' death in different ways?
2. What physical and emotional feelings would you have if you were crucified on a cross?

3. How would you feel if your best friend and "hero" were being crucified on a cross or undergoing a modern form of capital punishment?
4. What does it mean to you that Jesus died on the cross?
5. What does it mean to you that the veil of the temple was torn?
6. Why does Luke place so much emphasis on Jesus' innocence?

Luke 24

Fulfilling the Scripture

I. **INTRODUCTION**
We Buried Him Last Week

II. **COMMENTARY**
A verse-by-verse explanation of the chapter.

III. **CONCLUSION**
He Is Risen!
An overview of the principles and applications from the chapter.

IV. **LIFE APPLICATION**
Something Better to Offer
Melding the chapter to life.

V. **PRAYER**
Tying the chapter to life with God.

VI. **DEEPER DISCOVERIES**
Historical, geographical, and grammatical enrichment of the commentary.

VII. **TEACHING OUTLINE**
Suggested step-by-step group study of the chapter.

VIII. **ISSUES FOR DISCUSSION**
Zeroing the chapter in on daily life.

Quote

"If one refuses to believe in the possibility of miraculous occurrences altogether, the resurrection will seem an absurdity. But large numbers of 'modern, scientific' people recognize that science itself is merely descriptive rather than prescriptive. If a God exists, it is only natural to expect him to have powers beyond that which science has discovered or can explain and to be able to use them for his purposes. It is arguable that of all the alleged miracles in ancient history, the resurrection is actually the one with far and away the most historical support."

Craig L. Blomberg

Luke 24

IN A NUTSHELL

Jesus Christ rose from the dead in fulfillment of the Hebrew Scriptures, made appearances to his followers, promised them the Holy Spirit, and ascended to the Father.

Fulfilling the Scripture

I. INTRODUCTION

We Buried Him Last Week

*P*atsy Clairmont beautifully and movingly portrays the reality of recovering from grief. I quote her words because they are so strongly and lovingly written: "We buried my friend's 26-year-old son last week. An accidental gunshot took Jeff's life. We have more questions than answers. We are offended at people who have all the answers and no experience with devastating loss.

"I watched the heart-wrenching scenes as the family tried to come to grips with their tragedy. I can still hear the travailing of the mother's anguished heart. I can still see the wrenching of the father's grief-worn hands. I can still feel the distraught sobs that racked the sister's body as I held her. I can still smell the hospital and the funeral home. Memories march before my mind like soldiers, causing me to relive the agony. If it is this difficult for me, Jeff's godmother, how much more magnified it must be for his birth mother! I can't imagine.

"As I watched Jeff's mom, Carol, the week after his death, I observed a miracle. I saw her move from despair to hope. From franticness to peace. From uncertainty to assurance. From needing comfort to extending it.

"I witnessed a mom face her worst nightmare and refuse to run away. Instead, she ran to Him. When grief knocked the breath out of Carol, she went to the Breath Giver. I watched as the Lord placed His mantle of grace around her and then supported her with His mercy. The grief process has just begun for Jeff's loved ones. The Lord will not remove His presence from the Porter family. But there may be moments when He will remove their awareness of His presence. That will allow them to feel the impact of their loss. For He knows it would be our tendency to hide even behind His grace to protect our fragile hearts from the harsh winds of reality. He offers us refuge, but He also promises us wholeness. Wholeness means we are fully present with ourselves and with Him. Therefore, we have to own our pain. If we do not, part of who we are we must either shut down, avoid, or deny. That would leave us estranged from ourselves and divided in our identity. Also, we would never heal in a way that would allow us to minister to others" (*Under His Wings*, [Colorado Springs: Focus on the Family, 1994], 139ff.).

The death of Jesus Christ left his followers devastated with grief similar to the Porter family's. They had lost their best friend, their leader, and their life's goals, hopes, and dreams. All meaning had disappeared from life. Meeting the resurrected Christ gave them the assurance and power they needed to recover from their grief realistically, regain their wholeness, and renew their commitment to the goal Christ set before them. We have trouble feeling the same grief and loss the disciples felt at Jesus' death, but we can feel the glory of his resurrection and the joy of being part of his goal for living and for dying.

II. COMMENTARY

Fulfilling the Scripture

MAIN IDEA: *Jesus Christ rose from the dead, appeared to many of his followers, promised them the Holy Spirit, and ascended to the Father.*

A Christ Is Risen as Promised (24:1–8)

SUPPORTING IDEA: *The gospel stands or falls on the reality that Christ rose from the dead according to the Scriptures.*

24:1. The world's worst Sabbath finally dragged to a close. Sundown brought a new day, the first day of the week. Now the women could fulfill their duty to Jesus and do something concrete to express their grief. But sundown brought darkness, when they could not venture outside their homes, so again they had to wait. The first rays of morning sun gave them opportunity to accomplish their task. They hurried off to the tomb where they had seen Joseph of Arimathea place Christ's body.

24:2–3. The stone was rolled from the tomb. Yes, the large stone that resembled a millstone that donkeys might pull did not have to be moved. They could enter the tomb immediately. As they did, they saw that the tomb was empty.

24:4–5. What had happened? What could they do? How could they stand the loss of his body in addition to losing him to death? From out of nowhere two men in glistening garments appeared. Dazzled by it all, the women fell face down to the ground, afraid to look up. Then those angelic voices addressed them: Why do you look for the living among the dead?

24:6–8. Again the voices. He is not here. He is risen! The angels reminded the women of what Jesus had said in Galilee. Then they remembered!

B Telling the Resurrection Story (24:9–12)

SUPPORTING IDEA: *Qualified witnesses told the resurrection story with mixed initial reactions.*

24:9. The women had followed Jesus and supported his ministry in Galilee (8:1–3). They had faithfully watched at the cross (23:49). They were certainly qualified witnesses to recognize and tell the story of Jesus. In Luke the women believed the resurrection and told about it without even encountering the resurrected Lord. Here the disciples, with Judas missing, of course, must learn the central theme of the faith from the faithful women.

24:10. Luke carefully documents the women involved. Mary Magdalene and Joanna were listed in chapter 8 as supporting Jesus in his ministry in Galilee. Here Luke adds one prominent name—Mary, the mother of James— and does not include Susanna from chapter 8. Mark 15:40 identifies the second Mary as the mother of James-the-less. This is usually taken to mean he is the same as the apostle James the son of Alphaeus, as distinct from the apostle James the son of Zebedee and the brother of John. It is quite striking, however, that James and Joseph were also names of Jesus' brothers (Mark 6:3). This James became a strong leader in the Jerusalem church and probably is the author of the Epistle of James. Could it be that the early tradition of the church quietly identified Jesus' mother as the mother of their leaders James and Joses rather than as the mother of Jesus in a humble effort not to pay too much homage to Mary? Is it not reasonable that Jesus' mother would have been among those first women seeking to pay honor to the dead son and to fulfill the ritual requirements of burial? This view is seldom espoused in scholarship but should not be totally dismissed. Present-day respect for Mary does not demand that the early church would always identify her as the mother of Jesus.

24:11. The apostles knew the women well and had traveled long miles and hours with them. Still, the men did not believe the women. This may show the chauvinistic, patriarchal bent of their society and times. It may show how totally separated the disciples were at this time from Jesus. They played a very minor role at the cross. (Luke has not mentioned them specifically since Jesus' arrest.) The disciples, like the women, had ignored Jesus' passion predictions. They had no expectations of resurrection. The disciples had not seen or heard the "men" in the tomb. Resurrection and renewed fellowship with Jesus were something they did not even think about. They gathered for comfort in grief, not to find Jesus again. This apostolic skepticism is a major evidence for the truth of the resurrection. The apostles would not have invented the resurrection story. They had lost hope and sunk into despair at the arrest and death of Jesus.

24:12. Denying Peter was also impulsive, inquisitive Peter. The women's story pricked his conscience and challenged him to take a look for himself. Here the open tomb is taken for granted in the narrative. Peter easily entered the tomb. His response to such easy access was not recorded. The two "men" did not appear to Peter. All the evidence he had to go on were the cloths that had wrapped Jesus' body. They set him wondering. No one would remove the wrappings and then steal the body. Only a person needing to walk away would remove the cloths. Could the women's story be true?

C Jesus Reveals Himself on the Road to Emmaus (24:13–35)

SUPPORTING IDEA: *In the interpreting of Scripture and the breaking of bread, Jesus revealed himself as the resurrected one to two disciples who were walking to Emmaus.*

24:13. Perhaps still on the first day of the week, two disciples were going home to Emmaus after having been with the disciple band in Jerusalem. Modern scholars have no consensus about the precise location of Emmaus, although several sites have been suggested.

24:14. The two disciples had one topic of conversation—the events of the day. We will learn shortly what these events were.

24:15–16. Their conversation was interrupted by a new traveler. Jesus joined the pair on the way to Emmaus. As he walked quietly with them, they did not recognize him. But walking with strangers along the roads of Jerusalem must not have been unusual. Their lack of recognition did not come from his being a stranger. It came because God kept them from recognizing him until God was ready for the Son to be known.

24:17. For one entering into the middle of a conversation, Jesus asked the natural question: What are you talking about? His question halted their progress. Their immediate response came from their faces, not their mouths. Sadness and grief were inscribed all over their faces.

24:18. Finally, we learn the name of one of the disciples—Cleopas. Knowing the name does not do us a lot of good. It sounds and looks a lot like the Clopas of John 19:25, but the two should not be identified as the same person. We know nothing more about either person. Luke's church certainly knew Cleopas, but we do not share their information.

Cleopas was amazed that someone could have been in Jerusalem during the last couple of days and not heard the news. This must be a visitor, new in town today, he thought. Everyone knows about the crucifixion and rumors of angels and an empty tomb.

24:19. Jesus continued his probing, noticing how the disciples were reacting. They identified the central figure of their conversation: Jesus of Nazareth. They described him as a prophet whose words and actions showed he possessed unusual power. Jesus' actions were not hidden. He performed miracles and issued authoritative teaching in the open where both God and the people could witness. The implication is that both God and people saw, heard, and approved Jesus' words and actions.

24:20. Cleopas placed all the blame on the Jewish leaders for Jesus' death. They took the initiative to arrest and accuse him. They took him to the Roman authorities. The Romans shared guilt in that they carried out the crucifixion that the Jews demanded. Here is another strong piece of evidence for the death of the Messiah. His death was not in secret, hidden from the public. His death came at the hands of the leaders, very much in the public eye, who would later try to disprove his resurrection.

24:21. Christ's death ended apostolic hopes. Here Cleopas in a very important passage summarized the hopes of Jesus' disciples before Jesus' death. They thought Jesus would redeem Israel. This Greek verb for redeem (*lutroo*) appears only here and in Titus 2:14 and 1 Peter 1:18 in the New Testament. It has a strong Old Testament background, appearing ninety times in the Septuagint, usually as a translation of Hebrew *gal'al*, "to set free, redeem." It is rooted in the Exodus story of God redeeming Israel from Egyptian slavery (see Exod. 6:6). Luke used a related noun as Zechariah prophesied the work of his son John. God is coming to redeem his people. Anna explained the significance of the child Jesus to those who waited for the "redemption of Jerusalem" (2:38).

The term is often used in the process of paying a ransom or price to gain the freedom of a slave. Luke sees Israel in captivity just as they had been in the time of the Exodus. In sending John and Jesus, God had repeated the miracle of the Exodus. He had paid the ransom price and freed his people from slavery. But the freedom was not through military victory as in Egypt but through the work on the cross, paying the price for the slavery to sin. Paul used a related verb to confess that by Christ's death we are set free, redeemed, ransomed from our slavery to sin and death. Christ is the one who sets us free, that is, redeems us (Acts 7:35). He came to give his life as a means of liberating or redeeming us (Matt. 20:26).

The disciples saw in Jesus the one who would bring a new Exodus and free the nation from its Roman captors. Instead Jesus proved to be something much more—the Redeemer who freed them from sin and death. But at this point the two on the road to Emmaus had no idea of this.

The third day was important in many ways for the disciples in this context. By the third day the body would start to decay (cf. the four days of John 11:39). Three days should have given the news about Jesus time to circulate for all people to know about it. And three days was the time Jesus set for his being raised from the dead (Luke 9:22).

24:22–23. The disciples had not believed the women, but looking back on their story, they admitted their amazement at what the women said. They said Jesus was alive. Still, the disciples did not go out looking for Jesus. They did not stay together waiting for the risen Jesus to come to them. The disciples simply left Jerusalem for the safety and familiarity of Emmaus. Telling the story of resurrection did not elicit faith immediately from the disciples. It simply brought astonishment.

24:24. The women's story was verified. Some of the men went to check it out. This would probably include Peter's experience. The tomb was empty as the women said. But no Jesus. Stories of resurrection but no resurrection sightings. What did one do? What could one think? Could one believe?

24:25–27. Jesus had heard enough. He called the disciples foolish just as Paul referred to his Galatian readers (Gal. 3:1,3). The evidence stood before them, and they would not believe. They had not even placed this evidence over against the greatest source of knowledge they had. Scriptures pointed to Messiah's suffering before entering his glory. The disciples had it all reversed. They wanted Messiah to establish the glory of David's kingdom on earth before he died, his death probably marking the beginning of a new Davidic dynasty in Jerusalem. Jesus read Scripture in an entirely different way. He started with Isaiah 53 and saw suffering as the first necessity for Messiah. Only after suffering and death would glory be achieved, and this would be a glory entered after death, not a glory established on earth.

Then these two disciples received what each of us would give anything to have: Jesus' own interpretation of Scripture. Jesus showed just how the intention and wording of the Old Testament Hebrew Scriptures perfectly prepared the way for Jesus to come, minister, teach, heal, exorcise, be betrayed, suffer, die, and enter glory. What happened to Jesus was nothing new and unexpected. God had been preparing Israel for this all along. Scripture was full of Jesus. Any educated Israelite should be able to read Scripture and see Jesus.

24:28. Jesus started to leave the two disciples just as the conversation got interesting. He would let them go on home, and he would continue his journey.

24:29. The disciples would have none of that. They had a good excuse. Evening was falling. He could not go farther. He needed a place to stay. They had one. "Come on in. Let us continue the discussion. We want to hear more of what you say." Still, they did not recognize him or realize that his interpretation of Scripture pointed to no one but himself.

24:30. A major component of any meal was bread. Jesus acted as host, broke the loaf of bread, and distributed it to his disciples, just as he had often done, and especially just as he had done during the Last Supper. He said a prayer of thanks over the bread. The way he did it caught their attention. Now they focused on him.

24:31. Recognition came. It was Jesus. Immediately, he was gone, disappeared into thin air. This he could do in the resurrection body. He was now different from the way he had been before the crucifixion and resurrection.

24:32. They began immediately to share their thoughts and feelings with each other. Their grief had blinded them. Their attention to their own loss and sorrow prevented them from focusing on God and finding what God was doing for them at that very moment. And all this was a part of what God was doing, so they could hear Jesus out before they realized what was happening. A disciple could see the risen Lord without knowing he was seeing the risen Lord. Resurrection faith depended on more than just physical presence and physical sight. It depended on spiritual presence and spiritual sight. That came in the breaking of bread, a symbolic act that took them back to the night of the Lord's Supper. They knew their hearts burned. They knew something special was happening as they heard Jesus explain Scripture. But they did not know him until they broke bread together.

24:33. The two disciples had to share their experience. No one in Emmaus would understand. They had to go back to the other disciples. They found them in their gathering place in Jerusalem. The eleven apostles were there. This means the two going to Emmaus did not include an apostle.

24:34. The two from Emmaus were not the first. Their story was not unique. The several women could not convince them that Jesus was alive. Simon could. What was the difference? Jesus had appeared personally to Simon and revealed himself to him. Luke does not tell the story of revelation to Simon Peter. He simply reports that Simon's story had convinced the others of the reality of the resurrection. People could believe without seeing the risen Christ. Personal appearance was not necessary to make people believe. Strong personal testimony about being with the risen Jesus was the necessary ingredient to make the resurrection story believable.

24:35. The Emmaus Road walkers added their testimony. They emphasized that recognition came only in breaking of bread. Physical presence was not enough. They needed the spiritual presence of the supper with the Lord. In so doing they left the ongoing church a reminder. Jesus is present with his people as they break the bread of his supper and remember his body and his blood.

D Jesus Reveals Himself and the Meaning of Scripture to the Disciples (24:36–49)

SUPPORTING IDEA: *The resurrected Jesus revealed himself as one with the physical ability to eat and as the one whose life, death, and resurrection fulfilled Scripture.*

24:36. Unexpectedly, Jesus appeared. Again, he showed the nature of his resurrection existence. He could appear and disappear in surprising ways. The unexpected appearance brought the expected Hebrew or Aramaic greeting of *Shalom*—"peace, well-being, wholeness to all of you."

24:37. Telling one another about the resurrected Christ's reality, the disciples did not expect to see him. His was a surprise visit. They did not know how to react. Terror reigned in their hearts. Could this be a ghost? You just do not expect to see dead people walking. Intellectual belief had taken hold, but the sudden physical presence was too much for their emotions. The truth had not sunk in to become a part of their emotions. Intellectual acceptance did not drive out their emotional surprise.

24:38. Jesus knew their thoughts and feelings and read their faces. Body language spoke louder than words. Calmly, he asked, "Why do you react this way? No reason for fear and trembling. No reason to doubt the resurrection. It is really me. You can believe. You are seeing me. Calm your emotions. Clear your minds. Enjoy resurrection reality."

24:39. Come here! I will give you proof, he continued. Touch me. I still have flesh and blood like you do. I am not a ghost, some spirit without a body. Touch me and believe.

24:40–41. They looked at his hands and feet in particular. Apparently, they could still see the nail scars. Even this physical reality was not enough to overcome their emotional shock. It was too good to be true. They were so happy they could not believe it was really happening. They were so amazed they could not believe their eyes. Jesus had another approach. He showed he still had human needs. He was hungry. Could he have something to eat?

24:42–43. They found fish for him to eat. The resurrected Christ could do things humans cannot normally do, like appear and disappear. Still, the resurrected Christ shared certain realities with other people. He still retained the scars and wounds of life before death. All this took a while to sink in for the disciples. Resurrection faith was not easy, natural, and automatic. Resurrection faith took some time. It took getting used to. It required a calming of minds, a stirring of emotions, and a final unifying of mental and emotional faculties to believe that Jesus was risen.

24:44. As with the two followers going to Emmaus, so with the crowd in Jerusalem. Jesus opened Scripture and referred back to the passion predictions. Resurrection was a surprise. It should not have been if they had listened and absorbed his teachings. Scripture did not paint the kingdom the way they had been taught. Scripture did not paint Messiah in terms they expected. Scripture could be misread and misapplied. They had to read Scripture carefully and find what God wanted to say to them through it. Scripture read correctly points to Jesus, to all that Jesus experienced, especially his death, burial, and resurrection. Can you read? Can you hear the voice of God as you read? Do you see Christ as you read? Check how you read and understand Scripture. The first telling point is always this: Does it point you to Christ?

24:45. Scripture cannot be understood by the simple human mind. God has to open the mind to understand Scripture. Reading Scripture is not like any other reading assignment you might undertake. Reading Scripture must begin with a dedication of your mind and heart to God and with a willingness to listen to God as he speaks to you through Scripture. We understand Scripture only as God's Holy Spirit opens our minds and becomes our teacher.

24:46–48. Again, Jesus went back to his passion predictions. Old Testament Scriptures such as Isaiah 53 showed that the expected Messiah must suffer and die. They also indicated that he must be raised on the third day. This much is past happening. But all the Hebrew Scripture is not yet fulfilled. The mission is just beginning. What Messiah did must be proclaimed. This is why silent witnesses who knew Jesus well had to be at the cross. Eyewitness proclamation was in order. The result of Messiah's suffering, dying, and rising is forgiveness of sins. That is available only through repentance of sins. This comes only one way—by God's witnesses preaching all this in the name of Jesus.

Preach the name of Jesus, he told them. Call for repentance. Promise forgiveness. This is what the Scriptures said would happen. This is what you must do. This is your mission. The mission is worldwide. You cannot accomplish this immediately. You must have a starting point. That is right here where you are, here in Jerusalem. Start where you are and preach the name of Jesus, calling for repentance and promising forgiveness. Then Scripture will continue being fulfilled.

24:49. Not yet. You are not ready to go on mission yet, Jesus continued. One ingredient is lacking. You must have power to do it. The Father has promised that power. It is the power of the Spirit of God. It will come to you. Just wait. When God sends his power from on high to you, then you can begin the mission. Then Scripture will be fulfilled.

E Jesus Revealed Himself as He Ascended to Heaven and the Church Worshiped (24:50–53)

SUPPORTING IDEA: *Jesus is the ascended Lord, worshiped and obeyed by his church.*

24:50. Jesus led them toward his favorite place near Jerusalem, the city of Bethany across the valley north of Jerusalem where Mary, Martha, and Lazarus lived. He prayed for his followers and asked God's blessings on them.

24:51. Then the unexpected came. Jesus disappeared. This time he disappeared for good. He ascended to heaven. Luke gives no details of this. He simply ends Christ's earthly ministry with simple words. He left them and was taken to heaven. Jesus had said he would enter his glory (v. 36). Here he fulfills his word. Now the church cannot expect to see the resurrected Christ again. They must wait for the promised Spirit.

24:52–53. The church no longer grieves. Jesus' final disappearance does not bring mourning and sadness. It brings joy and worship. The church has heard the resurrection story. His followers have seen the resurrected Lord. They have experienced the spiritual presence in the breaking of bread. They believe in the resurrected Lord. They can tell the story of the resurrected Messiah. They can show that Scripture prepared for the Messiah to come to earth, minister, be betrayed, suffer, die, and be resurrected. They can preach in the name of Jesus. They can call for repentance. They can promise forgiveness. But only after the Spirit comes. Until then, stay in Jerusalem. Stay at the temple. Yes, work from the center of Judaism to preach Christ. Pray. Give thanks. Express joy. Worship. Wait for the Spirit. He will come in Volume Two: the Book of Acts.

MAIN IDEA REVIEW: *Jesus Christ rose from the dead, appeared to many of his followers, promised them the Holy Spirit, and ascended to the Father.*

III. CONCLUSION

He Is Risen!

The Lord is risen, indeed! This is the message that separates followers of Jesus Christ from all other people of the world. If Christ is not risen, we are of all people most foolish. The church must constantly ask why it believes in resurrection and what difference that belief makes. The Gospel writers faced the same questions as they wrote. They did not give philosophical answers. They did not engage in polemical debate. They simply testified to what the church had seen and how the church was different.

The first apostles did not believe the earliest testimony of the resurrection. They thought of it as an old wives' tale told by a bunch of grieving, delirious women. Quickly, they rethought their position. Better check it out. Peter found an empty tomb and discarded linen wrapping cloths. Then Jesus found Peter. His witness convinced the other apostles and followers of Jesus in Jerusalem. Jesus did not rely on only one appearance. He joined the pair on the road to Emmaus and let them recognize him in the breaking of bread. Thus, his followers would always know that when they met to remember him in the breaking of bread and drinking of the wine, they could encounter him. As the pair retreated to Jerusalem and shared their witness, Jesus again appeared, this time to all the disciples. He showed them he was not a spirit or a ghost. Even as he appeared in the resurrection body, they could see his physical reality in the scars in his feet and hands and in his need and ability to eat.

Jesus then showed them that his life, death, and resurrection had completed what Scripture had predicted. What is more, Scripture promised more to come. Repentance and forgiveness of sin must be preached to all the world. That job lay with the witnesses to and believers in the resurrection. So they were to stay put, wait for God's promised Spirit, and then start in Jerusalem and go to the nations in Jesus' name. Having received their mission, they watched as the risen Lord rose again, this time into the heavens to be with the Father. This brought not grief and sadness at their loss, but worship, joy, and praise. Life with the risen and ascended Lord is a life of joy, worship, and praise for his followers.

PRINCIPLES

- Jesus Christ is the risen Lord of the church.
- Resurrection faith differentiates followers of Jesus from all other people.
- The life, death, resurrection and mission of Jesus come directly from the expectations and teachings of the Hebrew Scriptures.
- Resurrection faith developed only after doubting disciples experienced the risen Christ, heard witnesses of the risen Christ, and were led by God to recognize the risen Christ.
- Christ is recognized as the church remembers him in the Lord's Supper.
- The resurrection body is different from but has continuity with the earthly body.
- Christ's followers witness in Jesus' name, calling people to repentance and promising forgiveness of sins.
- Christ's church witnesses to him in all the world.
- Christ's church can witness only as it receives power from the Holy Spirit.
- The church worships the risen Lord with joy and praise.

APPLICATIONS

- Study the Scriptures to learn about Jesus.
- Find assurance in the dark moments of life from your faith in the resurrection of Jesus.
- Be aware of Jesus' presence as you celebrate the Lord's Supper.
- Pray that God will make you aware of the power of the Holy Spirit in your life.
- Ask God how you can have a part in his mission to the rest of the world.

IV. LIFE APPLICATION

Something Better to Offer

Rosalee Mills Appleby introduces us to a young Brazilian boy named Matthias. Smallpox destroyed his left eye and permanently weakened the right eye. Poverty robbed him of any opportunity for an education. What little money he had came from playing his harp for dances. One night he headed for a dance, but a new kind of music caught his ear and haunted his soul. Through the windows of a mission church streamed out the melody of "Trust and Obey." Matthias stood spellbound. The service ended. The church members gradually disappeared to their homes. The melody reverberated in the young boy's mind. He could not escape it. He knew life had something better to offer him than what he had.

Matthias tried to play his ragtime dance music, but it roused only shame and disgust in his heart. The harp was good for only one thing: to be sold. Finding a way to have glasses to let him read, he finally learned to read the New Testament. Also, he took up a new business, selling thread and thimbles in the country districts. As he threaded his way along the rain forest paths from house to house, he carried on an even greater business. In his bag among the needles and thread were his real products: Bibles and tracts.

Appleby describes Matthias's mission: "His otherwise arduous task becomes a glorified one because a loving purpose tides him on and buoys him up. The naturally hostile people put him up for the night, and he preaches the gospel in their homes. Soon the humble, faithful tick-tack man will lay down his pack and go to live with the king. But his life will go on in this land of flowers. Boys and girls that now play beneath the palms will proclaim to others the message first heard from the lips of the peddler."

Thousands of such stories abound across the two thousand years since Jesus lived, died, rose again, and ascended to the Father. Each story has its own pathos and its own victories. Your story can be added to the growing list. Certainly you have all the qualifications and much more opportunity than did Matthias. You can express your faith in the living, resurrected Christ. You can accept his forgiveness for your sins. You can witness to others, calling them to repentance and promising them forgiveness in the name of Jesus. You can watch as persons whom you lead to Christ witness for him and lead hundreds of others to him. You can join Christ's church in worship, joy, praise, and witness. Jesus Christ suffered, died, and rose again, seeking and saving those who are lost, redeeming a sinful world. Join him in his mission today.

V. PRAYER

Resurrected Lord and Savior, I commit myself anew to you today. Thank you for forgiving my sins and saving me. Thank you for dying and rising again for me. Thank you for the great joy that fills my soul each time I think of you or hear your name. Send the power of your Holy Spirit upon my life so I may witness to others about your love and grace and lead them to repentance and forgiveness. Yes, Jesus, I praise your holy name. Amen.

VI. DEEPER DISCOVERIES

A. Holy Scriptures (24:7,26–27,32,44–49)

The Hebrew Scriptures serve as a foundation and source of authority for three world religions—Judaism, Islam, and Christianity. Each claims that their religion is based on these books. But each also adds something to the Hebrew Scriptures. Judaism adds the rabbinical interpretations called the Talmud. Islam adds Mohammed's Koran. Christianity adds the New Testament. Can all of these religions be right? The answer turns on how you read the Hebrew Scriptures. Jesus said you had to read all parts of the Scriptures—the Law or five books of Moses; the Prophets, including Joshua, Judges, Samuel, Kings, Isaiah, Jeremiah, Ezekiel, and the Book of the Twelve; and the Writings, including all the other books.

Jesus said one principle should guide your reading of Scripture. You should search the Scriptures to see how each part points to the life, death, resurrection, and mission of Jesus. Scripture is read correctly only when it is read in light of Jesus. Other readings of Scripture are in error because they miss the main point of the writing. The Hebrew Scriptures were not written to provide a history in preparation for Mohammed. They were not written to become a law book that formed the basis for the moral interpretations of the Talmud. They were written to prepare people to recognize Jesus of Nazareth as Son of God, Redeemer of Israel, and Savior of the World.

B. Resurrection (24:5)

Resurrection is the central fact on which Christianity and the church are built. Resurrection is unique from all that went before it. Some Old Testament heroes of faith were taken to heaven without enduring death—Enoch (Gen. 5:24) and Elijah (2 Kgs. 2:11). Jesus raised people from the dead (such as the son of the widow of Nain as well as Lazarus). These would die again. Jesus died. He was buried and stayed in the tomb parts of three days. Then he came out of the empty tomb alive, never to enter a tomb again. The resurrected Christ was then taken to heaven to rule with God forever.

Other religions and people without religion may claim to believe in a life after death. Without Jesus, however, they have no evidence for their belief, no reason for their hope. The historical example of Jesus Christ proves that the God and Father of Jesus Christ has power over sin, death, and the grave. The historical promise of Jesus Christ means that each of his followers can expect to participate in the resurrection of the dead and the rewards of Christ. A person who does not believe in Christ, who does not take up his cross, deny himself, and follow Jesus, has not received Christ's promises and cannot expect to join him in the rewards of eternal life after death.

This does not mean that all people will not experience resurrection. The Bible clearly teaches the resurrection of all people, both followers of Christ and those who reject Christ. Those who do not follow Christ will experience resurrection, but they will also receive the punishment for their sins that Christ bore for those who trust him. Thus, resurrection leads in two directions—to heaven and rewards for people who trust Christ and to hell and punishment for people without Christ.

C. The Christian Mission (24:47–49)

The resurrection story leads to mission. Jesus' purpose was to seek and save all the lost. Yet he never ministered outside Palestine and the surrounding countries. He left the rest of his mission to his church to accomplish. He gave his church the steps by which they are to accomplish this mission. He told the church to wait for power from the Spirit with prayer, joy, and worship. Then they were to minister in their home area and extend the work to the world. This is spelled out explicitly in Acts 1:8. Matthew 28:19–20 tells the church to act on the authority Jesus gives, since he has all authority in heaven and earth. That action should center on making disciples who are then to be baptized and taught. This is to be done in all the world.

From its very beginning, then, the message of Jesus Christ has sent people into the world, not kept them cloistered away from the world. The message of Jesus has never been restricted by any kind of limitations. The Book of Acts ends with Paul in jail preaching unhindered. This is what Jesus' message and mission are all about. His church under every circumstance is to preach the gospel to every person in every place in every age. The gospel offers forgiveness of sins and promise of resurrection and eternal life with Jesus after death. The gospel demands repentance of sins and taking up a cross to follow Jesus in mission.

VII. TEACHING OUTLINE

A. INTRODUCTION

1. Lead Story: We Buried Him Last Week

2. Context: Luke 24 makes the most remarkable transition in the history of literature. The hero is dead and buried at the command of the most powerful political force in world history. He has suffered the greatest shame and torment known to humanity. His closest followers are nowhere to be seen. Only some who know him along with a few women witness the crucifixion. They huddle together in mourning, frustration, wonderment, confusion, and despair. They had bet their

future on this man and lost. Life held nothing for them. They could not even ask the dreaded question, "What next?"

3. Transition: Suddenly, life is transformed, because one man has been transformed. Jesus of Nazareth is no longer captive and dead in a guarded tomb. He is alive and well. He appears to his followers. He eats with them and shows them his scars. The very man who died is alive. Why? He has fulfilled the Scriptures. He has done just what God long ago said would happen. Now only one part of the puzzle remains: the mission of the followers. They turn from grief to joy, from despair to worship, from confusion to mission. Luke 24 shows us how this great transformation occurred and what this wonderful mission is.

B. COMMENTARY

1. Christ Is Risen as Promised (24:1–8)
    a. The scene: women at tomb on first day of week (24:1)
    b. Surprise setting: stone rolled away; tomb empty (24:2–3)
    c. Heaven's action: angelic appearance (24:4)
    d. The women's reaction: reverence and fear (24:5a)
    e. The angelic response: why look for living among dead? (24:5b–7)
    f. The women's counter response: remembered his promise (24:8)
2. Telling the Resurrection Story (24:9–12)
    a. The scene: women and the eleven (24:9)
    b. Personnel: women identified (24:10)
    c. The disciples' reaction: disbelief (24:11)
    d. Peter's reaction: ran to tomb in wonder (24:12)
3. Jesus Reveals Himself on the Road to Emmaus (24:13–35)
    a. Scene A: two disciples on road to Emmaus (24:13–27)
        (1) The disciples' action: Jerusalem to Emmaus talking about Jesus' events (24:13–14)
        (2) The Master's action: join the walk (24:15)
        (3) God's action: hide Jesus' identity (24:16)
        (4) The Master's question: what are you talking about? (24:17a)
        (5) The followers' reaction: gloom (24:17b)
        (6) Cleopas's question: how have you not heard? (24:18)
        (7) The Master's response: what things? (24:19a)
        (8) The followers' response: things of Jesus we hoped would redeem Israel (24:19b–24)
        (9) The Master's response: believe the Bible (24:25–27)
    b. Scene B: the Master revealed (24:28–29)
    c. Scene C: Jesus is recognized (24:30–35)

4. Jesus Reveals Himself and the Meaning of Scripture to the Disciples (24:36–49)
   a. The Master's action: unexpected appearance (24:36a)
   b. The Master's greeting: peace (24:36b)
   c. The followers' reaction: scared of ghosts (24:37)
   d. The Master's response: do not doubt; touch and see (24:38–40)
   e. The followers' counter response: disbelief, joy, and amazement (24:41a)
   f. The Master's counter response: let us eat (24:41b–43)
   g. The Master's teaching (24:44–49)
      (1) My passion predictions and Scriptures are fulfilled (24:44–46)
      (2) Commission is yours: promise forgiveness, and preach repentance to all nations (24:47–48)
      (3) Wait for Father's promised power (24:49)
5. Jesus Revealed Himself as He Ascended to Heaven and the Church Worshiped (24:50–53)
   a. The scene: Jesus blessing followers at Bethany (24:50)
   b. God's action: Jesus' ascension (24:51)
   c. The followers' reaction: worship, return to Jerusalem, and stay at temple praising God (24:52–53)

C. CONCLUSION: SOMETHING BETTER TO OFFER

VIII. ISSUES FOR DISCUSSION

1. Do you believe Jesus of Nazareth died, was buried, was raised again the third day, and ascended to heaven? Why?
2. What difference does your belief or disbelief in Jesus' resurrection make in your life?
3. What makes Christianity different from all other world religions?
4. In what way are you carrying out the mission Jesus gave his church?
5. Do you know that your sins are forgiven and that you are going to be with Jesus when you die?
6. In what ways do you experience the presence of Jesus when your church observes the Lord's Supper?

Glossary

angel—A messenger from God who delivers God's message of instruction, warning, or hope

apostles—Men chosen by Jesus as his official messengers; this term refers generally to his twelve disciples

covenant—A contract or agreement expressing God's gracious promises to his people and their consequent relationship to him

cross—Two wooden beams shaped as a letter t or x used as an instrument to kill criminals by the Roman government; the wooden beams on which Jesus was killed and thus a symbol of Christian faith and responsibility

crucifixion—A form of execution by affixing a victim to a cross to die; Jesus' death on the cross for sinners

disciple—A follower and learner of Jesus Christ

eternal life—The quality of life that Jesus gives his disciples and unending life with God given to those who believe in Jesus Christ as Savior and Lord

faith—Belief in and personal commitment to Jesus Christ for eternal salvation

forgiveness—Pardon and release from penalty for wrongdoing; God's delivery from sin's wages for those who repent and express faith in Christ; the Christian act of freeing from guilt and blame those by whom one has suffered wrong

gospel—The good news of the redeeming work of God through the life, death, and resurrection of Jesus Christ

Gospels—The four New Testament accounts of the life of Jesus Christ. Matthew, Mark, and Luke are called Synoptic Gospels because they relate many of the same events and teachings of Jesus. John is the Fourth Gospel and tends to be more theological in nature, telling events and teachings not in the Synoptics.

Hades—The abode of the dead thought by some to be distinguishable from hell, the final state of the wicked

Herodians—An aristocratic Jewish group who favored the policies of Herod Antipas and thus supported the Roman government

Jerusalem—Capital city of Israel in the Old Testament; religious center of Judaism in the New Testament

Jesus Christ—The eternal Son of God; the Lord and Savior; the second Person of the Trinity

judgment—God's work at the end time involving condemnation for unbelievers and assignment of rewards for believers

kingdom of God—God's sovereign rule in the universe and in the hearts of Christians

Law—God's instruction to his people about how to love him and others. When used with the definite article "the," *law* may refer to the Old Testament as a whole but usually to the Pentateuch (Genesis through Deuteronomy).

Lord—A title for Jesus in the New Testament; means owner or master worthy of obedience

Messiah—The coming king promised by the prophets; Jesus Christ who fulfilled the prophetic promises; Christ represents the Greek translation of the Hebrew word *messiah*

miracle—An act of God beyond human understanding that inspires wonder, displays God's greatness, and leads people to recognize God at work in the world

parable—A short story taken from everyday life to make a spiritual point; Jesus' favorite form of teaching

passion—The suffering of Christ during his time of trial and death on the cross

Passover—The Jewish feast celebrating the Exodus from Egypt (Exod. 12); celebrated by Jesus and his disciples at the Last Supper

Pharisees—Jewish party or sect that used oral law and tradition to help Jews obey God in new situations not explicitly covered by the law; major opponents of Jesus

prophet—One who speaks for God

redemption—The act of releasing a captive by the payment of a price; Jesus' death provided our redemption from sin's power and penalty (Heb. 9:12).

resurrection—The raising of Jesus from the dead to eternal life; the raising of believers for eternal life with Christ; the raising of unbelievers to eternal punishment

Sabbath—The seventh day of the week corresponding to the seventh day of creation when people were called on to rest from work and reflect on God

Sadducees—A religious group that formed during the period between the Testaments when the Maccabees ruled Judah

Satan—The personalized evil one who leads forces opposed to God and tempts people

Savior—Jesus Christ, who brings salvation

scribe—A Jewish teacher of the law who studied and copied Scripture

Scripture—The Bible, the divinely-inspired record of God's revelation of himself and the authoritative source for Christian doctrine and teaching

Septuagint—Translation of the Hebrew Old Testament into Greek produced in the third century B.C.

shalom—Hebrew word for peace and wholeness meaning fullness of life through God-given harmony with God, the world, others, and oneself

Son of God—Title for Jesus emphasizing his divinity as coexistent with the Father

Son of Man—The title Jesus most frequently used for himself that emphasized both his divinity as the prophesied One in the Old Testament and his identification with people

temptation—The pull toward sin which all humans experience; it comes from Satan, not God

transfiguration—Jesus' appearance in full glory to Peter, James, and John

virgin birth—The miraculous birth of Christ in which Mary remained a virgin as she conceived and bore Jesus through the intervention of the Holy Spirit

Zealots—Militant radicals who act with great zeal for a cause. The term came to designate a particular segment of the Jewish population who continually tried to overthrow foreign oppression, especially the Roman rule in Palestine.

Bibliography

Arndt, William F. *The Gospel According to St. Luke*. St. Louis: Concordia, 1956.

Blomberg, Craig L. *Jesus and the Gospels*. Nashville: Broadman and Holman Publishers, 1997.

Bock, Darrell L. *Luke*. Baker Exegetical Commentary on the New Testament. 2 vols. Grand Rapids: Baker Books, 1994, 1996.

Conzelmann, Hans. *The Theology of Luke*. New York: Harper and Row Publishers, 1961.

Culpepper, R. Alan. "The Gospel of Luke," *The New Interpreter's Bible*, vol 9. Nashville: Abingdon Press, 1995.

Ellis, E. Earle. *The Gospel of Luke*. New Century Bible. Rev. ed. Grand Rapids: Wm. B. Eerdsman Publishing Company, 1974.

Fitzmyer, Joseph A. *The Gospel According to St. Luke*. The Anchor Bible, vols. 28, 28A. New York: Doubleday, 1981, 1985.

Green, Joel B. *The Theology of the Gospel of Luke*. Cambridge: Cambridge University Press, 1995.

Keck, Leander E., and Louis Martyn, J. eds. *Studies in Luke–Acts*. Nashville: Abingdon Press, 1966.

Lea, Thomas D. *The New Testament: Its Background and Message*. Nashville: Broadman and Holman Publishers, 1996.

Marshall, I. Howard. *The Gospel of Luke: A Commentary on the Greek Text*. Grand Rapids: Eerdsman, 1978.

Morris, Leon. *The Gospel According to St. Luke*. Tyndale New Testament Commentaries. Grand Rapids: Eerdmans, 1992.

Nolland, John. *Luke*. Word Biblical Commentary. 3 vols. Dallas: Word Publishers, 1989, 1993, 1993.

Stein, Robert H. *Luke*. New American Commentary. Nashville: Broadman Press, 1992.